COMMUNITY PSYCHOLOGY IN ACTION

Pulling together a range of responses to local and global challenges across different community settings, this book makes the case for community psychology as a responsive tool for social justice and liberation.

Using insights from both academia and professional practice, this book articulates key community psychology principles, practices and values and their role across "psy" and related professions. It draws on case studies from both the global north and south to show innovative ways in which communities have collectively taken action to demonstrate resistance and resilience, and describes creative psychological research methods that can be used to better understand and respond to the needs of communities. In so doing, it demonstrates the value of psychology which is both embedded within and reflective of its local community and challenges, and extends our understanding of what psychology is, how it is produced and to whom it belongs. Each chapter is supported by teaching and learning activities, including reflective exercises, discussion questions, embodied activities, stakeholder assessments, case study formulations and presentations.

Demonstrating how community psychology can support activities with local community members through meaningful examples of community action embedded in research, this is the ideal resource for psychology students. It may also interest professionals working in related fields, including clinical psychology, counselling psychology, health psychology, social psychology, social work and youth work.

Suzanne Wilson is a research fellow in social inclusion and community engagement at the University of Lancashire (UK). The research agenda is to work with communities to identify effective and sustainable means of increasing community capital. This expanding portfolio of research focuses on working-class coastal communities, often regarded as being "left-behind."

Rebecca Graber is a senior lecturer in health psychology at the University of Chichester. Her funded research focuses on how supportive friendships and peer relationships contribute to psychosocial resilience and wellbeing in the face of challenges such as ageing, socioeconomic marginalisation, substance addiction and LGBTQIA+ discrimination. She has formerly directed an MA in community psychology, has been a charity trustee and co-founded a network for Jewish academic and professional staff.

Carl Harris is a white, British, male clinical and community psychologist with 30 years' experience in the UK's National Health Service. Based in Birmingham neighbourhoods, working in community regeneration and mental health prevention, he writes from a practitioner-researcher critical perspective with a focus on inequality. He has been a member of Psychologists Against Austerity since 2010.

Maria Fernandes-Jesus is an assistant professor in psychology at the University of Sussex (UK). Her research focuses on collective action, climate justice, climate-linked mobilities, migration justice, youth participation, community solidarity and political imaginaries. She has been involved in several interdisciplinary, international and mixed-methods research projects related to these topics.

Topics in Applied Psychology Series

Series Editor

Graham Davey, Professor of Psychology at the University of Sussex, UK and former president of the British Psychological Society

Topics in Applied Psychology is a series of accessible, integrated textbooks ideal for courses in applied psychology. Written by leading figures in their field, the books provide a comprehensive academic and professional overview of the subject area, bringing the topics to life through a range of features, including personal stories, case studies, ethical debates, and learner activities. Each book addresses a broad range of cutting-edge topics, providing students with both theoretical foundations and real-life applications.

Counselling Psychology
Edited by Victoria Galbraith

Clinical Psychology, Third Edition
Edited by Graham Davey, Nick Lake and Adrian Whittington

Forensic Psychology
Edited by Neil Gredecki and Polly Turner

Work and Organizational Psychology, Third Edition
Sebastiaan Rothmann and Cary L. Cooper

Educational Psychology, Third Edition
Edited by Tony Cline, Anthea Gulliford and Susan Birch

Health Psychology, Third Edition
Charles Abraham, Mark Conner, Fiona Jones and Daryl O'Connor

Criminal Psychology, Third Edition
David Rowlands and David Canter

Community Psychology in Action
Striving Towards Social Justice and Wellbeing in Challenging Times
Edited by Suzanne Wilson, Rebecca Graber, Carl Harris and Maria Fernandes-Jesus

To find out more about this series, please visit: https://www.routledge.com/Topics-in-Applied-Psychology/book-series/TAP

COMMUNITY PSYCHOLOGY IN ACTION

Striving Towards Social Justice and Wellbeing in Challenging Times

Edited by

Suzanne Wilson, Rebecca Graber,
Carl Harris and Maria Fernandes-Jesus

Routledge
Taylor & Francis Group
LONDON AND NEW YORK

Designed cover image: Getty Image

First published 2026
by Routledge
4 Park Square, Milton Park, Abingdon, Oxon OX14 4RN

and by Routledge
605 Third Avenue, New York, NY 10158

Routledge is an imprint of the Taylor & Francis Group, an informa business

British Library Cataloguing-in-Publication Data
A catalogue record for this book is available from the British Library

ISBN: 9781032769387 (hbk)
ISBN: 9781032759975 (pbk)
ISBN: 9781003480464 (ebk)

DOI: 10.4324/9781003480464

Typeset in Times New Roman
by Deanta Global Publishing Services, Chennai, India

CONTENTS

LIST OF CONTRIBUTORS

Cinzia Albanesi (she/her) is a full professor of Community Psychology in the Department of Psychology at the University of Bologna, Italy. Her academic work centres on creating space for youth voices and empowerment in educational and community settings. She considers herself an advocate for the queer community, in particular transgender youth.

Nina Amelung, Institute of Social Sciences, Portugal, is a sociologist and research fellow in Political Sociology, Science and Technology Studies and Critical Migration Studies. She is co-chair of the Thematic Section on Knowledge, Science and Technology of the Portuguese Sociological Association, research network STS-MIGTEC and Cost Action DATAMIG.

Brendon Barnes is a professor of Psychology at the Institute for Social and Health Sciences, College of Human Sciences, at the University of South Africa. He writes in psychology, environmental health, and justice. He is chairperson and co-founder of the Climate, Environment and Psychology Division of the Psychology Society of South Africa. He has won teaching, mentorship, academic citizenship and research awards.

Laura Brito, SaMaNe collective, Portugal, is a co-founder of the SaMaNe collective.

Marina Passos Pereira Campos is a PhD candidate in Community Psychology at the Federal University of Ceará in co-tutorship with the Università degli Studi di Napoli Federico II. She is currently a CNPq-funded Research Fellow supporting Knowledge Dissemination, affiliated with the COSQUI – *Socio-environmental Conflicts, Suicide and Quilombos*.

Sofia Castanheira Pais is an assistant professor at the Faculty of Psychology and Education Sciences of the University of Porto (FPCEUP), and her research interests combine education, health, and well-being with vulnerable groups. She is co-coordinating the research group "Policies, Communities and Participation" at the CIIE-UP and integrates the Ethics Charter Monitoring Committee of the Portuguese Society of Educational Sciences.

Annalisa Cecconi (she/her) is a PhD student in the Department of Psychology at the University of Bologna, Italy. Her current research focuses on the secondary victimisation of gender-based violence survivors, alongside broader research interests in social justice, particularly youth participation and social work with marginalised groups.

Diptarup Chowdhury is an associate professor in Clinical Psychology at Lokopriya Gopinath Bordoloi Regional Institute of Mental Health, Tezpur, Assam, India. A clinical psychologist by training and a passionate teacher by calling, Diptarup Chowdhury spent two decades of his work-career searching for a more socially relevant and personally meaningful practice of psychology. In his pursuit to navigate through mainstream and the margins, he has found narrative ideas and practices to guide his engagements with clients and communities.

Carolina Coimbra, SaMaNe collective, Portugal, is a co-founder of the SaMaNe collective.

Karla Costa, SaMaNe collective, Portugal, is a co-founder of the SaMaNe collective.

Lynsey Crosthwaite is a specialist inclusion and diversity officer at Cumberland Council (UK), leading the council's approach to community cohesion. Lynsey has worked extensively in the field of community, inclusion and cohesion, specialising in service strategy, design and implementation to improve outcomes for marginalised communities. She holds a BA (Hons) in Community and Youth Work and is studying towards a Master's in Research.

Ana Stela Cunha, ICS-Social Sciences Institute, Portugal, passed away shortly after her contribution to this chapter. She was a linguist, postdoc anthropologist, street artivist and researcher. Among many projects, she coordinated VIBE (Voices of Iberia in the Black Europe – Cultural Fund Solidarity/DGArtes) with the musical band Yoka Kongo.

Bruno De Oliveira is a lecturer in Psychology at Chichester University, UK. His work is shaped by critical community psychology and is focused on participation, challenging frames of power, understanding poverty and wellbeing. He is the chair of the British Psychological Society Senate.

Evelyn De Simone, PhD in Human and Social Sciences, is research fellow in Social Psychology at the University of Salento, Italy. She is assistant editor of the international journal *Community Psychology in Global Perspective*. Her research interests focus on active participation, community resilience, sustainability and pro-environmental behaviours.

Raginie Duara is a researcher in health psychology specialising in youth wellbeing, visual methods and intersectional approach to mental health. Her current work at the University of Leeds blends visual storytelling – using photos, timelines and participatory filmmaking – to explore lived experiences of women journeying through addiction and recovery.

Amy Edwards-Smith is a lecturer in the School of Health, Social Work and Sport at the University of Lancashire (UK). Amy teaches across a range of subjects within the school. She has experience of working with individuals with additional learning needs and disabilities in education and social care settings. Amy's expertise is in Social Policy, in particular ideology, social justice and welfare.

Suzanne Elliott is a clinical psychologist. Suzanne uses Narrative and Community Psychology approaches to support people experiencing homelessness in Leicester UK.

Ana Eugenio da Silva, Black quilombola woman, is a PhD candidate in Social History at the Federal University of Ceará (UFC), funded by the Cearense Foundation for the Support of Scientific and Technological Development (FUNCAP). She holds a Master's in Humanities from UNILAB (University for the International Integration of the Afro-Brazilian Lusophony).

Raquel Farias Diniz, Department of Psychology, Federal University of Rio Grande do Norte, Brazil. She holds a Master's and a PhD in Psychology from the same university, where she is currently an assistant professor involved in teaching, research and extension activities at both undergraduate and postgraduate levels. She coordinates the Latin American Environmental Psychology Observatory (obPALA).

Maria Fernandes-Jesus is an assistant professor in Psychology at the University of Sussex (UK). Her research focuses on collective action, climate justice, climate-linked mobilities, migration justice, youth participation, community solidarity and political imaginaries. She has been involved in several interdisciplinary, international and mixed-methods research projects related to these topics.

Pedro D. Ferreira is an associate professor in the Faculty of Psychology and Education Sciences of the University of Porto (FPCEUP) and a member of the Centre for Research and Intervention in Education (CIIE). He has worked on issues of civic and political participation and political development, including how digital contexts and technologies are relevant to the practices and the construction of citizenship.

Micaela Gomes, Residências Refúgio, Portugal, is a project coordinator.

Beatriz Gomes de Figueiredo, Central European University, Austria, is a Political Science graduate and has a Master's degree in Sociology and Social Anthropology from Central European University.

Sangeeta Goswami, a pioneer in Counselling Psychology in Northeast India, founded MIND India, the region's first Institute on Positive Mental Health and Wellbeing. With 29 years of experience, she champions mental health awareness, counselling, training and research. She was awarded the Distinguished Service Award as Psychologist 2021 from AHPI.

Rebecca Graber is a senior lecturer in health psychology at the University of Chichester. Her funded research focuses on how supportive friendships and peer relationships contribute to psychosocial resilience and wellbeing in the face of challenges such as ageing, socioeconomic marginalisation, substance addiction and LGBTQIA+ discrimination. She has formerly directed an MA in Community Psychology, has been a charity trustee and co-founded a network for Jewish academic and professional staff.

Laura Hancox is a clinical psychologist. Laura uses Narrative and Community Psychology approaches to support people experiencing homelessness in Leicester UK.

Dani Harker-Brown is a clinical psychologist. Dani uses Narrative and Community Psychology approaches to support people experiencing homelessness in Leicester UK.

Natalie Hicks is an occupational therapist in the UK, currently leading and teaching the Community Health and Wellbeing Apprenticeship at Training 2000 and is a disability activist.

Gray Hutchins spent several years in leadership roles at The Clare Project, a community-led charity for trans, non-binary and intersex adults in Sussex. Beyond this, they are a community organiser and entrepreneur, combining intersectional lived and learnt experiences to invite perspective and enhance understanding. Gray currently works as a consultant specialising in the development, recovery and resilience of non-profits; alongside continuing to contribute to a variety of initiatives underpinned by intersectional feminism.

Davinia Jackson is a community organiser in Lancashire (UK) working for Citizens UK, with over 20 years of experience in voluntary and statutory services in the diverse and transient rural and coastal communities of Lancashire.

Katherine Jewell is a research assistant in Social Inclusion and Community Engagement at the University of Lancashire (UK). Katherine has experience working in local government Children's Social Care and also served as a full-time seconded union branch secretary. She holds an MA in Social Policy and a PhD in Political Ethnography, and her current research investigates the use of critical pedagogical methods in community civic education.

João Luís Joventino do Nascimento, also known as João do Cumbe, is a quilombola and PhD student in Social History at the Federal University of Ceará (UFC) under a quota system. He is a human rights defender, part of the leadership of the Quilombola Association of Cumbe/Aracati-CE and an activist in the Quilombola Movement of Ceará, the Movement of Artisanal Fishers (MPP/CE) and the Popular Organisation (OPA). He is also a researcher in the COSQUI-Mental Health Project.

Hannah Kessler is Creative Producer at Rosehill Arts Trust (Rosehill Theatre) in Cumbria, where she leads programmes for families, young people, inclusion, and artist development. With a background in participatory arts, facilitation, music, and theatre-making, she is passionate about creating opportunities for people to engage with the arts, develop their creativity, and build confidence through shared cultural experiences.

Koser Khan is a senior research associate at the University of Lancaster (UK), working with the NIHR-funded ARC Northwest Coast, with a background in welfare rights, local government and public health.

Alaa Kordia, Iscte - Instituto Universitário de Lisboa, Portugal, is a History graduate and has been a teacher in Syria for several years before the war. Currently, he is doing a master's degree in international studies focusing on Syrian refugees' lived experiences and perspectives on social inclusion in Portugal.

Alexander Kweh, Fórum Refúgio Portugal, Portugal, is a community organiser and the coordinator of Fórum Refúgio Portugal.

Anna Madill specialises in qualitative methods with a particular interest in visual approaches (see https://projectresilience.co.uk/). She is Chair in Qualitative Inquiry in the School of Psychology, University of Leeds, UK. Anna Madill is a chartered psychologist, Fellow of the British Psychological Society and Fellow of the Academy of Social Sciences. She co-founded and Chaired (2008–11) the British Psychological Society Qualitative Methods in Psychology Section. Anna Madill is a former associate editor of the *British Journal of Clinical Psychology* and is currently on the Editorial Boards of the *British Journal of Clinical Psychology*, *Qualitative Psychology and Qualitative Research in Psychology* and an editorial consultant for the *British Journal of Social Psychology*.

Terri Mannarini is a full professor in Social Psychology at the University of Salento, Italy. Founder of the international journal Community Psychology in a Global Perspective, her research interests focus on active citizenship and participatory processes, community cohesion and resilience, migration and gender issues.

Francisca Marleide do Nascimento, member of the National Coordination of the Articulation of Black Rural Quilombola Communities (CONAQ), quilombola, daughter of farmers, pedagogue, specialist in school management and psychopedagogy, holds a Master's in Humanities from UNILAB, poet, public school teacher in Fortaleza, activist, human rights defender and researcher in the COSQUI-Mental Health Project.

Elena Marta, PhD, is a full professor in Social and Community Psychology at Università Cattolica del Sacro Cuore Milano-Brescia, where she is Director of CERISVICO Research Centre on Community Development and Organisational Quality of Life. Her research topics are: social relationships of young people, NEET, rurality, volunteerism, risk behaviours, PAR.

Landu Yanick Matondo, Kazumba Association and Yoka Kongo!, Portugal, is an artist and co-creator of VIBE – Voices of Iberia in Black Europe, a project funded by Culture of Solidarity Fund/DGArtes.

Claudia Andréa Mayorga Borges holds a PhD in Social Psychology from the Complutense University of Madrid, Spain. She is currently a professor, researcher and community outreach practitioner in the Department of Psychology at the Federal University of Minas Gerais, Brazil. She coordinates the Núcleo Conexões de Saberes and conducts studies in community social psychology, feminisms and decoloniality.

Isabel Menezes has a degree and a PhD in Psychology and a habilitation in Education Sciences from the University of Porto, where she is a professor in Education Sciences. Her research explores if and how civic and political participation and non/formal education can generate more complex ways of relationship with the political, especially for groups of people in positions of vulnerability.

Ana Leia Morais Cardoso, from CONAQ/Quilombo do Pará, Brazil. Quilombola medical doctor and human rights activist, dedicated to implementing Black population health strategies and developing holistic health policies for quilombola communities. She works in emergency contexts, climate justice and racial equity.

James Ferreira Moura Junior, community psychologist, professor at the University for International Integration of the Afro-Brazilian Lusophony (UNILAB) and at the Postgraduate Programme in Psychology at the Federal University of Ceará. He is the principal investigator of the COSQUIMental Health Project – *Socio-environmental Conflicts, Suicide and Quilombos: strategies for promoting mental health through* (Transdisciplinary Studies in Public Health – CNPq/MS).

Dyoka Mukinay, Kazumba Association and Yoka Kongo!, Portugal, is an artist and co-creator of VIBE Voices of Iberia in Black Europe, a project funded by Culture of Solidarity Fund/DGArtes.

Joseph Murphy is founder and director of the Good Grace Foundation, an international initiative that connects communities through sustainable, nature-based and psychologically informed approaches. He has worked for over 25 years in statutory and third sector housing and homelessness services in Leicester, UK.

Bryan Nash is an expert in homelessness and exclusion by lived experience.

Sam Pywell is a lecturer in the School of Health, Social Work and Sport at the University of Lancashire (UK). She is the Social Prescribing Unit Coordinator. Sam is a Fellow of the Higher Education Academy. Sam also supervises postgraduate student research projects.

Dora Rebelo, Iscte – Instituto Universitário de Lisboa, Portugal, is a psychologist with a PhD in Anthropology, a Mental Health and Psychosocial Support consultant, a researcher and guest lecturer. Her research interests are migrant justice, solidarity and climate justice. She is a member of Fórum Refúgio Portugal and the European Community Psychology Association.

Manuel Riemer is a professor of community psychology and sustainability science at Wilfrid Laurier University, Canada. He is the director of the transdisciplinary Viessmann Centre for Engagement and Research in Sustainability (VERiS), with a focus on the intersection of climate change, sustainability, community and social justice.

Clementina Rios is assistant professor at Polytechnic Institute of Lusofonia, Lusophone Higher School of Education (ESEL–IPLUSO) and integrated researcher at CIIE–FPCEUP. With a PhD in Educational Sciences and 16 years in preschool teaching, she investigates Environmental and Early Childhood Education through pedagogical approaches, emphasising environmental citizenship and participation. At ESEL, she coordinates the master's in preschool and primary education.

Alessia Rochira is an associate professor in Social Psychology at the University of Salento, Italy. Currently editor-in-chief of the international journal *Community Psychology in a Global Perspective*, her research focuses on community diversity and sense of community, acculturation, interethnic contact, and social representations theory.

Fiona Routh is a lecturer in Children, Schools and Families at the University of Lancashire (UK). She previously worked for seven years as an associate for us within the Further Education sector. Fiona has experience in working within the Children, Schools and Families sector, having worked with children and young people aged 0–19 and their families over her career.

Cristina Santinho, CRIA – Center of Research in Anthropology, Portugal, has a PhD in Anthropology and led several action research projects aiming at the social inclusion of refugees, e.g., "Living in a Different Culture" – aiming at refugee students' inclusion in higher education. She is a member of Fórum Refúgio Portugal.

Mateus dos Santos Brito, from Brazil, is a quilombola from Lagoa de Maria Clemência (Bahia). He holds a Master's degree and is a PhD candidate in Public Health (ISC/UFBA), Ethnic-Racial Equity Advisor (Executive Secretariat/Ministry of Health), member of the National Quilombola Health Collective of CONAQ and alumnus of the Afro-Latin American Studies Certificate (ALARI/Harvard University).

Francisco Simões is an assistant researcher and full member of the Centre for Social Research and Intervention at ISCTE – University Institute of Lisbon. He is the Chair of the European Rural Youth Observatory. He has coordinated research projects and published several scientific papers on the psychosocial features of school-to-work transition in rural areas.

Penn Smith is associate professor and postgraduate programme lead for Counselling at York St John University, UK. She is deputy chair for the School of Education, Language and Psychology ethics committee and research lead for Counselling and the York St John Communities Centre. Penn is a chartered psychologist (CPsychol), senior fellow of the Higher Education Academy (SFHEA), and a counsellor with the British Association for Counselling and Psychotherapy (MBACP). Her research and therapeutic interests are in relational trauma, social justice, and working with creative approaches.

Ana Luisa Teixeira de Menezes is a professor of Psychology in the Graduate Programmes in Education and Professional Psychology at the University of Santa Cruz do Sul (UNISC). Between 2009 and 2013, she served as Pro-Rector of Extension and Community Relations at the same institution. She is the deputy leader of the CNPq research group PEABIRU: Amerindian Education and Interculturality (UFRGS/UNISC) and coordinates the project "Intercultural Learning with the Guarani and Kaingang Peoples in Basic Education."

Carlo Tomasetto (he/him) is a full professor of Developmental Psychology in the Department of Psychology at the University of Bologna, Italy. Most of his academic work has been focused on the impact of stereotypes, prejudice and social inequalities on children and adult members of stigmatized social groups.

Carlie D. Trott, associate professor in Psychology at the University of Cincinnati (USA), conducts research addressing the inequitable impacts of climate change, socially and geographically. Trott's climate justice research employs community-engaged, participatory and action research methods to centre the perspectives of those most affected by climate disruption and environmental injustice.

Suzanne Wilson is a research fellow in Social Inclusion and Community Engagement at the University of Lancashire (UK). The research agenda is to work with communities to identify effective and sustainable means of increasing community capital. This expanding portfolio of research focuses on working-class, coastal communities, often regarded as being "left-behind."

FOREWORD

Psychology is still one of the most popular subjects for study at the undergraduate degree level. As well as providing the student with a range of academic and applied skills that are valued by a broad range of employers, a psychology degree also serves as the basis for subsequent training and a career in professional psychology. A substantial proportion of students entering a degree programme in psychology do so with a subsequent career in applied psychology firmly in mind, and as a result, the number of applied psychology courses available at the undergraduate level has significantly increased over recent years. In some cases, these courses supplement core academic areas, and in others, they provide the student with a flavour of what they might experience as a professional psychologist.

The Topics in Applied Psychology series consists of nine textbooks designed to provide a comprehensive academic and professional insight into specific areas of professional psychology. The first eight texts cover the areas of clinical psychology, criminal psychology, educational psychology, health psychology, sports and exercise psychology, work and organisational psychology, counselling psychology and forensic psychology, and each text is written and edited by the foremost professional and academic figures in each of these areas.

It's now my pleasure to introduce this ninth book in the series, *Community Psychology in Action.* This book brings together principles, practices and values committed to the pursuit of social justice and wellbeing, linking the support of individuals with challenges to the processes of marginalisation that have created structures of distress over time. *Community Psychology in Action* aims to inspire and guide students, activists, researchers and practitioners across the world in applying community psychology approaches to address challenges in their own communities. For those new to the field or more experienced, the book brings together contributions from academics, activists and practitioners from around the globe to present a collection of guided case studies in how professional and "everyday" experts respond to global crises by promoting social justice. Examples are drawn from cutting-edge practice and research into issues including climate change, migration, rurality, housing, addiction recovery, clinical mental health practice and caregiving, with a mix of academic scholarship and practical advice.

Through successive editions, each textbook is based on a similar academic formula that combines a comprehensive review of cutting-edge research and professional knowledge with accessible teaching and learning features. The books are also structured, so they can be used as an integrated teaching support for a one-term or one-semester course in each of their relevant areas of applied psychology. Given the increasing importance of applying psychological knowledge across a growing range of areas of practice, we feel this series is timely and comprehensive. We hope you find each book in the series readable, enlightening, accessible and instructive.

Graham Davey
University of Sussex, Brighton, UK

ACKNOWLEDGEMENTS

We would like to express our sincere gratitude to Dr Katherine Jewell for her editorial assistance. Her immense patience and tireless administrative efforts throughout the publishing process provided significant support across a number of chapters.

We have, with gratitude, thanked our funders in individual chapters. We would like to gratefully acknowledge the support of our academic institutions, professional communities, mentors and key colleagues for their time, expertise and resourcing. Our students and community partners have been the audience we are writing towards. Importantly, we would like to acknowledge the contributions of the many community members whose engagement with the research and practice discussed here has made this book what it is. Their names will not be listed as authors but each chapter has been, in its way, written with them.

1 An invitation to participate

Striving towards social justice and wellbeing through community, research and action

Rebecca Graber, Carl Harris, Suzanne Wilson and Maria Fernandes-Jesus

Introduction

Welcome to this book. We hope this edited collection of case studies and activities will be of interest to students, practitioners, researchers and activists – and people who do not identify as any of these but who aspire to support justice and wellbeing in their communities, without yet having a clear role or direction for doing so.

We expect that many readers will already have some familiarity with "community psychology" (if only because they are most likely to pick up a book with "community psychology" in the title!), but we aim to be accessible, interesting and useful to those completely new to this field. Community psychology is a distinctive field, but it can also be practised within different disciplines of psychology (such as clinical psychology, health psychology or applied social psychology), other social sciences (such as sociology) and social or clinical contexts (such as youth work, social work or health care). We hope this book will be useful to any person who is concerned about how global challenges are playing out within their local communities and how communities can come together to address these challenges. We suggest starting where you are and don't worry about having a certain level of expertise or belonging to the "correct" group or organisation – if you have read this far, this book is probably for you.

How to use this book

The format and content of this book is informed by the different professional backgrounds of the four co-editors: Maria, Rebecca, Suzanne and Carl. Together, we hold experiences in teaching community psychology in higher education, research on topics and themes related to community psychology, clinical practice and training, leading community psychology groups, conducting and teaching participatory action research and community activism. We have worked directly within community psychology and incorporated community psychology principles and practices into projects that do not explicitly identify as being within this field. While no one piece of writing can be everything to everyone, our experiences in different kinds of settings encouraged us to continually ask expansive questions of ourselves and our contributing authors so that each of our imagined readers would gain something. Why does this matter? What did you learn? What were the messy or surprising parts of the process? What ideas and concepts underpinned or emerged from this work? What can others learn from your experience? And importantly, what might "social justice" or "wellbeing" look like in this context – how can we creatively envision something better?

DOI: 10.4324/9781003480464-1

Each chapter discusses how community psychology research and practice has been applied to a particular social problem such as migration, climate change or housing precarity and homelessness. We have organised these thematically into four parts: (i) Homes and movement, (ii) Transforming power, (iii) Crafting connection and (iv) Troubling medicalisation. We do not attempt to be comprehensive – geographically, topically or in any other meaningful way. One characteristic of community psychology is a confidence that more localised activities, when done a certain way, can have a transformative effect. This book is a sample of the type of work conducted by community psychologists and allies, but it is only a sample of what is being done across the world. We encourage curious readers to take their interest even further. We reached out through our extended networks to ask for work that would discuss a thematic strand of community psychology across a recognised global challenge, including case studies of inspiring research, practice and/or activism in local communities. We focused particularly on contributors who were using key methods such as participatory action research or creative methods and on case studies that could be written up to provide insights for learning. (And of course, not everyone we approached to contribute was able to say yes.) This book therefore reflects a starting point of interests and opportunities, rather than a finished conversation.

Chapters vary in format and thematic focus, but all contain the following elements. The authors lay out a *critical discussion* of the social problem, giving the reader context for understanding the issue from a community psychology perspective and aiming to enable you, the reader, to ask critical questions and undertake further action. The discussions use a *multi-level lens* whenever possible to describe and discuss this problem in terms of how individual, relational, community- and structural-level forces contribute to this particular social and historical moment, in the community in question. Chapters explore *what community psychologists can d***o** in this field, including challenges and opportunities. The authors provide one or more *case studies* of community psychology practice and research from their own work, explaining what they have done (and sometimes, still hope to do) to address this social problem: What knowledge was gained, what questions were raised and what was left unknown? What changes to communities have resulted from this work and what is still unknown or left to do? Our authors have been gracious in unpacking the *process* of their research and practice, including where things took an unexpected turn, to help inspire readers to apply this experience to their own contexts.

In an important addition to other community psychology texts, each chapter includes one or more *action for learning activities*. These are activities aiming to help you, the reader, enhance your own understanding and enact change through research, reflection, practice or activism using community psychology tools and techniques. They have been shaped by two community psychology principles of *praxis* (action shapes knowledge, which then shapes action, in an ongoing cycle) and *conscientização* (raising critical awareness and understanding as a form of empowerment and social change). For us, this means that learning must involve "doing" – and any meaningful discussion of a social problem has to then be turned over to you, the reader, to make something new out of it. Many of these activities are creative, involve little or no resources and can be undertaken alone or in groups. We hope you will use and adapt these activities in workshops, classrooms, community groups and self-reflection exercises – make them your own, so that you can start to apply your learning and seize on your inspiration straight away.

Chapters also include *discussion questions* which can be used to provoke conversation in workshops and small-group settings and *reflective questions* to help you apply and extend your investigation of a problem. Some authors have also included *additional resources* including books, articles or other media. We hope all of this will help you develop the skills, knowledge and attributes you will need going forward.

Themes

We now present a brief overview of each chapter, organised by thematic parts.

Homes and movement

Chapters 2, 3 and 4 are primarily concerned with what it is to be fully at home in the communities one lives in and belongs to, with dignity, meaningful participation and inclusion. The challenges of this task are starkly evident among migrant and refugee communities – who must re-make home out of urgency and for whom the yearning of home carries both recollections of memory and imaginings of undetermined futures. As Mannarini, Rochira and De Simone explore in Chapter 2, migration can be conceptualised as both a slow-onset stressor – a gradual process that prompts adaptation and change – and an ongoing societal challenge. Applying a richly drawn framework of community resilience, they explore ways in which the one striving to cope, eventually thrive in the face of upheaval is not the person, but the community itself. The authors suggest that migration offers opportunities for revitalisation, growth and meaning *because of*, not despite, the challenges posed to communities as they undergo transformation. Crucially, they identify *participation* and *sense of community* as pillars of resilient communities and show how these theoretical concepts played out in practice in the life of the city of Riace, Italy. In Chapter 3, Rebelo, Santinho, Cunha, Kordia, de Figueiredo and Amelung detail the creation of a collaborative research group striving to address barriers to social inclusion, using three case studies blending community psychology and anthropology in contexts of informal relationship building, obstetric health care and music research. The authors offer valuable and vulnerable reflections on how they successfully negotiated multiple perspectives, backgrounds and goals within the wider collective of project organisers, providing insight into the messiness of working with differences to avoid reproducing those social processes of exclusion and narrowing that they ultimately wish to disrupt. Those studying and working across other social contexts and problems will find much to learn from their experience.

Inequalities and precarity are also faced by unhoused people in their country of origin, as access to essential services and basic conditions of living are frequently tied to secure, predictable housing. In Chapter 4, De Oliveira, Elliott, Hancox, Harker-Brown, Murphy and Nash demonstrate participatory ways of working with "rough sleepers" in the UK to address immediate needs and inspire broader social change. They argue that relationshipbuilding, organisational flexibility and a willingness to understand lived experiences of homelessness can effectively challenge derogatory social stereotypes, social exclusion and the wariness of rough sleepers who have had negative experiences with prior outreach attempts. The arts are one way of bridging such divides, as is doing "street work" as part of service delivery.

Transforming power

While power can be conceptualised as an abstract concept, its impact is realised through access, resources and efficacy. While redistributing power can be one important goal of community psychologists, so can be a goal of transforming the nature of power and how it operates within a given social context or applied social problem. In Chapter 5, Moura, Jr, Silva, Marleide Nascimento, Joventino do Nascimento, Brito, Cardoso, Borges, Menezes, Diniz and Campos centre the use of participatory action research methods as, foremost, a political and ethical commitment which, when practised, aims to transform knowledge production. Their case study is situated within historically contested *quilombola* communities of Brazil, which are emblematic as sites of collective resistance and transformation. In the contemporary context, wellbeing is imagined as the flourishing of communal bonds, cultural resilience and self-determination. In the UK, Wilson, Jewell, Crosthwaite and Jackson (Chapter 6) engage with narratives of White working-class disconnection from the geographical and political centre. They develop and explain a concept of political peripherality where marginalisation as related to feelings of being "left-behind" can be challenged through participatory approaches that can particularly engage young people in making an imprint in local communities. Here, interestingly, there is less desire to overturn traditional power structures but more a concern with physical and symbolic ways to co-create within those structures.

The approach taken by Fernandes-Jesus, Trott, Barnes and Riemer in Chapter 7 exemplifies how community psychology articulates the link between complex global challenges, such as climate change and social justice, embedding an individual within a multi-level system. Community psychology principles and practices are applied to the pursuit of distributive, intergenerational, procedural and recognitional forms of climate justice, using examples of collaborative and participatory projects in Haiti, Canada and South Africa. This represents an important transition from focusing on individual-level responses to climate change, such as anxiety or pro-environmental behaviour, towards using psychology to support community-level change, transforming power and advancing social justice while addressing climate-related issues.Further, in Chapter 8, Menezes, Rios, Pais and Ferreira show how participatory research processes can foster hope even amidst the troubling, seemingly intractable challenges faced by a generation of youth facing significant climate change. Here, young people in the Porto Metropolitan Area in Portugal were empowered to conduct research, identify significant issues impacting their locality and devise hopeful and actionable proposals for solutions through a community profiling methodology. The authors reflect on the ethical and methodological commitments of stewarding young people through a transformation of power within their own areas of influence and the importance of creating diverse and pluralistic spaces for young people to co-create their futures. The chapter provides useful inspiration for those wanting to disrupt existing models of policy towards something more responsive, actionable and hopeful.

Crafting connection

Ultimately, humans in communities are humans in relationship, yet discussions of community-building do not always centre the relational dimensions of this work. Wilson, Graber, Jewell and Kessler (Chapter 9) explore relational practice in the context of the challenges faced by unpaid caregivers in the UK, attending to the emotional tenor of loneliness and social exclusion often faced by those undertaking this role, as many of us may do over the course of a life. The authors ask how to bring relationships *as relationships* more strongly into community psychology practice and research and apply a novel framework for developing a person's capacity and power through relationshipbuilding. They detail a grassroots case study of using creativity and the arts to develop an inclusive, multi-generational community space to nourish, empower and connect. Linking this with research practice, they discuss how to actively foster relational approaches to empowerment and impact for social change. Social connection is also at the centre of Graber, Duara, Goswami, Chowdhury and Madill's exploration of recovery to, and prevention of, substance addiction in urban areas of Assam, India (Chapter 10). They argue that substance addiction is a community-level risk to wellbeing, impacted by (and impacting) social inequalities and relationships. The authors draw on a series of case studies of creative, arts-based techniques in research and mental health practice to traverse the various chasms of social exclusion facing young people experiencing addiction. The examples show how creativity can practically empower people in addiction recovery to use their experience to inform compassionate, culturally sensitive understandings of addiction that may support recovery and prevent further harm in the at-risk communities they live in. The authors offer encouragement that creative, arts-based techniques can inspire those working on social problems to break out of existing practices and generate new, hopeful visions for a healthy and socially connected future.

In Chapter 11, Cecconi, Tomasetto and Albanesi connect the individual and the systemic, approaching intimate partner violence against women through the concept of secondary victimisation. They use an intersectional multi-level lens to articulate how service providers and institutions who aim to support victims/survivors may (unwittingly) re-traumatise women and, frequently, their children. The authors define the problem of secondary victimisation, and crucially, they identify steps towards social justice. They apply a concept of dynamic empowerment to suggest theory-based tools and strategies to transform formal settings to restore power to women who have had it wrenched from them. The ability to weave theory and practice, individual wellbeing and systemic justice, is an ambition of community psychology. Simões and Marta close this part with Chapter 12 by using community psychology to frame the experience of young people in rural settings, which in the European context, are frequently depicted as lacking meaningful opportunities for the next generation compared to urban settings. They probe whether there can be spaces for participation within existing cultures of decision-making for younger generations to contribute, harnessing young people's interests in being socially active to solve concrete problems. They convincingly argue that fostering participation depends on building a relational environment underpinned by trust and detail the use of specific youth-led participatory action research methods to create a skilled environment for intergenerational collaboration and cooperation in policy, governance and community action. Their chapter provides inspiration for using similar strategies in other geographical contexts to connect decision-making mechanisms with the needs of community members.

Troubling medicalisation: perspectives from the UK

Community psychology perspectives can be usefully – if sometimes disruptively – integrated with other disciplines and forms of professional practice, particularly where medical models tend to dominate narratives and discourses of "wellbeing." This is a long process, often requiring patience in striving to work towards ideals of participation in settings which have been shaped by alternative models of service delivery. Here we focus particularly on the UK, its National Health Service (NHS) and related systems of social and health care. Edwards-Smith, Pywell, Routh, Khan and Hicks (Chapter 13) apply the multilevel approach to families, conceptualising family wellbeing as a goal for health and exploring the potential for NHS-led social prescribing techniques as a way to counter the effects of social inequalities through improving families' access to support, education and wellbeing services. This approach embeds community psychology practices and values into the health service, although with several challenges to implementation, including tailoring for different age groups, resource constraints and organisational cultures. Smith and Madill, in Chapter 14, consider the challenges of applying concepts of empowerment and social justice within a multi-agency setting servicing people with profound, complex mental health needs. Here, the use of research techniques aimed at empowering service users (such as photo-led interviews) can be seen to pose ethical challenges when weighed against other principles such as safeguarding and confidentiality and the ability of participants to engage day-to-day. The authors provide a clear, step-by-step route in for practitioners and researchers wanting to introduce these kinds of potentially empowering approaches into similar multi-agency settings with highly vulnerable people and discuss how this kind of research provides opportunities for participants to reflect on connection, integration and community.

In Chapter 15, Hutchins aims to create space for community psychologists to contribute to movements for person-centred healthcare for trans and non-binary (TNB) people. Drawing on their grassroots experience working within communities, developing project-based initiatives and advising health policymakers and practitioners in the southeast of England, the author argues for the necessity of community-led initiatives and commissioning structures that move beyond "representation" to "participation." Social justice and wellbeing are conceptualised as the ability of TNB people to have all health needs met, above and beyond care that affirms their gender, within a system that is designed with, and for, gender-diverse people. The tensions of working within or outside of existing systems can be deeply felt, and a map of a way forward can be valuable. Harris, Bostock, Hagan, Stirzaker and Young close the part (Chapter 16) by describing how, working separately, a group of clinical psychologists in different areas of the NHS have aimed to integrate community psychologist values and practices into mental health care. The authors note that many clinical psychologists are aware of the ways in which social inequalities such as poor housing, precarity, poverty and loneliness contribute to poor mental health outcomes but feel a lack of opportunities within service provision to operate in a community-centred way. The chapter explores practical ways in which clinicians have created entry for community psychology in their fields, often through collaboration with other kinds of services, creative tools and the creation of accessible and impactful guidance documents. Readers seeking inspiration for what to "do" with their learning will find many ideas and can take heart that incremental changes in mainstream settings can lead to significant benefits for communities and individuals.

Finally, in our concluding Chapter 17, we as co-editors (Fernandes-Jesus, Wilson, Graber and Harris) reiterate an urgent call to action: to engage in a continuous commitment to challenge the structural roots of adversity, contest power and oppression and progress towards a future of social justice through the values, practices and principles of community psychology. We encourage all readers, regardless of their backgrounds, to bring their resources and skills to mobilise towards social change, and caution against the dangers of populist and oppressive ideologies that may promise betterment at the expense of others. Ultimately, we strive towards a future of liberation without oppression, where empowerment is realised without reproducing or creating additional forms of suffering. If this seems a lofty goal, we are heartened by the practical steps forward offered in this book and in community psychology more broadly.

Defining community psychology and its key principles and practices

We will not attempt to give a definitive definition of community psychology, as there are many useful ones from researchers and professional groups, but will highlight some we like. Describing the development of Latin American community psychology, one of the main geographical centres of this field, Montero (2008) shows that community psychology became a transformative discipline in which both participants and researchers are seen as main actors in a participatory research and action process that is capable of giving meaningful answers to people's needs; where there is a focus on theoretical plurality and critical revision of knowledge; and a liberating and ethical character is increasingly important, so that people can solve the problems that bother them and enact changes to the environment and social context. In the UK, Kagan and Burton (see Burton et al., 2007) state that community psychology presents a framework for working with marginalised people that leads to self-aware social change through a process of value-based, participatory work underpinned by effective alliances. It is presented as an alternative to individualistic psychology because intervention and analysis go above the levels of the individual and their immediate interpersonal context. Bhatia and Sethi (2007) explain that as communities are social systems that function to meet a person's needs, community psychology can be understood as a different framework for understanding the needs of a person and the resources available to meet them, with interventions aiming to provide opportunities for wellbeing within this context. Community psychology extends a global outreach but has particularly strong histories within Latin America, Europe, the United States and Canada, Australia and New Zealand, South Africa and India.

Our own definition of community psychology draws from these and many others. Community psychology is a discipline of psychology with a set of recognisable principles, practices and values which can pragmatically and conscientiously be embedded within adjacent disciplines and is premised upon the idea that humans exist in communal relationships. Issues of wellbeing are viewed through a lens of power and empowerment, where an individual is nested within multiple layers of interconnected systems that interact to affect conditions, processes and outcomes, so that social justice is an intrinsic part of wellbeing. Part of psychological knowledge-making therefore involves understanding this interplay and bringing it to attention. A sense of action and purpose underpins community psychology work, so that change to social conditions, as well as alleviation of immediate suffering, becomes part of the psychological project of understanding human behaviour and supporting wellbeing. Community psychology tends not only towards the radical and disruptive, but also towards the collective. It is underpinned by participation – doing with, instead of doing to or doing for – as a way of making knowledge, transforming practice and shifting power and resources. Community psychology can be done in many places – a classroom, a therapy clinic, a local government meeting, a youth centre or a beach, but it cannot be done alone. Community psychology entails meaningful, productive relating between people of a community, and, in the right conditions, between members of a marginalised community and those with more resources and power. And while we are not sure that it is *required*, we think that maintaining a sense of hope can make engagement with these complex challenges feel more sustainable and help us imagine new ways of doing.

Distinctive principles and practices of community psychology

It will be helpful to be familiar with some key concepts from community psychology before reading the rest of the book. Many of the chapters explore these concepts in detail. All these terms are subject to much discussion and debate; we encourage you to take your reading further.

In community psychology, the *ecological levels of analysis* are a framework for understanding problems by examining their impact across multiple environmental layers, from the individual to the broader society (Kelly, 1986). This multi-level approach, which is also often seen in developmental psychology, involves concepts like the microsystem (immediate surroundings, like the family or the school), mesosystem (interactions between the microsystems), exosystem (indirect influences, like social care services or a parent's workplace) and macrosystem (cultural and economic systems such as a particular health policy or values of individualism or collectivism) (Bronfenbrenner, 1979, 1994). By analysing these interconnected systems, community psychologists identify key areas for intervention and foster positive, lasting change within communities. Each individual is seen as nested within these interconnected systems, so that a more complete analysis of a particular social issue or example of mental distress will attend to all, or some, of these levels.

While people belong to groups and are subject to social forces, community psychology is built on the idea that we do not just group together but form real or imagined *communities* based on geography, identity, shared purpose or other commonalities. This sense of community is a fundamental human need that promotes psychological wellbeing, provides emotional and practical support and buffers individuals against stress and isolation (Baumeister & Leary, 2017). A sense of *belonging* is therefore a core component of community psychology, encompassing feelings of connection, acceptance and shared identity within a group (McMillan & Chavis, 1986). A strong sense of belonging is associated with better adjustment, stronger social support and a greater ability to identify with group goals and values (Sarason, 1974; Goodenow, 1993). Some communities have been historically or are even now *marginalised*: the outcome of a process where structural disadvantages, transfer of adversity across generations and individual vulnerabilities interact so that members of these communities have comparatively less access to the social power, resources and capacity needed to engage productively with society (Kagan et al., 2019).

Empowerment is a key approach to reversing the negative effects of marginalisation and resource imbalances by building capacity and shifting *power* dynamics (Rappaport, 1987; Zimmerman, 2000; Zimmerman & Rappaport, 1988). Empowerment can be economic, social or psychological (Rappaport & Seidman, 2000). It can be fostered in numerous ways, including community-driven solutions (Christens, 2019), increased access and skills, participatory approaches (Fine & Torre, 2019) and peer support (Mario et al., 2009). *Participatory approaches* are critical within community psychology. They involve collaboration, shared decision-making and community ownership in research and interventions, aiming to empower communities and address social problems from within (Lewin, 1946). Key methods include Community-Based Participatory Research (CBPR) and Participatory Action Research (PAR), which focus on incorporating community voices to develop solutions that align with their needs and cultural contexts (Fine, 2018; Wallerstein et al., 2017). These approaches break down the traditional power dynamic between external experts and communities, fostering mutual respect and a focus on social justice (Fals-Borda and Rahman, 1991).

One way of doing this is through *conscientização*. *Conscientização* is a Brazilian Portuguese term for critical consciousness or consciousness-raising, a concept developed by educator and philosopher Paulo Freire (Freire, 2017). A central tenet of his critical pedagogy, it is the process through which people become aware of the social, political and economic contradictions that oppress them and take action to transform their reality. Conscientização is more than simply gaining knowledge; it is a profound shift in perspective that combines critical reflection with action, a process Freire called *praxis*. These concepts have been widely applied within liberation and community psychology, with an explicit focus on social justice and social action (Martín-Baró, 1996; Prilleltensky, 2001).

Action-orientation and *social change* are fundamental principles of community psychology, which views psychological wellbeing as deeply interconnected with social conditions and aims to empower communities to address systemic issues through collective action (Montero, 2011, 2012). Community psychologists conduct participatory, action-oriented research to understand and reduce the impact of factors like poverty, discrimination and political policies on marginalised groups, fostering solidarity and collective action to achieve social justice goals (Balcazar et al., 1998).

An invitation to participate

The process of co-editing this book has itself been *praxis*. In applying community psychology principles and practices to this collaboration, we have come to better understand what these are. Over two years of work, we came to identify several values that underpin this book and inform our collective vision of what community psychology can and should be. These values are: respectful dialogue, curiosity, humanisation, willingness to be in relationship, social justice and wellbeing, hopefulness and liberation without oppression. We offer these as a complement to and extension of the practices identified in the previous part, showing the evolution of the discipline as we have come to practice it.

First, we aim towards *respectful dialogue* with each other, with authors and with knowledge. We hope readers can be in genuine conversation with this book and with their worlds, being in continual relation to a multiplicity of others and always under active construction. While dialogue is often enriching, inspiring and enlightening, at times it is tense, provocative and challenging. When working closely together to examine significant issues of our time, we found that we did not always agree: sometimes holding competing understandings or priorities despite our many common values or realising that we have come to experience the world in different ways. We were challenged by the chapters, our authors, each other and events unfolding in the world. A commitment to respectful dialogue, to building knowledge and understanding together, needs continual renewal: a promise in good faith to listen, learn, speak, reflect and connect. Underpinning this is a commitment to *curiosity*: a desire to engage in knowing, grounded in a humility and acknowledgement that there is much we do not, or perhaps cannot, know. Participatory and collaborative approaches to knowledge-making must be grounded in curiosity for them to retain a level of respect for the dignity and wisdom of all of those participating. This differs from an extractive approach to knowledge-making, where something is done *to* a person or a patronising approach where people are not seen as able to contribute to knowledge-making processes and where their experiences and worldviews are therefore deemed less valid.

A criterion for recognising this curiosity in action is seeing whether an interaction is fundamentally humanising. Does an interaction – a piece of writing, a study, a professional body, an interpersonal relationship, etc. – appear to treat a person as a full and complex person, with dignity, rights, a history, a full and rich inner life, a culture? Does this interaction treat members of a group or community as a collective of humans, seen this way? *Humanisation* can be a powerful counter to the polarisation that we observe across facets of society. This is partly recognisable in acknowledging the complexity and richness of a given person or community. It is also recognisable in a perceived willingness to engage in contact with another. One needs contact to build strong relationships within communities, and eventually one needs intergroup contact, under careful conditions, to achieve empowerment and move past extraordinary divisions (e.g., White et al., 2019). We are particularly struck by the role of human relationship in underpinning this remaking: to relate to an excluded other, to relate to one's community, to relate to one's self, to forge points of empathetic connection, are suggested throughout these chapters as a necessary precondition for meaningful social change. Community psychology can and should disrupt the status quo and its social systems; but a community psychology that dehumanises an Other, that relies upon disconnection, division or discrediting, is one which risks reproducing existing injustices or bringing new ones into the world. A *willingness to be in relationship,* to allow *oneself* to be changed through sustained interaction and engagement, is therefore crucial.

Global challenges threaten communities in profound and diverse ways, but we remain hopeful for viable alternatives. We believe *hopefulness* is truly radical. It is, arguably, easy to critically identify problems – this is a foundational and valuable activity of social science, activism and clinical work. It is therefore understandable to feel burdened by despondency over the many injustices facing communities across the globe and the suffering and divisions seen day to day. Each of us struggled with this at times over the years, as our own lives were impacted in different ways by some of the problems faced in this book and more. But, without hope, it is hard to live. And without hope, it is hard to imagine, much less enact, better. We challenged our authors to imagine what *social justice and wellbeing* could look like in the context of their work, taking a communities-led approach. Some of us, authors and editors, struggled to put this affirmative vision into words. In doing so we came to understand that this imagining was a fundamental act of hope and that work underpinned by hope offers potential for meaningful action to not only disrupt injustice but reorient processes of change. At the same time, hopefulness without a critical understanding of social issues may lead to imaginaries of the future that reproduce existing injustices. We therefore deliberately do not offer a singular vision of social justice and wellbeing, recognising that these are necessarily contested concepts. Instead, we seek to foster a shared commitment to an ongoing practice of working towards *liberation without oppression*, in which members of diverse communities are empowered to flourish together without harm to self, other beings or the environment. We aim to equip ourselves and readers with the resources to bring this to fruition. We may not finish the work, but it is as good a time as any to get started.

References

Balcazar, F. E., Keys, C. B., Kaplan, D. L., & Suarez-Balcazar, Y. (1998). Participatory action research and people with disabilities: Principles and challenges. *Canadian Journal of Rehabilitation, 12*, 105–112.

Baumeister, R. F., & Leary, M. R. (2017). The need to belong: Desire for interpersonal attachments as a fundamental human motivation. In *Interpersonal development* (pp. 57–89). Routledge.

Bhatia, S., & Sethi, N. (2007). History and theory of community psychology in India: An international perspective. In S. M. Reich, M. Riemer, I. Prilleltensky, & M. Montero (Eds.), *International community psychology* (pp. 180–199). Springer.

Bronfenbrenner, U. (1979). *The ecology of human development: Experiments by nature and design.* Harvard University Press.

Bronfenbrenner, U. (1994). Ecological models of human development. *International Encyclopedia of Education, 3*(2), 37–43.

Burton, M., Boyle, S., Harris, C., & Kagan, C. (2007). Community Psychology in Britain. In S. Reich, M. Riemer, I. Prilleltensky, & M. Montero (Eds.), *International Community Psychology*. Springer.

Christens, B. D. (2019). *Community power and empowerment*. Oxford University Press.

Fals-Borda, O., & Rahman, M. A. (Eds.). (1991). *Action and knowledge: Breaking the monopoly with participatory action-research.* Apex Press.

Fine, M. (2018). *Just research in contentious times: Widening the methodological imagination.* Teachers College Press.

Fine, M., & Torre, M. E. (2019). Critical participatory action research: A feminist project for validity and solidarity. *Psychology of Women Quarterly, 43*(4), 433–444.

Freire, P. (2017). *Pedagogy of the oppressed.* Penguin Classics.

Goodenow, C. (1993). The psychological sense of school membership among adolescents: Scale development and educational correlates. *Psychology in the Schools, 30*(1), 79–90.

Kelly, J. G. (1986). Context and process: An ecological view of the interdependence of practice and research. *American Journal of Community Psychology, 14*(6), 581–589.

Lewin, K. (1946). Action research and minority problems. *Journal of Social Issues, 2*(4), 34–46.

Mario, J., Osorio, F., Montero, M., & Sonn, C. C. (2009). *Psychology of liberation: Theory and applications.* Springer.
Martín-Baró, I. (1996). *Writings for a liberation psychology.* Harvard University Press.
McMillan, D. W., & Chavis, D. M. (1986). Sense of community: A definition and theory. *Journal of Community Psychology*, *14*(1), 6–23.
Montero, M. (2008). An insider's look at the development and current state of community psychology in Latin America. *Journal of Community Psychology*, *36*(5), 661–674.
Montero, M. (2011). A critical look at critical community psychology. *Social and Personality Psychology Compass*, *5*(12), 950–959.
Montero, M. (2012). From complexity and social justice to consciousness: Ideas that have built a community psychology. *Global Journal of Community Psychology Practice*, *3*(1), 1–13.
Prilleltensky, I. (2001). Value-based praxis in community psychology: Moving toward social justice and social action. *American Journal of Community Psychology*, *29*(5), 747–778.
Rappaport, J. (1987). Terms of empowerment/exemplars of prevention: Toward a theory for community psychology. *American Journal of Community Psychology*, *15*(2), 121–148.
Rappaport, J., & Seidman, E. (Eds.). (2000). *Handbook of community psychology.* Springer Science & Business Media.
Sarason, S. B. (1974). *The psychological sense of community: Prospects for a community psychology.* Jossey-Bass.
Wallerstein, N., Duran, B., Oetzel, J. G., & Minkler, M. (Eds.). (2017). *Community-based participatory research for health: Advancing social and health equity.* John Wiley & Sons.
White, F., Turner, R., Verrelli, S., Harvey, L., & Hanna, J. (2019) Improving intergroup relations between Catholics and Protestands in Northern Ireland via E-contact. *European Journal of Social Psychology*, *49*(2), 429–439.
Zimmerman, M. A. (2000). Empowerment theory: Psychological, organizational and community levels of analysis. In J. Rappaport & E. Seidman (Eds.), *Handbook of community psychology* (pp. 43–63). Springer US.
Zimmerman, M. A., & Rappaport, J. (1988). Citizen participation, perceived control, and psychological empowerment. *American Journal of Community Psychology*, *16*(5), 725–750.

Further reading

Barrett, M., & Zani, B. (2015). *Political and civic engagement: Multidisciplinary perspectives.* Routledge.
Francescato, D., & Aber, M. S. (2015). Learning from organizational theory to build organizational empowerment. *Journal of Community Psychology*, *43*(6), 717–738.
Freitas, M. D. F. Q. D. (1998). Inserção na comunidade e análise de necessidades: reflexões sobre a prática do psicólogo. *Psicologia: reflexão e crítica*, *11*, 175–189.
Kagan, C., Akhurst, J., Alfaro, J., Lawthom, R., Richards, M., & Zambrano, A. (2022). *Routledge international handbook of community psychology*. Routledge.
Kagan, C., Burton, M., Duckett, P., Lawthom, R., & Siddiquee, A. (2019). *Critical community psychology: Critical action and social change*. Routledge.

PART I

Homes and movement

2 Community resilience, sense of community and participation in the context of contemporary migration

Terri Mannarini, Alessia Rochira and Evelyn De Simone

The chapter explores community resilience in the context of international migration, presenting migration as a slow-onset stressor and ongoing challenge. It examines how a sense of community and participation enable communities to adapt to migration-related changes. The authors argue that community resilience is not a fixed outcome, but a dynamic process of adaptation. Through theoretical analysis and empirical studies, including a case study of Riace, Italy, the chapter discusses how communities can transform migration challenges into opportunities for social revitalisation by cultivating an inclusive sense of community and promoting collective action. Key themes include the importance of inclusive social interactions, participatory approaches and the need to address structural inequalities while fostering collective empowerment and cultural understanding.

Migration as a slow-onset stressor and an ongoing challenge

According to the United Nations, international migration is a global issue and a major public concern worldwide. The latest Migration Report of the UN International Organisation for Migration (McAuliffe & Oucho, 2024) underlines that international migration is a complex phenomenon, significantly influenced by economic and political dynamics, socio-demographic transitions and environmental and technological changes taking place on a global scale. Although migration is a global issue, it does not manifest itself as a single phenomenon. Rather, it emerges in distinct patterns and configurations that depend on the specific contexts in which it occurs and are shaped by various economic, political, social, demographic and environmental factors.

In this sense, international migration represents a slow-onset stressor, that is, an "anthropogenic driver of change" (Verbena et al., 2021; Wilson, 2012) with the term "stressor" referring not to a negative evaluation of migration but to a process that prompts communities to adapt and potentially transform over time. Slow-onset stressors represent complex, multidimensional phenomena that result not from discrete events, but from the convergence of multiple conditions and circumstances over long periods of time (Staupe-Delgado, 2019). Slow-onset processes occur in all areas of the world, although their manifestation and the corresponding community responses vary considerably among populations (Rochira et al., 2022).

Unlike far-reaching events – particularly large-scale and exceptional crises such as natural disasters, health emergencies and wars – slow-onset stressors lack precise points of origin and produce gradual transformations in communities. These processes unfold through gradual, incremental changes and

DOI: 10.4324/9781003480464-3

show significant interconnectedness, ultimately producing adverse impacts that can significantly affect communities and fundamentally alter their profile and functioning (Faulkner et al., 2018). These transformations eventually come to be perceived as routine aspects of social life because their effects appear less dramatic than sudden catastrophic events. Consequently, their potential for risk and damage to the environment and community health often goes unnoticed until they escalate into acute crises or rapid-onset disasters (Amirzadeh & Barakpour, 2021; Vargo Hsu, 2019).

International migration is an example of a slow-onset stressor, as it continues to evolve through subtle changes. The gradual nature of migration-related changes creates a unique dynamic for continued system transformation and adaptation. Indeed, international migration can be seen as a "continuous challenge," forcing communities to gradually expand and adapt to accommodate newcomers, thereby fostering more sustainable integration processes. Understanding migration as a slow-onset stressor and continuous challenge provides valuable insights for community psychologists in both research and practice and highlights the importance of sustainable, adaptive approaches that can address both the challenges and opportunities presented by gradual community change.

Community resilience as a theoretical framework for addressing migration challenges

The ability of communities to deal creatively with ongoing challenges is usually referred to as community resilience. This concept has received considerable attention from both academics and practitioners and has generated extensive discourse on its utility in understanding systemic responses to both acute environmental disturbances, such as natural disasters, terrorist attacks and armed conflicts (Magis, 2010; Ostadtaghizadeh et al., 2015) and continuous challenges, such as climate change and international migration (Rochira et al., 2022; Staupe-Delgado, 2019). Community resilience has evolved conceptually over time, from early definitions that focused on a community's ability to recover from disruptions to more nuanced understandings of adaptive processes. Bonanno et al. (2015) made an important distinction between acute stressors, which represent relatively isolated traumatic events, and chronic stressors, which exert repeated and cumulative effects over extended periods. While extensive research has addressed community resilience in response to acute stressors (Abramowitz, 2005; Kendra & Wachtendorf, 2003; Tobin & Whiteford, 2002), investigation of community resilience in the context of chronic stressors is still in its infancy (Rochira et al., 2022).

Community resilience is far from a single concept. Norris et al. (2008) conceptualised community resilience as resulting from the interaction of four adaptive capacities, namely (1) economic development based on resource volume, diversity and accessibility; (2) social capital, which includes network structures and connections; (3) information and communication systems; and (4) community competence such as collective action and decision-making. Building on this foundation, Matarrita-Cascante et al. (2017) proposed a synthesis through three fundamental dimensions: (1) change processes as resilience manifests when communities encounter stressor-induced change; (2) contextual factors, recognising that different types of stressors produce different psychological and social outcomes; and (3) components of resilience, acknowledging that operational definitions depend on specific constituent elements (Vaneeckhaute et al., 2017).

Despite a variety of conceptualisations and measurement approaches, community resilience continues to be a valuable construct for both research and practice (Carpenter, 2014; Klein et al., 2003). The current scenario of polycrisis – including the COVID-19 pandemic, armed conflicts and climate change

– has intensified interest of both researchers and decision-makers in community resilience processes. These recent applications have particularly highlighted the social components of community resilience such as the role of social media and new technologies (Gatti & Procentese, 2024; Karami & Keshavarz, 2024) and social networks and capital (Carter & Cordero, 2022; Hall et al., 2023; Kristanti et al., 2021; Perach et al., 2023) in fostering adaptive capacities and have also highlighted the need for an intersectional approach (Siller & Aydin, 2022).

Regardless of the specific contexts in which it is embedded, contemporary approaches tend to view community resilience as a process, a capacity of communities to respond not only to sporadic events, but also and especially to continuous stressors (Cardinali et al., 2024; Rochira et al., 2022; Tavares et al., 2022). As Staupe-Delgado (2019) has noted, models based on "pre-" and "post-disaster" phases are inadequate to capture community responses to slow-onset disasters characterised by protracted temporal development such as international migration. Full recovery or a return to stability proves virtually impossible amidst ongoing challenges (Staupe-Delgado, 2019). Instead, communities experiencing slow-onset challenges prioritise maintaining optimal functional capacity despite chronic vulnerability and ongoing adaptation demands. In the context of continuous challenges, community resilience manifests as a persistent adaptive process that allows social systems to persist and evolve through an interplay of strengths and vulnerabilities, involving both adaptive and maladaptive responses (Imperiale & Vanclay, 2016). The heterogeneous nature and manifestations of slow-onset processes suggest that community resilience does not function as a universal formula (Faulkner et al., 2018) but rather evolves as a context-specific and dynamic configuration of adaptive capacities (Norris et al., 2008). While important unresolved questions remain, the continued interest in this construct suggests that community resilience may serve as a valuable theoretical framework for analysing and studying slow-onset stressors.

In the specific context of international migration, several dimensions of community resilience emerge as particularly relevant. Social connectedness and networks provide crucial support systems that facilitate integration and mutual understanding between newcomers and established residents. Community competence enables collective problem-solving and the development of innovative responses to demographic changes. Transformative potential allows communities not only to adapt to migration-related changes, but also to evolve in ways that promote social cohesion and cultural enrichment. These dimensions highlight how resilience frameworks can help communities approach migration not only as a challenge to be managed, but also as an opportunity for positive transformation.

In sum, the multiplicity of definitions, operationalisations and domains of application that we have outlined so far leads us to suggest that rather than being a uniformly definable and measurable construct, community resilience is more appropriately a framework for addressing ongoing societal challenges, in particular how communities persistently strive to resist, adapt and transform in response to the changes brought about by migration.

Migration as a community challenge: Sense of community and participation as pillars of resilient communities

Migration is both a global phenomenon and a locally situated and context-dependent process that acquires distinctive characteristics based on the specificities of the community in which it takes place (Nair & Safra, 2024; Olcese et al., 2024; Verbena et al., 2021). Furthermore, as a continuous phenomenon, its characteristics and manifestations are not static but evolve over time, progressing through incremental transitions punctuated by periodic significant transformations.

Considering this argumentation, community resilience is the preferred conceptual framework for approaching how migration becomes a lived everyday experience for individuals living in local communities. Given these premises, a sense of community and participation stands out as a key mechanism for recognising how the impact of immigration is felt locally by migrants and receiving communities, beyond a narrow focus on the internal processes of individuals (Ayers & Forsyth, 2009; Ensor et al., 2018; Forsyth, 2013).

Sense of community can enhance our understanding of how community emerges as a valued dimension of self-concept and acquires distinct meanings for the diverse people who inhabit it, both host community members and immigrants (Buckingham et al., 2018). Participation in community life can be a second lever for building resilience at both individual and community levels, as it serves as a mechanism through which community members, especially migrants, strive to make meaningful social contributions and assert their importance in their communities, even in the face of structural inequalities and social barriers (Marzana et al., 2019) of stressors (Carter-Pokras et al., 2007; Chen et al., 2007).

In the following sections, we will explore how a sense of community and participation operates in migration contexts. We will first examine the sense of community processes (*Sense of community from the perspective of community members faced with migration*) and then explore participation through the case study of Riace, Italy (*Community participation as a driver and an outcome of community resilience: the riace case study*).

Rather than presenting a systematic literature review, we will discuss empirical findings from a series of studies conducted primarily in Italy and the US between 2012 and 2022, using both qualitative (Buckingham et al., 2018; Fedi et al., 2019; Brodsky et al., 2022) and quantitative (Verbena et al., 2021) methodologies to investigate the experiences of both receiving community members and migrants. Three university-based research teams, composed of faculty, postdoctoral researchers, graduate and undergraduate students diverse in age, gender, language and ethnicity, including both immigrant and native-born individuals, led the research. Notably, none of the team members identified as first- or second-generation immigrants from the communities represented by our participants. The research teams deliberately leveraged the intersectional expertise and experiences of their members while carefully and openly incorporating the unique insider perspectives and knowledge of our participants.

Sense of community from the perspective of community members faced with migration

Unlike the notion of community resilience, there is almost unanimous agreement among academics and practitioners on the conceptualisation and measurement of sense of community (Mannarini & Fedi, 2009; Mannarini et al., 2012; McMillan & Chavis, 1986; Sarason, 1974; Talò & Mannarini, 2015). McMillan and Chavis (1986) have defined it as "*a feeling that members have of belonging, a feeling that members matter to one another and to the group, and a shared faith that members' needs will be met through their commitment to being together*" (p. 9). Their framework includes four key components: Membership, Shared Emotional Connection, Integration and Fulfilment of Needs and Mutual Influence. Membership includes feelings of identification, acceptance of shared symbols, belonging to an organised system and a sense of security. Shared Emotional Connection refers to the common ground established through regular interactions, shared experiences and significant events that enrich the community's history and collective memory, thereby facilitating members' identification and integration of new experiences. Integration and Fulfilment of Needs – which McMillan (1996) later characterised as an "economy of social trade" – describes how communities provide opportunities for members to satisfy both psychological (affective) and material needs, fostering individual commitment and interpersonal interdependence. Mutual Influence reflects the cohesive forces that promote compliance with community norms, with members both accepting the influence of the community and recognising their own impact on fellow members and the community structure.

Local communities are both the settings where a sense of community develops and the places where intercultural processes and relationships unfold. According to this perspective, the way community members make sense of their community and form their sense of community is also a process of adjustment to an increasingly multicultural environment. Conversely, the process of intercultural adjustment which takes place within community contexts continuously shapes and reshapes people's sense of community. This theme has been central to the work of an international research group (senior researchers Anne Brodsky, Sara Buckingham, Angela Fedi, Terri Mannarini and Alessia Rochira) composed of scholars from three universities, two in Italy – the University of Salento and the University of Turin – and one in the US (the University of Maryland Baltimore County). This collaboration spanned approximately ten years since, eventually expanding to include the University of Alaska Anchorage. Cross-sectional data were collected between 2012 and 2020 in the two national contexts while both countries faced significant, though different, immigration challenges, showing ambivalent or negative attitudes towards migrants and revealing a tension between assimilation and civic ideologies in the US and the rejection of cultural pluralism in Italy.

Analysing our empirical findings through the community resilience framework and conceptualising immigration as an ongoing systemic challenge, we argue that sense of community processes and outcomes follow different paths in different communities. In some cases, often among receiving community members with limited contact with people from different ethnocultural groups (Fedi et al., 2019), sense of community leads to a return to a pre-adversity equilibrium state – that is the condition before the presence of immigrants increases in the community (Bonanno et al., 2015)—voicing a desire to maintain existing power structures. Here the perception of similarity serves as the primary symbolic resource, with homophily and proximity being essential elements of membership (Neal, 2017; Rochira, 2018), that is people tend to interact with those who are perceived similar. While many receiving members claim to value diversity, this is often at odds with the expectation that newcomers will conform to existing community norms: despite recognising the benefits of multiculturalism, many believe that new members must adapt to be "accepted" (Buckingham et al., 2018). Typically, immigrants are expected to follow the customs of established residents, and these expectations lead to both overt and subtle discrimination. This form of sense of community based on the preference for immigrant assimilation somehow aims to maintain the status quo by neglecting the internal ethnic diversity of communities.

This argument is consistent with the results of another study (Verbena et al., 2021) that we conducted in the southern Italian context (Lecce) with the aim of examining the relationships between community resilience, individual resilience and the acculturation expectations held by members of the receiving society (i.e., multiculturalism, melting pot, segregation and exclusion, according to Berry's (2005) acculturation model). We found that the perception of the community of belonging as resilient and endowed with a variety of resources does not necessarily coincide with support for cultural diversity. Rather, the willingness to share community resources appears to depend on the degree of cultural adaptation of immigrants. Members of the receiving communities show greater willingness to share resources when immigrants adopt dominant cultural practices, while expressing resistance when they maintain their cultural distinctiveness.

In contrast, regular social exchanges between locals and immigrants can facilitate the negotiation of common ground through mutable cultural features (e.g., food traditions, festivals and celebrations), potentially developing a "culturally based similarity" that allows for the appreciation of diversity (Fedi et al., 2019). The opportunity to cultivate relationships between new and established community members seems critical to building more inclusive forms of sense of community. This works best in diverse settings that bring together newcomers and autochthonous residents, such as schools, workplaces and community organisations, where people can build connections through shared activities, characteristics and values (Buckingham et al., 2018), ultimately cultivating their belonging in both micro and macro communities. Indeed, newcomers belong to multiple communities at once (Brodsky & Marx, 2001), with relationship-based communities being more meaningful than those based on shared territory. Smaller, more intimate and personally relevant communities appear to be most effective in building a sense of community, whereas larger territorial communities (e.g., cities or regions) are often seen only as places where people settle (Buckingham et al., 2018). While relationship-based communities are more accessible, regardless of immigration status, and allow for more inclusive forms of sense of community, immigration policies create barriers for newcomers to participate in territorial communities. Without citizenship rights, migrants are unable to engage in formal civic activities such as voting and struggle with basic needs such as finding well-paid work.

In the face of societal barriers that undermine community resilience, immigrants quite often engage in internally focused resilient strategies to pursue their psychological adjustment in the face of significant obstacles in community settings where resources and risks are unequally distributed between newcomers and established community members (Brodsky et al., 2022). From this perspective, sense of community may function as a personal resource that can buffer the negative effects of discrimination. However, for sense of community to act as a catalyst of community resilience, it is necessary to promote collective action. There is evidence that psychosocial mechanisms (e.g., social identity, efficacy) underlying collective action develop among members of both immigrant and host communities (e.g., Block et al., 2017; Ford-Paz et al., 2020; Gleeson & Sampat, 2018; Hsia, 2009), particularly when addressing common challenges (e.g., access to education, community safety and economic opportunity). These shared concerns can serve as starting points for developing cross-community coalitions that ultimately promote resilient communities.

Community participation as a driver and an outcome of community resilience: The Riace case study

Recent theoretical developments have highlighted the dynamic relationship between participatory processes and resilient communities. Mahajan et al. (2022) have introduced the concept of "participatory resilience" as a way of understanding how communities survive, recover and improve through collective action. This notion represents a significant advance in our understanding of how communities actively engage in recovery and development processes, as it allows us to move beyond traditional top-down models of community intervention and instead emphasises the importance of collective agency and shared responsibility. Indeed, participation serves as both an outcome and a driver of group resilience, creating a virtuous circle that strengthens community bonds and enhances adaptive capacity (Verbena et al., 2021).

Concrete illustrations are essential for understanding how these processes unfold in real-life contexts. The case of Riace, a small town in southern Italy, provides a remarkable example of how participatory resilience can work in practice.

The story of Riace's transformation is set in the context of the significant rural decline that characterised many southern Italian municipalities in the late twentieth century. Situated in the economically depressed region of Calabria in southern Italy, Riace exemplified the plight of many rural communities facing massive outmigration since the 1960s and 1970s. As documented by Driel (2020), the town had experienced a dramatic demographic decline, with its population falling from 2,500 in the 1950s to just 800 in the late 1990s. This decline represented not only a demographic crisis, but a wider threat to the cultural and economic survival of the community, leaving behind an ageing population, several abandoned properties and deteriorated public services, including a local school facing closure due to insufficient enrolment.

The emergence of the "Riace Model" as a community response was triggered by the fortuitous arrival of Kurdish refugees in 1998. This arrival occurred at a significant moment: Italy was experiencing increased migration flows from conflict zones but lacked formal national asylum reception systems (Zavaglia, 2018). This period coincided with the diplomatic crisis surrounding Abdullah Ocalan, the leader of the Kurdistan Workers' Party (PKK), who had sought asylum in Italy. Kurdish refugees had fled persecution in Iraq and Iran, with many initially viewing Italy as merely a transit country en route to established Kurdish communities in northern Europe (Sasso, 2018). Under the leadership of future mayor Domenico "Mimmo" Lucano, who was initially among the local volunteers responding to this emergency, what began as an improvised response gradually evolved into a deliberate strategy. This approach was partly inspired by a similar, though ultimately unsuccessful, experiment in nearby Badolato, where Kurdish refugees had arrived in December 1997 (Sasso, 2018).

The approach developed in Riace demonstrates how strong local leadership, combined with community engagement, can create innovative solutions to meet both refugee settlement needs and community revitalisation goals. The integration practices developed in Riace exemplify a sophisticated understanding of how participation can facilitate meaningful social integration. The success of the model was built on creating multiple opportunities for genuine interaction between locals and newcomers (Driel & Verkuyten, 2022). The restoration of abandoned houses in the historic centre, rather than creating separate facilities for refugees, was used as a deliberate strategy to facilitate natural, everyday interactions between residents, applying the contact theory principles (Allport, 1954). The community created the conditions for optimal intergroup contact through equal status in social interactions, common goals through joint projects, intergroup cooperation and support from the local authorities. These conditions were reinforced by practical initiatives such as joint workshops, cultural events and joint economic enterprises.

The Riace experience makes a significant contribution to our understanding of social inclusion in rural contexts. Beyond simple integration, the model demonstrates how newcomers can become an integral part of the community fabric, contributing to its economic and cultural revitalisation. The impact was multi-dimensional, ranging from demographic revitalisation (population growth to around 1,800 inhabitants) to a qualitative transformation of community life through the reopening of local schools, the revival of traditional crafts and the establishment of new businesses. A particularly significant outcome has been the transformation of local identity. Rather than experiencing cultural dissolution, the community developed what Alrawadieh et al. (2024) describe as genuine hospitality, characterised by authentic intercultural relationships and mutual support networks. This development of local identity demonstrates how participatory approaches to integration can strengthen rather than threaten community cohesion.

Several key factors emerged as critical to the success of the Riace model. Strong political leadership combined with genuine community engagement created the conditions for innovative problem-solving. The integrated approach to housing, employment and social interaction provided a comprehensive framework for sustainable integration. The emphasis on genuine relationships and mutual benefit created a foundation for lasting community change. However, significant challenges also emerged. Mainly, the dependence on external funding (government funding and EU grants, as well as donations from foundations and affluent private supporters) and political support, which made this experience vulnerable to changes in the wider political environment. These challenges underline the complexity of sustaining participatory resilience initiatives over time and call for strategies aimed at promoting self-sustained development: microeconomies based on productive activities, valorisation of local resources, diversification of revenue sources, development of income-generating activities aligned with community values, investment in community financial management skills and establishment of communal ownership of key resources.

The relationship between participation and resilience can be further understood through three complementary theoretical frameworks. First, the notion of community capacity building, "the interaction of human, organisational and social capital that exists within a given community and can be used to solve collective problems and improve or maintain the wellbeing of that community" (Chaskin, 2001, p. 295). This perspective enriches our understanding of how participatory processes contribute to building sustainable resilient communities. Second, Dempsey et al.'s (2011) social sustainability framework. Their emphasis on social interaction, participation in collective groups, community stability, pride/sense of place and security closely aligns with the outcomes observed in successful integration initiatives. This framework helps to explain how participatory processes can contribute not only to immediate integration goals, but also to longer-term social sustainability. Third, the concept of transformative resilience (Pelling, 2011). In contrast to traditional conceptualisations of resilience that focus on returning to a pre-existing state, transformative resilience emphasises how communities can use challenges as opportunities to restructure social relations and power structures. Kirby et al. (2024) reinforce this understanding by highlighting how bottom-up participation can drive transformation processes and create more resilient social systems.

Drawing on the theoretical framework of participatory resilience (Mahajan et al., 2022) and the empirical evidence provided by the Riace case study (Driel & Verkuyten, 2022), several conclusions can be drawn about the relationship between participation and community resilience in the context of migration. First, that participatory processes can serve as a fundamental means by which communities build and maintain their resilience while addressing complex social challenges, in line with recent findings on community responses to ongoing stressors (Cardinali et al., 2024; Kaim et al., 2024). Second, that community regeneration efforts require a holistic approach that integrates spatial, economic and social strategies rather than treating them as separate domains, a finding that resonates with recent research on crisis management and community transformation (Bronfman et al., 2024; Whetstone & Demiroz, 2023). Third, that strong local leadership is a crucial catalyst in facilitating participatory processes, creating spaces for dialogue and collaboration, while maintaining a clear vision for community development, as observed in similar contexts (Carter & Cordero, 2022; Hall et al., 2023). Finally, and perhaps most importantly, the Riace case highlights the need to build sustainable local capacity and gradually reduce reliance on external support to ensure long-term community resilience, echoing findings from recent research on social solidarity economy (Sotnyk et al., 2024) and community capacity building (Perach et al., 2023).

Looking forward, this case suggests several important implications for both research and practice in community psychology. In the first place, it highlights the value of conceptualising community resilience as a broad framework that can incorporate multiple theoretical perspectives and practical approaches (Rochira et al., 2022; Tavares et al., 2022). Moreover, it demonstrates the importance of examining how participatory processes operate in different contexts and at different scales, particularly when addressing social inequalities through an intersectional approach (Siller & Aydin, 2022). Finally, it highlights the need for further research into how communities can build sustainable participatory structures that enhance their resilience in the face of ongoing migration challenges (Olcese et al., 2024). As communities around the world continue to face migration tests, the emphasis on participation as a key mechanism offers a promising framework for addressing not only migration-related challenges, but also broader social issues facing communities in an increasingly interconnected world (Gatti & Procentese, 2024; Karami & Keshavarz, 2024).

Conclusion

Community resilience has proved to be a fruitful Community Psychology framework for understanding both the challenges and opportunities in the migration context. Within this framework, sense of community and participation can act as catalysts for social justice and societal transformation. The vision of social justice that emerges from this discussion is one of inclusion, equity and collective empowerment, which acknowledges the structural barriers and systemic injustices that migrants face while envisioning pathways to build equitable communities. In this context, wellbeing is reimagined as transcending individual psychological states to encompass collective and cultural dimensions. It is about fostering environments where migrant communities can experience safety and belonging, and therefore develop multiple senses of community and also have access to resources and opportunities for individual and collective agency, which are foundational to community resilience. However, for community psychologists, significant challenges persist in applying this resilience-based framework:

1. Global–local connections: Migration today is driven by planetary processes of resource depletion, economic inequality, conflict and climate crisis. While community psychologists need to remain responsive to local needs and capacities, they also need to navigate these global dynamics.
2. Structural inequalities: Migrants face persistent forms of exclusion and limited access to services. Overcoming these challenges requires community psychologists to adopt systemic approaches that go beyond individuals to address the root causes of inequality.
3. Cultural sensitivity: Promoting community resilience through an inclusive sense of community and collective action requires an understanding of diverse cultural experiences, values and coping strategies to ensure that interventions are contextually relevant and empowering.

Despite these challenges, the community resilience framework provides community psychologists with two basic, often intertwined, strategies: adopting and disseminating participatory methodologies that centre migrant voices, promote self-organisation and foster collective agency and ownership of solutions and strengthening connections, social networks and community coalitions while validating and preserving diverse cultural identities. Both these strategies are central to promoting equitable resilient communities, along with social wellbeing and collective strength.

Action for learning: Community resilience mapping workshop

This workshop (Figure 2.1) is designed as a structured yet flexible process, through which participants can develop a deeper understanding of social justice, wellbeing and resilience in migrant communities, while identifying practical pathways for meaningful intervention and support.

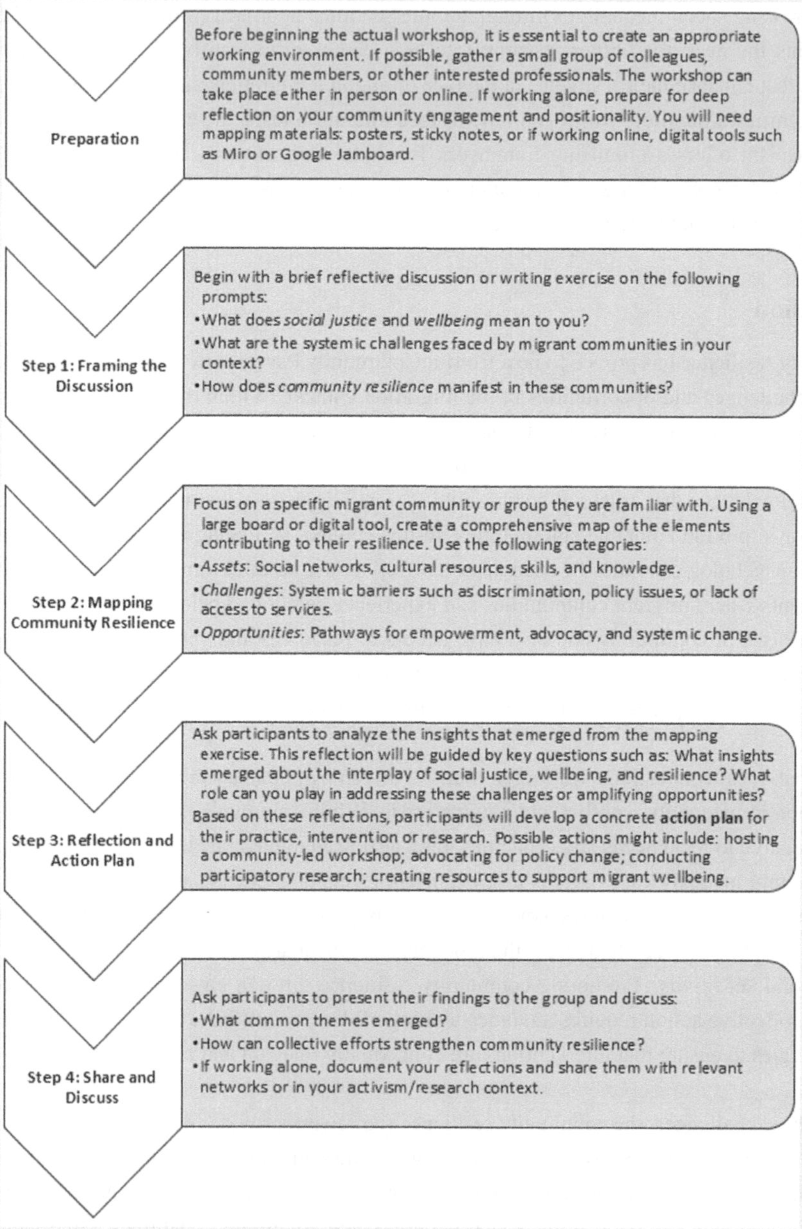

Figure 2.1 Community resilience mapping workshop

References

Abramowitz, S. A. (2005). The poor have become rich, and the rich have become poor: Collective trauma in the Guinean Languette. *Social Science & Medicine*, *61*(10), 2106–2118. https://doi.org/10.1016/J.SOCSCIMED.2005.03.023

Allport, G. W. (1954). *The nature of prejudice*. Perseus Books.

Alrawadieh, Z., Altinay, L., Urbančíková, N., & Hudec, O. (2024). Refugees at home: The role of hospitableness in fostering pro-social attitudes and behaviours towards refugees. *International Journal of Contemporary Hospitality Management*, *36*(9), 3052–3071. https://doi.org/10.1108/IJCHM-04-2023-0546

Amirzadeh, M., & Barakpour, N. (2021). Strategies for building community resilience against slow-onset hazards. *International Journal of Disaster Risk Reduction*, *66*, 102599. https://doi.org/10.1016/J.IJDRR.2021.102599

Ayers, J., & Forsyth, T. (2009). Community-based adaptation to climate change. *Environment*, *51*(4), 22–31. https://doi.org/10.3200/ENV.51.4.22-31

Berry, J. W. (2005) Acculturation: Living successfully in two cultures. *International Journal of Intercultural Relations*, *29*(6), 697–712. https://doi.org/10.1016/j.ijintrel.2005.07.013

Block, S., Longoria, M., & Hunt, J. J. (2017). *ATU division 757 letter to union members, transit riders, and the greater Portland community. Amalgamated Transit Unit 757.* Amalgamated Transport Union.

Bonanno, G. A., Romero, S. A., & Klein, S. I. (2015). The temporal elements of psychological resilience: An integrative framework for the study of individuals, families, and communities. *Psychological Inquiry*, *26*(2), 139–169. https://doi.org/10.1080/1047840X.2015.992677

*Brodsky, A., Buckingham, S., Fedi, A., Gattino, S., Rochira, A., Altal, D., & Mannarini, T. (2022). Resilience and empowerment in immigrant experiences: A look through the transconceptual model of empowerment and resilience. *American Journal of Orthopsychiatry*, *92*(5), 564–577. https://doi.org/10.1037/ORT0000634

Brodsky, A., & Marx, C. M. (2001). Layers of identity: Multiple psychological senses of community within a community setting. *Journal of Community Psychology*, *29*(2), 161–178. https://doi.org/10.1002/1520-6629(200103)29:2<161::AID-JCOP1011>3.0.CO;2-1

Bronfman, N. C., Nikole, G. M., Castañeda, J. V., Cisternas, P., & Repetto, P. B. (2024). Relationship between social vulnerability and community resilience: A geospatial study in the context of natural disasters. *International Journal of Disaster Risk Reduction, 112*. https://doi.org/10.1016/J.IJDRR.2024.104774

Buckingham, S. L., Brodsky, A., Rochira, A., Fedi, A., Mannarini, T., Emery, L., Godsay, S., Miglietta, A., & Gattino, S. (2018). Shared communities: A multinational qualitative study of immigrant and receiving community members. *American Journal of Community Psychology*, *62*(1–2), 23–40. https://doi.org/10.1002/AJCP.12255

Cardinali, P., Olcese, M., Antichi, L., & Migliorini, L. (2024). Cumulative trauma and perceived community resilience: A serial mediation model. *Journal of Community Psychology*, *52*(1), 276–288. https://doi.org/10.1002/JCOP.23097

Carpenter, A. C. (2014). Community resilience to sectarian violence in Baghdad. *Community Resilience to Sectarian Violence in Baghdad*, 1–156. https://doi.org/10.1007/978-1-4614-8812-5/COVER

Carter, E. D., & Cordero, M. L. (2022). Salir Adelante: Social capital and resilience during the Covid-19 pandemic in Argentina. *Health and Place*, *77*. https://doi.org/10.1016/J.HEALTHPLACE.2022.102870

Carter-Pokras, O., Zambrana, R. E., Mora, S. E., & Aaby, K. A. (2007). Emergency preparedness: Knowledge and perceptions of Latin American immigrants. *Journal of Health Care for the Poor and Underserved*, *18*(2), 465–481. https://doi.org/10.1353/HPU.2007.0026

Chaskin, R. J. (2001). Building community capacity. *Urban Affairs Review*, *36*(3), 291–323. https://doi.org/10.1177/10780870122184876

Chen, S., Poland, B., & Skinner, H. A. (2007). Youth voices: Evaluation of participatory action research. *Canadian Journal of Program Evaluation*, *22*(1), 125–150. https://doi.org/10.3138/CJPE.022.006

Dempsey, N., Bramley, G., Power, S., & Brown, C. (2011). The social dimension of sustainable development: Defining urban social sustainability. *Sustainable Development*, *19*(5), 289–300. https://doi.org/10.1002/SD.417

Driel, E. (2020). Refugee settlement and the revival of local communities: Lessons from the Riace model. *Journal of Modern Italian Studies*, *25*(2), 149–173. https://doi.org/10.1080/1354571X.2020.1716538

Driel, E., & Verkuyten, M. (2022). Contact theory and the multiethnic community of Riace, Italy: An ethnographic examination. *Journal of Community Psychology*, *50*(5), 2326–2343. https://doi.org/10.1002/JCOP.22778

Ensor, J., Forrester, J., & Matin, N. (2018). Bringing rights into resilience: Revealing complexities of climate risks and social conflict. *Disasters*, *42*, S287–S305. https://doi.org/10.1111/DISA.12304

Faulkner, L., Brown, K., & Quinn, T. (2018). Analyzing community resilience as an emergent property of dynamic social-ecological systems. *Ecology and Society*, *23*(1), art24. https://doi.org/10.5751/ES-09784-230124

Fedi, A., Mannarini, T., Brodsky, A., Rochira, A., Buckingham, S., Emery, L., Godsay, S., Scheibler, J., Miglietta, A., & Gattino, S. (2019). Acculturation in the discourse of immigrants and receiving community members: Results from a cross-national qualitative study. *American Journal of Orthopsychiatry*, *89*(1), 1–15. https://doi.org/10.1037/ort0000325

Ford-Paz, R. E., Santiago, C. D., Coyne, C. A., Rivera, C., Guo, S., Rusch, D., St. Jean, N., Hilado, A., & Cicchetti, C. (2020). You're not alone: A public health response to immigrant/refugee distress in the current sociopolitical context. *Psychological Services*, *17*(S1), 128–138. https://doi.org/10.1037/ser0000381

Forsyth, T. (2013). Community-based adaptation: A review of past and future challenges. *Wiley Interdisciplinary Reviews: Climate Change*, *4*(5), 439–446. https://doi.org/10.1002/WCC.231

Gatti, F., & Procentese, F. (2024). Ubiquitous processes strengthening neighbourhood communities: How neighbourhood-related social media can foster the active involvement of citizens and build resilient communities. *Journal of Community and Applied Social Psychology*, *34*. https://doi.org/10.1002/casp.2862

Gleeson, S., & Sampat, P. (2018). Immigrant resistance in the age of Trump. *New Labor Forum*, *27*(1), 86–95. https://doi.org/10.1177/1095796017744778

Hall, C. E., Wehling, H., Stansfield, J., South, J., Brooks, S. K., Greenberg, N., Amlôt, R., & Weston, D. (2023). Examining the role of community resilience and social capital on mental health in public health emergency and disaster response: A scoping review. *BMC Public Health*, *23*(1). https://doi.org/10.1186/S12889-023-17242-X

Hsia, H.-C. (2009). The making of a transnational grassroots migrant movement. *Critical Asian Studies*, *41*(1), 113–141. https://doi.org/10.1080/14672710802631186

Imperiale, A. J., & Vanclay, F. (2016). Experiencing local community resilience in action: Learning from post-disaster communities. *Journal of Rural Studies*, *47*, 204–219. https://doi.org/10.1016/J.JRURSTUD.2016.08.002

Kaim, A., Tov, M. S., Kimhi, S., Marciano, H., Eshel, Y., & Adini, B. (2024). A longitudinal study of societal resilience and its predictors during the Israel-Gaza war. *Applied Psychology: Health and Well-Being*, *16*(3), 1479–1496. https://doi.org/10.1111/APHW.12539

Karami, R., & Keshavarz, M. (2024). The emergence of online social capital during the COVID-19 outbreak and its impact on individual coping and community resilience in rural areas. *Current Psychology*, *43*(19), 17787–17800. https://doi.org/10.1007/S12144-023-05167-Y

Kendra, J. M., & Wachtendorf, T. (2003). Elements of resilience after the World Trade Center disaster: Reconstituting New York City's Emergency Operations Centre. *Disasters*, *27*(1), 37–53. https://doi.org/10.1111/1467–7717.00218

Kirby, N., Stasiak, D., & von Schneidemesser, D. (2024). Community resilience through bottom–up participation: When civil society drives urban transformation processes. *Community Development Journal*. https://doi.org/10.1093/cdj/bsae031

Klein, R. J. T., Nicholls, R. J., & Thomalla, F. (2003). Resilience to natural hazards: How useful is this concept? *Global Environmental Change Part B: Environmental Hazards*, *5*(1–2), 35–45. https://doi.org/10.1016/J.HAZARDS.2004.02.001

Kristanti, D., Edison, E., Yunanto, M. K., Alfiandri, A., Utari, D. S., Samnuzulsari, T., Akbar, D., Suyito, S., Solina, E., & Yudiatmaja, W. E. (2021). Strengthening social capital of urban community during COVID-19 disaster. *E3S Web of Conferences*, *331*. https://doi.org/10.1051/E3SCONF/202133101013

Magis, K. (2010). Community resilience: An indicator of social sustainability. *Society and Natural Resources*, *23*(5), 401–416. https://doi.org/10.1080/08941920903305674

Mahajan, S., Hausladen, C. I., Argota Sánchez-Vaquerizo, J., Korecki, M., & Helbing, D. (2022). Participatory resilience: Surviving, recovering and improving together. *Sustainable Cities and Society*, *83*, 103942. https://doi.org/10.1016/J.SCS.2022.103942

Mannarini, T., & Fedi, A. (2009). Multiple senses of community: The experience and meaning of community. *Journal of Community Psychology*, *37*(2), 211–227. https://doi.org/10.1002/JCOP.20289

Mannarini, T., Rochira, A., & Talò, C. (2012). How identification processes and inter-community relationships affect sense of community. *Journal of Community Psychology*, *40*(8), 951–967. https://doi.org/10.1002/JCOP.21504

Marzana, D., Martinez Damia, S., Atallah, D., & Loreto Martinez, M. (2019). The resilience of Peruvian immigrants through participation in community-based organizations in urban Chile. *Journal of Community Psychology*, *48*(5), 1327–1346. https://doi.org/10.1002/jcop.22284

Matarrita-Cascante, D., Trejos, B., Qin, H., Joo, D., & Debner, S. (2017). Conceptualizing community resilience: Revisiting conceptual distinctions. *Community Development*, *48*(1), 105–123. https://doi.org/10.1080/15575330.2016.1248458

McAuliffe, M., & Oucho, L. A. (2024). *World Migration Report 2024*. International Organization for Migration. https://publications.iom.int/books/world-migration-report-2024

McMillan, D. W. (1996). Sense of community. *Journal of Community Psychology*, *24*(4), 315–325. https://doi.org/10.1002/(SICI)1520-6629(199610)24:4<315::AID-JCOP2>3.0.CO;2-T

McMillan, D. W., & Chavis, D. M. (1986). Sense of community: A definition and theory. *Journal of Community Psychology*, *14*(1), 6–23. https://psycnet.apa.org/record/1987-03834-001

Nair, P., & Safra, L. (2024). Interconnected protective factors and adversities: Adaptation and resilience in refugees during intensified containment and COVID-19 in Lesbos, Greece. *Adversity and Resilience Science*. https://doi.org/10.1007/s42844-024-00149-w

Neal, Z. P. (2017). Taking stock of the diversity and sense of community debate. *American Journal of Community Psychology*, *59*(3–4), 255–260. https://doi.org/10.1002/AJCP.12132

Norris, F. H., Stevens, S. P., Pfefferbaum, B., Wyche, K. F., & Pfefferbaum, R. L. (2008). Community resilience as a metaphor, theory, set of capacities, and strategy for disaster readiness. *American Journal of Community Psychology*, *41*(1–2), 127–150. https://doi.org/10.1007/s10464-007-9156-6

Olcese, M., Cardinali, P., Camilleri, A. P., & Migliorini, L. (2024). Feeling community during war: Community resilience of Ukrainian women refugees in Italy. *Journal of International Migration and Integration*. https://doi.org/10.1007/S12134-024-01147-8

Ostadtaghizadeh, A., Ardalan, A., Paton, D., Jabbari, H., & Khankeh, H. R. (2015). Community disaster resilience: A systematic review on assessment models and tools. *Disasters, PLoS Currents*, *7*. https://doi.org/10.1371/CURRENTS.DIS.F224EF8EFBDFCF1D508DD0DE4D8210ED

Pelling, M. (2011). *Adaptation to climate change: From resilience to transformation*. Routledge. https://www.routledge.com/Adaptation-to-Climate-Change-From-Resilience-to-Transformation/Pelling/p/book/9780415477512

Perach, R., Fernandes-Jesus, M., Miranda, D., Mao, G., Ntontis, E., Cocking, C., McTague, M., Semlyen, J., & Drury, J. (2023). Can group-based strategies increase community resilience? Longitudinal predictors of sustained participation in Covid-19 mutual aid and community support groups. *Journal of Applied Social Psychology*, *53*(11), 1059–1075. https://doi.org/10.1111/JASP.12995

Rochira, A. (2018). What is the role of sense of community in multiracial societies? A contribution to the community-diversity dialectic: A genetic psychology approach. *Journal of Community Psychology*, *46*(8), 972–982. https://doi.org/10.1002/jcop.21985

Rochira, A., De Simone, E., & Mannarini, T. (2022). Community resilience and continuous challenges: A qualitative analysis of the functioning of communities in the aftermath of persistent and ordinary stressors. *Journal of Community Psychology*, *51*(3), 1106–1123. https://doi.org/10.1002/jcop.22987

Sarason, S. B. (1974). *The psychological sense of community prospects for a community psychology*. Jossey-Bass. https://www.scirp.org/reference/referencespapers?referenceid=2080506

Sasso, C. (2018). *Riace, terra di accoglienza*. Edizioni Gruppo Abele.

Siller, H., & Aydin, N. (2022). Using an intersectional lens on vulnerability and resilience in minority and/or marginalized groups during the COVID-19 pandemic: A narrative review. *Frontiers in Psychology*, *13*. https://doi.org/10.3389/FPSYG.2022.894103

Sotnyk, I., Kubatko, O., Chortok, Y., Kostenko, A., Kupenko, O., Karintseva, O., & Tarasenko, S. (2024). Social solidarity economy during the war: The sources of individual and community resilience. *Problems and Perspectives in Management*, *22*(3), 542–555. https://doi.org/10.21511/PPM.22(3).2024.41

Staupe-Delgado, R. (2019). Can community resettlement be considered a resilient move? Insights from a slow-onset disaster in the Colombian Andes. *The Journal of Development Studies*, *56*(5), 1017–1029. https://doi.org/10.1080/00220388.2019.1626836

Talò, C., & Mannarini, T. (2015) Measuring participation: Development and validation the participatory behaviors scale. *Social Indicators Research*, *123*, 799–816. https://doi.org/10.1007/s11205-014-0761-0

Tavares, L. P., Luís, S., Henriques, J., Marujo, H. Á., Gonçalves, S. P., & Rivero, C. (2022). *Responding to everyday problems and crises: Measuring community resilience*. https://doi.org/10.1002/jcop.22933

Tobin, G. A., & Whiteford, L. M. (2002). Community resilience and volcano hazard: The eruption of Tungurahua and evacuation of the faldas in Ecuador. *Disasters*, *26*(1), 28–48. https://doi.org/10.1111/1467–7717.00189

Vaneeckhaute, L. E., Vanwing, T., Jacquet, W., Abelshausen, B., & Meurs, P. (2017). Community resilience 2.0: Toward a comprehensive conception of community-level resilience. *Community Development*, *48*(5), 735–751. https://doi.org/10.1080/15575330.2017.1369443

Vargo Hsu, K. (2019). *The relationship between social support and resilience among school nurses*. [Doctoral Dissertation, Walden University] Walden Dissertations and Doctoral Studies.

Verbena, S., Rochira, A., & Mannarini, T. (2021). Community resilience and the acculturation expectations of the receiving community. *Journal of Community Psychology*, *49*(2), 390–405. https://doi.org/10.1002/jcop.22466

Whetstone, C., & Demiroz, F. (2023). Understanding intersectionality and vulnerable populations: A missing part in building disaster resilient communities? *Intersectionality and Crisis Management: A Path to Social Equity*, 18–37. https://doi.org/10.4324/9781003184621-2/understanding-intersectionality-vulnerable-populations-crystal-whetstone-fatih-demiroz

Wilson, G. A. (2012). Community resilience, globalization, and transitional pathways of decision-making. *Geoforum*, *43*(6), 1218–1231. https://doi.org/10.1016/j.geoforum.2012.03.008

Zavaglia, P. D. (2018). *Bronzi, santi e rifugiati. Il caso di Riace*. Castelvecchi Editore.

3 "*Bem-vindos a Portugal,*" they said

A community-engaged collaborative research based on the lived experiences of migrants and refugees

Dora Rebelo, Cristina Santinho, Ana Stela Cunha, Alaa Kordia, Nina Amelung, Beatriz Gomes de Figueiredo, Micaela Gomes, Alexander Kweh, Carolina Coimbra, Karla Costa, Laura Brito, Landu Yanick Matondo and Dyoka Mukinay

Introduction

Research with migrant communities has been biased by a power imbalance between those who call themselves "researchers," and those who "participate" in research (Saltsman & Jacobsen, 2021). Reflecting on this concern, in January 2022, the co-authors of this chapter gathered a team of critical researchers in Anthropology, Psychology and Sociology and ten people with lived experiences of migration and refugee reception in Portugal, from eight nationalities, including Syria, Afghanistan, Nigeria, Liberia, Guinea-Bissau, Togo, the Democratic Republic of the Congo and Angola. Our intent was to engage in an experimental exercise of knowledge co-production, inspired by Community Psychology and Public Anthropology methodologies, using a reflexive, community-based, interdisciplinary and collaborative approach.

Stimulated by previous work conducted by critical community psychologists (e.g., Ciofalo, 2022; Dutta, 2018), we wanted to challenge the power imbalance between researchers and marginalised communities, in order to amplify historically disregarded voices, integrate diverse knowledges and experiment with collaborative research methods. We have also been motivated by the developments made within Public Anthropology (e.g., Borofsky & De Lauri, 2019; Vine, 2011), namely the discipline's engagement with social issues and community participation, as well as its collaborative methodologies of knowledge production (Lassiter, 2008).

Co-authors started by establishing weekly collaborative research sessions for a period of five months until May 2022. The team was then divided into three research groups, each with the purpose of addressing one specific subject. The first group, led by the first and second authors, studied the lived experiences of refugees in Lisbon; the second, led by the founders of SaMaNe – a collective of Black mothers - studied healthcare inequalities experienced by migrant and Afro-descendant women; and the third, led by

DOI: 10.4324/9781003480464-4

the third co-author, alongside musical band *Yoka Kongo!* – comprised of 13 musicians from Angola, the Democratic Republic of Congo, Brazil and Cuba – worked on an auto-ethnography of the band members' lived experiences as Black migrant men.

The chapter is organised into six sections. First, we explore our positionalities and collaborative approach. Then, we describe our theoretical inspirations and the methodologies that we experimented with in the three case studies. Additionally, we propose an action for a learning activity based on our experience. In sections four and five, we delve into the main findings of each of our case studies. Finally, we end the chapter with some reflections on the significance of our collaborative exercise.

Situating ourselves and our collaborative approach

We start by acknowledging that Ana Stella Cunha, the third co-author, who accompanied our collaborative research from 2022 to 2023 and co-wrote a subsection of this chapter, unfortunately passed away a few months after we finished our collaboration, due to a fatal illness. As she wished to publish her work, we include it as an homage to a committed and brilliant colleague, expressing our collective sincere gratitude for her wonderful contribution and dedicate this chapter to her.

As we sat together for the first time, at the large meeting table of project *Residências Refúgio*, a project aimed at the social inclusion of refugees, led by a partnership between associations *Largo Residências*, *Fórum Refúgio Portugal* and *Aga Khan Foundation,* we took a moment to contemplate the faces in the room. Ana Stela, a researcher and community organiser from Brazil, member of the musical band *Yoka Kongo!*; Alaa, a refugee and researcher from Syria; Alexander, a refugee and community organiser from Liberia, now coordinator of *Fórum Refúgio Portugal* – a civil society platform aiming at improving refugee inclusion; Beatriz, Cristina and Dora, researchers from Portugal, engaged with fieldwork with refugees (see Rebelo et al., 2020); Nina, a researcher from Germany now based in Lisbon; Micaela, coordinator of the project *Residências Refúgio;* and Laura, a founder of *SaMaNe*. Together, we assumed the role of co-organisers of the collaborative research process that followed.

We decided to begin our collective endeavour by recognising our *lugar de fala*, i.e., our "place of speech," a concept coined by the Brazilian feminist scholar Djamila Ribeiro (2019) to illustrate the intersectionalities embodied by different subjects in relation to multiple societal oppressions (e.g., racism, homophobia, sexism, classism, etc.). Using this framework, we situated one another regarding our migrant and refugee experiences, attempting to occupy our rightful place in the collective conversation. While we all allowed ourselves to participate in the discussions, we learned not to forget each other's subjectivities, diverse perspectives and lived experiences. In fact, we often brought up to the conversation how our *lugar de fala* potentially conditioned our perceived right to speak and to use silence. In order to genuinely engage in an exercise of reflexive collaboration, we felt we needed to set up a "safe enough" space, i.e., to recognise power and privilege as persistent variables in our group dynamics. We aimed at making the often silenced and invisibilised experiences of oppression and resistance noticeable, amidst our group. We also aimed to make our multiple "us and them" – our implicit hierarchies – explicit. To establish such a "safe enough space," we acknowledged that the academic researchers in our group, having invited people racialised as migrants and refugees to become research partners, were perhaps biased by a professional curiosity and the structures of power that come with it. We also acknowledged that refugees and migrants in the group have been living in Portugal in logics of belonging that reflect what Yuval-Davis (2006) named "boundaries that separate the world population into 'us' and 'them'" (p. 204). Ana Stela, Beatriz, Cristina, Micaela and Nina – White researchers working within academic institutions – are committed to engaging with the collective work with constant reflexivity. We acknowledged that academia contains, within itself, a power that can be misused in community relations. By bringing this acknowledgement into light, during the first encounters, we tried to uncover potential unspoken rules and expectations often enfolded in academic discourses *about* migrants and refugees. Our collective goal was to make sure that all perspectives in the room were considered and included, as plural and diverse knowledge. Also, we aspired that members of our group who are often put in a place of subalternity, based on racism and xenophobia, would become, through this approach, critical and knowledgeable research contributors.

Combining Community Psychology and Public Anthropology through an interdisciplinary approach

Community Psychology has focused on working alongside communities, aiming at improving both their resources and their agency (Trickett, 2009), even though the discipline's views of "helping" and "giving voice" to others have sometimes been criticised by decolonial scholars (e.g., Ciofalo, 2022; Fernández et al., 2021). Public Anthropology (Borofsky & De Lauri, 2019) emerged as a subfield of Anthropology that attempts to purposefully engage researchers with public issues, social concerns and emergent debates, cultivating community participation (e.g., Borofsky & De Lauri, 2019; Lassiter, 2008). Both disciplines have been attempting to find alternative ways of centring empirical research in communities' diverse knowledges, employing collective perspectives and lived experiences. Furthermore, both disciplines often recur to research methodologies that combine activism, artistic practices and collaborative writing. Public anthropologists (e.g., Lassiter, 2008) suggest that the theory/practice divide needs to be challenged, to openly address equity and social justice. Likewise, decolonial community psychologists contest mainstream psychology research practices and call for a more engaged approach, employing methods such as participatory action research (Lykes, 2017).

Both Community Psychology and Public Anthropology privilege lived experiences as valuable sources of knowledge. Community psychologists (e.g., Kessi, 2017) state that collaborative research with marginalised communities can help to mitigate the epistemic injustices often produced and exercised against those "being researched" by contributing to the exclusion, silencing, distortion or misrepresentation of the community's own meanings and contributions. According to Inge et al. (2024), epistemic injustice occurs when a person's or group's knowledge is systematically undervalued, misrepresented, mistrusted or silenced. We tried, instead, to root our collective work in locality, epistemic justice and resistance, reflecting on ways to dismantle theories about the "Other" that can dehumanise the racialised communities we are part of. By including communities as contributors and co-authors, we aim at creating, instead, a *co-citizenship* (Lassiter, 2008), i.e., a citizen-based partnership aimed at democratising knowledge production using epistemic justice and amplifying the resistance of migrant and refugee communities in Portugal.

Action for learning activity: collaborative ethnography

Collaborative ethnography is an approach rooted in collaboration that aims at producing knowledge based on lived experiences. In this activity, we encourage the readers to create a group of people that share common experiences. All group participants will become observers of their own lives, to make, collectively, sense of the social interactions and interpersonal exchanges that shape their communal lives. We recommend that the activity is done regularly and consistently by the same group of participants. Ideally, participants should meet every week over a period of at least three months in order to gather enough and diverse perspectives to assemble a collective reflection.

- Step 1 – Decide the topic of research that you want to focus on. Try to make it specific enough. For example, you could work together to explore "How are people around me expressing and/or experiencing hospitality?"
- Step 2 – Decide which methodology will best capture the reality that you are observing and reflecting on. Please privilege auto-ethnographic accounts, to avoid speaking "about" or on behalf of others. For example, you can use a notebook to write your impressions, an audio recorder to capture your own voice or meaningful conversations that you were a part of, a camera to take pictures, or even a scrapbook or collage to create your own art. It is important that you use the same methodology consistently and regularly and follow ethical considerations (e.g., informed consent in case you are using conversations with others).
- Step 3 – Weekly roundtable. Each participant presents their weekly reflections based on the collected observations/notes/images/other materials. It is important that each participant situates their impressions within their lugar de fala to better integrate individual contributions within the collective work. Reflect on your positionality, how your background and past experiences may have shaped your views and how certain privileges or the lack thereof have influenced your perspectives. The group decides, each week what the main insights are that should be retained and recorded (by writing/audio/collage) to assemble their collective reflection.
- Step 4 – Collective reflection. In order to create collective knowledge, participants may identify step-by-step learned knowledge that evolved from the previous exchanges, progressively developing common perspectives and understandings, which may change over time. Once they feel the group reaches a common understanding, yet acknowledging and respecting differences in views, they can articulate the group's diverse contributions in a shared written reflection, enriched by the documentation of the whole process.

Lived experiences of migrants and refugees in Portugal: three case studies

We developed three case studies led by members of our author collective, who then invited others in the community to participate. The first group, based in the project *Residências Refúgio*, used regular meetings, around a table with homemade cakes and hot beverages, to stimulate relaxed and informal discussions on refugee reception and social inclusion. First and second co-authors facilitated the dialogues, but the experience-sharing was mostly spontaneous, usually a reaction to a series of "surprises" and curiosities that were found in social events and interactions. From one week to the next, the group developed "homework" (further exploring and reflecting on the research subject). Sometimes, opinions differed quite significantly, and the group tried to hold multiple perspectives simultaneously.

The second case study, led by three founders of the *SaMaNe* collective, analysed recently collected data on the interactions between Black mothers and the Portuguese healthcare system. The study used *SaMaNe's* own fieldwork research, an anonymous online survey on racialised women's experiences in the healthcare system, and a series of conversation circles, activist actions and advocacy endeavours.

Figure 3.1 Co-authors' weekly meeting, Lisbon, April 2022.
Source: Photo by Ana Stela Cunha

Co-authors and *SaMaNe* founders Carolina Coimbra, Karla Costa and Laura Brito led the exercise and then co-wrote it.

The third case study was led by co-author Ana Stella Cunha, who has been a part of *Yoka Kongo!* for 13 years, during which time she developed multiple musical and anthropological research projects. She developed a collective autoethnography, based on the band members' own lived experiences as Black migrant men living in Portugal. Autoethnography is a method that uses personal experiences to describe and interpret practices, beliefs and cultural impressions and to bring visibility to societal and cultural issues (Hernandez-Carranza et al., 2021).

As we moved forward, in each of the three case studies summarised above, we shared our findings in regular collective conversations between co-authors and collaborators. Our discussions, initially disjointed, progressively became more entwined and correlated, helping us to organise the next subsection of findings and reflections.

Collective reflections based on our case studies

"Refugeeness": A reverse outlook to the social inclusion of refugees in Portugal

Our group started its collective work by acknowledging and reflecting on the knowledge that has already been produced on refugee inclusion in Portugal. Many of us have been familiarised with a series of reports and academic literature (e.g., Santinho, 2016; Vacchiano, 2018; Rebelo et al., 2020) hinting at the inconsistencies between the speeches produced about Portugal's "welcoming environment" and the data collected by practitioners and academics. However, the actual voice of refugees has been seldom utilised in research, which led us to contribute new evidence based on refugee lived experiences and perspectives.

It was not easy for refugees in our group to build close relationships in Portugal, which made us think that Portuguese people are more "closed" than most of us initially thought. This is an extract of our first dialogue, where we reflect on this first impression.

A: Relationships in Portugal are closed, not open. They say they are true friends, but they are not.

R: Portuguese are closed and not very welcoming. Sometimes I think this person is a friend, but then I learn that he is just an acquaintance ("conhecido," in Portuguese). What is a *conhecido*?

A: Yes, in our culture we don't have this word "conhecido." These are social barriers that we only noticed when we came here.

R: I always feel lonely in the street. I say "hi" when I see a person I met before – someone that I shared conversations with, someone I thought I knew – but afterwards, I always feel lonely. It's like we represent nothing to them.

E: As a Nigerian, I tend to have more Nigerian friends because speaking Portuguese is a little difficult, and we speak English all the time (...) it is difficult to find someone outside of our culture.

(*Residências Refúgio*, group discussion, January 2022)

As the group shared their views about what it means to welcome others and feel socially included, we got more acquainted with the rituals of hospitality performed in Syria, Liberia, Nigeria and Afghanistan. One commonality that immediately stood out was the way through which diverse societies celebrate the "stranger." A, a refugee from Afghanistan, stated, *"*It's almost mandatory to immediately invite someone over, to eat with us, or even to stay over for a few days and enjoy our hospitality." R, a refugee from Syria, added, "We do not need to 'break barriers,' to bring the 'stranger' into our most intimate spaces.*"*

Three members of our group reported that, soon after arriving, they felt an uncomfortable sense of "othering" and difficulty connecting to the host society. Their reception centre used a series of rules and norms (e.g., curfews, logistical constraints, etc.) that made them feel institutionalised. This was perceived by members of our group as a process of subalternity, which made them feel powerless and, at times, almost child-like. Group members also declared that they sometimes felt "policed" by their reception institutions. Often, conviviality decisions were made for them. For instance, the utilisation of common spaces (e.g., the kitchen) was restricted by rigid schedules and the way they could prepare and eat food was regulated (e.g., some personal items were forbidden). *"*We were almost encouraged to hide our personal belongings from others, and to portray an image of 'neediness', to be accepted*"* (R, Syrian refugee). In the accounts of our research colleagues, very few opportunities were made available to proactively participate in processes of social inclusion. On the contrary, they felt compelled to make efforts to learn about the Portuguese host society and to behave according to what their hosts expected of them, something we connect to our readings on epistemic injustice (e.g., Inge et al., 2024).

The lived experiences reported by our colleagues made us reflect that refugee status becomes a sort of filter, which we named "refugeeness," through which all refugees are seen by institutional actors. When these actors provide services, they often pressure refugees to demonstrate their "refugeeness," a performative submission that entails a constant pleading for help and an exaggerated politeness. In this sense, gratitude became a kind of barter that refugees must always carry along. Charities' employees have also been observed by co-authors using the filter of "refugeeness" for their own benefit. For instance, "borrowing" refugees' stories and pictures to plead for financial aid in fundraising events. In other instances, the filter of "refugeeness" is used to justify symbolic acts of violence, such as withholding or stalling services, when refugees confront them with complaints.

Our group noted yet another interesting manifestation of "refugeeness," when institutional actors exhibit "pity" for the living conditions of refugees. Group members witnessed that, out of sight from their employers, these actors may sometimes offer informal support and alternate ways to solve their problems. Understanding the ways through which these informal "small powers" interact with "refugeeness," our colleagues concluded that their social inclusion is often more dependent on "luck" than on policy.

A, a Syrian researcher in our team doing a master's in international studies, collected impressions about social inclusion among a group of Syrian refugees living in Portugal. As a peer and trusted friend, A held long conversations around a coffee or a meal with his research collaborators. A reported that their perception of social inclusion in Portugal was marked by an overall sense of being welcomed and having personal freedom (e.g., Muslims in Portugal often decided which religious norms and rules to follow and which ones to discard, like eating *halal* meat). However, the acknowledgement of hospitality and personal freedom did not prevent them from experiencing a sense of solitude in Portugal. Close and meaningful relationships were perceived as hard to build, despite the fact that A's interviewees had lived in Portugal for four to five years when he collected his data. In fact, none of them had yet expanded their social circle beyond the Syrian/refugee community.

A's findings further showed that Syrians missed the sense of being part of a wider community. A noticeable aspect impacting his participants' sense of inclusion concerned the size of their families. A, himself, belongs to a family of more than 500 people, including parents, siblings, uncles, aunts and cousins, while, in Portugal, as all other Syrians, he feels restricted to a nuclear family. One reason is, of course, the limit imposed by the reunification policies – families are allowed to reunite with spouses and children and, at most, a grandfather or a grandmother. This has been experienced by many as a loss of not only familial, but also communal bonds. A's interviewees further reflected that Portugal is far from being a desirable country to settle in the long run. They mentioned Germany and Sweden as much more appealing destinations, not due to more advantageous economic opportunities, but rather to the presence of a bigger and more established Syrian diaspora.

In Portugal, Syrian refugees' lives are perceived by the participants as precarious, both for those who are employed and for those who study. It is not uncommon for labour relations in Portugal to include exploitation (e.g., working beyond working hours) and precarity (e.g., extremely low wages and short-term contracts). Refugee workers in our group have also shared a series of labour mistreatments that range from control and authoritarianism to abusive language and belittling from Portuguese/white coworkers. They further noted that there is a resistance to denounce such situations of abuse among the refugee community, understandably caused by the fear of losing means of survival. Refugee activists in our group challenge these everyday violences using communal practices of care and support (e.g., grassroots organising, advocating for refugees' rights, partnering with civil society allies) to enhance collective resistance.

In the case of refugee students, challenges begin in the admission process to university – with extremely slow and complex bureaucracies – continuing throughout all academic life. I, a Syrian student in our group, shared his personal impressions of social inclusion at the university:

> Nobody tells me directly that they prefer not to talk to me. But their expressions, their body language, and even some sentences, show mistrust, or even a fear of interacting with me. 'Put the mask

> on, put the mask on', is an example of what they told me recently. I understood that this insistence comes from the fact that I'm not Portuguese, and not because I'm not wearing a mask at that moment. They don't tell me directly: 'Now you have to wear the mask because you are Syrian and I don't trust you', but this is what I read in the subtitles.

These shared reflections and multiple lived experiences led us to conclude that the social inclusion of refugees in Portugal needs further contributions from refugees themselves in both academic and institutional projects. We believe that it is important to "break" the filter of "refugeeness" to see refugees as they are.

An intersectional perspective on access to health care through the lenses of racialised women

This subsection was written by the *SaMaNe* collective and aims at bringing visibility – in the social and academic debate – to the obstetric experiences of Black women in Portugal. *SaMaNe* has been conducting fieldwork research using four main methods: (1) an anonymous online survey that collects racialised women's experiences in the healthcare system; (2) conversation circles around empowerment of motherhood experiences; (3) participation in social networks, academic events and advocacy efforts; and (4) public health policy proposals to better include racialised women living in Portugal.

Portugal has a universal healthcare system, accessible to everyone regardless of their economic and social conditions, including reproductive health care (Martins, 2014). Over the decades, improvements in the country's socioeconomic conditions and healthcare services helped to progressively overcome the high rates of maternal and infant mortality, registered until the 1980s (Pintassilgo, 2014). However, social movements for the humanisation of childbirth have been consistent in denouncing the high rates of excessive medical intervention and obstetric violence (Associação Portuguesa pelos Direitos da Mulher na Gravidez e Parto, 2020). Regarding racialised migrant women, research has shown that they have less satisfactory experiences when accessing health care in Portugal (Dias & Rocha, 2009; Topa, 2016; Martins, 2014). With this in mind, the SaMaNe collective gathered the descriptions of 150 Black women's interactions with the Portuguese health services, during the obstetric period (prenatal, delivery and postpartum). The following two excerpts are illustrative of such:

> It happened once in hospital X, the nurse asked me four times about my birthplace. She thought it was strange for me to be from [Lisbon] and she also asked several times about my schooling.
>
> (Luso-Cape Verdean, Lisbon, 28 years old)

> Compared to my first pregnancy, this second one was very bad. Without a general practitioner, at 24 weeks, I only had 3 medical appointments [...] During the pregnancy, I bled, but the doctors, including in hospitals (in emergency rooms), said it was normal.
>
> (São Tomé migrant, Lisbon, 30 years old).

These discriminated bodies of Black women in the obstetric scenario bring us the (late) need to address intersectional aspects of body-race-health. These, and other similar descriptions, are not yet included in the official narrative about experiences of pregnancy in Portugal. The collection of data such as race and ethnicity has been constantly hampered by the State, due to an alleged "protection from discrimination" rule. Several researchers (Matos, 2019; Roldão, 2016) believe that the non-disclosure of race and ethnicity data makes it extremely difficult to create policies aimed at specific populations, considering their socioeconomic characteristics, using an intersectional and social justice perspective. Looking specifically at the health of racialised women in Portugal, the consequences of the institutional narrative of "protection from discrimination," highlight a reality hitherto silenced. The SaMaNe collective believes that this silencing is part of a broader context of structural racism, which permeates Portuguese society and its institutions, resulting in a refusal to address it broadly, as a political and social problem. Despite the difficulty in gathering data, the statements above do not represent isolated cases, either in the country or in other scenarios, where the topic has been widely studied and debated, both socially and politically (Leal et al., 2017). One of the few studies available in Portugal on this topic aimed to make an intersection between migration and sexual and reproductive health, looking at its impacts on social development and on the wellbeing of individuals and communities. The descriptions collected in the study corroborate the ones shown above, as the authors pointed out that women racialised as migrants were deemed more vulnerable during the period of pregnancy and postpartum (Dias & Rocha, 2009). During these crucial periods, there were greater risks of negative obstetric outcomes for migrant mothers and babies than for the native population (Dias & Rocha, 2009).

Many questions remain open in this particular research subject. The SaMaNe collective will continue to contribute to this debate by bringing into public discussion the multiple oppressions, microaggressions and inequalities that racialised women experience in the obstetric scenario and beyond in order to break the silence on this topic. We aim for racialised women (migrants, or not), living in Portugal, to lead this endeavour, as protagonists of their own stories and experiences. Organising in community-based collectives that work both with activism and research is our proposal to make this happen in other contexts.

Living in Portugal as Black migrants: a decolonial auto-ethnographic reflection

The notes we bring to this sub-section result from 13 years of conviviality built within the musical group *Yoka Kongo!*, a band formed in Portugal, by members with connections to Central Africa, specifically the *Bakongo* People and their diaspora. We consider this collective work to be a contribution to both Community Psychology and Public Anthropology, in the sense that it has been co-produced by a group of researchers, musicians and artists, to illuminate diverse perspectives and knowledges.

We come from four countries (DRC, Angola, Cuba and Brazil) and ten ethnicities and our ages range from 21 to 64 years. Throughout the years, the band has changed its composition, bringing in new members and replacing others, but it has always kept the same communal circle. Through music-making and other performative arts, the group explores Black Atlantic musicalities based on personal experiences and ongoing training. The music is a reflection of the politics and personal paths that brought individual members together to their present lives.

The disjunction of different migration flows led us to a demographic plurality and a reshaping of our understanding of borders. We look at them as spaces of multiple belongings. Our diversities configure a strategic movement towards communal resistance, and we "translate" our ontologies through musicality.[1] Diversity represents a radical rhetoric for the separation of totalised cultures, which are based on the utopia of a unique collective identity. As a collective, we decided to bring to this collaborative chapter some concerns that depart from a long debate and observation exercise, stemming from our lived experiences. Led by our Brazilian colleague, we came to question our subjectivities as Black migrant men, through six months of reflections and discussions on social inclusion, in a collaborative exercise of auto-ethnography. Our collective debate touched relevant issues affecting our integration, such as xenophobia, racism, loneliness, fears and anguish. We talked to each other in casual meetings, on Sundays, when, lonely and exhausted, after a full week of heavy work (usually in construction), we got together to cook, watch a football match and drink.

In order to find our place in Portuguese and European society, we had to submit to the exploitation of our Black bodies, our strength and physical labour and to the stereotyped objectifications of our image as Black migrants. Loneliness is only one of the innumerable consequences of maintaining an archetype that lingers between virility, dehumanisation, physical strength and intellectual capability – we believe we are perceived as the socio-racial group with the lowest level of education, be it due to our late enrolment in the school system, early abandonment, poor academic achievement, significant age-grade distortion or the low turnout to schooling.

We consider that White masculinity has dehumanised us as Black men, so when we reflect specifically on Black masculinity we do it, before anything else, as an exercise to claim back our humanity. Living in a host society that has been contributing to the disaggregation of Black communities and discouraging the association between Black people, discussing the loneliness of Black men is part of a much-needed decolonial dialogue. For many years, we believe we have been mainly viewed as useful objects, able to provide joy and pleasure through our art and offer strength through our manual labour. These seem to be the only places where we are perceived as having some value in the host society. As Black migrants with low social capital, we have progressively adapted to racist stereotypes, reinforcing our social roles and functions of meagre prestige, our low financial turnout and fragile positions in the labour market.

In our minuscule universe of Congolese migrants, we remain (most of us) single. Most of us left our wives or significant others in our home countries. The possibility of engaging in interracial relationships is hindered by the language barrier. But there are other social and cultural barriers to forming relationships with Portuguese women. For example, their expectations around motherhood, financial independence and gender roles. Among our group, many assert that relationships with African and Afro-descendant women are also extremely hard because, *"when Black migrant women reach Europe, they transform."* When asked to further describe these transformations, members of our group say: *"they start to demand the same treatment as white women."* One of the major "problems" reported by the group concerns the perceived changes in African women, after pregnancies, namely through the way they become the "owners" of children's social allowances and/or children's due tax credits. According to members of our group, many of the women move into a "reverse gender role" in the relationship, as they begin controlling family finances. This reversal of gender roles generates discomfort and stirs with our conceptions of masculinity, already weakened by the embodiment of migration and racism that we experience as Black men.

We firmly believe that transformations may arrive with self-reflection. The processes of questioning ourselves have been pertinent for us to understand who we are, where we are and how we relate to one another. As Black men, we have created complex strategies to renegotiate our masculinities under the rules and systems of values of our host society. Understanding that there are "hegemonic" masculinity codes, we attempt to subvert them through our own views and values. Some elements of our Black symbolic repertoire in the musical band became allies in this mission that we consider to be one of (re) humanisation. Maybe due to this resistance and self-reflection, this music band has shown, throughout the years, singular stories of empowerment. It is in this space of artistic freedom that our bodies gain visibility and act not only as unqualified manpower or objects of pleasure, but as full body-spaces that make themselves present and are able to disturb.

Conclusion

In this collaborative chapter, we presented diverse perspectives, experiences and acts of resistance shared by refugee and migrant communities living in Portugal. Our first goal was to contribute to widening the academic and institutional understanding of what social inclusion entails for people racialised as migrants and refugees. We also hinted at important aspects of social and epistemic justice that should be considered in research, such as the direct participation and co-authorship of marginalised communities using an intersectional lens.

We end this collective journey feeling that more than just experimenting with collaborative research, we engaged in a truly expansive learning experience. Our exercise helped us to reflect and situate our diverse positionalities in an open-ended, informal and pragmatic way, which helped us to collect new apprehensions and understandings about what it takes to feel more welcomed and included.

In our case studies, we showed the importance of lived experiences as irreplaceable contributions to rethink policies, practices and services of social inclusion. Namely, we illustrated many ways through which migrant and refugee communities feel disempowered and constrained by the ways through which different Portuguese actors and institutions relate to them. The second and third case studies highlight the value of using an intersectional lens in research, potentiating the sociocultural knowledge, resistance and resources of racialised communities.

Our interdisciplinary approach suggests that practitioners and academics can add value to their work by establishing partnerships based on co-citizenships with racialised communities. We understand this practice as a form of critical solidarity, i.e., a critical engagement with communities as citizens, aiming at improving social justice. More specifically, our author collective defends the right of migrants and refugees to be the protagonists of academic research that concerns their own lives.

We end this chapter by inviting all community researchers to reflect on how they can contribute to amplifying the knowledges, struggles and resistances of racialised communities affected by multiple discriminations using interdisciplinary and collaborative approaches that may widen their reflections. Please consider the questions below to help you reflect on this.

Reflective questions

1. How can you make use of your *lugar de fala* in community research?
2. How can you integrate collaborative methodologies in your current community work or research?
3. How can you contribute to not only produce but also disseminate knowledge that engages and includes marginalised and racialised communities affected by multiple discriminations?
4. How can you foster and sustain co-citizenship and allyship with these communities?

Acknowledgements

Nina Amelung's funding is based on an FCT grant entitled "Affected (non)publics: Social and political implications of transnational biometric databases in migration and crime control (AFFECT)," Individual Research Grant Fellow FCT CEECIND/03611/2018/CP1541/CT0009.

Note

1 Over the last two years, the VIBE project (www.blackeurope.pt) has hosted a series of in-person and virtual meetings, with some participants forming the musical collective Yoka Kongo! The band went on to record two studio singles as well as perform in concerts across Portugal. In 2020, Yoka Kongo! was selected for a residency in Lisbon, at Largo Residencias. The space was used for rehearsal as well as to host seminars with religious leaders from Afro-Cuban, Afro-Brazilian and Central African faiths.

References

Associação Portuguesa pelos Direitos da Mulher na Gravidez e Parto. (2020). *Experiências de parto em Portugal: Inquérito às mulheres sobre as suas experiências de parto* (2nd ed.). https://associacaogravidezeparto.pt/campanhas-e-eventos/inquerito-experiencias-de-parto-em-portugal-2-a-edicao/

Borofsky, R., & De Lauri, A. (2019). Public anthropology in changing times. *Public Anthropologist, 1*(1), 3–19. https://doi.org/10.1163/25891715-00101002

Ciofalo, N. (2022). Making the road caminando de otra manera: Co-constructing decolonial community psychologies from the Global South. *American Journal of Community Psychology, 69*(3–4), 426–435. https://doi.org/10.1002/ajcp.12562

Dias, S. F. & Rocha, C. F. (2009) *Saúde sexual e reprodutiva de mulheres imigrantes africanas e brasileiras* (Vol. 32). Observatório da Imigração, ACIDI, IP.

Dutta, U. (2018). Decolonizing "community" in community psychology. *American Journal of Community Psychology, 62*(3–4), 272–282. https://doi.org/10.1002/ajcp.12281

Fernández, J. S., Sonn, C. C., Carolissen, R., & Stevens, G. (2021). Roots and routes toward decoloniality within and outside psychology praxis. *Review of General Psychology, 25*(4), 354–368. https://doi.org/10.1177/10892680211002437

Hernandez-Carranza, G., Carranza, M., & Grigg, E. (2021). Using auto-ethnography to bring visibility to coloniality. *Qualitative Social Work, 20*(6), 1517–1535. https://doi.org/10.1177/14733250211039514

Inge E., Pérez-Aronsson A., Ibrahim K., Aljeshy R., Sarkadi A., & Warner, G. (2024). Ameliorating epistemic injustice in practice: communication strategies in a research project with refugee youth coresearchers. *Health Expect, 27*, e13926. https://doi:10.1111/hex.13926

Kessi S. (2017). Community social psychologies for decoloniality: An African perspective on epistemic justice in higher education. *South African Journal of Psychology, 47*(4), 506–516. https://doi.org/10.1177/0081246317737917

Lassiter, L. E. (2008), Moving past public anthropology and doing collaborative research. *NAPA Bulletin, 29*, 70–86. https://doi.org/10.1111/j.1556–4797.2008.00006.x

Leal, M., Gama, S. G. N., Pereira, A. P. E., Pacheco, V. E., Carmos, C. N., & Santos, R. V. (2017). A cor da dor: iniquidades raciais na atenção pré-natal e ao parto no Brasil. *Cadernos de Saúde Pública, 33*(1), 1–17. https://doi.org/10.1590/0102-311X00078816

Lykes, M. B. (2017). Community-based and participatory action research: Community psychology collaborations within and across borders. In M. A. Bond, I. Serrano-García, C. B. Keys, & M. Shinn (Eds.), *APA handbook of community psychology: Methods for community research and action for diverse groups and issues* (pp. 43–58). American Psychological Association. https://doi.org/10.1037/14954-003

Matos, A. L. (2019). *A legitimidade da recolha e processamento de dados relativos à raça e à origem étnica: Impactos na esfera privada dos indivíduos e no combate à discriminação* [Master's thesis, Faculdade de Direito da Universidade do Porto]. Repositório Aberto da Universidade do Porto. https://repositorio-aberto.up.pt/bitstream/10216/126089/2/384586.pdf

Martins, M. (2014). 'O programa de assistência pré-natal nos Cuidados de Saúde Primários em Portugal – uma reflexão'. *Revista Brasileira de Enfermagem*, *67*(6), 1008–1012. https://doi.org/10.1590/0034–7167.2014670621

Pintassilgo, S. (2014). *O risco e as condições sociais e assistenciais da maternidade em Portugal* [Doctoral dissertation, ISCTE – Instituto Universitário de Lisboa]. Repositório do ISCTE-IUL. https://repositorio.iscte-iul.pt/bitstream/10071/7898/1/phd_sonia_cardoso_pintassilgo.pdf

Rebelo, D., Abdullah, A., & Hussein, M. (2020). Solidarity with refugees in Portugal: A collaborative research. *Community Psychology in Global Perspective*, *6*(1), 36–51. https://doi.org/10.1285/i24212113v6i1p36

Ribeiro, D. (2019). *Lugar de fala*. Pólen Produção Editorial Ltda.

Roldão, C. (2016, October 27). *Os afrodescendentes no sistema educativo* [Conference presentation]. Encontros Mensais sobre Experiências Migratórias, Faculdade de Letras da Universidade de Lisboa.

Saltsman, A., & Jacobsen, K. (2021). Power in forced migration research methods. *Journal of Refugee Studies*, *34*(3), 2511–2521.https://doi.org/10.1093/jrs/feab058

Santinho, M. C. (2016). Refugiados e requerentes de asilo em Portugal: Contornos políticos no campo da saúde (Vol. 48). *Observatório das Migrações*, ACM, IP, Portugal.

Topa, J. (2016). *Cuidados de saúde materno-infantis a imigrantes na região do grande Porto: Percursos, discursos e práticas* (Vol. 47). Observatório das Migrações, Alto Comissariado para as Migrações, I. P.

Trickett, E. J. (2009). Community psychology: Individuals and interventions in community context. *Annual Review of Psychology*, *60*(1), 395–419. https://doi.org/10.1146/annurev.psych.60.110707.163517

Vacchiano, F. (2018). On marginal inclusion: Refugees at the fringes of citizenship in Portugal. In *Changing societies: Legacies and challenges. Vol. 1: Ambiguous inclusions—Inside out, outside in* (pp. 99–112). Imprensa de Ciências Sociais. https://repositorio.ulisboa.pt/bitstream/10451/35589/1/ICS_FVacchiano_On.pdf

Vine, D. (2011). "Public Anthropology" in its second decade: Robert Borofsky's center for a public anthropology. *American Anthropologist*, *113*(2), 336–339. https://doi.org/10.1111/j.1548–1433.2011.01334.x

Yuval-Davis, N. (2006). Belonging and the politics of belonging. *Patterns of Prejudice*, *40*(3), 197–214. https://doi.org/10.1080/00313220600769331

4 "Count me in"[1]

Participation and inclusion in the context of UK homelessness

Bruno Basilio De Oliveira, Suzanne Elliott, Laura Hancox, Dani Harker-Brown, Joseph Murphy and Bryan Nash

What has psychology got to do with homelessness?

It is estimated that 4,667 individuals slept rough in the UK in autumn 2024, based on the government definition of rough sleeping (Department for Levelling Up, Housing and Communities, 2024). Whilst profound, this figure is likely an underestimate given the restrictions of the definition used, the practical challenges of counting people and the transient nature of homelessness.

Social, material, racial and other kinds of disadvantage and discrimination have been consistently recognised as contributing to poorer life chances with increased psychological distress and chances of becoming ensnared in cycles of offending (Sheppard, 2002; Viner et al., 2012; Wilkinson & Pickett, 2010). However, these are frequently not attended to by support systems that medicalise, individualise and pathologise. The "Hard Edges" report (Bramley & Fitzpatrick, 2015) outlines how the combined impact of homelessness, substance use and contact with criminal justice services alongside lack of access to education, poverty and difficult family relationships has a profound influence on health and quality of life during adulthood. Unsurprisingly then, a growing body of literature indicates high levels of psychological distress and difficulty amongst homeless people (e.g., St. Mungo's, 2014). Despite this, research suggests that people experiencing homelessness face significant barriers to accessing mental health support (e.g., Marmot et al., 2010) for a number of reasons, including low levels of GP registration and high levels of mobility (Owen & Khalil, 2007), lack of flexibility in appointment systems and discharge procedures (Spence, 2009), lack of responsibility placed on services to seek out vulnerable non-attendee's (Crane & Warnes, 2001) and stigma (O'Reilly et al., 2009).

With increased awareness that people experiencing homelessness are more likely to have endured traumatic histories and face ongoing challenges, many public sector services have adopted a "Psychologically-Informed Environments" approach (Wittington, 2007) to everyday practice. This approach, which has become known as "PIE," aims to support people experiencing homelessness to make changes in their lives with the help of workers who have completed training that introduces psychological models and ways of implementing these theories into daily practice (Keats et al., 2012). The definition of a PIE given by the authors of the guidelines is that if asked why a service is run in a particular way, "the staff would give an answer couched in terms of the emotional and psychological needs of the service users, rather than giving some more logistical or practical rationale, such as convenience, costs, or health and safety regulations" (Johnson et al., 2010). One of the guideline's strengths is its

DOI: 10.4324/9781003480464-5

adaptability; it does not specify which models should or should not be included in the "psychological framework" which services use. We consider the guidelines to be compatible with community psychology praxis in that the whole document is linking a sociopolitical phenomenon (homelessness) with distress and advocates interventions targeted at the social context and systems in which people experiencing homelessness find themselves, rather than an individualised psychological approach of locating the problem within the person.

In Leicester, one of the psychological models informing our PIE framework is Community Psychology (CP) because it offered a good fit with the experiences of frontline homeless staff who are painfully aware of the impact of toxic social policy and political choices on wellbeing and human suffering. We often draw from Bronfenbrenner's Ecological theory (1977) when talking with staff from homelessness services about the impact of wider social and political forces on individuals' wellbeing. CP also offered psychologists an evidence base which avoided individualising, internalising, blaming or pathologising narratives. CP informed an understanding of homelessness are much more likely to emphasise structural factors within society, such as unemployment, poverty and shortage of affordable and accessible housing (Orford, 2008).

Homelessness in the UK: Leicester and Brighton

In this chapter we are focussing only on UK homelessness, because the context of homelessness and meanings of "home" varies so much across the globe. In some areas of the world, war, famine or "natural" disasters play a significant role in creating homelessness. There is extreme variation in the degree of social support available to those experiencing homelessness in different parts of the world, often depending on political choices. Some countries are considered to have "conquered" homelessness completely. The UK, however, is thought to have one of the highest rates of homelessness in Europe (Yanatma, 2024).

Homelessness in Leicester, like other cities across the UK, has increased year on year since 2021, which marked the end of the "Everyone In" COVID-19 emergency response to homelessness, whereby there were no conditions to the provision of emergency shelter. The city council reported an increase from 4,756 households seeking help with homelessness in 2018–19 to over 5,000 households in 2021–22 (Leicester City Council [LCC], 2023). In Brighton, most recent figures (Department for Levelling Up, Housing and COmmunities, 2024) suggest that there was an increase in rough sleeping of 46% from 2023 to 2024. The *Rough Sleeping Snapshot in England* report (Department for Levelling Up, Housing and Communities, 2025) together with the Leicester Homelessness Strategy (2023) and the Brighton Homelessness and Rough Sleeping Strategy (Brighton & Hove City Council, 2020) will provide readers with more detailed demographic information for those who have been identified as homeless in Leicester and Brighton. In Leicester, in 2017, a survey was conducted by De Montfort University (Richardson, 2017) which gives further indication of the "support needs" of respondents experiencing homelessness. Any data are likely to be underestimates because of the hidden nature of homelessness.

Community psychology and homelessness

Community Psychology (CP) emphasises the interplay between individuals and their communities, focusing on social change, empowerment and liberation. In the context of homelessness in the UK, CP adopts a holistic approach to address the root causes and consequences of homelessness, integrating participatory action research and community engagement. Community psychologists have significantly influenced research, theory, intervention and policy on homelessness since the 1980s.

Community psychologists have employed ecological–developmental perspectives to study homelessness, recognising the interplay between individual development and multiple levels of social organisation. To illustrate, Haber and Toro (2004) emphasised that while homeless individuals often face resource scarcity and adverse events, they also possess adaptive potential and resilience. This nuanced understanding has led to more holistic research approaches that consider both risks and strengths within homeless populations. Haber and Toro (2004) have highlighted how family dynamics, community resources and societal structures contribute to homelessness by integrating ecological frameworks, challenging simplistic explanations and underscoring the need for holistic approaches such as Participatory Action Research (PAR).

PAR can be defined as a collaborative research approach that actively involves participants as co-researchers in identifying issues, generating knowledge and enacting change, with the dual aim of producing rigorous insight and empowering communities to transform their conditions (De Oliveira, 2023). Interventions enhance self-efficacy, dignity and community integration by focusing on existing resources and adaptive capacities. This contrasts with deficit-based models which emphasise the assumed deficiencies of individuals or groups, leading to their portrayal as the root cause of the issue. According to Townley et al. (2018), PAR can be used to engage homeless individuals in developing community-based solutions by using participatory and cross-cultural engagement with the community.

CP offers a transformative approach to addressing homelessness by shifting the focus from individual shortcomings to systemic factors and community liberation. Community psychologists challenge the view that homelessness results from personal failings, instead highlighting the complex interplay of societal issues such as economic inequality, lack of affordable housing and deep social inequalities. CP seeks to create sustainable solutions to homelessness by focusing on systemic change and community empowerment. This approach involves advocating for policies that address the root causes of homelessness, such as increasing affordable housing, enhancing social services and supporting community initiatives that promote social change (Hopper, 2013).

CP seeks to liberate individuals to understand and critically challenge the systemic forces perpetuating their marginalisation. Homelessness is a consequence of structural oppression, economic disparity, social exclusion and policies that prioritise the privileged while disregarding the needs of the most vulnerable. CP aligns with this by working with participatory methods, advocacy and grassroots mobilisation to address homelessness as a social justice and human rights issue, shifting the narrative away from blaming individuals for their homelessness and instead focusing on solidarity, dialogue and social action. Community psychologists seek to change the focus of research and practice to humanising approaches that restore dignity and agency to people experiencing homelessness, rather than treating them as passive "subjects" by challenging and transforming the structures that keep them marginalised.

Actions undertaken by community psychologists

We would like to highlight four future directions for CP praxis in homelessness, which include an increased focus on prevention. First, people applying CP can advocate for policies that address the structural factors contributing to homelessness, using research evidence. For example, research highlighting the correlation between housing instability and poor mental health (e.g., Kang, 2022) can be instrumental in advocating for just housing policies. Community psychologists are well placed to use research findings such as these to argue for policy interventions that ensure individuals at heightened risk of housing instability are proactively housed. This could be through lobbying government, challenging discriminatory practices, promoting equal access to resources and opportunities or by highlighting the evidence base when responding to calls for evidence (e.g., St. Mungo's, 2014).

Second, initiatives that promote social inclusion and reduce stigma associated with homelessness are also important. People experiencing homelessness are often subjected to significant stigma and marginalisation, which can impact their mental health and hinder access to support services (Phelan et al., 1997; O'Reilly et al., 2009). Social inclusion can be achieved through public awareness campaigns, community engagement activities and cultivating inclusive community environments (Sampson et al., 2013). We would argue that focusing on the strength, resistance and resilience of individuals experiencing homelessness, rather than their deficits, is an essential part of a CP approach to homelessness.

Third, community psychologists can continue contributing to the evidence base through community-based research which promotes an understanding of homelessness as a complex issue influenced by multiple systems (e.g., economic, social, political). Use of PAR invites community psychologists to collaborate with individuals with lived experience of homelessness, ensuring their perspectives are central to the issue they seek to explore. This approach to research and social change generates valuable insights and empowers participants by validating their experiences, recognising their expertise and promoting their active involvement as co-researchers (Jason, 2013). A participatory approach can be essential to identifying best practice, measuring outcomes and informing policy and practice (De Oliveira, 2018). Unfortunately, there remains a need to tackle stigma and ill-informed narratives, promoting more inclusive societal narratives and challenging dehumanising depictions of homelessness. We know the power of these narratives and research (see praxis case study 2) is one way to change the stories told about people experiencing homelessness so that the stories lived are less painful.

Fourth, community psychologists can look for community development opportunities, collaborating with policymakers, community organisations and other stakeholders to develop and implement effective interventions (Evans et al., 2014). Actions might include training community members and service providers, developing local support networks and promoting collaboration between sectors and agencies (Kloos et al., 2012). To illustrate, Canada's Calgary Homeless Foundation (CHF, 2018) and Leicester's partnership working approach (Blackburn, 2019) utilise a collaborative approach that integrates services across various sectors to provide holistic support to people experiencing homelessness. This model demonstrates the potential of cooperative networks in addressing the multifaceted nature of homelessness.

Praxis case study 1: Psychology on the streets

What?

Dominant narratives of exclusion, based on socially constructed ideas of the homeless population as "criminal" or "dangerous," feed into reinforcing a powerfully stigmatising discourse of "us versus them" (Toolis & Hammack, 2015) which may make it particularly challenging for people who are rough sleeping to use mainstream service provision. Building familiarity and relationships with people rough sleeping in order to challenge assumptions and provide disengaged communities with the services they are entitled to has been seen to enhance collaborative working and improve take-up of offers of support

(Cullen et al., 2007; Durcan et al., 2017). Therefore, innovative ways of steadfastly reaching out to people who are sleeping rough are key to adequately supporting this community.

In 2016, people with lived experience of rough sleeping advised us that part of the homeless community was missing the chance of support because they would not come to see us at the usual venues we worked in. Inspired by the principles of PIE, CP and a passionate Street Outreach team manager determined to connect rough sleepers with healthcare professionals, the Homeless Mental Health Service in Leicester took psychologists to the streets.

We initially looked to the evidence base to guide our work. There is a broad international consensus that multi-agency partnership working is essential in order to support people to avoid or recover from homelessness (Anderson et al., 2005; Department for Communities and Local Government [DCLG], 2012; Luchenski et al., 2018; Homeless Link, 2022; Sheikh & Teeman, 2018; Taylor, 2024). Multi-agency partnership working is also a key principle of the standards of the Faculty for Homeless and Inclusion Health (Hewitt, 2018). However, we could find no research into street outreach in partnership or the value of psychologically informed street outreach. When we came across a project founded on CP principles in London, we were inspired. Music and Change (MAC-UK) was set up in 2008 to support and empower disenfranchised young people who were considered "hard to reach" (Durcan et al., 2017); a phrase often used to describe people who sleep rough. Psychologists from MAC-UK were able to connect with the people they supported by capitalising on their relationships with influential key "community gatekeepers" by allowing self-referral and by "hanging out" where those people spent time. The only driver to initial contact was to build trust. Relationship building was "front and centre" and if the person then asked for support, whether immediately or later, then it was responded to. Once trust was established, it was possible to enquire about the person's interests and passions, and this then led to conversations about developing projects together in those areas. In Leicester, we agreed to take this approach as a model underpinning our work with people rough sleeping.

How?

With this in mind, clinical psychologists joined the Outreach team fortnightly. The Outreach team was a small but highly specialist group of passionate staff, respected and valued by the homeless community, with decades of experience and presence on the streets. We identified that this team were our "community gatekeepers" (Durcan et al., 2017) who could help us "gain entry" into the community (Toolis & Hammack, 2015). If the Outreach team showed the people we met that the psychologists could be trusted, this would give us an opening to build trust that might otherwise be unlikely due to the barriers mentioned previously.

Within the psychology and Outreach teams" organisations, there was some concern about what psychologists would be able to achieve when out in public spaces, beyond the comfort and privacy of the therapy room. We also met assumptions that we would not be able to offer anything effective if the people we were talking to did not have their "basic needs" of shelter, warmth and food met first. However, we were aware of the anti-racist critiques of Maslow's theory of human motivation (e.g., Blackstock, 2011; Rutledge, 2011) and our conclusion was that the infamous "hierarchy" he proposed is actually more like a "web of needs" with all "levels" or aspects of it intersecting and coming to prominence at different points in time depending on the person's circumstances and context.

Considering our work from this position enabled us to reserve judgement about whether it was possible to have conversations on the street until we started the work. It also freed us up to give consideration to what kinds of conversations we could have on the street. In our clinical work with people experiencing homelessness over 15 years, we have found it helpful to attend to the structural barriers to psychological wellbeing, highlighted by CP, whilst at the same time offering conversations that were useful to people recovering from challenging life experiences prior to and during homelessness. Rather than framing what we were doing on street outreach using "mental health" language like "assessment" or "therapy" we opened up conversations about "what is important to this person?"; "What are they passionate about?" or "What do they give value to in life?" This approach structured safety by avoiding pushing the people we met into very personal conversations about trauma. At the same time, if, after building trust with the psychologist during outreach, people we met wanted support with their mental health, the psychologist could act as a "bridge" to the wider homeless mental health team in which we sit.

Feedback

One person we met through street work made a self-referral to the team. This person told us that he was able to self-refer because he felt familiar and trusting towards the psychologist due to meeting with them on several occasions on the streets. This person said that he had learned more about what psychology can offer and what it might mean to see a psychologist; myths such as being "sectioned" were dispelled for him after having conversations about accessing mental health services. Another person we met on the street was passionate about our planet, and after discovering this we were able to offer meetings with this person in a less urban, more wild environment, which nurtured connection with nature and allowed us to have more meaningful conversations. These are powerful examples of how our wellbeing is inseparable from social inequalities such as poverty, racism, climate injustice and social exclusion. It also illustrates how, contrary to dominant discourses in UK mental health services, people experiencing homelessness often actively seek support with their mental health (Elliott, 2015).

Feedback from the Outreach team following the initial 10-month pilot of this project outlined that one of the most important aspects of the work, from their standpoint, was building connections between agencies. The team suggested that this connection between the teams reflected the ultimate goal of nurturing trust with people rough sleeping (i.e., the connection between the homeless community and the psychology team was improved through the psychology team's association with the Outreach team). Also, the deepened connection between the psychology team and the Outreach team gave the Outreach team better knowledge of mental health and wellbeing; they were better able to share this with people rough sleeping.

The psychology team moved beyond the comfort of a clinical interview room to "be with" people who are living on the streets every day. However, it was extremely troubling to witness people asleep on the concrete floor, in all weathers, surrounded by constant noise and unceasing bright city lights. The reality of rough sleeping was brought into sharp focus and has allowed the psychologists a greater sense of the profound impact that life circumstances can have on people. Witnessing this together also brought the two teams closer. Perhaps this was because of the power that shared experiences can have in helping us to relate to one another, and also perhaps because those experiences cemented the shared vision of our work. The psychologists learned from people sleeping rough that sometimes rough sleeping felt the better of two limited options because of a culture in temporary accommodation that can be intimidating and expose further vulnerability. We also witnessed the sense of community that can exist amongst people who are homeless.

We hope that an ethic of transparency within these reflections might offer an account of the messy, imperfect, iterative nature of CP praxis which usually results in multi-directional growth and change. We see ourselves as part of an interconnected network of citizens who are changed by the process of taking social action as well as setting out to influence social change.

Praxis case study 2: In today's news: Tackling simplistic media's narrative of homelessness with Participatory Action Research

The participation of people with lived experience of homelessness in contesting their marginalisation is central to CP's commitment to amplifying marginalised voices, promoting agency and co-creating solutions (Kagan et al., 2011a). As an approach that can be identified by CP values, PAR disrupts traditional power imbalances in research by positioning individuals who have experienced homelessness as co-researchers rather than passive subjects, focusing on collaborative knowledge production and social action (Watts et al., 2003). De Oliveira (2018) participated with residents ("companions") at Emmaus Brighton and Hove, seeking to challenge dominant media discourses on homelessness, an initiative that exemplifies CP's commitment to critical consciousness (Freire, 1970) and ecological validity (Bronfenbrenner, 1979). Emmaus provides a unique and innovative solution to homelessness by supporting community living, economic participation and social support, mirroring CP's emphasis on structural interventions rather than individualised solutions.

De Oliveira's (2018) case study demonstrates how CP's core principle of participatory empowerment, collaborations between academics, artists and individuals with lived experience, contests stigmatising discourses and creates opportunities for challenging power structures (Orford, 2008). The research highlights how dominant narratives often stigmatise homelessness, reinforcing individual blame rather than recognising structural determinants such as housing policy, welfare reform and labour market conditions. By collaborating with individuals who have lived experiences, the study aims to exemplify CP's commitment to shifting power dynamics and fostering collective action (Zimmerman, 1995). Furthermore, the research aimed to transcend conventional academic boundaries by integrating the praxis that underpins CP's activist–researcher position, embodying Freirean principles of dialogue and problem-posing education. This approach positions research as a platform for fostering critical consciousness and social change (Freire, 1970). The PAR demonstrates how people with lived experience can reclaim narratives, shift public discourse and influence policy through media engagement. The originality and value of this research lie in its demonstration of the emancipatory potential of collaboration between academics and people with lived experiences. CP-informed approaches can challenge oppressive social representations and seek alternatives, such as strength-based narratives, by advocating for a more inclusive, participatory and justice-oriented approach to researching homelessness. This approach aims to reshape public perceptions and drive policy reform (Prilleltensky & Nelson, 2017). Thus, research becomes a space of resistance and action rather than extraction. This approach challenges the individualisation of social problems and reinforces the CP principle that sustainable solutions must centre those most impacted. CP challenges structural inequalities and dominant narratives through critical engagement, participatory action and a commitment to social change, offering an alternative framework rooted in justice, empowerment and collective wellbeing.

Action for learning activity 1: Forum Theatre on homelessness

Aims

This action-learning activity aims to engage students with the issue of homelessness through Forum Theatre. This participatory theatre form can enable students to explore the complexities of homelessness in a dialogical manner.

Introduction

Forum Theatre, developed by Augusto Boal as part of the Theatre of the Oppressed, can be a powerful pedagogical tool (Dahal et al., 2022; Wrentschur, 2008) for exploring social issues and enabling community engagement (Jackson & Boal, 2005). This activity encourages participation, critical thinking and collective problem-solving that educational institutions and community organisers can use when working with local communities.

Set-up

Preparation (1 hour)

Reading Assignment: Before the activity, students are encouraged to read key texts on homelessness and Forum Theatre, including Boal's "Games for Actors and Non-Actors" (Jackson & Boal, 2005) and recent studies on homelessness (e.g., Toro, 2007).
Discussion: In class, facilitate a brief discussion on the readings to ensure students understand the basic concepts and the social context of homelessness.

Scene development (2 hours)

Group Formation: Divide students into small groups (4–6 members).
Story Cr3eation: Each group will create a short scene (5–10 minutes) on homelessness. The scene should highlight issues such as the causes of homelessness, daily challenges, interactions with social services, and public perceptions.

Forum Theatre Act (2 hours)

Introduction: The audience (spect-actors, i.e., spectator and actor) can intervene in the scene to propose solutions or alternative actions (Jackson & Boal, 2005).
Development: Each group performs its scene once without interruption.
Interventions: After the initial performance, invite spect-actors to suggest changes. The scene is re-enacted with the spect-actors' interventions, allowing them to step into roles and assess their ideas.

Debriefing (1 hour)

Reflection: Facilitate a debriefing session where students discuss their experiences. Questions to guide the discussion include:

What new insights did we gain about homelessness?

How did the interventions change the outcome of the scenes?

How can these insights inform our practices?

Suggested follow-up assignment

Reflective Essay: Participants can write a reflective piece discussing the impact of the Forum Theatre activity on their understanding of homelessness and its implications for community interventions.

Action for learning activity 2: Where are they at? A two-stage exercise

It is essential when taking social action around homelessness that you give careful, honest consideration to the reasons driving your project. This is stage one; when you have done this and shared with your co-activists, you can move to stage two: Stakeholder Analysis.

Stage one: Personal reflexive exercise

Working in homelessness is working with complexity. Done well, it meets and connects with a web of systems, many of which are imperfect. Working with complexity requires activists to nurture their capacity for acknowledging and engaging with a multitude of factors simultaneously, both individual and systemic. The following exercise has been inspired by the work of activist psychologist Vikki Reynolds (n.d.) and Gesturing Towards Decolonial Futures Collective (n.d.).

Give some time to reflect on your own values, power and aspirations in relation to your homelessness project. Developing your own knowledge of yourself and your assumptions and biases (we all have them!) is called "reflexivity" and will help you to build relationships with the homeless community and the network of services around them. Going into these relationships without first reflecting on your own position could make it more likely that your initiative will not be welcomed or accepted by those already involved in the community. Here are some questions that can be used to start your reflections; they can be used for independent reflection or you could consider each of these questions as topics for meetings with your co-activists:

1. What does "home" mean to you? Where do you find belonging? How were you recruited into these ideas about "home"? Where did these ideas come from? What alternative definitions of "home" might exist? How are these allowed or disqualified by society? What alternative definitions might or might not be acceptable to you?
2. Unmask your privilege: create a "brick wall" out of post-it notes or postcards writing on each one things (both physical items and relational items such as love and warmth) which you had access to as a baby and small child which enabled you to survive and thrive. These things

continue to influence us as adults (Gerhardt, 2004). When you have done this, take away the items which you know people in the local homeless community did not have access to. This exercise will help you to consider things you have in common with people experiencing homelessness which could bring you into solidarity with them and ways in which you might have privilege, which could be barriers to solidarity.

3. What is driving you to take social action about homelessness? What brings you to the work? Whose interest is served by this? What if the process is costly in some way for you? How do you respond in situations where there are multiple truths, layers of meaning and power? To what extent have you been exposed to different stories of and about the world? Who would you like to be accountable to and what do you need from them?
4. What is the best use of you? When are you at your best and most connected with your ethics? How do you know when you are in this zone (the zone which Reynolds calls the "Zone of Fabulousness")? What keeps your "believed-in-hope" alive (Reynolds, n.d.)?

When you have reflected on your position in relation to these questions, discuss them with your co-activists and consider how your ideas and what you give value to may differ and complement each other. When you have done this, you will be ready for Stage Two.

Stage two: Stakeholder analysis

It is crucial that you do not duplicate initiatives that are already on offer, as this can undermine work already being done and thereby increase risk to people already living on the fringes of society. Instead, ideally, you will work in partnership with others who are already involved with the community and where there is mutual respect. These are your "community gatekeepers" who will help you "gain entry" into the community. This may mean working in partnership with those who do not share your values; but we cannot stress enough how important it is to avoid duplication and avoid further damaging people experiencing homelessness. It can be helpful to consider working with people who do not share your values as one of the challenges to be met in the work.

Who do you need to be in solidarity with locally in order to take social action together? In their "Critical Community Psychology" textbook, Kagan et al. (2011b) suggest mapping stakeholders onto quadrants of a square as a way to reflect on the power and influence they might hold in relation to your project. Stakeholder Mapping offers a helpful tool to consider who you might approach in allyship in order to offer something meaningful to people who are excluded. Equally, stakeholder mapping can make visible those who may stand in the way of your project or present barriers. Use Kagan et al.'s stakeholder mapping exercise (Figure 6.9 on page 153) to map out those individuals and organisations/groups who are present in your community with a "stake" in homelessness. Your "community gatekeepers" will sit in quadrant B.

Social justice and wellbeing in homelessness

We hope that the projects described here demonstrate a reduction in stigma related to mental health, making it acceptable to talk about our psychological wellbeing on the streets. Through the two projects described here, people who are homeless are more visible to those who are housed, and housed people, including psychologists and other health professionals, are more approachable to people experiencing homelessness.

These projects have not only attempted to challenge exclusionary oppressive narratives in society, but have simultaneously challenged the practices of exclusion employed by traditional patriarchal, colonial public institutions which can intimidate, medicalise, frighten and patronise people who may already have been betrayed and abused throughout their lives. Through the projects presented in this chapter, people who have experienced homelessness have opportunities to contribute to society, and the systems around them respond by moving towards them and including them.

Co-production is essential in a CP approach to social action on homelessness. It is often aspired to in institutions like the NHS and academia; however, genuine collaboration with people who have experienced homelessness is too easily undermined by the power of systems, over-reliance on good literacy and the willingness of stakeholders to genuinely listen. There is understandable distrust of institutions, like the NHS and education, amongst people who have experience of homelessness. These institutions have betrayed people who have experience of rough sleeping in the past and we do not want to add to this damage or rekindle the impact of it by making tokenistic gestures at co-production. In psychology, this is known as "retraumatisation" and will not be in the direction of CP ethics. For example, the welcome initiative of inviting people who have no safe place to stay into a warm room with tea and biscuits to co-produce with us is undermined if later we invite them to contribute "take home messages," with no thought as to the weight of the word "home." Those we have met during the course of the projects described here are adept at spotting "people with clipboards" and are acutely aware of what they have described as "the power of the lanyard."

If we can surmount institutional barriers, people experiencing homelessness can be heard. Their valuable talents, expertise and special skills can contribute to improving our communities. They can challenge systems to adapt in ways which make them more humane, and their words can support efforts to campaign for statutory changes to policy. This could mean mental health services which no longer turn away from people who have experienced homelessness and which all people feel confident to approach if necessary. It might mean mental health services which no longer blame people for the damage which society has done to them. Without institutional barriers, we might all hear good news stories about homelessness in the media, stories which celebrate the diversity of our communities and include rather than ostracise.

Challenges for community psychologists in addressing homelessness

Homelessness is a multifaceted social issue that requires a critical and social justice-based approach with an emphasis on liberation, dialogue and participation. One of the difficulties people aiming to challenge homelessness can face is navigating the very same structural and systemic barriers that create and perpetuate homelessness. There are powerful interests which do not want these structures to be changed. For example, psychologists may meet challenges within their institutions about spending their time on the street or undertaking "engagement" pre-intervention work. This work can be time-consuming and difficult to measure. We have found that our skills in evaluating our work (for example, through collecting accounts from people we meet about the value of this work) are useful and this data can be called upon if we are challenged. The signs and signals of institutional power are barriers that can compromise a CP approach. Contributing to justice and wellbeing in your community may first require addressing institutional barriers which could otherwise trip you up when you reach out to the community.

Conducting CP research alongside people experiencing homelessness presents unique ethical challenges. Researchers must navigate power imbalances and ensure their work genuinely benefits participant–researchers rather than merely advancing academic or personal interests. PAR is not immune to this; however, it is a research process that can offer a space in which contesting marginalisation is possible (De Oliveira, 2023).

Conclusion

In conclusion, homelessness remains a profound societal challenge in the UK, affecting thousands of individuals who face significant barriers to stability, health care and support services. Homelessness is not a question of lacking a home; it is deeply entwined with broader systemic issues such as social inequality, marginalisation, discrimination and economic hardship. CP frameworks, including the PIE approach, offer a valuable opportunity to address these challenges. Community psychologists can foster meaningful, systemic change by emphasising empowerment, social justice and participatory action. The examples of praxis given in this chapter illustrate the need to engage with individuals experiencing homelessness through collaboration, creativity and respect for the expertise that their lived experience brings. These projects not only provide psychological support but also challenge harmful narratives and offer a platform for those affected by homelessness to reclaim agency with opportunities to influence informal and formal social and health policies.

Governments pour billions into band-aid solutions – shelters, sweeps and surveillance – while failing to address structural roots like unaffordable housing, precarious labour and welfare erosion. CP demands we stop blaming individuals and start holding systems accountable, prioritising empowerment, participation and policy reform over punitive measures because homelessness is not a personal failure – it's a societal one. Homelessness is far from a UK-exclusive crisis; it is a problem across the globe. The praxis projects in this chapter illustrate community-driven, relationship-based interventions which are transferable beyond the UK. The Brighton media discourse project shows the power of narrative change, a strategy applicable across contexts where the media reinforces harmful stereotypes. The "Psychology on the Streets" project highlights the importance of embedding psychological outreach within existing community structures, an approach applicable in countries with high distrust of formal services. By integrating CP principles like empowerment, structural critique and participatory decision-making, other nations can adapt these approaches to fit local cultural, political and economic realities.

If we want to avoid the risk of further punishing, patronising and damaging people who find themselves without shelter, practitioners, policymakers and communities must embrace innovative and inclusive strategies. We must prioritise prevention, dismantle stigma, cut through disabling red tape and bureaucracy and ensure marginalised voices are at the centre of decision-making processes. In doing so, we can make significant strides towards eradicating homelessness and achieving a more just and equitable society for all.

Note

1 From a note written by someone who was homeless inviting him to collaborate on a psychology project in Leicester.

References

Anderson, I., Baptista, I., Wolf, J., Edgar, B., Sapounakis, A., & Schoibl, H. (2005). *The changing role of service provision: Services for homeless people and Inter-agency working*. European Observatory on Homelessness. https://www.feantsaresearch.org/download/2005_interagency_working1556858412630774889.pdf

Blackburn, P. (2019). All too exceptional. *The Doctor*, *10*, 6–11. https://issuu.com/thebma/docs/the_doctor___issue_10__june__2019/6

Blackstock, C. (2011). The emergency of the breath of life theory. *Journal of Social Work Values and Ethics*, *8*, 1. https://doi.org/10.55521/10-008-100

Bramley, G., & Fitzpatrick, S. (2015). *Hard edges: Mapping severe and multiple disadvantage (England)*. LankellyChase Foundation.

Brighton & Hove City Council. (2020). *Homelessness and rough sleeping strategy 2020–2025*. https://www.brighton-hove.gov.uk/housing/homelessness-and-rough-sleeping-strategy-2020-2025

Bronfenbrenner, U. (1979). *The ecology of human development: Experiments by nature and design*. Harvard University Press.

Calgary Homeless Foundation. (2018). *Annual Report 2017–2018*. https://www.calgaryhomeless.com/wp-content/uploads/2021/01/CHF-Annual-Report-2017.pdf

Crane, M., & Warnes, A. W. (2001). Primary health care services for single homeless people: Defects and opportunities. *Family Practice*, *18*(3), 272–276. https://doi.org/10.1093/fampra/18.3.272

Cullen, S., Byrne, S., & Hayes, P. (2007). *Good practice guide: Homelessness, Early intervention and prevention*. Shelter. https://assets.ctfassets.net/6sxvmndnpn0s/2yLo7OA3hr8guxOrYkD003/f03274618d6efde3b919e8fd070dbf9a/Homelessness_early_identification_prevention.pdf

Dahal, P., Joshi, S. K., & Swahnberg, K. (2022). Does forum theater help reduce gender inequalities and violence? Findings from Nepal. *Journal of Interpersonal Violence*, *37*(13–14), NP12086-NP12110. https://doi.org/10.1177/0886260521997457

Department for Communities and Local Government. (2012). *Making every contact count: A joint approach to preventing homelessness*. https://www.gov.uk/government/publications/making-every-contact-count-a-joint-approach-to-preventing-homelessness

De Oliveira, B. (2018). On the news today: Challenging homelessness through participatory action research. *Housing, Care and Support*, *21*(1), 13–25. https://doi.org/10.1108/HCS-01-2018-0002

De Oliveira, B. (2023). Participatory action research as a research approach: Advantages, limitations and criticisms. *Qualitative Research Journal*, *23*(3), 287–297. http://dx.doi.org/10.1108/QRJ-08-2022-0101

Department for Levelling Up, Housing and Communities (2025). *Rough sleeping snapshot in England: Autumn 2024*. https://www.gov.uk/government/statistics/rough-sleeping-snapshot-in-england-autumn-2023/rough-sleeping-snapshot-in-england-autumn-2023

Durcan, G., Zlotowitz, S., & Stubbs, J. (2017). *Meeting us where we're at*. Centre for Mental Health. https://www.centreformentalhealth.org.uk/publications/meeting-us-where-were/

Elliott, S. (2015). On 'defensive psychology': Should we push people who are homeless away or strive to see those who are 'invisibled'? *Clinical Psychology Forum*, *265*, 9–12. https://doi.org/10.53841/bpscpf.2015.1.265.9

Evans, S. D., Rosen, A., & Nelson, G. (2014). Community psychology and social justice. In C. V. Johnson, H. L. Friedman, J. Diaz, Z. Franco, & B. K. Nastasi (Eds.), *Praeger handbook of social justice and psychology: Fundamental issues and special populations; Well-being and professional issues; Youth and disciplines in psychology* (pp. 143–163) Praeger.

Freire, P. (1970). *Pedagogy of the oppressed*. Continuum.

Gerhardt, S. (2004). *Why love matters: How affection shapes a baby's brain*. Routledge.

Gesturing Towards Decolonial Futures. (n.d.). *Home*. https://decolonialfutures.net/

Haber, M. G., & Toro, P. A. (2004). Homelessness among families, children, and adolescents: An ecological–developmental perspective. *Clinical Child and Family Psychology Review*, *7*, 123–164. https://doi.org/10.1023/b:ccfp.0000045124.09503.f1

Hewitt, N. (Ed.). (2018). *The faculty for homeless and inclusion health service standards for commissioners and service providers.* Pathway. https://www.pathway.org.uk/resources/the-faculty-for-homeless-and-inclusion-health-service-standards-for-commissioners-and-service-providers/

Homeless Link. (2022). *Shaping the future together*. Homeless Link. https://homeless.org.uk/news/shaping-the-future-together-homeless-links-strategy-to-end-homelessness/

Hopper, K. (2013). Revisiting the unseen: Some unresolved issues in homeless advocacy and research. In A. J. Katz, A. Lurie, & C. Vidal (Eds.), *Critical social welfare issues* (pp. 31–52). Routledge.

Jackson, A., & Boal, A. (2005). *Games for actors and non-actors*. Routledge.

Jason, L. (2013). *Principles of social change*. Oxford University Press.

Johnson, R., & Haigh, R. (2010). Social psychiatry and social policy for the 21st century—New concepts for new needs: The "psychologically-informed environment". *Mental Health and Social Inclusion, 14*(4), 30–35.

Kagan, C., Burton, M., Duckett, P., Lawthom, R., & Siddiquee, A. (2011a). *Critical community psychology*. BPS Blackwell.

Kagan, C., Duggan, K., Richards, M., & Siddiquee, A. (2011b). Community psychology. In P. R. Martin, F. Cheung, M. C. Knowles, M. Kyrios, L. Littlefield, J. B. Overmier, & J. M. Prieto (Eds.), *IAAP handbook of applied psychology* (pp. 471–499). Wiley-Blackwell.

Kang, S. (2022). The cumulative relationship between housing instability and mental health: Findings from the panel study of income dynamics. *Journal of Social Distress and Homelessness, 31*(2), 191–203.

Keats, H., Maguire, N., Johnson, R., & Cockersell, P. (2012). *Psychologically informed services for homeless people: Good Practice Guide*. DCLG.

Kloos, B., Hill, J., Thomas, E., Wandersman, A., Elias, M. J., & Dalton, J. H. (2012). *Community psychology*. Cengage Learning.

Leicester City Council. (2023). *Leicester homelessness strategy 2023–2028.* https://www.leicester.gov.uk/your-council/policies-plans-and-strategies/housing-and-homelessness/leicester-homelessness-strategy-2023-2028/#Homelessness%20in%20Leicester on 23/03/25

Luchenski, S., Maguire, N., Aldridge, R. W., Hayward, A., Story, A., Perri, P; Withers, J., Clint, S., Fitzpatrick, S., & Hewett, N. (2018). What works in inclusion health: overview of effective interventions for marginalised and excluded populations. *Lancet, 391*(10117), 266–280.

Marmot, M., Allen, J., Goldblatt, P., Boyce, T., McNeish, D., Grady, M., & Geddes, I. (2010) *Fair society, healthy lives: The Marmot review*. Institute of Health Equity. https://www.instituteofhealthequity.org/resources-reports/fair-society-healthy-lives-the-marmot-review

Nelson, G. B., & Prilleltensky, I. (2005). *Community psychology: In pursuit of liberation and well-being*. Bloomsbury.

O'Reilly, M., Taylor, H., & Vostanis, P. (2009). "Nuts, schiz, psycho": An exploration of young homeless people's perceptions and dilemmas of defining mental health. *Social Science & Medicine, 68*(9), 1737–1744. http://dx.doi.org/10.1016/j.socscimed.2009.02.033

Orford, J. (2008). *Community psychology: Challenges, controversies and emerging consensus*. Wiley.

Owen, S., & Khalil, E. (2007). Addressing diversity in mental health care: A review of guidance documents. *International Journal of Nursing Studies, 44*(3), 467–478. https://doi.org/10.1016/j.ijnurstu.2006.08.024

Phelan, J., Link, B. G., Moore, R. E., & Stueve, A. (1997). The stigma of homelessness: The impact of the label" homeless" on attitudes toward poor persons. *Social Psychology Quarterly, 60*, 323–337. https://doi.org/10.2307/2787093

Prilleltensky, I., & Nelson, G. (2017). *Doing psychology critically: Making a difference in diverse settings*. Bloomsbury Publishing.

Reynolds, V. (n.d.). *Home.* https://vikkireynolds.ca/

Richardson, J. (2017). *The European end street homelessness campaign: Leicester city report.* De Montfort University. https://actionhomeless.org.uk/wp-content/uploads/2017/10/end-street-homelessness-in-leicester-report-nov-2017.pdf

Rutledge, K. (2011). Social networks: What Maslow misses. *Psychology Today*. https://www.psychologytoday.com/gb/blog/positively-media/201111/social-networks-what-maslow-misses-0

Sampson, E., Gridley, H., & Turner, C. (2013). Community psychologists advocating for action on poverty and social inclusion. *The Australian Community Psychologist*, *25*(1), 13–32. https://psychology.org.au/aps/media/acp/acp-25(1)-sampson-et-al.pdf

Sheppard, M. (2002). Mental Health and Social Justice: Gender, Race and Psychological consequences of unfairness. *British Journal of Social Work*, *32*(6), 779–797. http://dx.doi.org/10.1093/bjsw/32.6.779

Sheikh, S. & Teeman, D. (2018). *A rapid evidence assessment of what works in homelessness services*. Social Care Institute for Excellence. https://www.crisis.org.uk/media/238843/a_rapid_evidence_assessment_of_what_works_in_homelessness_services_2018.pdf

Spence, S. A. (2009). Roofless in a steel city: Learning from the homeless mentally ill. *Psychiatric Bulletin*, *33*(2), 64–69. https://doi.org/10.1192/pb.bp.107.018994

St. Mungo's. (2014). *Down and out? The final report of St Mungo's call 4 evidence*. St. Mungos.

Taylor, G. (2024). *Radical safeguarding toolkit – Homelessness*. National Children's Bureau. https://www.researchinpractice.org.uk/media/dhbntuyr/radical-safeguarding-toolkit-for-homelessness-pt_web.pdf

Toolis, E. E., & Hammack, P. L. (2015). "This is my community": Reproducing and resisting boundaries of exclusion in contested public spaces. *American Journal of Community Psychology*, *56*, 368–382. https://doi.org/10.1007/s10464-015-9756-5

Toro, P. A. (2007). Toward an international understanding of homelessness. *Journal of Social Issues*, *63*(3), 461–481. https://doi.org/10.1111/j.1540–4560.2007.00519.x

Townley, G., Brown, M., & Sylvestre, J. (2018). Community psychology and community mental health: A call for reengagement. *American Journal of Community Psychology*, *61*(1–2), 3–9. https://doi.org/10.1002/ajcp.12225

Viner, R. M., Ozer, E. M., Denny, S., Marmot, M., Resnick, M., Fatusi, A., & Currie, C. (2012). Adolescence and the social determinants of health. *Lancet*, *28*, 1641–1645. https://doi.org/10.1016/s0140-6736(12)60149-4

Watts, R. J., Williams, N. C., & Jagers, R. J. (2003). Sociopolitical development. *American Journal of Community Psychology*, *31*(1–2), 185–194. https://psycnet.apa.org/doi/10.1023/A:1023091024140

Wilkinson, R. & Pickett, K. (2010). *The spirit level: Why equality is better for everyone*. Penguin.

Wittington, D. (2007). *Beaten into violence: Anger, masculinities, alcohol, narcotics*. AuthorHouse.

Wrentschur, M. (2008). Forum theatre as a participatory tool for social research and development: A reflection on 'nobody is perfect'—A project with homeless people. In P. Cox, T. Geisen, & R. Green (Eds.), *Qualitative research and social change: European contexts* (pp. 94–111). Palgrave Macmillan.

Yanatma, S. (2024). As homelessness across the continent spikes, how do European countries compare? *Euronews*. https://www.euronews.com/my-europe/2024/07/15/homelessness-on-the-rise-in-uk-and-france-how-do-european-countries-compare

Zimmerman, M. A. (1995). Psychological empowerment: Issues and illustrations. *American Journal of Community Psychology*, *23*, 581–599. https://doi.org/10.1007/BF02506983

PART II

Transforming power

5 Participatory Action Research (PAR) as a tool for liberation in the Community Psychology from Quilombos in Brazil

James Ferreira Moura Junior, Ana Eugenio da Silva, Francisca Marleide Nascimento, João Luís Joventino do Nascimento, Mateus dos Santos Brito, Ana Leia Morais Cardoso, Claudia Andréa Mayorga Borges, Ana Luisa Teixeira de Menezes, Raquel Farias Diniz and Marina Passos Pereira Campos

Introduction

The enduring legacies of colonialism and systemic racism continue to shape the lives of quilombola communities in Brazil, underscoring the multifaceted social problems that form the core of this research. Quilombos, established as spaces of resistance against slavery and oppression, remain sites of struggle against contemporary structural inequities (Santos & Nyamien, 2022). Quilombos are Afro-Brazilian communities originally formed by people who escaped slavery and built autonomous settlements in resistance to the colonial regime. Historically, these communities were structured around principles of collective land use, mutual aid, cultural continuity and territorial self-governance. While the colonial state criminalised quilombos as insurgent and illegal, they endured through centuries as spaces of refuge, cultural preservation and political resistance. Today, quilombos are legally recognised in Brazil as traditional communities with distinct ethnic, cultural and territorial identities, protected under the Brazilian constitution. They continue to struggle for land rights, recognition and social justice, particularly in the face of racism, environmental destruction and extractive economic policies (Santos, 2019).

These challenges operate on multiple levels – individual, community and policy – highlighting the complex interplay of historical and modern dynamics perpetuating marginalisation. At the individual level, members of quilombola communities face pervasive psychological and social barriers rooted in systemic racism, economic precarity and cultural erasure (Santos & Nascimento, 2019). Experiences of exclusion often manifest as heightened vulnerability to mental health challenges, including depression and anxiety, exacerbated by limited access to culturally sensitive healthcare. The stigmatisation of traditional healing practices further alienates individuals from mental health services, diminishing their autonomy and wellbeing (Moura & Silva, 2024). On a community level, the quilombos face collective struggles tied to land insecurity, environmental degradation and socio-economic marginalisation (Silva & Moura, 2025). The encroachment of agribusiness, renewable energy projects and extractive industries

DOI: 10.4324/9781003480464-7

disrupts communal life, undermining traditional livelihoods like fishing and agriculture. These activities threaten the physical territories of quilombos and fracture their social and cultural cohesion, intensifying the challenges of collective resistance (Silva et al., 2025). At the policy level, systemic neglect and institutional racism perpetuate inequities. Quilombola communities often remain invisible in national and local policy frameworks, receiving inadequate protection under Brazil's land titling and environmental legislation (Santos, 2019). Policies addressing racial and ecological justice frequently fall short, either in enforcement or inclusivity, leaving quilombos vulnerable to exploitation and violence. Furthermore, recent political shifts toward austerity and deregulation exacerbate these vulnerabilities, weakening protections for marginalised groups and prioritising corporate interests over community wellbeing (Silva et al., 2025).

This chapter is co-authored by quilombola researchers and allied academics committed to decolonial praxis and community-based knowledge production. Several authors – Ana Eugênio, Marleide Nascimento, João do Cumbe, Mateus Brito and Ana Leia Morais – are quilombola researchers rooted in their territories, bringing ancestral knowledge and lived experience. Others are university-based scholars from diverse disciplines and institutions across Brazil. Our varied positionalities – as Black, quilombola, feminist, community-rooted and institutionally situated – shaped the research at every stage. Grounded in trust and co-responsibility, we worked collaboratively to challenge extractivist models of research and honour the epistemologies of quilombola resistance and re-existence.

Historical development of Community Psychology in Latin America

Community Psychology in Latin America has emerged as a response to systemic oppression and structural inequalities. It emphasises empowerment, liberation and transformation through collective action and dialogical practices. Influenced by the works of Ignacio Martín-Baró, Maritza Montero and Paulo Freire, the field integrates critical reflection and action to address historical injustices and promote social change (Freire, 1987; Martín-Baró, 1985; Montero, 2006). Latin American Community Psychology departs from traditional paradigms by centring marginalised voices and addressing the socio-historical contexts of oppression. Freire's concept of conscientisation underpins the critical awareness needed for transformative change, emphasising the interplay of reflection and action (Freire, 1987). Martín-Baró (1986) further stresses that liberation psychology seeks to dismantle the psychological and material conditions that sustain inequality. His work, alongside Freire, highlights the importance of empowering oppressed populations to reclaim their agency and challenge systemic injustices through collective praxis.

As articulated by Fals Borda, PAR builds on this foundation, rejecting extractive research practices and positioning communities as co-researchers (Fals Borda, 1999). PAR, championed by Orlando Fals Borda, aligns with these goals by fostering collaboration and co-creation of knowledge, making it a cornerstone methodology in the region. In Latin America, PAR has effectively addressed issues such as land rights, racial inequalities and health disparities. For instance, interventions in rural and with quilombola communities have employed PAR to empower local populations, advocate for their rights and foster sustainable social change. These efforts underscore the transformative potential of integrating PAR into Community Psychology frameworks (Góis, 2005).

The foundation of PAR lies in Paulo Freire's concept of conscientisation, a process through which individuals develop a critical awareness of their social realities. Freire (2001) argued that conscientisation enables communities to recognise the systemic roots of oppression, transitioning from a passive to an active role in shaping their futures. This approach is crucial in PAR as it transforms community members into active agents of change, creating a reciprocal dynamic where researchers and participants engage in mutual learning. Freire's emphasis on dialogical methods ensures that PAR is not just a tool for research but a transformative process aimed at collective social change. Incorporating Martín-Baró's liberation psychology into PAR deepens its potential for social transformation. Martín-Baró (1983, 1986) emphasised that research in marginalised contexts must address the structural determinants of inequality while fostering community agency. PAR operationalises this by integrating a praxis-oriented approach combining critical reflection and action.

PAR is a methodological approach involving communities in knowledge creation, ensuring that research serves their interests and leads to tangible social change. Rooted in empowerment, praxis and collaboration, PAR has become essential for addressing systemic oppression and fostering liberation. This section explores the defining characteristics of PAR, emphasising its application in community settings and its transformative potential. At the heart of PAR is the commitment to collective participation. Unlike traditional research paradigms, PAR prioritises the voices and experiences of community members as co-researchers. This horizontal approach creates a shared space for dialogue and decision-making, empowering participants to take ownership of the research process and its outcomes (Freire, 1987; Montero, 2006). In working with quilombola communities, for example, PAR has enabled individuals to identify and challenge the structural determinants of their marginalisation (Ximenes & Moura, 2015).

Community Psychology in practice: Participatory Action Research in quilombola territories

This section explores how community psychology takes shape PAR in quilombola communities in Brazil. In this field, PAR is not merely a methodological choice but a political and ethical commitment to co-producing knowledge and fostering social transformation alongside historically marginalised populations. Integrating PAR into Community Psychology exemplifies the field's commitment to social justice and transformative praxis. By centring marginalised communities and fostering collaborative knowledge production, PAR is a powerful tool for addressing the socio-political complexities of Latin America. Orlando Fals Borda's contribution to PAR aligns seamlessly with the values of Community Psychology. His methodology rejects the traditional hierarchies of academic research, instead fostering an egalitarian approach that centres on the knowledge and experiences of marginalised communities. This approach has been instrumental in addressing socio-political challenges, particularly in contexts where structural violence and historical marginalisation persist (Fals Borda, 1999; Montero, 2006).

PAR's collaborative nature extends beyond the immediate community, including partnerships with various stakeholders. Networking with local organisations, NGOs and government institutions can amplify the reach and effectiveness of PAR initiatives. For instance, interdisciplinary collaboration in Fortaleza, Brazil, demonstrated how PAR can align diverse resources to address complex issues such as poverty and violence (Góis, 2008; Moura et al., 2014). This networking approach ensures a holistic and sustainable impact. There is an emphasis on community ownership, ensuring that the community controls the research process and its outcomes. This shifts the power dynamics typically seen in conventional research, where knowledge is extracted and analysed externally. By fostering shared leadership, PAR empowers communities to make decisions that align with their cultural, social and economic needs. For example, in the networked interventions in Fortaleza, Brazil, women participants co-led projects that addressed their community's most pressing issues, from health disparities to structural violence (Moura et al., 2014).

PAR integrates vital elements that align with the principles of Community Psychology (Fals Borda, 1999):

1. **Dialogue and Reciprocity**: Informed by Freirean pedagogy, PAR emphasises mutual learning and co-creation of solutions, fostering deep connections between researchers and communities.
2. **Empowerment and Transformation**: By actively involving community members, PAR promotes a shift from passive subjects to empowered agents of change.
3. **Critical Praxis**: PAR's iterative cycle of reflection and action embodies the liberatory praxis central to both Freire's and Martín-Baró's frameworks, enabling communities to address their realities critically and collectively.

Cultivating critical consciousness is a central goal rooted in Freire's pedagogical framework. Critical consciousness enables individuals to perceive the underlying structures of power and oppression in their lives and to collaborate to transform these realities. Through dialogical processes, PAR facilitates the co-creation of knowledge, encouraging participants to question societal norms and challenge systemic inequalities. In quilombola communities, this approach has been instrumental in empowering residents to advocate for land rights and cultural preservation (Freire, 2001; Ximenes & Moura, 2015). By engaging participants in collective reflection and action, the methodology strengthens the social fabric of communities, promoting mutual support and collective agency. This is particularly evident in marginalised settings, where systemic oppression often fragments communities (Góis, 2008; Moura et al., 2014).

The effectiveness of PAR lies in its capacity to address intersectional issues affecting marginalised communities. It considers the interconnectedness of race, gender, class and other identity markers in shaping experiences of oppression. In quilombola communities, PAR has highlighted the unique struggles faced by Black women, addressing how systemic racism and patriarchy intersect to deepen inequality. By centring these lived experiences, PAR provides a pathway for more inclusive and equitable interventions (Montero, 2006; Moura et al., 2014). One of the defining characteristics of PAR is its focus on sustainability through local capacity building. By involving community members as co-researchers, PAR equips them with the skills and knowledge needed to address challenges independently in the future. This approach ensures that the outcomes of PAR are not only immediate but also enduring. In Fortaleza, the creation of interdisciplinary networks helped community members access resources and develop strategies for long-term resilience and self-determination (Moura et al., 2014; Ximenes & Moura, 2015). Montero (2006) and Góis (2005) note that researchers often encounter resistance from institutions and actors invested in maintaining the status quo. Additionally, in quilombola communities, historical disenfranchisement and land insecurity compound the difficulties of fostering sustainable change. However, as Freire (2001) suggested, the iterative nature of PAR – grounded in reflection and action – allows for continuous adaptation and resilience, enabling communities to overcome obstacles and drive long-term transformation.

A solid ethical commitment is foundational to the communities involved. Reflexivity ensures that researchers continuously evaluate their positionality and the power dynamics within the research process. This ethical stance is vital in maintaining trust and ensuring the research serves the community's best interests (Montero, 2006). In quilombola communities, reflexivity has been vital to adapting methodologies to their specific needs and realities, ensuring meaningful and equitable participation (Ximenes

& Moura, 2015). In practice, this reflexivity has involved a continuous process of listening to community voices, revising research questions based on local priorities and co-creating strategies that align with quilombola ways of knowing and organising. For example, in fieldwork conducted in the communities of Alto Alegre and Serra do Evaristo, local leaders requested that group discussions be held in formats that mirrored their traditional gatherings – roundtables under shade trees or in community centres – rather than conventional classroom or clinical spaces. Researchers responded by adjusting the timing, language and structure of data collection to align with the rhythms of community life, such as agricultural cycles and religious festivities. Reflexivity also meant acknowledging power asymmetries, such as those between university-based researchers and quilombola youth, and actively working to democratise the process by including young people as co-facilitators of workshops and co-authors of educational materials. This grounded, relational approach helped build trust and fostered a research environment that was not only participatory but transformative. Participatory Action Research embodies the principles of liberation, empowerment and collaboration. By actively involving communities as co-researchers, integrating cultural knowledge and addressing systemic inequalities, PAR serves as a powerful tool for social transformation.

Community Psychology is pivotal in advancing social justice by engaging in actions that prioritise empowerment, collective agency and dismantling systemic oppression. In contexts like those of quilombola communities in Brazil, the community psychologist often operates as a facilitator, mediator and advocate, employing a praxis that combines critical reflection with transformative action. Their work extends across multiple disciplines and settings, reflecting the diverse contexts in which social inequalities are experienced. CPs engage in a wide range of actions designed to empower marginalised populations. They facilitate community-building processes, create spaces for participatory decision-making and support grassroots movements advocating for systemic change. PAR's strength is its ability to foster a sense of shared purpose and collective agency. The project envisions social justice as the reclamation of agency and cultural identity by quilombola communities, resisting systemic oppression through collective action and knowledge co-creation. This perspective embraces diverse visions of justice, such as land sovereignty, equitable access to culturally relevant healthcare and recognising traditional practices as legitimate forms of knowledge. Wellbeing is imagined not merely as the absence of distress but as the flourishing of communal bonds, cultural resilience and self-determination. For quilombola communities, this includes mental health practices rooted in collective rituals, spiritual traditions and environmental harmony – visions that challenge hegemonic definitions of wellbeing and assert the need for frameworks that integrate cultural and historical contexts.

Praxis case study: Building Participatory Action Research with quilombola communities in Brazil

The application of Community Psychology in quilombola territories offers a vital framework for understanding and transforming the psychosocial realities of Black rural communities in Brazil. Grounded in values of social justice, collective wellbeing and critical reflexivity, Community Psychology provides tools not only to analyse the effects of structural racism and historical exclusion but also to co-develop practices of resistance, resilience and healing. In the quilombola communities of Ceará, this approach has proven essential for building research processes rooted in trust, accountability, and reciprocity. Rather than viewing communities as passive recipients of aid or of data, the Community Psychology lens affirms them as active producers of knowledge and agents of social change.

This case study focuses on a PAR process developed in partnership with quilombola communities in the Baixo Jaguaribe and Maciço de Baturité regions, State of Ceará. The work emerged from longstanding relationships with local leaders, youth and elders and from a collective desire to address intergenerational trauma, environmental injustice and violations of the right to health and land. The research was intentionally designed to be dialogical, incorporating culturally grounded methods such as storytelling, community mapping and roundtable discussions. By centring lived experience and epistemologies rooted in quilombola memory and spirituality, this PAR initiative reflects the core tenets of Community Psychology: promoting liberation, fostering collective agency and dismantling oppressive systems from the ground up.

Quilombos are emblematic Afro-Brazilian communities that emerged as spaces of resistance against the systemic violence of slavery and colonisation. More than just territorial entities, quilombos embody collective resilience, cultural preservation and sustainable relationships with the environment (Santos, 2019). They continue to represent resistance today, though systemic challenges such as territorial insecurity, socio-environmental conflicts and structural racism persist (Santos & Nyamien, 2022). Central to quilombola identity is their connection to the land. Land is not merely a resource but a cultural and spiritual anchor. However, many communities lack formal land recognition, exposing them to ecological degradation and systemic exclusion (Santos, 2023). Addressing these challenges requires methodologies like PAR that prioritise community voices, integrate traditional knowledge and advocate for structural change.

Quilombos represent alternative models of social organisation based on biointeraction and self-sustainability (Santos, 2023). He emphasises that quilombos offer a worldview that opposes the prevailing capitalist and ecocidal model. The term ecocidal refers to practices and policies that lead to large-scale environmental destruction, often with irreversible impacts on forests, rivers and traditional ways of life (Santos, 2023). In contrast, quilombos offer a vision of society grounded in biointeraction – a relational ethic of living well with the land, the community, and the spiritual world. From this perspective, to be a quilombola is to adopt a way of life that values the interdependence between people and nature, as opposed to individualism and unbridled exploitation. Biointeraction is a harmonious and organic way of relating between humans and nature, through which knowledge, meanings and ways of life are constructed (Santos, 2023). Santos (2019) points out that one of the people's strategies against colonisers has been to weaken colonial words. He emphasises that a war of denominations is taking place, and in this war, the Quilombola people are using defence art and naming words with new meanings. Thus, Quilombola Participatory Research is based on orality, a compelling ancestral technology for the Quilombola people. It is an ancestral technology for preserving history, transmitting cultural values and sustaining resistance. This form of knowledge-making draws its strength from generations of elders, griots, midwives and community leaders who have kept alive the experiences and teachings that formal archives have erased or silenced. To name orality as an ancestral technology is to recognise its political and epistemological weight. It challenges dominant Western models of knowledge that prioritise written documentation and institutional validation (Santos, 2023). Instead, it affirms that legitimate, complex and actionable knowledge can be spoken, sung, danced or lived in ritual. In practice, this meant that the research process was guided by community narratives – oral testimonies that emerged in rodas de conversa (dialogue circles), on church steps, or under cashew trees – spaces where knowledge flows relationally and collectively. By rooting PAR in these traditions, the research not only honoured the epistemologies of quilombola communities but actively subverted the colonial hierarchies that continue to devalue non-written forms of knowing.

According to Jesús and Marques (2017), "Memory/orality and History/scholarly knowledge can be intertwined and mobilised to guide the projects for a society that the quilombolas want to defend, improve or build" (p. 268). It is from this sharing of research that the intention is for non-quilombola subjects to listen to, read and share the production that the quilombolas emphasise so that the words echo with the desire for them to germinate into articles, booklets and public policies in order to guarantee quilombola living.

The trajectory of PAR with quilombola communities in Brazil reflects a deepening engagement with their articulated needs, culminating in a series of interconnected research projects. Each initiative responded to specific demands while building on insights and relationships developed in earlier work. The first research with people from the remaining quilombos was qualitative and conducted in 2021 as part of a broader investigation into the relationships between structural violence and human rights among university students in Brazil. The study adopted a decolonial and intersectional lens and was carried out at the University for the International Integration of Afro-Brazilian Lusophony (UNILAB) in Redenção, Ceará. It involved focus groups with students from multiple social markers, including Black, Indigenous, African and quilombola backgrounds – disaggregated by gender to deepen the analysis of intersectional experiences. The quilombola participants in particular voiced the need for the sessions to occur in roundtable formats and within their communities, suggesting that the research process itself be an intervention. These dialogues explored conceptions of violence, human rights and reparation, surfacing how colonial legacies continue to inform the everyday experiences of racism, exclusion and marginalisation. Methodologically grounded in thematic narrative analysis (Riessman, 2008) and critical bifocality (Weis & Fine, 2012), the research revealed how macro-structures of oppression intersect with the subjective experiences of historically silenced populations. It laid the foundation for a participatory research agenda that not only documents injustice but also co-creates strategies for reparation rooted in quilombola memory, resistance and ancestral knowledge. It took a critical approach, but in this research, the quilombola leaders were only asked if they would like to take part in an investigation into human rights violations and structural violence. Black people, Indigenous people, people living in poverty and quilombolas were invited to take part. However, in the focus group with quilombolas, there was a call from the quilombola participants to hold that focus group in a round table format in the quilombola communities of the state of Ceara, in the north-east of Brazil and also to carry out an intervention.

Collaborations with quilombola students revealed how systemic racism pervades academic spaces, creating additional barriers to inclusion. Co-researchers emphasised the role of their communities in shaping resistance and perseverance, advocating for institutional reforms that celebrate their cultural heritage while dismantling racist practices. This project bridged academic and community spaces, ensuring the voices of quilombola students reached decision-makers. During the same period and in the action research format, a study was carried out jointly with quilombola leaders focusing on evaluating mental health services in quilombola territories. In this research, the quilombolas were also researchers who carried out the research and led the research methods. Using a mixed-method approach that combined surveys, focus groups and PhotoVoice, the project highlighted the critical role of traditional healing practices. The PhotoVoice is a participatory visual method that enables participants to capture aspects of their lived experience through photography. These images then served as prompts for collective reflection and critical discussion during the group sessions, encouraging a deeper analysis of social realities and empowering participants to express themselves beyond verbal narratives (Wang & Burris, 1997). Participants shared how practices like herbal medicine, collective rituals and storytelling acted as buffers against the psychological distress caused by structural violence and territorial conflicts. It was conducted between 2022 and 2023 as part of a broader project on mental health vulnerabilities and protective factors in traditional communities in Ceará, supported by the PPSUS programme. The study engaged with quilombola communities such as Nazaré, Córrego dos Iús, Cumbe, Capuãn, Ubaranas, Alto Alegre and Serra do Evaristo (Figure 5.1).

Fieldwork involved multiple visits, where researchers facilitated focus groups, conducted semi-structured interviews, and organised participatory workshops in collaboration with local leaders. These encounters took place in the territories themselves, privileging oral narratives and collective reflection in familiar communal spaces. Conversations addressed issues like access to mental health care, experiences of racism, environmental degradation and traditional healing practices. The research was also marked by the active participation of quilombola co-researchers, who helped shape the questions and methods. This co-construction of knowledge laid the groundwork for a more expansive participatory action research agenda that continues to evolve in partnership with the communities. The findings emphasised the value of integrating traditional knowledge into mental health interventions. It identified cultural and social assets, such as collective farming, oral traditions and spiritual practices, as critical to fostering resilience. This project demonstrated how protective factors rooted in quilombola traditions could be leveraged to inform public health policies tailored to their unique contexts.

The research activities carried out in the territory always began with a song that brought back memories of the resistance of the quilombos. The action became a daily practice in the research process. The researchers carried out a community clinic process in which they created spaces for listening and empowerment for people in Quilombo who were suffering. The quilombo researchers discussed the need for these community clinic spaces for people from the quilombos in dialogue with the leaders. Although health and mental health services are public and free in Brazil, it is difficult for people in the territory to access them because of the high demand. Therefore, creating these reception spaces in the

Figure 5.1 Conversation circle in 2022 in Quilombo de Capuãn, Ceará, Brazil.

Source: Author's collection

quilombos works as a counter-colonial strategy to strengthen and resist structural racism, colonial genocide and the erasure of the quilombos' history of struggle in Brazilian society.

In these welcoming spaces, the Cumbe quilombo, located on the east coast of the state of Ceará, brought up specific stories of suffering caused by the implementation of renewable energies, such as wind farms, which have had a central negative effect on the community dynamics. In addition, the Cumbe quilombo has suffered environmental damage due to shrimp farming in its mangrove territory and the heavy exploitation of real estate. These socio-environmental conflicts have caused a series of fights in the territory and impoverishment of the community due to the negative impacts on the quilombo's fishing and agriculture. The quilombola researchers then proposed carrying out a new national research project in partnership with the National Coordination of Quilombola Articulation (CONAQ) and funded by the Ministry of Health and CNPQ under the Transdisciplinary Studies in Collective Health programme to investigate the mental health of quilombola peoples nationwide in situations of socio-environmental conflict. The research carried out with quilombola communities in Ceará was the basis that led us to expand it into a new national study called Socioenvironmental Conflicts and Quilombos (COSQUI). The study seeks to analyse the impacts of climate change and socio-environmental conflicts on suicide, violence and the mental health of quilombola communities (Figure 5.2).

This research adopts a gendered and life-cycle perspective, focusing on how systemic inequities exacerbate vulnerabilities across different stages of life. Quilombola women and youth have emerged as central figures in this work, advocating for mental health promotion strategies rooted in their ancestral knowledge and practices. The project underscores the importance of holistically addressing systemic inequities to improve mental health outcomes. The projects collectively highlight how structural violence – manifested through land disputes, socio-economic inequalities and systemic racism – affects quilombola communities. However, they also underscore the resilience of these communities, rooted in their cultural practices, communal living and intergenerational knowledge (Santos, 2019). These findings have informed advocacy efforts for policy changes that address the unique needs of quilombos. In this way, we obtained funding to valorise the work of quilombola researchers and expand it in confluence

Figure 5.2 Conversation circle in 2024 in Quilombo do Cumbe, Ceará, Brazil.
Source: Author's collection

with other Brazilian quilombos. We will maintain the community clinic strategies and expand the community training process for future quilombola researchers in different Brazilian territories.

Likewise, throughout this process of building participatory action research with quilombola communities, there is constant attention to strengthening the political struggle. We are not just doing research. We are acting in the political struggle to guarantee land rights, health, education, food sovereignty and culture. Research practices feed the political struggle, and the political struggle for quilombola rights feeds the research. There is no division between activism and research because there are no dichotomies or separations in doing PAR with quilombos. The countercoloniality you articulate challenges the foundations of coloniality that structure our lives and institutions. It demands a critique of hegemonic forms of power and knowledge and the construction of alternatives rooted in ancestral and community knowledge. This perspective guides our commitment to research that not only denounces oppression but also creates possibilities for collective resistance. Working in dialogue with quilombola peoples has taught us that counter-colonial knowledge is not an exercise in abstraction but a living practice, situated and deeply rooted in relationships with the land, with the collective and with ancestry.

The epistemologies of the South intertwine with care practices, promoting what is known as confluent knowledge: a space where academic knowledge meets lived knowledge, where science listens and is transformed through dialogue with communities. Countercoloniality here is not just a critique of the system but a practice of transformation that involves coalitions between different agents: academics, communities and social movements. This spirit of confluence inspires us to create spaces where multiple worlds can meet and collaborate in doing PAR with quilombos in Brazil. Across these projects, collaborative networks have been vital. Partnerships with universities, local NGOs and health professionals have facilitated interdisciplinary approaches to complex socio-political challenges. By integrating cultural, academic and policy-oriented perspectives, these networks have strengthened the sustainability of research outcomes while fostering community empowerment. The cumulative experience of conducting PAR with quilombola communities demonstrates the transformative potential of this methodology. Each project has contributed to a deeper understanding of structural violence, cultural resilience and mental health in quilombos by centring community voices. These initiatives highlight the importance of sustained collaboration between researchers and quilombola leaders in building equitable and culturally sensitive strategies for social change.

Each research project has prioritised the active participation of quilombola communities, ensuring their perspectives guide the research process. For example, in the 2022–23 project, focus groups revealed the role of territorial conflicts in exacerbating mental health disparities. Quilombola leaders emphasised the need for culturally sensitive mental health services that integrate traditional practices, such as herbal medicine and spiritual rituals (Santos & Nyamien, 2022). Quilombola women have been central to the research process, serving as cultural custodians and community leaders. Their participation has illuminated the intersectional challenges they face, such as gender-based violence and limited access to health care. Their leadership in advocating for land rights and mental health services underscores their critical role in sustaining community resilience (Santos, 2023).

While each research project faced challenges, including resource constraints and bureaucratic hurdles, the commitment to PAR methodologies facilitated meaningful engagement. The emphasis on dialogue, co-creation and cultural sensitivity ensured that the research addressed immediate issues and contributed to long-term empowerment and policy advocacy (Freire, 1987).

In order to strengthen the ongoing struggle of quilombola communities for land rights, cultural recognition and the dismantling of structural racism, Quilombola Participatory Research must be developed by quilombola communities in coalitions with other peoples and social groups. Santos (2023) discusses the importance of alliances between quilombolas and other peoples as a fundamental strategy for counter-colonisation. He emphasises that resistance to colonising processes cannot be done in isolation. Unity between different communities, including indigenous peoples and other traditional communities, is vital to confront the threats posed by contemporary colonising and capitalist forces. During enslavement, many Africans formed communities in partnership with indigenous peoples and poor Whites. These communities, called counter-colonisers by Mestre Quilombola Nego Bispo Santos (2023), shared the land and its resources sustainably and communally. The formation of quilombos like Palmares is a clear example of how these alliances worked in the past and continue serving as a collective resistance model. According to Costa (1995), the complexity of the alliances formed between quilombolas and other subaltern groups during the Brazilian colonial and imperial periods is emphasised. The author highlights that these alliances were crucial to the collective resistance and survival of the quilombos. Despite cultural and linguistic differences, these groups shared a joint position of subjugation under colonial rule. This condition created a basis for solidarity and the formation of alliances. The Palmares quilombo was not only made up of Africans but also of indigenous people and other marginalised people, such as deserted soldiers and fugitives from justice.

Developing PAR with quilombola communities is based on strengthening organic knowledge. According to Mestre Quilombola Nego Bispo Santos (2019), organic knowledge has been invisibilised by scientific rationality. Non-White people have been recognised as savages (Fanon, 2008), as have quilombola peoples since colonial times. Organic knowledge seeks to break with the dichotomies established by colonising hegemonic knowledge, bringing together what should never have been separated: the individual and the social, theory and practice and grounding them. Participatory Action Research with quilombola communities involves the participation of all the people based on themes that are deeply linked to the territories. Thus, there must be a combination of action and research to tackle and solve concrete problems while generating knowledge that is also organically linked to the territory. The research seeks to break away from the production of epistemic knowledge. This chronology of research with quilombola communities illustrates the transformative potential of PAR. By centring quilombola voices and addressing systemic injustices, these projects have contributed to academic knowledge and community empowerment. The ongoing collaboration between researchers and quilombola leaders remains vital to advancing social justice and fostering resilience in these historically marginalised communities.

Action for learning: Cultivating collective knowledge through participatory workshops

A key aspect of participatory action for learning is fostering spaces where dialogue, reflection and collective action can occur. The following section outlines a structured Participatory Workshop on Community-Centred Solutions, designed to be interactive, reflective and transformative. It is adaptable for a range of audiences – students, community members, educators, activists or policymakers – and is rooted in community psychology principles of empowerment, collective agency and co-production of knowledge.

Workshop title: "Reimagining Community Solutions: A Participatory Approach"

Objective: To engage participants in critically examining systemic inequalities and collaboratively developing community-centred solutions that prioritise equity, cultural resilience and sustainable change.

Ideal number of participants: 12 to 25 people (small enough for meaningful dialogue, large enough for diverse perspectives).

Duration: 2–3 hours, depending on the depth of discussion and the number of participants.

Materials needed: Flip chart or large paper sheets; sticky notes (multiple colours); markers or pens; projector or screen (optional for presenting guiding questions or visual stimuli); open space with movable seating (to encourage flexibility in groupings).

Pre-workshop preparation (for facilitators): Reflect on the context and objectives of the group:

- Is the focus mental health, education, environmental justice or another issue?
- Prepare a brief opening presentation with 3–5 guiding questions and key definitions (e.g., structural inequality, resilience, community-based solutions).
- Print out case studies or quotes from community members, if available, to anchor the discussion in lived experience.
- Be familiar with dialogical facilitation methods and principles of PAR.

Workshop structure and steps:

1. Welcome and framing (15–20 minutes)
   - Begin with a land acknowledgement or moment of reflection.
   - Explain the workshop goals and the participatory approach.
   - Present 2–3 key concepts (e.g., systemic inequality, community resilience).
   - Invite participants to share their name and one word they associate with "community."
2. Visual mapping of challenges (30 minutes)
   - On a wall or flipchart, create a large visual map titled: "What are the systemic challenges our communities face?"
   - Ask participants to write challenges they observe or experience on sticky notes (one per note) and place them on the map.
   - Group the notes thematically and facilitate a brief collective reflection on patterns observed.
3. Small group breakouts: Root cause analysis (30 minutes)
   - Divide participants into 3–5 groups.
   - Each group chooses one challenge from the map and explores:
   - What are the root causes of this issue?
   - Who is most affected?
   - What community knowledge or practice already addresses this?
   - Groups document their discussion on large sheets.
4. Co-creation of solutions (40 minutes)
   - Using the previous analysis, each group develops one concrete, community-centred proposal for action.
   - Encourage them to reflect on feasibility, cultural relevance and who must be involved.
   - Each group presents its proposal in a short 3-minute pitch.

5. Collective reflection and next steps (20–30 minutes)
   - Reassemble and reflect:
   - What did we learn from each other?
   - What surprised us?
   - How can these ideas be mobilised in real settings?
   - Optionally, close with a round of commitments or a symbolic gesture (e.g., each person writes one thing they will carry forward on a note and posts it on a "Tree of Action").

Post-workshop: Facilitators can compile key takeaways and share a collective summary or community letter. If appropriate, invite participants to form a working group to continue developing one of the proposals.

Conclusion

PAR with quilombola communities in Brazil exemplifies the transformative potential of Community Psychology to address systemic inequities through culturally rooted and participatory methodologies. By centring quilombola voices and traditions, this approach highlights the power of collective agency and resilience in challenging structural violence and socio-environmental conflicts. PAR bridges the gap between academic knowledge and lived experience, fostering a reciprocal learning process that promotes justice, wellbeing and empowerment. The projects described in this chapter demonstrate the importance of co-creating solutions grounded in the historical and cultural contexts of the communities involved. From addressing mental health disparities to advocating for land rights, PAR has facilitated sustainable, community-driven change. These initiatives also underscore the necessity of interdisciplinary collaboration and the integration of ancestral knowledge systems to counter-colonial frameworks that perpetuate marginalisation. As we move forward, the lessons from this work call for a continued commitment to equity and collective action. Community psychologists, policymakers and activists must embrace PAR to understand and transform the realities of oppressed communities. By doing so, they can contribute to a more just and inclusive society that values its most marginalised members' knowledge, agency and resilience. The ongoing struggle for quilombola rights reminds us that research is not merely an academic exercise but a vital component of broader social and environmental justice movements.

References

Costa, F. C. (1995). Quilombolas e Revoltas Escravas no Brasil. *Revista USP*, *28*, 14–39. https://doi.org/10.11606/issn.2316–9036.v0i28p14-39

Fals Borda, O. (1999). *People's participation in social change.* Tercer Mundo Editores.

Fanon, F. (2008). *Black skin, white masks* (R. Philcox, Trans.). Grove Press. (Original work published 1952).

Freire, P. (1987). *Pedagogia do oprimido.* Paz e Terra.

Freire, P. (2001). *Educação como prática da liberdade.* Paz e Terra.

Góis, C. W. L. (2005). *Psicologia Comunitária: atividade e consciência.* Publicações Instituto Paulo Freire de Estudos Psicossociais.

Góis, C. W. L. (2008). *Saúde Comunitária Pensar e Fazer*. HUCITEC.

Jesús, E. M., & Marques, F. S. (2017). Memory/orality and history/scholarly knowledge. *Revista Estudos Interdisciplinares em Ciências Humanas*, *11*(2), 255–270.

Martín-Baró, I. (1983). *Acción e ideologia: Psicología Social desde Centro America*. UCA Editores.

Martín-Baró, I. (1985). El papel del psicólogo. *Boletín de Psicología UCA*, *3*(17), 99–112.

Martín-Baró, I. (1986). *Psicología de la Liberación*. Trotta.

Montero, M. (2006). *Teoría y práctica de la psicología comunitaria*. Paidós.

Moura Jr., J. F.,Rebouças Júnior, F. G., Alencar, A. B., Porto, A. K. S. M. O., Pinho, A. M. M., Ximenes, M. V., & Gadelha, A. K. S. (2014). Intervención comunitaria con mujeres a partir de la actuación en red en Psicología Comunitaria: Una experiencia en una comunidad en Brasil. *Psicoperspectivas*, *13*(2), 133–143. https://dx.doi.org/10.5027/psicoperspectivas-Vol13-Issue2-fulltext-419

Moura, J. F., & da Silva, A. C. (2024). Tecendo redes participativas a partir de uma pesquisa-ação com povos indígenas e quilombolas no Ceará: Relato de experiência do processo de investigação social. *Revista Inter-Legere*, *7*(39). https://doi.org/10.21680/1982–1662.2024v7n39ID33168

Riessman, C. K. (2008). *Narrative methods for the human sciences*. Sage.

Santos, A. B. (2019). *Colonização, quilombos: Modos e significações*. INCTI – UnB.

Santos, A. B. (2023). *A terra dá, a terra quer*. Ubu Editora.

Santos, A. N. S., & Nascimento, E. R. (2019). Proposições de cuidado cultural à enfermagem frente a aspectos da saúde reprodutiva de mulheres quilombolas. *Revista Baiana de Enfermagem*, *33*, 1–15. http://dx.doi.org/10.18471/rbe.v33.33375

Santos, H. A. L. dos, & Nyamien, F. R. da G. (2022). A relação humano-natureza na comunidade quilombola Manoel Ciriaco dos Santos: Racismo ambiental e possibilidades de resistência. *Revista da Associação Brasileira de Pesquisadores/as Negros/as (ABPN)*, *14*(Especial), 52–72.

Silva, E. C., Guerrero-Moreno, M. A., Oliveira, F. A., Dias-Silva, K., Juen, L., Moura Junior, J. F., De Carvalho, F. G., & Oliveira-Junior, J. M. B. (2025). Socio-environmental conflicts and traditional communities in protected areas: A scientometric analysis. *Journal for Nature Conservation*, *86*, 126936. https://doi.org/10.1016/j.jnc.2025.126936

Wang, C., & Burris, M. A. (1997). Photovoice: Concept, methodology, and use for participatory needs assessment. *Health Education & Behavior*, *24*(3), 369–387. https://doi.org/10.1177/109019819702400309

Weis, L., & Fine, M. (2012). Critical bifocality and circuits of privilege: Expanding critical ethnographic theory and design. *Harvard Educational Review*, *82*(2), 173–201. https://doi.org/10.17763/haer.82.2.v1jx34n441532242

Ximenes, V. M., & Moura Jr., J. F. (2015). Relações da Psicologia Comunitária com a Libertação a partir da dialética dominação-opressão. *Teoría y Crítica de la Psicología*, *6*, 140–161.

6 Claiming our voices, choices and rights

Challenging political peripherality through Community Psychology

Suzanne Wilson, Katherine Jewell, Lynsey Crosthwaite and Davinia Jackson

Introduction

> *Whether you believe the issues lie with posh politicians who've never tasted desperation, ruthless exploitation by corporate elites or misguided, thin-skinned idealists, too short in the tooth to understand the real world, there is arguably one unifying theme which connects many of Britain's current difficulties – proximity... Proximity is how close we are to the action and how that affects the ways in which we assess, relate and respond to it... Britain is riddled with problems of proximity across key institutions and at every level of governance.*
>
> (Darren McGarvey, 2022, *The Social Distance Between Us*, pp. 5–6)

Low-income, coastal communities without developed tourist economies have recently been identified as a significant area for research within the health and social sciences (Whitty, 2021). These communities are subject to social exclusion on multiple levels (Levitas et al., 2007), including political exclusion and alienation. This chapter is authored by a group of individuals who position themselves as a coalition of passionate citizens and community activists, living and working along the north-west coast of England. We have all worked with both the public and third sectors and are always seeking to challenge injustice and fight for social inclusion in all that we do. The motivations behind this chapter are to help people understand why communities often feel left out of "the action" and inspire them to work with communities to become politically energised and engaged.

In the coming pages, we demonstrate how communities feel politically peripheral and how this feeling of distance impacts on cohesion and engagement with civic institutions. When we discuss political peripherality, we refer to the perception of physical and symbolic distance from local and national political institutions, leading to disengagement and discontent with both politics and broader civil society. We explore how participatory research methods (Ledwith, 1997) and co-production (Durose & Richardson, 2015) can enhance social, cultural and political connectedness in coastal communities, promoting cohesion and challenging white-working-class narratives around disengagement and the "othering" of socially excluded groups. This chapter is about working with communities to create the conditions for them to claim their voices, choices and rights.

DOI: 10.4324/9781003480464-8

Based at the University of Lancashire's campus in West Cumbria, we draw on ten years of participatory action research (PAR) within communities along the West Cumbrian Coastline, all of which sought to understand and foster social inclusion. Boxes 6.1 and 6.2 summarise two significant projects. We also present two praxis case studies to demonstrate how relational practice can encourage proximity rather than distance in areas experiencing both physical and symbolic peripherality.

Box 6.1 Connected Communities (2017–22)

Figure 6.1 Connected Communities. A chaperone supporting a young researcher to conduct a doorstep survey in a local housing estate.

Source: Photograph by the author.

"Connected Communities Cumbria" trained 120 children and young people mainly aged between nine and seventeen years old as community researchers. They conducted 646 doorstep interviews with residents from the four low-income coastal communities in which they lived. The research used a survey tool developed by the University of Lancashire to understand residents' social networks, resources, health and wellbeing and perceptions of the local community (Parsfield et al., 2015). The young researchers shared their results at public events and collaborated with community stakeholders to co-create interventions to meet the community's needs as identified by the research. The research findings shaped a co-produced "Children's Charter" adopted by Copeland Borough Council and informed the creation of three new organisations, collectively raising over £10,000 for community projects. Moreover, opportunities for children and young people to build relationships with the local authorities and other significant stakeholders such as the police promoted social inclusion, citizenship and a sense of belonging.

A key finding of the research was that only nine out of 646 residents interviewed reported they would approach the Council or a Councillor if they wanted to make a positive change in their community, which inspired the design for "Community Power," the next project which will be discussed.

Box 6.2 Community Power (2021–26)

Figure 6.2 Nine participants conducting a roundtable discussion. Community Power event.

Source: Photograph by the author.

"Community Power" was designed as relationally-based community-level PAR, aiming to foster collaboration between the local Council and communities across the policy development cycle. Working closely with 40 residents in four low-income coastal communities, workshops explored enablers and barriers to civic and democratic participation. Particular attention was given to perceived and aspirational relationships between stakeholders before facilitating co-creative forums. These forums provided new opportunities to collaborate in co-creating innovative approaches to promote engagement in the local democratic system.

The research revealed unquestioning narratives concerning local government held within the communities, these being:

1. *A lack of trust in local government to act for the benefit of the community.*
2. *A belief that council decisions are predetermined.*
3. *A feeling that policy actors assume superiority over the community.*
4. *A consensus that "local government does not care about us."*

The local Councl responded to these findings by forming an independent group of community network organisations to review and make recommendations on new policies and engagement materials they produced.

Imagined Communities, Intersectionality and Place-Based Identity

Coastal areas in the UK are more likely to have higher levels of deprivation than non-coastal towns, attributed to factors such as slower economic growth and declining industries (Telford, 2021; Telford & Lloyd, 2020). This is the case with the low-income coastal communities in post-industrial, ex-mining towns included in our research, all located directly on the Cumbrian coastline (Figure 6.3), which display characteristics similar to those known as "left-behind" communities or those that "suffer from significant levels of economic and social deprivation based on existing accepted definitions" (Local Trust, 2019, p. 11). The communities face significant social exclusion in terms of educational outcomes (Ovenden-Hope & Passy, 2019; Richards, 2022), employment and development opportunities for young people (Wenham, 2020) and political disillusionment (Rodríguez-Pose et al., 2023).

Figure 6.3 Study Locations. Research sites at Maryport, Workington, Whitehaven, and Millom.
Source: Google Maps, n.d.

As well as being geographically defined, we regard these coastal communities as imagined communities (Anderson, 1983), in which collective identities are constructed through shared histories, cultural narratives, and common experiences of place. The industrial heritage of mining and manufacturing, experiences of economic decline, and perceptions of neglect by political and economic institutions contribute to powerful local narratives that continue to shape collective understandings of belonging. In this sense, the communities are not simply locations on a map but social and cultural formations through which residents make sense of their circumstances and identities. Anderson's concept is particularly useful for understanding how agency, structure, conflict, and cooperation operate within communities that frequently perceive themselves as overlooked by mainstream institutions and national policy agendas.

However, collective identities are never uniform. Despite shared experiences of place and history, residents occupy different social positions and experience belonging, exclusion, and disadvantage in diverse ways. This is particularly important in white working-class coastal communities, where experiences of deprivation are often discussed as though they are homogeneous. In reality, factors such as age, gender, disability, educational background, family circumstances, and employment status shape how individuals experience both community life and socioeconomic disadvantage. Understanding these differences requires attention not only to the collective identity of the community but also to the multiple and intersecting inequalities that influence individual lives.

To explore these dynamics, we draw on intersectionality. Originally developed by Black feminist scholars and activists to explain the multiple and intersecting forms of oppression experienced by Black women (Crenshaw, 1989), intersectionality has increasingly been applied to understand how different social identities and inequalities interact across a variety of contexts (e.g., France & Roberts, 2017). While attention to race and racialisation remains fundamental to the framework, scholars have argued that intersectionality can also illuminate the experiences of other marginalised groups, including white working-class communities (Taylor Hill, 2024). Within the context of Cumbrian coastal communities, intersectionality provides a useful lens for examining how different aspects of identity interact to shape experiences of inclusion, exclusion, aspiration, opportunity, and belonging.

At the same time, the application of intersectionality to white working-class communities requires careful consideration. Developed within the specific historical and political context of the United States, the framework emerged to explain how race and gender intersect to produce particular forms of oppression (Crenshaw, 1989). Its application to class-based disadvantage in contemporary Britain is therefore not straightforward. One challenge concerns the relationship between privilege and disadvantage. Residents of white working-class coastal communities may experience racial privilege relative to ethnic minority populations while simultaneously facing severe economic marginalisation, restricted opportunities, and diminished social mobility. Although intersectionality acknowledges the coexistence of privilege and disadvantage, it offers limited guidance regarding how these different dimensions should be weighed against one another. Questions therefore arise about the extent to which racial privilege can be meaningfully understood in communities where employment opportunities have contracted, public services have been reduced, and pathways for socioeconomic advancement have become increasingly limited.

A related concern is that some applications of intersectionality focus primarily on groups experiencing multiple marginalised identities, potentially rendering severe economic hardship among white populations less visible. This issue is particularly salient in post-industrial coastal communities, where poverty, unemployment, poor health outcomes, and educational disadvantage are often deeply embedded within local histories of industrial decline. Residents may understand their experiences principally through class and place-based identities rather than through other dimensions of social difference. Consequently, analyses that focus exclusively on intersecting identities risk overlooking the significance of collective experiences of economic dislocation and territorial stigma that shape life in many coastal communities.

Furthermore, while intersectionality offers a powerful framework for understanding identities, inequalities, and power relations, it is less well equipped to explain the broader structural transformations that have affected many white working-class coastal areas. Processes such as deindustrialisation, labour market restructuring, automation, globalisation, and the movement of capital have fundamentally altered the economic foundations of communities across the Cumbrian coast and beyond. These structural changes have contributed to declining employment opportunities, outmigration among younger populations, and a growing sense of disconnection from centres of political and economic power. As such, understanding disadvantage in these communities requires attention not only to intersecting identities but also to the wider political-economic forces that shape local realities.

Consequently, we employ intersectionality as one component of a broader analytical framework. Rather than viewing it as a comprehensive explanation for the experiences of white working-class coastal communities, we use it alongside analyses of place, history, and economic change. This enables us to examine how experiences of exclusion and belonging are produced through both individual social positions and the structural conditions that shape community life.

Traditionally, imagined communities have been used to explain the formation of national identities (Anderson, 1983). We suggest, however, that the concept can also be applied at a regional and local level. The coastal communities examined in this study are characterised by distinctive histories, cultural memories, and shared narratives of industrial decline, resilience, and marginalisation. These narratives contribute to a collective sense of identity that distinguishes them from other places and influences how residents interpret social and economic change. By combining the concepts of imagined communities and intersectionality, we are able to examine not only how white working-class coastal identities are collectively constructed but also how they are experienced differently by individuals occupying diverse social positions within the same locality. In doing so, we seek to understand the dynamic relationship between place, class, identity, and belonging, while remaining attentive to the broader structural forces that continue to shape life in contemporary coastal Britain.

In developing our understanding of what it means to be a "peripheral community," we have drawn on both research evidence and shared critical reflection on over 55 collective years of promoting social justice and social inclusion in the public and third sectors (Figure 6.4). Using this, we aim to explain the social construction of physical, social, cultural and political peripherality and structural inequalities, shaped by the geo-political-historical context along the Cumbrian coast, which is often referred to as the "white working-class."

However, we believe that notions of the working class need to reflect the rich ethnic diversity within communities, particularly in the North of England, so we also declined to use the term "left-behind." "Left-behind" has been widely criticised as emphasising negative characteristics to the detriment of the communities it seeks to describe (Antink, 2019). Instead, in response to the nuanced context of the area and the complex dimensions of the communities we worked with, we draw on the concept of peripherality (Bickerstaff, 2022).

The term peripheral was initially inspired by reflections on the peripheral, or isolated, nature of the West Cumbrian coastline. In November 2008, the surrounding area experienced severe flooding, which essentially left every road and train line inaccessible. Research found that residents along the West Cumbrian coast felt deeply isolated (Wilson, 2024c). Although basic infrastructure is routinely available in some places, travel and connectivity to the rest of the UK remain a challenge with poorly maintained and overcrowded road networks alongside unequal access to reliable public transport for the 25% of West Cumbrian residents without access to a car (Büscher et al., 2022).

It was from this starting point that one of the authors, Suzanne, began to think about how the communities we were working with felt not only physically distant from the rest of the UK, but also symbolically, particularly in terms of democracy. Reflecting on research she had conducted locally, she identified four key components that contribute to the subjective experience of peripherality in communities: structural inequalities, a deep collective history, a strong collective identity and perceived political peripherality.

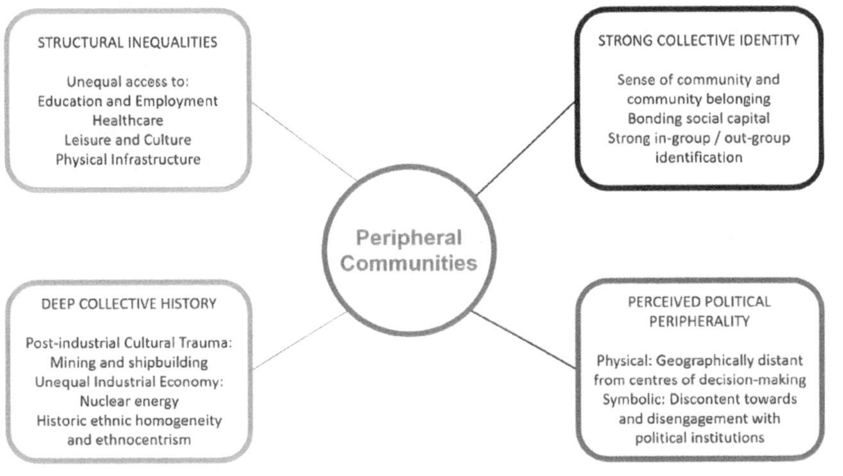

Figure 6.4 Peripheral communities (Wilson, 2024c). A diagram showing four characteristics of peripheral communities: structural inequalities, strong collective identity, deep collective history, and perceived political peripherality.

Structural inequalities

Most of the communities included in the research were within the 10% most deprived areas in the county, with a few sections of the community being in the top 20% (IMD, 2019). The 2019 Index of Multiple Deprivation revealed the limited and unequal outcomes in these areas, including education, employment, income and health care (IMD, 2019). More recent data from the 2021 Census suggest that these levels of deprivation and inequality persist, with all communities reporting high levels of economic inactivity, long-term unemployment and disability rates compared to local and national averages (Census 2021, n.d.). These indicate structural inequalities within these peripheral communities, an assessment strengthened by data concerning limited access to leisure and culture (Arts Council England, 2024). This deprivation should also be viewed in the context of geographical location: as well as experiencing the wider north–south divide, these West Cumbrian communities also contrast starkly with the neighbouring Lake District, highlighting the deeply unequal distribution of Cumbria's economic development.

Deep collective history

The West Cumbrian coast has a rich history deeply rooted in the historic steel and mining industries; however, these industries have not been operational for several decades, contributing to economic decline. As seen elsewhere, the end of mining took with it a fundamental basis of the community's collective identity and solidarity (Strangleman, 2001). The nuclear industry in West Cumbria became a dominant part of the local economy and social life in the 1980s, partly due to the decline of traditional extractive and secondary industries. Relatively elevated salaries within the nuclear industry present a dual economy: those who work within the sector and those who do not, with some of the highest median wages in the UK alongside high rates of disadvantage (Wylie et al., 2020).

The historical dominance of White British ethnicity continues to characterise West Cumbria, with 98.4% of those living in the research sites identifying as White British compared with the UK average of 81.0% (Census 2021, n.d.). Local research and practice revealed that many residents feel a strong sense of ethnocentrism, characterised by three dominant narratives, including resentment over a perceived preferential allocation of resources, fear of the unknown and feeling socially obligated to be "politically correct" (Wilson et al., 2025). This adds to evidence from other areas, which suggests that a process of "othering" different cultures also occurs in similarly non-diverse communities (Fenton, 2012; Spracklen, 2018). These attitudes towards difference are influenced by the intersection of race, place, class and positionality within the context of local geography, history and politics (Crenshaw, 2013). Our findings mirror other studies which link these preconditions with an increased level of support for more extreme, right-wing views and anti-immigrant narratives, as presented above.

Strong collective identity

Many communities along the Cumbrian Coast show a profound sense of collective solidarity and belonging (Wilson & Morris, 2020, 2023a, 2023b; Wilson et al., 2020). Within this context, we relate collective solidarity to the concept of social capital (Guzhavina, 2018; Oosterlynck et al., 2017; Portes & Landolt, 2000; Putnam, 2000), where strong bonding social capital describes cases where individuals relate closely to one another and behave altruistically within their imagined community. However, it can also result in rigid ingroup/outgroup identities (Tajfel & Turner, 1979), which reinforce the tendency to "other" those that are not seen to belong and can take the form of exclusionary solidarity (Daly & Silver, 2008; Hopman & Knijn, 2022). The research suggests these attitudes arise from contexts where communities feel they are in the process of recovering from a past dominated by large-scale employment in steelworks and coal mining. Collective grief and trauma underpin the shared collective identities of the communities. This is again reflected in existing research concerning community identity in similarly non-diverse post-industrial, working-class communities, particularly in relation to the construction of clear in-group/out-group distinctions (Spracklen, 2018).

Perceived political peripherality

Our collective research and experience show that communities along the Cumbrian Coast feel tangibly distant from local politics and other civic institutions (Wilson, 2024a, 2024b). The impact of this perceived peripherality is evident in the most common form of political engagement: voting. Local elections for the new Cumberland Council in May 2022 saw all communities return fewer votes than the 36.1% county average (UK Parliament, 2023). This has been shown to be common voter behaviour in communities that are considered left-behind (Abreu & Jones, 2021; Telford, 2021, 2023; Telford & Lloyd, 2020). Arguably, perceived political peripherality is the product of the other dimensions as seen through our research: structural inequalities and collective history produce a strong collective identity, which reinforces the perception of political peripherality.

Community Psychology in action: Praxis case studies

Community Psychology can be utilised to foster critical dialogue among communities, enabling them to co-create recommendations for inclusive policy development (Hill & Wilson, 2003; Huddy, 2001; Hunter, 2003). Through participatory approaches, community psychologists can utilise creative methods to facilitate the sharing of stories, realising critical consciousness and developing pedagogical material (Pinedo et al., 2024) with all political actors: citizens, grassroots organisations, local authorities, even central government or beyond. Here, we present two case study examples of how co-production and participatory methods have been applied within community settings to make a real difference in terms of community participation and cohesion.

Chatty Bus, Blackpool, UK

In our first case study, Davinia Jackson tells us about her time working for Blackpool, on the northwest coast of England, where she worked with communities to organise and engage with formal institutions.

Citizen inquiry for social inclusion

For many Britons, Blackpool calls to mind certain cultural imagery: bright lights, fun in the sun, fish and chips, a stick of "rock" and a "kiss me quick" hat. All make for pleasurable memories and nowadays great social media content, but what happens when the sun goes down and the lights go out – what about those who are living in the dark, damp shadows of low educational achievement, poor housing, low unemployment, high rates of suicide and more health inequalities than can be listed in this book? Shared Future Community Interest Company has developed and delivered a model of citizens' inquiries, juries and assemblies across the country and on a variety of issues. Residents involved are then supported through a ten-week process to share their experiences and opinions on the issue. They can then listen to expert evidence, meet with commentators and workers in the relevant field of specialism and make recommendations on how they would like to influence and change public policy.

Shared Futures was commissioned to work in a housing area with buildings of multiple occupancy and a transient community, all of whom were living in deprivation but rich in experience and driven by passion and anger at injustice and inequality, wanting change. Many of the group were unemployed; those in employment were on part-time or temporary contracts, and there was a reliance on welfare benefits for various reasons. At first, most of the 23 residents were reluctant to voice their opinions and experiences; hesitant and suspicious of whether there was an ulterior motive. As the time together increased and the process unfolded, there was more opportunity to discuss things that really mattered to them, such as drug use in the area, safety, cleanliness and the standard of housing.

As they explored the issues in depth, they found differences of opinion and experiences, but often a common ground that things needed to change. After the nine Inquiry sessions, the group hosted a launch event at which the group's recommendations were shared and discussed with invited local stakeholders. Following the Inquiry process, ten members of the group agreed to continue meeting to consider how the recommendations could be implemented and acted upon in their community. Despite some entrenched issues, the group felt that their main priority was to address the social isolation within the community.

After trying out different ideas, the group chose to develop a *chatty bus* and a *chatty cuppa* (In England, a cuppa is an informal way of saying a cup of tea.). Local service providers and businesses were approached for support – some offering financial assistance to hire the bus, while others provided a driver or tea bags and cups. Eight local volunteers led a wide range of conversations at ten locations over a total of 360 *chatty brews* (In England, a brew is another informal way of saying a cup of tea.). In all, the group gave 155 volunteer hours, and 65 professionals from local services attended.

Along with an array of personal benefits to individuals in the community, such as increased access to health services, eight members of the local group all significantly improved their own health and wellbeing by working together for the common good of their community. They gained confidence, attended training and gained new skills and qualifications, which led to three of the group being offered employment.

The group was keen to further develop this model and came up with project plans and ideas to share with existing partners and potential funders. However, the organisation that had initially commissioned the citizens' inquiry had been unsuccessful in securing any longer-term funding to support the work. The Inquiry took place in 2019, but by March 2020, the world had changed dramatically due to the COVID-19 pandemic. Priorities of local authorities and community services shifted to react to the unfolding crisis that was sweeping the world.

Broad-based community organising for sustainable change

On reflection, this group gained a great deal, but the oversight of the entire process and the "professionals" involved, including myself, was to overlook the power that the residents in that area held. Not allowing this work to be led by the residents, allowing them to continue to believe that they were being done to, rather than worked with, was a serious failing in the process. I have since become a community organiser for Citizens UK, where the method of Broad-based organising is used to build alliances of institutions in communities.

At the heart of this method is identifying and developing leaders, strengthening institutions, and engaging with civil society. To do this, the key is to organise people and money, to have some autonomy from the state and the market. Broad-based community organising encourages institutions to build alliances and organise their resources and people, giving them autonomy to take action on issues affecting the collective's members. This also allows autonomy from the state and the market, which can give the alliance power to call for their accountability. Within this autonomy, the approach advocates for cultivating relationships with those who hold power, such as the local authorities, engaging in constructive dialogue to effect social change. We do this because institutions are deep-rooted in the community, but people come and go, especially in transient coastal communities.

The citizens' inquiry model organised individuals to consider how to influence change; yet once the funding and process had concluded, they felt powerless again due to lacking the strength in numbers and a lack of funding. The alternative, broad-based method of community organising has a rich history in creating long-term systemic change. Examples from the civil rights movement and in the UK saw the launch of the Real Living Wage campaign in 2011, which has helped uplift millions of people out of in-work poverty.

If this method had been applied to the work of the citizens' inquiry group, and in some small parts it did, then I strongly believe that they would still be functioning and growing in numbers and strength. Power conjures up so many negative connotations for many; however, in its simplest meaning, it is the ability to act. And therefore, we all have it; we are just not encouraged to believe we can or to use that ability against the structures and systems that we must navigate in our small, coastal and often forgotten communities.

Community street art, Young Cumbria

In this second case study, Lynsey Crosthwaite shares a project she developed while serving as project manager at Young Cumbria, describing how community street art was used to mobilise and energise young people to express their concerns about their local community.

One of the main objectives of Young Cumbria was to ensure that young people felt invested in their communities, and had an increased sense of connection, belonging and contribution to their community. As one means of promoting this, we developed a community cohesion programme that ran over ten weeks, aiming to give young people a deeper understanding of important community and social issues through educational workshops and artistic social engagement.

Figure 6.5 Community street art, example 1. Colourful graffiti art centring around the word "poverty" with images and statistics.

Source: Photography by the author.

Figure 6.6 Community street art, example 2. Graffiti art depicting a cheetah's head with one side healthy amongst flowers and the other side a burned skull and flames.

Source: Photograph by the author.

Each ten-week programme had a broad theme focusing on poverty, inclusion, gender and sexuality, and the environment, and explored the topic within local, national and global contexts. Groups were presented with a variety of themes and asked to choose one that best met the specific needs and interests of their community. Young people worked together in weekly sessions to improve their understanding of the chosen theme, develop a greater tolerance of difference, and hone art-based skills, which were then applied to create a piece of public street art displayed within the local community. This showcasing not only helped solidify the learning that had taken place, but also sought to transcend the confines of the sessions by raising awareness among the local community.

Another essential aspect of this delivery was that it could encourage the involvement of other community members, which helps to enhance the programme content and increase the dialogue and learning of everyone involved. This ranged from having community activists assist in aspects of awareness raising and delivery to having parents/carers attend specific sessions to contribute to debate and discussion.

As a Youth and Community work organisation, our core focus was always the social and personal development of disadvantaged young people, developing coping skills for the future and providing positive activities that enrich the lives of those we work with. It was our experience that combining street art and youth work is a great way to engage young people in social issues that affect their lives and offer more significant opportunities for personal growth, beyond simply engaging in art. The use of street art as a medium for spreading their message is a truly powerful one, allowing communities to challenge their own assumptions and those of society via a means that taps into cultural consciousness and social commentary.

During the programme, the young people spent time designing and creating pieces of artwork based on the topics discussed; these designs were then merged to form the basis of the large community artwork. This community artwork was located within the local area, on the side of a local youth centre or an unused property, in a highly visible spot to area residents. Part of the work process involved securing a location for the artwork to be displayed; this was something that the young people did themselves, depending on their ability and willingness.

The act of integrating this artwork into the community was the heart of our artistic social engagement strategy. Additional outcomes include developing a sense of community pride, aesthetic improvement and providing underrepresented groups of young people with a platform to challenge social issues. At the end of each programme, we aimed to offer the young people an "experience" based upon the social issue they had been exploring. This was delivered in the form of an educational visit or by a guest speaker. For example, if the social issue was "poverty," we may have taken the young people to a food bank. Alternatively, a representative from the food bank could be invited into the session to talk to them.

An unexpected outcome was how much the young people thrived by taking collective action to convey a message using art. The art was the culmination of their shared learning, enabling them to convey a message to the community. The incremental knowledge building, which came with emotion and motivation, provided the art with a purpose and focus. Members from almost all groups wanted to remain involved, and so we developed a youth group to bring them all together to harness that motivation. We did not have funding to run this group, so we covered the rent of the space and acted primarily as facilitators, and they organised themselves. This group went on to secure commissions for pieces of art that covered their materials and expenses. They worked at festivals and community organisations.

This case demonstrates how participatory methods can create the conditions for enacting community power and political proximity. In securing buildings to display their street art, the young people claimed their power to engage with institutions and to creatively express their views on social policy issues important to them. Personal agency and collective power were further enabled through the young people's ownership of the project's direction and their leadership of commissioned pieces of art, aiming for wider impact, demonstrating the potential of creative practice to bridge distance and foster proximity.

Action for learning exercise 1: Creatively connecting

Think about different creative tools that can be used to help people express themselves. They may include writing, drawing, singing or photography, amongst many other methods.

How might these be applied to help people communicate their voices, choices and rights with local politicians?

Action for learning exercise 2: Reflective exercise

Take ten minutes to sit quietly and reflect on a time you felt powerless. This could be in any context: home, school, work or with friends, for example.

1. What do you think happened?
2. How did you feel?
3. How did this influence your future behaviour?

Now, apply these thoughts, feelings and behaviours within a local political context.

The local refuse collection service is on strike during the school summer holidays. This means that the bins have not been collected in a local community for three weeks.

How will this feel for the following people? What forms of power do they possess in this situation? In what ways may they be feeling powerless?

- A local refuse collector?
- A mother of three children, including a 2-month-old baby
- A local Councillor

Social justice and political peripherality: Co-production to develop an inclusive policy process

This chapter presents social justice through the lens of participatory social inclusion, calling for those who can enable the conditions for communities on the edges of the mainstream to claim their voices, choices and rights. Our collective experience has shown us that people seek to work dialogically with those with shared values around reciprocity. There is a desire to build trusting and equitable relationships in which residents can become informed and empowered actors. Communities do not necessarily want to be involved in structural or formal decision-making processes, nor do they wish to overturn traditional power structures. Rather, they seek a physical and symbolic space in which power is distributed equally and communities' views, concerns and preferences are considered legitimate as those of the local authority.

Our case studies demonstrate that co-productive approaches can foster conditions that support active and meaningful community engagement, giving people the confidence and skills to take the lead in shaping services to suit their needs and circumstances in a way that is impossible under traditional methods. To achieve authentic, sustainable community power, local authorities must commit to co-production processes that position communities as active partners and contributors in the democratic process. This includes, but is not limited to:

- Understanding what pride and agency mean within local communities and how connected they feel, safe and secure they feel.
- Adopting culture and arts-based engagement strategies to begin conversations with communities.
- Providing opportunities to co-create ways for communities to participate in local democracy and allocate resources to ensure co-produced strategies are implemented.
- Establishing lived experience advisory groups, with the support of key third-sector organisations, to ensure that the voices of those experiencing inequalities are at the centre of policy development.
- Forming local governance structures to ensure that community representatives play an active role in decision-making and holding the authorities to account.

Co-production is not linear, with a clearly defined beginning and end. It involves a cultural shift in thinking and practice, which necessitates a critical examination of power dynamics within co-productive policy (Durose & Richardson, 2015; Beebeejuan et al., 2014). Barriers to successful implementation may include resistance and even hostility towards changing practices, from both elected members and officers. This hostility, as our research found, may be rooted in a sense of powerlessness within institutions themselves. Therefore, it is essential that all actors, including both community and policy, are included in the journey towards co-production and community empowerment.

Competing priorities can also impede inclusive and co-produced practice; it is expensive and time-consuming, a luxury many local authorities may feel they cannot afford. Promoting a culture that appreciates long-term public cost savings can be a valuable tool for gaining institutional support (Improta & Mannoni, 2024). Moreover, implementing cultural change within an institution may be hindered by short-term policy cycles, which often provide only short-term strategies that seek quickly observable outcomes. This can be countered by challenging hegemonic structures and promoting sustainable, long-term systems beyond traditional policy cycles (Bartels & Wittmayer, 2019).

From peripherality to power and proximity: Challenges and opportunities for community psychologists

At a time when political tensions are escalating, marked by a rise in right-wing populism across Europe and beyond (Falcó-Gimeno, et al., 2026), the need to apply community psychology in practice to effect change is crucial. In this chapter, we present several psychological theories that help explain how communities feel and act, as well as why, including solidarity and social capital (Daly & Silver, 2008; Putnam, 2000) and identity theory (Tajfel & Turner, 1979). However, there is also a need to consider the complex intersections of psychological, social and structural conditions that drive inclusionary and exclusionary practices, such as hostility and antipathy towards different marginalised groups.

Drawing on ecological-systems theories, such as Bronfenbrenner (1989), can provide a holistic understanding of the wider influencing impact of peripherality experienced by the communities we work with. This includes, but is not limited to, appreciating the interdependent relationships between personal relationships (which are highly valued in peripheral communities), local social systems, networks, and institutions (which are sometimes strained) and the dominant beliefs and ideologies held by peripheral communities (Figure 6.7).

Community psychologists have a role to play in reducing the social distance between peripheral communities and political institutions by appreciating the value of relational practice and skills in bringing people together to facilitate conversations that create a space where groups can understand the perspectives of others. Within these dialogical spaces, the purpose is not necessarily to create a consensus

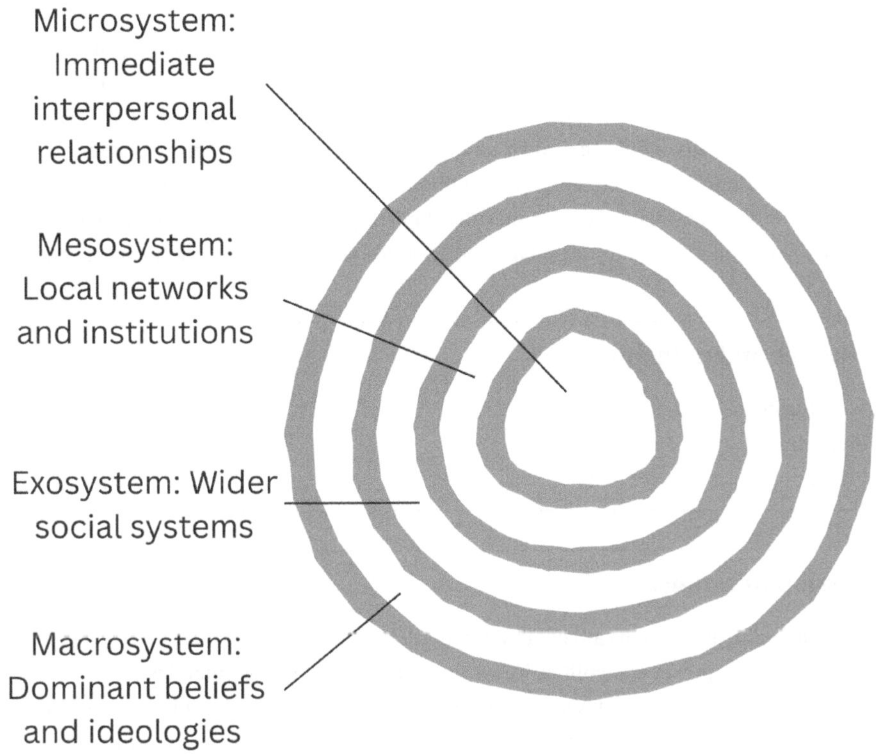

Figure 6.7 Bronfenbrenner's Ecological Systems Model (Bronfenbrenner, 1989). Concentric circles illustrating the relationship between microsystems (innermost), mesosystems, exosystems and macrosystems (outermost).

between different groups, but rather to create a space where groups can "disagree agreeably." We argue that feeling heard and understood, rather than merely being in agreement, is the key to building greater community coherence in peripheral communities, and thus reducing the risk of populist support, divisive politics and civil unrest.

Along with relational practice, a participatory approach has the potential to overcome disengagement and disenfranchisement in peripheral communities, which should be embraced by local and national governments in their policy development. This, however, takes time and money, both of which are in short supply. Moreover, a radical culture change is required by holders of traditional power, from one characterised by systems and dominance to one of unity and collaboration.

Conclusion

Coastal communities in the UK face several intersecting disadvantages, resulting in perceptions of both geographical and political peripherality, which in turn lead to distrust in government organisations and politicians. Feeling unheard and neglected contributes to that distrust and to poor relationships with institutions. Through our research and experience, participatory and co-production approaches that prioritise relationship building and redressing oppressive power dynamics can allow communities to experience increased trust and agency to make positive improvements to their quality of life; however, local government practitioners and political representatives have a vital role to play in working with third sector organisations to bring about a cultural shift in support of challenging traditional power structures. Building on our success in coastal communities, we are developing plans to test our methods beyond the coastal context in other post-industrial communities that appear to be experiencing similar political peripherality, albeit with their own unique challenges. Transforming hegemonic structures in disadvantaged communities, by creating the conditions needed to develop co-productive practices that share power and decision-making over issues that impact people's lives, has the potential to turn the most socially and economically disadvantaged neighbourhoods in England into thriving communities.

Key values and principles

- Social justice
- Inequalities
- Power

Discussion questions

1. How do political decisions affect our daily lives?
2. How do we see power and politics in our families, schools or communities?
3. If you were tasked with changing the ways power was distributed within a group/class/political system, what barriers would you anticipate encountering and how would you propose to overcome them?

Reflective questions

1. Have you ever been in a group situation when you disagreed with a decision made by the group? How did that feel? How did you act?
2. Look at the different systems in Bronfenbrenner's ecological systems theory. What different actors influence your life on each level?

Position statements

Suzanne Wilson

I self-identify as a White, heterosexual female who grew up in a working-class household but now holds a professional position. I strongly identify with my northern English heritage and have recently become a mother for the first time, and would describe myself as a mother–scholar–activist. Throughout my adult life, I have been dedicated to promoting social inclusion, demonstrating this commitment through both practical efforts and research. My various paid and voluntary positions include clinical psychology and community mental health, educational governance and community development. As an applied and socially conscious researcher, my ambition is that all my research contributes to promoting social inclusion through recommendations for local and central government and third-sector organisations.

Katherine Jewell

A White, heterosexual, married female, I immigrated to the UK, alone at age 19. Originally from an upper-middle class family, my adult life has been spent both working with and living amongst disadvantaged communities in the north of England. My husband and I collaborate to raise and home-school our three boys and care for their elderly grandfather, and we have recently relocated to West Cumbria with the intention of permanence. I have worked for over 17 years to promote social justice, through children's social care, trade unionism, community activism and academic/third sector research. My interests and expertise include social identity theory, political ethnography and community activism.

Lynsey Crosthwaite

I was born and raised in West Cumbria. I left the area aged 19 to study and returned 17 years later. During that time, I lived and worked in various cities but settled for ten years in East London. I have a career of 27 years, primarily working in the fields of housing and homelessness, youth work and inclusion and diversity, and have worked within some of the most disadvantaged and diverse communities in the UK. I have an unwavering commitment to the principles of social justice, social inclusion and community activism. This, rooted within a framework of anti-oppressive practice, is the basis of my practice.

Davinia Jackson

Davinia Jackson is the Community Organiser with Citizens UK in Lancashire. She was born and raised in Blackpool and has always lived on the Fylde Coast. She has rooted her career and interests in the area in both voluntary and statutory services, including public health, community education, housing, substance misuse and youth provisions. She is keen to embed the methods and principles of community organising to bring about long-term social change.

References

Abreu, M., & Jones, C. (2021). The shadow of the Pithead: understanding social and political attitudes in former coal mining communities in the UK. *Applied Geography, 131*, 102448. https://doi.org/10.1016/j.apgeog.2021.102448

Anderson, B. (1983) *Imagined communities*. Verso.

Antink, B. (2019). *Our towns have not been 'left behind', they have been actively excluded.* RSA. https://www.thersa.org/blog/2019/05/left-behind

Arts Council England. (2024). *The active lives survey.* https://www.artscouncil.org.uk/research-and-data/active-lives-survey

Bartels, K., & Wittmayer, J. (2019). *Action research in policy analysis*. Routledge. https://doi.org/10.4324/9781315148724

Beebeejuan, Y., Durose, C., Rees, J., Richardson, J., & Richardson, L. (2014). 'Beyond text': Exploring ethos and method in co-producing research with communities. *Community Development Journal, 49*(1), 37–53. https://doi.org/10.1093/cdj/bst008

Bickerstaff, K. (2022). Living on with Sellafield: Nuclear infrastructure, slow violence, and the politics of quiescence. *Transactions of the Institute of British Geographers, 47*(4), 955–970. https://doi.org/10.1111/tran.12540

Bronfenbrenner, U. (1989) Ecological systems theory. In R. Vasta (Ed.), *Annals of child development, six theories of child development: Revised formulations and current issues* (Vol. 6, pp. 187–249). JAI Press.

Büscher, M., Clark, J., Colderley, R., Kirkbride, A., Larty, J., McCulloch, S., Moody, E., Mullis, E. Phillips, I., Vaudrey, W., & Willshaw, K. (2022). Cumbria 2037: Decarbonising mobility futures. DecarboN8 Research Network. https://eprints.whiterose.ac.uk/id/eprint/194665/1/Cumbria%202037%20-%20Decarbonising%20Mobility%20Futures.pdf

Census 2021. (n.d.). Census maps. https://www.ons.gov.uk/census/maps/

Crenshaw, K. W. (1989). Demarginalizing the intersection of race and sex: A Black feminist critique of antidiscrimination doctrine, feminist theory and antiracist politics. *University of Chicago Legal Forum*, *1989*(18), 139–167. https://chicagounbound.uchicago.edu/uclf/vol1989/iss1/8

Crenshaw, K. W. (2013). Mapping the margins: Intersectionality, identity politics, and violence against women of color. *Stanford Law Review*, *43*(6), 1241–1299. https://doi.org/10.2307/1229039

Daly, M., & Silver, H. (2008). Social exclusion and social capital: A comparison and critique. *Theory and Society*, *37*, 537–566. http://doi.org/10.1007/s11186-008-9062-4

Durose, C., & Richardson, L. (2015). *Designing public policy for co-production: Theory, practice and change*. Policy Press.

Falcó-Gimeno, A., Jurado, I., & Wagner, M. (2026). Left-Wing Governments and Far-Right Success. *British Journal of Political Science*, 56, e5.

Fenton, S. (2012). Resentment, class and social sentiments about the nation: The ethnic majority in England. *Ethnicities*, *12*(4), 465–483. https://doi.org/10.1177/1468796812448023.

France, A., & Roberts, S. (2017). *Youth and social class: Enduring inequality in the United Kingdom, Australia and New Zealand*. Palgrave Macmillan.

Google Maps. (n.d.). West Cumbrian coast from Millom to Maryport. Retrieved August 8, 2024, from https://www.google.com/maps/@54.5033448,-3.3859492,88468m/data=!3m1!1e3?authuser=0&entry=ttu&g_ep=EgoyMDI1MDkwOS4wIKXMDSoASAFQAw%3D%3D

Guzhavina, T. Y. A. (2018). Social capital of the urban community: Trust, solidarity, responsibility. *Economic and Social Changes: Facts, Trends, Forecast*, *11*(4), 252–268. http://doi.org/10.15838/esc.2018.4.58.16

Hill, J., & Wilson, T. M. (2003). Identity politics and the politics of identities. *Identities: Global Studies in Culture and Power, 10*(1), 1–8.

Hopman, M., & Knijn, T. (2022). Understanding solidarity in society: Triggers and barriers for in-and outgroup solidarity. In M. A. Yerkes & M. Bal (Eds.), *Solidarity and social justice in contemporary societies: An interdisciplinary approach to understanding inequalities* (pp. 29–39). Springer International Publishing.

Huddy, L. (2001). From social to political identity: A critical examination of social identity theory. *Political Psychology*, *22*(1), 127–156. http://doi.org/10.1111/0162-895X.00230.

Hunter, S. (2003). A critical analysis of approaches to the concept of social identity in social policy. *Critical Social Policy*, *23*(3), 322–344. https://doi.org/10.1177/02610183030233002.

Hvenegård-Lassen, K., Staunæs, D., & Lund, R. (2020). Intersectionality, yes, but how? Approaches and conceptualizations in nordic feminist research and activism. *Nordic Journal of Feminist and Gender Research*, *28*(3), 173–182. https://doi.org/10.1080/08038740.2020.1790826

IMD. (2019). *Indices of multiple deprivation map*. http://dclgapps.communities.gov.uk/imd/iod_index.html

Improta, M., & Mannoni, E. (2024) Government short-termism and the management of global challenges. *The British Journal of Politics and International Relations*, *27*(2), 612–627. https://doi.org/10.1177/13691481241280172

Ledwith, M. (1997) *Participating in transformation: Towards a working model of community empowerment*. Venture Press.

Levitas, R., Pantazis, C., Fahmy, E., Gordon, D., Lloyd, E., & Patsios, D. (2007). *The multi-dimensional analysis of social exclusion*. http://dera.ioe.ac.uk/6853/1/multidimensional.pdf

Local Trust. (2019). *Left behind? Understanding communities on the edge*. https://localtrust.org.uk/insights/research/left-behind-understanding-communities-on-the-edge/

Oosterlynck, S., Schuermans, N., & Loopmans, M. (2017). Beyond social capital: Place, diversity and solidarity. In S. Oosterlynck, N. Schuermans, & M. Loopmans (Eds.), *Place, diversity and solidarity* (pp. 1–18). Routledge. https://doi.org/10.4324/9781315622866

Ovenden-Hope, T., & Passy, R. (2019). *Educational isolation: A challenge for schools in England*. Plymouth Marjon University and University of Plymouth. https://www.marjon.ac.uk/educational-isolation/Education-Isolation-Report.pdf

Parsfield, M., Morris, D., Bola, M., Knapp, M., Yoshioka, M., & Marc, G. (2015). *Connected capital: The value of connected communities*. RSA.

Pinedo, A., Diemer, M. A., & Frisby, M. B. (2024). Critical consciousness and youth political activism. *Annual Review of Developmental Psychology*, *6*, 351–372. https://doi.org/10.1146/annurev-devpsych-010923-113449

Portes, A., & Landolt, P. (2000). Social capital: Promise and pitfalls of its role in development. *Journal of Latin American Studies*, *32*(2), 529–547. https://doi.org/10.1017/S0022216X00005836

Putnam, R. (2000). *Bowling alone: The collapse and revival of American community*. Simon & Schuster Paperbacks.

Richards, G. (2022). Are we expecting too much? Aspirations and expectations of girls living in an ex-mining community. In R. Simmons & K. Simpson (Eds.), *Education, work and social change in Britain's former coalfield communities: The ghost of coal* (pp. 197–222). Springer International Publishing.

Rodríguez-Pose, A., Terrero-Dávila, J., & Lee, N. (2023). Left-behind vs. unequal places: Interpersonal inequality, economic decline, and the rise of populism in the US and Europe. *Journal of Economic Geography*, *23*(5), 951–977. https://doi.org/10.1093/jeg/lbad005

Spracklen, K. (2018). Theorising northernness and northern culture: The north of England, northern Englishness, and sympathetic magic. In G. Riches, K. Spracklen, & S. Swain (Eds.), *Northernness, northern culture and northern narratives* (pp. 4–16). Routledge. https://doi.org/10.4324/9781315144641

Strangleman, T. (2001). Networks, place and identities in post-industrial mining communities. *International Journal of Urban and Regional Research*, *25*(2), 253–267. https://doi.org/10.1111/1468–2427.00310

Tajfel, H., & Turner, J. C. (1979). An integrative theory of intergroup conflict. In W. G. Austin & S. Worchel (Eds.), *The social psychology of intergroup relations* (pp. 33–47). Brooks/Cole.

Taylor Hill, S. (2024). Unraveling the white working-class conundrum: A closer look at its utility and pitfalls. *Ethnicities*, *24*(6), 835–853. https://doi.org/10.1177/14687968241240787

Telford, L. (2021). 'There is nothing there': Deindustrialization and loss in a coastal town. *Competition & Change*. https://doi.org/10.1177/10245294211011300

Telford, L., & Lloyd, A. (2020). From "infant Hercules" to "ghost town": Industrial collapse and social harm in Teesside. *Critical Criminology*, *28*(4), 595–611. https://doi.org/10.1007/s10612-020-09523-3

Telford, L. (2023). 'Levelling Up? That's never going to happen': Perceptions on Levelling Up in a 'Red Wall' locality. *Contemporary Social Science, 18*(3–4), 546–561.

UK Parliament. (2023). Local election 2023: Results and analysis. https://commonslibrary.parliament.uk/research-briefings/cbp-9798/

Wenham, A. (2020). "Wish you were here"? Geographies of exclusion: Young people, coastal towns and marginality. *Journal of Youth Studies*, *23*(1), 44–60. https://doi.org/10.1080/13676261.2019.1704408

Whitty, C. (2021). *Chief medical officer's annual report 2021: Health in coastal communities*. https://www.gov.uk/government/publications/chief-medical-officers-annual-report-2021-health-in-coastal-communities

Wilson, S., & Morris, D. (2020). *Connected communities woodhouse*. https://clok.uclan.ac.uk/34922/1/UCLan%20Connected%20Communities%20Woodhouse%20Sept%2020.pdf

Wilson, S., & Morris, D. (2023a). *Ormsgill stronger together*. https://clok.uclan.ac.uk/47472/1/UCLan%20Connected%20Communities%20Ormsgill.pdf

Wilson, S., & Morris, D. (2023b). *Moorclose stronger together*. https://clok.uclan.ac.uk/45901/1/UCLan%20Connected%20Communities%20Moorclose%20March%202023.pdf

Wilson, S. (2024a). A 'left behind' Habitus? Understanding local political disengagement using bourdieu. *Space and Polity*, *28*, 1356–2576. https://doi.org/10.1080/13562576.2024.2407146

Wilson, S. (2024b). *Community power: Co-creating approaches to participatory democracy*. https://clok.uclan.ac.uk/51696/1/Community%20Power_Co-Creating%20Approaches%20to%20Participatory%20Democracy_UCLan.pdf

Wilson, S. (2024c). *Levelled up or left behind? A relational approach to social inclusion in low-income coastal communities* [Doctoral thesis, University of Lancashire]. https://clok.uclan.ac.uk/id/eprint/53725/

Wilson, S., Jewell, K., & Crossthwaite, L. (2025). *Peripherality and community cohesion in predominantly white, low-income coastal communities*. Women and Equalities Committee. https://clok.uclan.ac.uk/id/eprint/55528/

Wylie, R., Heaslip, M., Fyfe, J., Slavin, W., Haraldsen, S., & Wilson, S. (2020). Polycentric policy communities and the public value profile of the nuclear industry in West Cumbria. In R. Wylie (Ed.), *Public value management: Institutional design and decision for the common good* (pp. 215–239). Rowman & Littlefield. https://clok.uclan.ac.uk/id/eprint/35097/

Further reading

Books

Bolton, M. (2017). *How to resist: Turn protest into power*. Bloomsbury.
Alinsky, S. (1971). *Rules for radicals: A pragmatic primer for realistic radicals*. Vintage Books.
Chambers, E. T. (2018). *Roots for radicals: Organising for power, action and justice*. Bloomsbury.

Podcasts

Listen, Organise, Act: Organising and Democratic Politics – Luke Bretherton.
Everyday People Making Every Day Change – Citizens UK.

7 Action for climate justice

Community Psychology tackling climate change in an unjust world

Maria Fernandes-Jesus, Carlie D. Trott, Brendon Barnes and Manuel Riemer

Introduction

As we finish writing this chapter, we reflect on the many extreme weather events that have impacted communities worldwide during the past year. We saw devastating floods, communities battling wildfires, persistent droughts and flooding. In addition, 2024 was the world's hottest year on record (National Centres for Environmental Information [NOAA], 2024) and the first year ever to exceed the 1.5°C limit in average global temperatures (Copernicus Climate Change Service (C3S), 2025). These and other climate events have profound implications for the lives of communities, leading to food and water scarcity, economic insecurity, increased health risks, displacement and losses of livelihoods (Vestby et al., 2024). These are just some examples. The reality of climate change is, unfortunately, devastating in many other ways and interacts with several social issues, often exacerbating existing inequalities and affecting communities' wellbeing.

Despite (or because of) our diverse experiences and backgrounds, we, the four co-authors of this chapter, all share an understanding of climate change as a matter of social justice. Inspired by many activists, social movements and critical scholars, we argue that climate change is fundamentally a social justice issue and, as such, it requires a climate justice lens (e.g., Fernandes-Jesus et al., 2020; Newell et al., 2021; Sultana, 2022; Trott et al., 2022). As explained by Trott et al. (2022):

> climate justice perspective recognises that climate risks and vulnerabilities, as well as the benefits and burdens of climate actions, are anything but equally distributed, and that climate shocks often exacerbate existing inequalities. Further, enacting climate justice means working with communities on the frontlines of extreme climate impacts to reverse these trends.
>
> (p. 231)

As a discipline grounded in social justice principles (e.g., Evans et al., 2014), community psychologists can play a critical role in the face of devastating climate events. In recent years, there have been several calls and empirical attempts within Community Psychology to examine both the impacts of climate change and climate action – i.e., efforts to tackle climate change and its impacts – from a climate justice perspective (e.g., Barnes et al., 2022; Dobai & Riemer, 2024; Fernandes-Jesus et al., 2020; Riemer & Reich, 2011; Trott et al., 2022). In this chapter, we discuss how Community Psychology can contribute to advancing climate justice, grounded in examples of our research and praxis. While acknowledging

DOI: 10.4324/9781003480464-9

that (in)justice related to climate change can take many forms across a variety of settings and scales, we focus on the four pillars of climate justice proposed by Newell et al. (2021):

- Distributive: related to the distribution of burdens and benefits of climate change and climate action.
- Intergenerational: concerned with the obligations towards younger and future generations.
- Procedural: focused on the processes for making decisions and involving communities in such processes.
- Recognitional: related to the rights, needs, values and practices of marginalised, minoritised and underrepresented groups.

In discussing these pillars or dimensions of climate justice, we address key principles in Community Psychology, such as social justice, conscientisation, participation, liberation, power and empowerment. We also highlight critical and participatory action research as privileged methodological approaches to address climate change while striving for the wellbeing of communities across the world. Before we move to our discussion of the four pillars, it should be noted that Community Psychology approaches to climate justice are still an emergent and developing field. Rather than discussing what is missing within the field, which we recommend as further reading (see, for example, Dittmer et al., 2023; Fernandes-Jesus et al., 2020), in this chapter, we invite you to engage with some examples of research that, we believe, can help to tackle climate change while contributing to overcoming social injustices and fostering wellbeing.

Distributive justice: Climate justice from an international perspective

Climate change is a major global challenge, increasingly impacting every single country. There are, however, fundamental differences in how climate change impacts communities, raising issues related to a fair distribution of the burdens of climate change and climate action (Grasso, 2010; Islam, 2022) and the differentiated historical and current responsibilities in producing climate change (Grasso, 2010). According to the World Inequality Report, when considering both historical and current average emissions, the wealthiest countries in the world (the so-called global North) are far more responsible for climate change than the poorest countries (the so-called global South) (Chancel, 2021). Specifically, countries in the global North are responsible for around 92% of the "climate breakdown" (Hickel, 2020). Moreover, there are also inequalities within countries, including in countries in the global North, with poor and Indigenous communities in the global North experiencing significantly higher negative impacts (e.g., Islam & Winkel, 2017).

Despite contributing very little to the causes of climate change, unfairly, countries in the global South and historically underserved communities everywhere are the ones suffering the most from climate change (Babatunde, 2020; Islam, 2022). They also tend to have fewer resources and capacity to adapt to the impacts of climate change (Joshi et al., 2021). For example, the most climate-vulnerable regions (i.e., South Asia and Sub-Saharan Africa) have been allocated less climate funding (i.e., financial resources for tackling climate change), reproducing distributive injustice in adaptation funding allocation (Islam, 2022; Juhola et al., 2022). Similarly, as we have seen in the Conference of the Parties last year (COP29), the world's high-income countries (i.e., the main polluters) reject their obligation to compensate countries for economic and non-economic (e.g., displacement, loss of culture) loss and damage at the level and scale needed (Schalatek, 2024). As wellbeing is "something that is actively constituted through the interplay of personal, social and environmental processes" (Walker-Springett et al., 2017, p. 66), the increasing distributive injustices across the world (in both climate change impacts and climate action) have implications for people's health and wellbeing (Adger et al., 2022; Lawrance et al., 2022; Walinski et al., 2023). From a community perspective, climate change is drastically affecting the physical (e.g., land, water) and social living conditions of communities (e.g., displacements), which in turn is impacting their community wellbeing (Dorji et al., 2023). A critical understanding of the global dimensions of climate justice and the compound impacts of climate change on social justice and well-being is key to advancing the role of community psychology in tackling climate change. The concept of "conscientização" or conscientisation (i.e., sometimes also referred to as critical consciousness) proposed by Paulo Freire in the 1970s – and widely used within liberation and community psychology – is particularly relevant. Conscientisation can be defined as the process of learning to understand the existing social, political and economic conditions and ambiguities and to take action against the oppressive elements constraining our realities (Freire, 1974). As conscientisation requires a historical commitment (Freire, 1974), advancing distributive justice in climate change calls for critical awareness of the brutal impact of capitalism and colonialism in producing climate change and reproducing and amplifying existing inequalities (Sultana, 2022). Thus, transforming the historical and existing structures that are responsible for climate justice requires conscientisation – i.e., reflecting critically on how existing structures and systems exert oppression over people and communities. Research within community psychology has started to contribute to this, for example, by documenting how climate change impacts people's lives across the world and supporting communities in reclaiming power in the face of climate injustices (e.g., Barnwell et al., 2020; Cidade et al., 2020).

Action for learning: Viewing the world through a distributive justice lens

For this activity, we invite you to look at the distorted world maps presented in the Carbon Map, which can be found via this link: https://www.carbonmap.org/. See also Figure 7.1, for an example.

Start by exploring how the world is often seen and compare it with the actual area, population size and wealth. Then, explore what the world looks like when considering countries' responsibility for climate change regarding the extraction of fossil fuels, current emissions, consumption, historical emissions and fossil fuel reserves. Finally, examine the country sizes from a lens of "vulnerability," considering the number of people at risk and which countries are exposed to rising sea levels and poverty levels. Think about the concept of distributive justice described above. Note that distributive justice is about the distribution of burdens and benefits of climate change and climate action. What are the main contradictions in these world maps? Once you have identified a list of contradictions, select one of the most climate-vulnerable countries in the world. Write down the name of the country and reflect on the following: What (if any) social connections do you have with this country? Perhaps you were born there or have a friend living there?

Now, try to find examples of how communities (from the country you have selected) are trying to overcome existing climate injustices. Try to find a wide range of examples of actions that communities are taking. You may find some examples using the following resources:

- The EJAtlas – Global Atlas of Environmental Justice, https://ejatlas.org/
- The Transition Network, https://transitionnetwork.org/

- The Global Ecovillage Network, https://ecovillage.org/ecovillages/
- The Solidarity Economy Network, https://neweconomy.net/solidarity-economy/

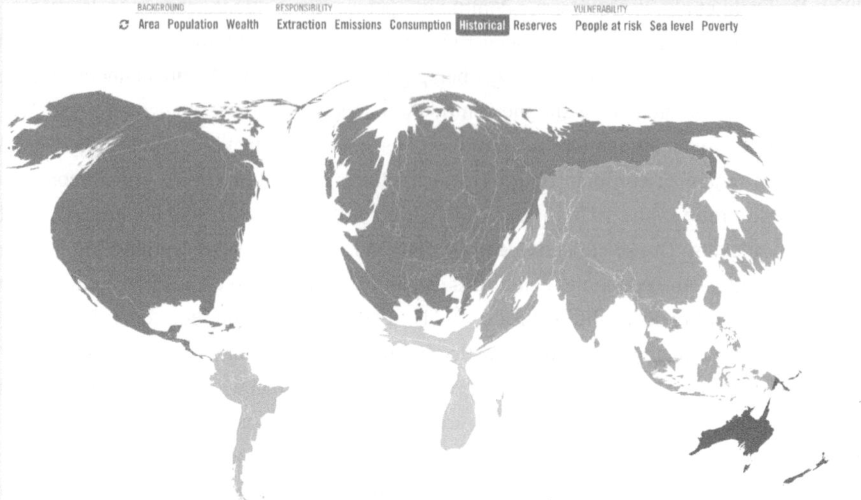

Figure 7.1 A world map showing historical CO2 emissions from energy use released between 1850 and 2011. Image retrieved from the Carbon Map.

Source: https://www.carbonmap.org/#Historical

Describe what these communities are doing. What do you think are the most promising forms of action? Now, take action in your own community. It can be anything, including writing a letter to politicians, organising a film screening or talking about distributive justice with a friend.

Intergenerational justice: Youth action towards just futures

A key dimension of climate justice is a commitment to advancing intergenerational justice. An intergenerational justice perspective recognises that generations alive today have obligations towards younger and future generations, chief among them to ensure liveable planetary conditions. Today's younger generations face disproportionate harms from climate breakdown over the course of their lives, "despite not being the ones responsible for causing it" (Piispa & Kiilakoski, 2022, p. 904). Unfortunately, despite facing uneven consequences, today's young people remain largely excluded from formal spaces of decision-making and action on climate change mitigation and adaptation (Intergovernmental Panel on Climate Change [IPCC], 2022; Thiery et al., 2021).

Aligning with the goals of intergenerational justice, the field of Community Psychology has long recognised the importance of taking young people's perspectives seriously, given the pervasiveness of adultism in family, school, community and research settings (Lam & Trott, 2024; Malafaia, 2022). Adultism refers to "the ideology of adult supremacy" (DeJong & Love, 2015, p. 490) as well as its consequences in the form of young people's subordinate position within society, their limited power to make decisions and exercise agency and their lower sociopolitical status compared to adults (Bertrand et al., 2023; DeJong & Love, 2015). When it comes to addressing the climate crisis, dominant, disempowering narratives of young people's capabilities often underlie adults' implicit or explicit disregard for their perspectives and actions (Trott, 2024a). Given the disproportionate harms faced by young people and future generations, adultism is the "insult" layered onto the "injury" of climate breakdown (Trott, 2024b).

The climate justice goal of centring the views and experiences of groups who are most impacted by climate disruption means recognising that today's young people have a critical role to play in voicing their concerns and taking action to avert catastrophic climate change. Across psychology's sub-disciplines, community psychologists have been at the forefront of research aimed at facilitating justice-driven, community-engaged work addressing the climate crisis alongside young people (Barnes, 2021; Dittmer & Riemer, 2012; Dittmer et al., 2018; Fernandes-Jesus et al., 2020; Trott, 2024c). To centre young people's perspectives, amplify their voices and catalyse their action, community psychologists have developed youth-focused programmes and partnerships in collaboration with community groups and organisations integrating arts-based, participatory and action-oriented research methods (e.g., Lam & Trott, 2022; Riemer et al., 2016).

Praxis case study: Partnering with young people in Haiti

For seven years, I [Trott] have been partnering with Jakmel Ekspresyon (JE), a community arts centre in Jacmel, Haiti that is dedicated to youth-led education and community action. To date, we have co-developed environmental programming inspired and informed by the interests of JE youth. In total, we have worked together to design, implement and evaluate four courses that integrate the arts and sciences and invite youth to investigate and address local environmental issues, ranging from access to clean water and deforestation to (plastic) pollution. Courses have incorporated youth photography, social data mapping, water quality testing and robotics design – positioning young people as co-researchers, environmental communicators and critical change agents in their communities. Two courses culminated in short documentary films screened at community events to showcase young people's accomplishments, raise awareness of critical environmental and health threats, urge action by adults and young people and prompt discussion around the need for structural and policy change. Findings from surveys and interviews conducted with JE staff and students found that JE youth were challenging dominant cultural narratives that marginalise Haiti on the world stage and marginalise young people as key actors for advancing sustainability in their communities (Trott et al., 2020b, 2024). We also worked together to develop a methodological framework that emphasises how art–science integration can be used to facilitate: (1) transdisciplinary learning, focusing on local sustainability challenges; (2) participatory process, bringing experience-based knowledge into conversation with research-based knowledge; and (3) collaborative sustainability action, inviting community members to envision and enact sustainable alternatives that are locally meaningful (Trott et al., 2020a).

As an international, interdisciplinary and intergenerational group of collaborators, we have navigated multifaceted challenges – traversing language and cultural barriers, disciplinary boundaries, differential access to resources and technology and power imbalances rooted in age, nationality and professional status. In alignment with JE's mission to be "a space of non-discrimination for all people to learn, explore and create," we have navigated these diverse challenges through open communication and a unifying commitment to the community psychology principles of collaboration and empowerment. First, our collaboration aims to "promote genuine representation and respect for all community members, and act to legitimize divergent perspectives on community and social issues" (Society for Community Research

Figure 7.2 Photography excursion at Baie de Jacmel.
Source: Photo by Larry Jean of Jakmel Ekspresyon

and Action [SCRA], 2024, "Community Inclusion and Partnership" section). Moreover, we share a commitment to collective empowerment, aiming to "support communities that have been marginalized in their efforts to gain access to resources and to participate in community decision-making" (SCRA, 2024, "Empowerment" section). For example, a particular challenge arose in the spring of 2020 when one of our planned courses – originally intended to be carried out in person and facilitated by US collaborators – required reorganisation due to pandemic-related travel restrictions. Additionally, post-program data collection via interviews – originally planned to be conducted by US collaborators – suddenly required a new approach. After discussing possible next steps collaboratively as a team, we proceeded to reformulate the course for virtual delivery and train JE staff to conduct post-program interviews. Despite the numerous challenges and interruptions posed by the pandemic, a strength of this new approach was that interviews were conducted in Haitian Creole, rather than requiring real-time translation. Moreover, JE staff obtained research training and acquired interview skills, which the team has relied upon in the years since. Looking back, it is now clear that the research training that enabled JE-led data collection positioned our team to better navigate language and cultural barriers, while also reducing power imbalances on the research team.

Like gender or race, age and nationality not only shape how climate change is experienced by different groups within society, but also, age and nationality can be sources of differential power, status and wealth that often place adults and those living in the global North in positions of relative power and privilege compared to young people and those living in the global South (Elsen & Ord, 2021). Similarly, my social identities and professional status as a White US university professor place me in a position of relative power and privilege compared to my JE collaborators. To work against these power imbalances – and ultimately to sustain and strengthen our youth-focused collaborative work for collective empowerment and climate justice – engaging in ethical, reflective practice has been critical. Drawing on Community Psychology practice competencies (SCRA, 2024), this has meant continuously working to grow in my ability to: (1) recognise ethical issues when they arise and take action to responsibly address them and (2) articulate how my values, assumptions, and life experiences influence my work with JE – and, relatedly, to continuously reflect on the strengths and limitations of my own perspective. An important ethical consideration, for example, is to ensure that the voices and perspectives of JE students and staff are accurately represented in research dissemination. Towards this goal, all empirical articles resulting from our collaboration have been co-authored with JE collaborators.

Procedural justice: Fair and meaningful participation in climate action

Climate actions generally have two main targets: mitigate the causes of climate change and/or prevent or reduce the negative impacts of climate change. Procedural climate justice "is fundamentally about processes for making decisions about the impacts of and responses to climate change that are fair, accountable, and transparent" (Newell et al., 2021, p. 4). Advocates of procedural justice emphasise the critical need for the inclusion of those most vulnerable to climate change impacts and their meaningful participation in planning, key decisions and actions aimed at preventing or reducing the negative consequences of exposure to extreme weather and other negative impacts (Haque, 2024; IPCC, 2022; Newell et al., 2021). Participation, including in environmental decision-making, has long been an important concept within Community Psychology (Culley & Hughey, 2008; Dittmer et al., 2023; Rich et al., 1995).

In addition to dealing with climate change impacts, fair and meaningful participation and accountability are also critical in the context of mitigative or sustainability actions (Dobai & Riemer, 2024). The exclusion of people with disabilities from planning and decision-making regarding public transportation or waste management planning, for example, can result in inaccessible sustainability solutions that further exacerbate existing inequalities for people with disabilities (Bevan et al., 2024). Exclusion can happen simply by not holding public engagement opportunities in accessible locations. Another example is the issue of free, prior and informed consent (FPIC) regarding land acquisition and resource extractions, especially on Indigenous territories. The production of technology-based renewable energy solutions, such as solar panels, often requires significant amounts of minerals, a majority of which are located on Indigenous territory (Owen et al., 2023). The right to self-determination principle of FPIC is central to the United Nations Declaration on the Rights of Indigenous Peoples Act and, in theory, allows Indigenous Peoples to provide or withhold/withdraw consent regarding projects that impact their territory (Office of the High Commissioner for Human Rights [OHCHR], 2007). In practice, however, this right has some limitations and is often circumvented with negative consequences for the wellbeing of the Indigenous people on that land (Kelly et al., 2024). Mandated participatory processes are often executed in a very tokenistic way and in ways that are not conducive to the engagement of equity-deserving groups (Champagne, 2020).

Praxis case study: Overcoming power challenges in municipal climate action

A core concept within community psychology that is critical to considerations of procedural justice is social power, which we will illustrate with a case study. For this purpose, we are drawing from two dimensions of power within the three-dimensional power cube model developed by Gaventa and colleagues (Gaventa, 2007; Gaventa et al., 2011): forms of power and spaces. The goal of the project in this case study was to improve procedural climate justice by working towards a decolonial approach to engaging with Black and Indigenous community members within a municipality in Southern Ontario, Canada (see Teelucksingh et al., 2026). The project was co-led by a Black and Indigenous scholar and me [Manuel], a White settler. The need the project was trying to address is that engagement strategies of municipalities are often a one-size-fits-all and are grounded in Western colonial worldviews, practices and interests. This has historically resulted in a lack of participation of Black and Indigenous community members in climate action planning and decision-making.

At the core of the project were two workshops with staff and managers from the municipality and Black and Indigenous community members. The objectives were to improve relationships and engagement between the community and the municipality and to co-design a decolonised engagement approach that shifts power from the municipality to the community. The workshops were guided by *Etuaptmumk* (Two-Eyed Seeing) approaches that braid together different knowledge systems and ways of knowing for the benefit of all. This braided approach was developed by Mi'kmaw Elder Albert Marshall to integrate Western and Indigenous perspectives into a shared vision in a culturally respectful way and facilitate cross-cultural collaboration, co-learning and co-creation, building upon the strengths of each knowledge system (Bartlett et al., 2012).

While the workshops generally went well, there were power challenges both in the planning of the workshops and in the follow-up. During the planning, for example, we were affected by the hierarchical power structure within the city, in which power is concentrated in the hands of a few powerful top managers, a form of visible power (Gaventa et al., 2011). After a few months of planning primarily with the Director of the Office of Equity, Diversity and Inclusion, who is relatively low within the municipal power structure, a top manager suddenly decided that our workshops were too high risk and that they would withdraw. While we were able to persuade them to continue, the degree to which they participated and committed to using the outcomes of the workshops was significantly reduced. We also were hoping to create a form of a neutral claimed space, which is when relatively powerless groups create new spaces rather than being invited to spaces dominated and controlled by the relatively powerful (Gaventa et al., 2011). This included involving community groups in the planning of the workshops. Yet, over the course of the planning process, the municipality used their hidden power to control the conditions of the workshop. Hidden forms of power are used by the relatively powerful "to maintain their power and privilege by creating barriers to participation, by excluding key issues from the public arena, or by controlling politics 'backstage'" (Gaventa et al., 2011, p. 11). Examples in this case included influencing the date and format of the workshop, who should be invited and not, and what the nature of the participation for the municipal staff would be (i.e., listening only rather than committing to engage with the outcomes of the workshops). This significantly delayed our workshops and resulted in some community members no longer being interested. It also shaped the workshops more towards a format that was more geared towards the municipal staff. Despite these challenges, the workshops resulted in some good ideas for an engagement process grounded in a two-eyed seeing approach, and the community members were eager to continue working on this engagement framework. The top manager of the municipality, however, decided to withdraw from any further engagement with the community and stated they would engage with the communities on their own terms in the future, keeping the current power relations, using once again their visible power to do so.

Recognition justice: Acknowledging differences within communities

Recognition justice focuses on recognising the rights, needs, values and practices of marginalised, minority and underrepresented groups (Whyte, 2011). Recognition justice is often relevant to issues affecting First Nations, Indigenous and other ethnic minorities. However, recognition injustice also extends to gender, class, culture and language and, importantly, misrecognising local ways of knowing (Benjaminsen & Svarstad, 2021). Misrecognition has often resulted in harm or unintended consequences for local communities. For example, reforestation initiatives for carbon sequestration in Africa have displaced people who use that land for their livelihoods (Massarella et al., 2020) and reinforced neo-colonial dependency between the global North (who typically fund these initiatives) and African countries (Macia et al., 2023). Similarly, a South African fishing regulation to conserve aquatic fish and shellfish stocks through licensing has resulted in criminalising First Nations groups who responsibly foraged for fish and shellfish (Mbhele, 2024). Importantly, and linked with procedural justice, because First Nations and Indigenous communities' values and practices are undervalued, disrespected or located in Western legal frameworks, their voices and concerns are often excluded from decision-making.

Several definitions of recognition justice exist (see, for example, Van Uffelen, 2022). However, we will identify a few characteristics of recognition justice that may be useful for this discussion. Recognition justice focuses on *difference*, namely that there are differences between different groups, and it is important to incorporate those differences in climate justice initiatives (Whyte, 2017). Second, recognition justice encourages us to focus on understanding *local* contexts, actors and dynamics. Indigenous scholars encourage us to appreciate differences in dynamics and processes even between First Nation groups. Western scholars tend to simplify indigeneity, but it is important to recognise and appreciate local nuances and political dynamics in climate justice within minority groups. Minority leaders may themselves be pro-extractivist or be complicit with problematic development initiatives. It is important, therefore, to not only understand local dynamics but also hold traditional leaders accountable (Whyte, 2017). Recognition justice also extends to misrecognising people's relationships with the natural world, especially when marginalised are constructed as harmful to nature, for example, in some conservation models (Martin et al., 2016).

Third, recognition justice can refer to both structural injustices (for example, legal frameworks and governance structures that are not sensitive to marginalised groups) and *discourse* (Benjaminsen & Svarstad, 2021). Often, misrecognition is embedded in moral hierarchies of being (some groups are superior to others, and humans are superior to the natural world). Discourses shape rights and entitlements, including who can speak, what they can speak about and under what conditions. For example, African women youth climate activists' voices are often undermined based on assumptions about their youth (they are too young to know), their gender (they are overly emotional) and geopolitical location (they should stick to local African issues because they cannot speak about global climate change) (Barnes, 2024a). Similarly, the discursive "promotion" of climate change as a cause of mass displacement in Syria may lead to the obfuscation of age-old structural underpinnings of conflict in those areas (Benjaminsen & Svarstad, 2021).

Praxis case study: Grassroot resistance in Eastern Cape province of South Africa

A current project focuses on the climate and environmental resistance in the biodiverse yet poverty-stricken northern part of the Eastern Cape province of South Africa. I [Barnes] have ancestral roots among the traditional amaMpondo people in the area, and it was the last part of South Africa to be officially colonised in 1894. Communities are currently resisting several separate threats: prospective titanium mining, prospective exploration of natural gas in the seabed, the construction of a national road that cuts through a biodiverse-rich area and, more recently, the construction of a luxury tourist lodge to bring in wealthy tourists, which will restrict community access to public spaces (Mbuthuma, 2022). The project explores historical land and environmental dispossession with current activism (see Barnes, 2024b). The communities are divided about these projects. Some people believe that the projects will bring much-needed income into the area. Others are firmly against the projects, given the history of exploitation of the area and the dubious history of some of the proposed developers and development projects in the area. Those opposed point out that these projects will have negative impacts on biodiversity and ancestral sites, climate adaptation and there is a low likelihood that the projects will make a difference to poverty. They also promote alternative development models, such as eco-tourism, as there is already a growing tourist hiking industry focusing on eco and cultural tourism, including overnight homestays in traditional dwellings. Local traditional authorities are often overlooked and have been largely ineffective in opposing the developments in the face of strong support from government authorities. Amidst legal battles, particularly about poor consultation and the enshrining of communities' rights to say no, there has also been violent intimidation of those resisting, including the murder of one activist (Healy, 2022).

In addition to contestation about distribution and procedural justice, there have also been several examples of misrecognition, including flawed environmental assessments that ignored how ancestral and cultural heritage is inherently co-constituted with local ecology. For example, the assessments of natural gas exploration in the sea misrecognised the fact that the sea is not just about the aquatic ecosystem but also holds immense spiritual value for amaMpondo (Mbuthuma, 2022). The development projects overlooked local dynamics, including divisions within communities about the projects. The projects also misrecognised the history of oppression and land dispossession through colonisation and apartheid, which forms an important part of ecological and political consciousness in the communities. For example, many families, including my own ancestors, were forcibly displaced to build a casino and golf resort in the 1970s, and reparations for the displacement have not been fully resolved (Makhaye & Mkhize, 2021; Beinart, 2021). A good example of misrecognition occurred when developers of the proposed local luxury tourist lodge diverted footpaths allegedly so that tourists would not see local people as they traversed the landscape (see Transkei Stories, 2024). This seemingly innocuous intervention misrecognised the spiritual and cultural role of footpaths linking villages and places of spiritual importance.

Social justice and wellbeing in the context of climate change

Throughout this chapter, we have described four pillars of climate justice that are key to research and action within Community Psychology: distributive, intergenerational, procedural and recognitional. While we have presented these pillars separately, they are intrinsically linked. For example, some scholars argue that to be useful, distributive and procedural justice should be underpinned by recognition justice (e.g., Whyte, 2011). It is important to recognise and respectfully understand marginalised groups' relationships with the environment if we are to consider the distribution of climate hazards and their participation in decision-making. Also, in general, it is assumed that processes rooted in procedural justice principles lead to more equitable and fair outcomes, such as distributive justice (Haque, 2024).

Likewise, research that attends to the intergenerational dimensions of climate disruption can map onto the full range of the aforementioned pillars of justice. Working alongside young people to facilitate youth-led climate decision-making and action can advance procedural justice, while taking seriously young people's specific needs and diverse perspectives and working to redress their heightened vulnerabilities and risks are forms of recognition and distributive justice, respectively.

As the climate crisis intensifies, research and action for climate justice will become even more pressing. Community Psychology, particularly in its critical and decolonial forms (Sonn et al., 2024; Watkins, 2019), has the conceptual and methodological tools to advance climate justice by focusing on distributive, intergenerational, procedural and recognition aspects. The commitment to social justice (e.g., Evans et al., 2014), strong focus on the role of context, and preference for systems thinking approaches (Lawlor & Metta, 2023) place Community Psychology in a privileged position to contribute to forwarding social justice and community wellbeing in times of climate change. Rather than focusing merely on individual responses to climate change (e.g., pro-environmental behaviour) as mainstream psychology still tends to do (e.g., for a detailed critique see Adams, 2021), Community Psychology highlights the role of communities in tackling climate change and the processes of resistance and empowerment that are crucial for building transformative and just climate futures (Fernandes-Jesus et al., 2020; Barnes et al., 2022). By acknowledging the importance of looking at individual and psychological processes – embedded and influenced by social structures and oppressive forces – community psychologists can complement existing approaches to climate justice in other fields and disciplines (e.g., human geography, sociology). Community Psychology's transdisciplinary nature (Stark, 2012) can also help to cross disciplinary boundaries and bring academics, practitioners, activists and local communities closer together. For example, community psychologists can work alongside communities towards their liberation by supporting, making sense of, and engaging with critical action in their communities (e.g., Barnwell et al., 2020). They can collaborate with policymakers to incorporate climate justice principles into climate adaptation and mitigation measures (e.g., Teelucksingh et al., 2026). They can facilitate inclusive decision-making processes that ensure that marginalised communities and young generations are included in decision-making processes and that their experiences and needs are not disregarded (e.g., Trott et al., 2020b, 2024). Finally, they can practise accompaniment – i.e., "to create an ethics of being alongside of, of learning together, of acting in solidarity and co-shouldering necessary risks" (Watkins, 2019, p. 2) – by working towards solidarity with those most affected by climate injustices. This "action-orientation" nature of Community Psychology research deserves to be highlighted as a distinctive element from other disciplines and subdisciplines. In fact, Community Psychology's preference for "research with rather than on" communities is still a marginal approach. As we have demonstrated via our praxis case studies, working with communities using participatory action research methods has the potential to facilitate climate justice while increasing people's awareness, empowerment and engagement with climate change (e.g., Trott et al., 2020b, 2024).

The examples presented and discussed throughout the chapter illustrate how Community Psychology can contribute towards climate justice and community wellbeing. With these examples, we hope to have offered some concrete directions on how to foster climate justice locally, nationally and internationally by applying community principles and values to our attempts to tackle climate change and build more just and healthier climate futures. One does not have to identify as a community psychologist to follow such approaches. Indeed, action-orientation and participatory methodologies can be helpful for everyone who seeks to work with communities in facilitating climate justice (e.g., activists, eco-psychologists, community organisers, social workers, etc.).

Reflective questions

Based on what has been discussed in this chapter, we now invite you to reflect on the following:

- How is climate change changing your community?
- How is climate change related to social inequality?
- What are the four pillars of climate justice? Choose two pillars and provide examples of what climate injustice might look like where you live. For each pillar, what can be done to advance climate justice?
- How does climate action impact underserved communities in your country?
- In what ways can community psychologists contribute to climate change policy and action?
- Imagine a future where climate justice prevails. How would you describe such a future?

References

Adams, M. (2021). Critical psychologies and climate change. *Current Opinion in Psychology*, *42*, 13–18. https://doi.org/10.1016/j.copsyc.2021.01.007

Adger, W. N., Barnett, J., Heath, S., & Jarillo, S. (2022). Climate change affects multiple dimensions of well-being through impacts, information and policy responses. *Nature Human Behaviour*, *6*(11), 1465–1473. https://doi.org/10.1038/s41562-022-01467-8

Babatunde, E. O. (2020). Distributive justice in the age of climate change. *Canadian Journal of Law & Jurisprudence*, *33*(2), 263–292. https://doi.org/10.1017/cjlj.2020.13

Barnes, B. R. (2021). Reimagining African women youth climate activism: The case of Vanessa Nakate. *Sustainability*, *13*(23), 13214. https://doi.org/10.3390/su132313214

Barnes, B. R. (2024a). Racism and youth climate activism: What can we learn from racism allegations about the image exclusions of black women activists? In J. O'Connor (Ed.), *The handbook of youth activism* (pp. 196–209). Edward Elgar.

Barnes, B. R. (2024b). Colonial constructions of friendship and land dispossession: Implications for contemporary land and environmental defending. In C. Sonn, J. Siham Fernandes, J. Ferreira Moura Jr., M. Eviandaru Madyaningrum, & N. Malherbe (Eds.), *Handbook of decolonial community psychology* (pp. 337–353). Springer.

Barnes, B. R., Barnwell, G., & Hendricks, L. (2022). Psychology, environment and climate change: Foregrounding justice (part one). *Psychology in Society*, *63*, 1–5. https://doi.org/10.57157/pins2022Vol63iss1a5438

Barnwell, G. C., Stroud, L., & Watson, M. (2020). 'Nothing green can grow without being on the land': Mine-affected communities' psychological experiences of ecological degradation and resistance in Rustenburg, South Africa. *Community Psychology in Global Perspective*, *6*(2), 87–109. https://doi.org/10.1285/i24212113v6i2-2p87

Bartlett, C., Marshall, M., & Marshall, A. (2012). Two-eyed seeing and other lessons learned within a co-learning journey of bringing together indigenous and mainstream knowledges and ways of knowing. *Journal of Environmental Studies and Sciences*, *2*, 331–340. https://doi.org/0.1007/s13412-012-0086-8

Beinart, W. (2021). Restitution and land rights in the Eastern Cape: The Hlolweni, Mgungundlovu and Xolobeni cases. In W. Beinart, R. Kingwell, & G. Kapps (Eds.), *Land, law and chiefs in rural South Africa: Contested histories and current struggles* (pp. 247–265). Wits University Press.

Benjaminsen, T. A., & Svarstad, H. (2021). Recognising recognition in climate justice. *IDS Bulletin*, *53*(4), 1–18. https://doi.org/10.19088/1968–2022.136

Bertrand, M., Brooks, M. D., & Domínguez, A. D. (2023). Challenging adultism: Centering youth as educational decision makers. *Urban Education*, *58*(10), 2570–2597. https://doi.org/10.1177/004208592095913

Bevan, A., Buettgen, A., Riemer, M., Spadafore, B., Scanlon, H., & Whitney, S. (2024). *Operationalizing accessibility in environmental sustainability efforts: Challenges, barriers, and opportunities* [manuscript submitted for publication]. Viessman Centre for Engagement and Research in Sustainability, Wilfrid Laurier University.

Champagne, D. (2020). Urban sustainability policies in neoliberal Canada: Room for social equity? *Current Sociology*, *68*(6), 761–779. https://doi.org/10.1177/0011392119892668

Chancel, L. (2021). *Climate change and the global inequality of carbon emissions 1990–2020*. World Inequality Lab Study. https://wid.world/document/summary-of-climate-change-the-global-inequality-of-carbon-emissions-1990-2020-study-world-inequality-lab-working-paper-2021-21/

Cidade, C. E., Junior, F. M. J., & Ximenes, M. V. (2020). Impacts of climate change on rural poverty in the Brazilian Northeast and South. *Community Psychology in Global Perspective*, *6*(2/2), 124–138. https://doi.org/10.1285/i24212113v6i2-2p125

Copernicus Climate Change Service (C3S). (2025). *Copernicus: 2024 is the first year to exceed 1.5°C above pre-industrial level*. Global Climate Highlights. https://climate.copernicus.eu/copernicus-2024-first-year-exceed-15degc-above-pre-industrial-level

Culley, M. R., & Hughey, J. (2008). Power and public participation in a hazardous waste dispute: A community case study. *American Journal of Community Psychology*, *41*(1–2), 99–114. https://doi.org/10.1007/s10464-007-9157-5

DeJong, K., & Love, B. J. (2015). Youth oppression as a technology of colonialism: Conceptual frameworks and possibilities for social justice education praxis. *Equity & Excellence in Education*, *48*(3), 489–508. https://doi.org/10.1080/10665684.2015.1057086

Dittmer, L. D., Mugagga, F., Metternich, A., Schweizer-Ries, P., Asiimwe, G., & Riemer, M. (2018). We can keep the fire burning: Building action competence through environmental justice education in Uganda and Germany. *Local Environment*, *23*(2), 144–157. https://doi.org/10.1080/13549839.2017.1391188

Dittmer, L. D., & Riemer, M. (2012). Fostering critical thinking about climate change: Applying community psychology to an environmental education project with youth. *Global Journal of Community Psychology Practice*, *4*(1), 1–12.

Dittmer, L. D., Reimer-Watts, K., Dobai, J., & Riemer, M. (2023). Contributions, missed opportunities, and future directions: A critical reflection on global climate change and environmental sustainability in *AJCP* over five decades. *American Journal of Community Psychology*, *72*(3–4), 288–301. https://doi.org/10.1002/ajcp.12720

Dobai, J., & Riemer, M. (2024). Closing the equity deficit: Sustainability justice in municipal climate action planning in Waterloo region. *American Journal of Community Psychology*, *73*(1–2), 118–132. https://doi.org/10.1002/ajcp.12675

Dorji, T., Morrison-Saunders, A., & Blake, D. (2023). Understanding how community wellbeing is affected by climate change: Evidence from a systematic literature review. *Environmental Management*, *72*, 568–586. https://doi.org/10.1007/s00267-023-01833-w

Elsen, F., & Ord, J. (2021). The role of adults in "youth led" climate groups: Enabling empowerment. *Frontiers in Political Science*, *3*, 641154. https://doi.org/10.3389/fpos.2021.641154

Evans, S. D., Rosen, A. D., & Nelson, G. (2014). Community psychology and social justice. In C. V. Johnson, H. L. Friedman, J. Diaz, Z. Franco, & B. K. Nastasi (Eds.), *The Praeger handbook of social justice and psychology: Fundamental issues and special populations; Well-being and professional issues; Youth and disciplines in psychology* (pp. 143–163). Praeger/ABC-CLIO.

Fernandes-Jesus, M., Barnes, B., & Diniz, R. D. (2020). Communities reclaiming power and social justice in the face of climate change. *Community Psychology in Global Perspective*, *6*(2/2), 1–21. https://doi.org/10.1285/I24212113V6I2-2P1

Freire, P. (1974). Conscientisation. *CrossCurrents*, *24*(1), 23–31. https://www.jstor.org/stable/24457877?seq=2

Gaventa, J. (2007). 12 levels, spaces and forms of power: Analysing opportunities for change. In F. Berenskoetter & M. J. Williams (Eds.), *Power in world politics* (pp. 204–224). Routledge.

Gaventa, J., Pettit, J., & Cornish, L. (2011). *Power pack, understanding power for social change*. Institute for Developmental Studies. https://www.powercube.net/wp-content/uploads/2011/04/powerpack-web-version-2011.pdf

Grasso, M. (2010). An ethical approach to climate adaptation finance. *Global Environmental Change*, *20*(1), 74–81. https://doi.org/10.1016/j.gloenvcha.2009.10.006

Haque, M. A. (2024). Conceptualizing climate justice. *Journal of Climate Policy*, *3*(1), 12–30. https://doi.org/10.47941/jcp.1625

Healy, H. (2022). Struggle for the sands of Xolobeni–From post-colonial environmental injustice to crisis of democracy. *Geoforum*, *133*, 128–139.

Hickel, J. (2020). Quantifying national responsibility for climate breakdown: An equality-based attribution approach for carbon dioxide emissions in excess of the planetary boundary. *The Lancet Planetary Health*, *4*(9), e399–e404. https://doi.org/10.1016/S2542-5196(20)30196-0

Intergovernmental Panel on Climate Change (IPCC). (2022). Summary for policymakers – Climate -change 2022: Impacts, adaptation and vulnerability. In H. O. Pörtner, D. C. Roberts, M. Tignor, E. S. Poloczanska, K. Mintenbeck, A. Alegría, M. Craig, S. Langsdorf, S. Löschke, V. Möller, A. Okem, & B. Rama (Eds.), *Contribution of working group II to the sixth assessment report of the intergovernmental panel on climate change*. Cambridge University Press. https://doi.org/10.1017/9781009325844.001

Islam, M. M. (2022). Distributive justice in global climate finance – Recipients' climate vulnerability and the allocation of climate funds. *Global Environmental Change*, *73*, 102475. https://doi.org/10.1016/j.gloenvcha.2022.102475

Islam, S. W., & Winkel, J. (2017). *Climate change and social inequality. DESA Working Paper No. 152.* Department of Economic and Social Affairs. https://www.un.org/esa/desa/papers/2017/wp152_2017.pdf

Joshi, A., Chappin, E., & Doorn, N. (2021). Does distributive justice improve welfare outcomes in climate adaptation? An exploration using an agent-based model of a stylized social–environmental system. *Sustainability*, *13*(22), 12648. https://doi.org/10.3390/su132212648

Juhola, S., Heikkinen, M., Pietilä, T., Groundstroem, F., & Käyhkö, J. (2022). Connecting climate justice and adaptation planning: An adaptation justice index. *Environmental Science & Policy*, *136*, 609–619. https://doi.org/10.1016/j.envsci.2022.07.024

Kelly, S., Heiret, Y. S., Guerra-Schleef, F., Fajardo Mazorra, A., Lorini Formiga, N., Acosta-Rodríguez, S., & Greenleaf, M. (2024). Epistemic justice as energy justice: Reflections from a transnational collaboration on hydropower and Indigenous rights. *Climate and Development*, 1–14. https://doi.org/10.1080/17565529.2024.2369608

Lam, S., & Trott, C. D. (2022). Children's climate change meaning-making through photovoice: Empowering children to learn, care, and act through participatory process. *Educação, Sociedade & Culturas*, *62*, 1–25. https://doi.org/10.24840/esc.vi62.478

Lam, S., & Trott, C. D. (2024). Intergenerational solidarities for climate healing: The case for critical methodologies and decolonial research practices. *Children's Geographies*, 1–10. http://dx.doi.org/10.1080/14733285.2023.2301546

Lawlor, J. A., & Metta, K. R. (2023). From parts to whole: Embracing systems science in community psychology. *American Journal of Community Psychology*, *72*(3–4), 366–377. https://doi.org/10.1002/ajcp.12711

Lawrance, E. L., Thompson, R., Newberry Le Vay, J., Page, L., & Jennings, N. (2022). The impact of climate change on mental health and emotional wellbeing: A narrative review of current evidence, and its implications. *International Review of Psychiatry*, *34*(5), 443–498. https://doi.org/10.1080/09540261.2022.2128725

Macia, E., Allouche, J., Sagna, M. B., Diallo, A. H., Boëtsch, G., Guisse, A., Sarr, P., Cesaro, J. D, & Duboz, P. (2023). The great green wall in Senegal: Questioning the idea of acceleration through the conflicting temporalities of politics and nature among the Sahelian populations. *Ecology and Society, 28*(1), art31. https://doi.org/10.5751/ES-13937-280131

Makhaye, C., & Mkhize, N. (2021, September 9). The battle for the ground Sol Kerzner used for Wild Coast Sun is still raging. *Daily Maverick.* https://www.dailymaverick.co.za/article/2021-09-09-the-battle-for-the-ground-sol-kerzner-used-for-wild-coast-sun-is-still-raging/

Malafaia, C. (2022). 'Missing school isn't the end of the world (actually, it might prevent it)': Climate activists resisting adult power, repurposing privileges and reframing education. *Ethnography and Education, 17*(4), 421–440. https://doi.org/10.1080/17457823.2022.2123248

Martin, A., Coolsaet, B., Corbera, E., Dawson, N. M., Fraser, J. A., Lehmann, I., & Rodriguez, I. (2016). Justice and conservation: The need to incorporate recognition. *Biological Conservation, 197*, 254–261. http://dx.doi.org/10.1016/j.biocon.2016.03.021

Massarella, K., Sallu, S. M., & Ensor, J. E. (2020). Reproducing injustice: Why recognition matters in conservation project evaluation. *Global Environmental Change, 65*, 102181. https://doi.org/10.1016/j.gloenvcha.2020.102181

Mbhele, S. (2024, October 17). Local fishing communities struggle against exclusion and ocean industrialization. *Mail and Guardian.* https://mg.co.za/thought-leader/2024-10-17-local-fishing-communities-struggle-against-exclusion-and-ocean-industrialisation/

Mbuthuma, N. (2022). Resisting extractivist development. *New Agenda: South African Journal of Social and Economic Policy, 83*, 90–94. https://hdl.handle.net/10520/ejc-nagenda_v2022_n83_a18

National Centers for Environmental Information (NOAA). (2024). 2024 was the warmest year in the modern temperature record. https://www.climate.gov/news-features/featured-images/2023-was-warmest-year-modern-temperature-record

Newell, P., Srivastava, S., Naess, L. O., Torres Contreras, G. A., & Price, R. (2021). Toward transformative climate justice: An emerging research agenda. *Wiley Interdisciplinary Reviews: Climate Change, 12*(6), e733. https://doi.org/10.1002/wcc.733

Office of the High Commissioner for Human Rights (OHCHR). (2007). United Nations declaration on the rights of indigenous peoples. https://www.ohchr.org/sites/default/files/Documents/Publications/Declaration_indigenous_en.pdf

Owen, J. R., Kemp, D., Lechner, A. M., Harris, J., Zhang, R., & Lèbre, É. (2023). Energy transition minerals and their intersection with land-connected peoples. *Nature Sustainability, 6*(2), 203–211. https://doi.org/10.1038/s41893-022-00994-6

Piispa, M., & Kiilakoski, T. (2022). Towards climate justice? Young climate activists in Finland on fairness and moderation. *Journal of Youth Studies, 25*(7), 897–912. http://dx.doi.org/10.1080/13676261.2021.1923677

Rich, R. C., Edelstein, M., Hallman, W. K., & Wandersman, A. H. (1995). Citizen participation and empowerment: The case of local environmental hazards. *American Journal of Community Psychology, 23*(5), 657–676. https://doi.org/10.1007/BF02506986

Riemer, M., & Reich, S. M. (2011). Community psychology and global climate change: Introduction to the special section. *American Journal of Community Psychology, 47*(3–4), 349–353. https://doi.org/10.1007/s10464-010-9397-7

Riemer, M., Voorhees, C., Dittmer, L., Alisat, S., Alam, N., Sayal, R., Bidisha, S. H., De Souza, A., Lynes, J., Metternich, A., Mugagga, F., & Schweizer-Ries, P. (2016). The youth leading environmental change project: A mixed-method longitudinal study across six countries. *Ecopsychology, 8*(3), 174–187. https://doi.org/10.1089/eco.2016.0025

Schalatek, L. (2024, November 22). COP29: Is the loss and damage fund becoming an empty promise? *Heinrich Boll Stiftung.* https://www.boell.de/en/2024/11/22/cop29-loss-and-damage-fund-becoming-empty-promise

Society for Community Research and Action (SCRA). (2024). *Community psychology practice competencies.* https://scra27.org/resources/practitioners/community-psychology-practice-competencies/

Sonn, C., Fernández, J., Moura, J. F., Madyaningrum, M. E., & Mallberbe, N. (2024). *Handbook of decolonial community psychology*. Community Psychology book series, Springer.

Stark, W. (2012). Community psychology as a linking science potentials and challenges for transdisciplinary competencies. *Global Journal of Community Psychology Practice*, *3*(1), 42–49. http://dx.doi.org/10.17161/gjcpp.v3i1.20880

Sultana, F. (2022). The unbearable heaviness of climate coloniality. The unbearable heaviness of climate coloniality. *Political Geography*, *99*, 102638. https://doi.org/10.1016/j.polgeo.2022.102638

Teelucksingh, C., Riemer, M., & Sioui, M. (2026). *Decolonizing and Transforming the Engagement of Indigenous and Black People Within Municipal Planning* – Lessons Learned. Action Research, 0(0). https://doi.org/10.1177/14767503261461952.

The Carbon Map. (2025). *Historical responsibility*. https://www.carbonmap.org/#Historical

Thiery, W., Lange, S., Rogelj, J., Schleussner, F., Gudmundsson, L., Seneviratne, S. I., Andrijevic, M., Frieler, K., Emanuel, K., Geiger, T., Bresch, D. N., Zhao, F., Willner, S. N., Büchner, M., Volkholz, J., Bauer, N., Chang, J., Ciais, P., Dury, M., ... Wada, Y. (2021). Intergenerational inequities in exposure to climate extremes. *Science*, *374*(6564), 158–160. https://doi.org/10.1126/science.abi7339

Transkei Stories. (2024). *Two ears & One mouth – Conflict on the wild coast about the Gwe Gwe Beach lodge development. Documentary* [Video]. Youtube.. https://www.youtube.com/watch?v=irtpgElZFMA

Trott, C. D. (2024a). Ambivalent adultism: Theorizing hostile and benevolent adultism as barriers to intergenerational climate justice [Manuscript submitted for publication]. *PsyArXiv*. https://doi.org/10.31234/osf.io/p9t8u

Trott, C. D. (2024b). "It can't just be the younger people": Exploring youth activists' perspectives on intergenerational solidarities for climate justice. *Journal of Community & Applied Social Psychology*, *34*(6), e70001. https://doi.org/10.1002/casp.70001

Trott, C. D. (2024c). Rewriting the climate story with youth climate justice activists. *Geographical Research*. https://doi.org/10.1111/1745–5871.12662

Trott, C. D., Even, T. L., & Frame, S. (2020a). Merging the arts and sciences for collaborative sustainability action: A methodological framework. *Sustainability Science*, *15*(4), 1067–1085. https://doi.org/10.1007/s11625-020-00798-7

Trott, C. D., Reimer-Watts, K., & Riemer, M. (2022). In pursuit of a practical utopia: Transitioning towards climate justice. In C. Kagan, R. Lawthom, M. Richards, J. Alfaro, A. Zambrano, & J. Akhurst (Eds.), *The Routledge international handbook of community psychology: Facing global crises with hope*. Taylor & Francis. https://doi.org/10.4324/9780429325663-19

Trott, C. D., Rockett, M. L., Gray, E., Lam, S., Even, T. L., & Frame, S. M. (2020b). "Another Haiti starting from the youth": Integrating the arts and sciences for empowering youth climate justice action in Jacmel, Haiti. *Community Psychology in Global Perspective*, *6*(2), 48–70. https://doi.org/10.1285/i24212113v6i2-2p48

Trott, C. D., Weinberg, A. E., Frame, S. M., Jean-Pierre, P., & Even, T. L. (2024). Civic science education for youth-driven water security: A behavioral development approach to strengthening climate resilience. *International Journal of Behavioral Development*, *48*(2), 145–155. https://doi.org/10.1177/01650254231188661

Van Uffelen, N. (2022). Revisiting recognition in energy justice. *Energy Research & Social Science*, *92*, 102764. https://doi.org/10.1016/j.erss.2022.102764

Vestby, J., Schutte, S., Tollefsen, A. F., & Buhaug, H. (2024). Societal determinants of flood-induced displacement. *Proceedings of the National Academy of Sciences*, *121*(3), e2206188120. https://doi.org/10.1073/pnas.2206188120

Walinski, A., Sander, J., Gerlinger, G., Clemens, V., Meyer-Lindenberg, A., & Heinz, A. (2023). The effects of climate change on mental health. *Deutsches Arzteblatt international, 120*(8), 117–124. https://doi.org/10.3238/arztebl.m2022.0403

Walker-Springett, K., Butler, C., & Adger, W. N. (2017). Wellbeing in the aftermath of floods. *Health & Place*, *43*, 66–74. https://doi.org/10.1016/j.healthplace.2016.11.005

Watkins, M. (2019). Toward a decolonial approach to psychosocial accompaniment from the "Outside". In G. Stevens & C. Sonn (Eds.), *Decoloniality, knowledge production and epistemic justice in contemporary community psychology*. Springer.

Whyte, K. (2017). The recognition paradigm of environmental injustice. In R. Holifield, J. Chakraborty, & G. Walker (Eds.), *The Routledge handbook of environmental justice* (pp. 113–123). Routledge.

Whyte, K. P. (2011). The recognition dimensions of environmental justice in Indian country. *Environmental Justice*, *4*(4), 199–205. https://doi.org/10.1089/env.2011.003

8 Climate community profiling by children and youth

Fostering collective (political) hope in community contexts

Isabel Menezes, Clementina Rios, Sofia C. Pais and Pedro D. Ferreira

Introduction

Environmental issues have been at the core of citizens' concerns for many decades, highlighting, in particular, the injustices and environmental vulnerabilities that lead to the destruction of ecosystems, the occurrence of natural disasters, and the extinction of species (Cutter-Mackenzie & David, 2019). Furthermore, socio-environmental injustices profoundly affect the lives and livelihoods of the most vulnerable and disadvantaged populations, as well as the future of coming generations. Examples include the unequal distribution of and access to natural and economic resources (Agyeman et al., 2016), the increase in climate change refugees (Bates, 2002), the proliferation of new diseases and viruses resulting from exposure to unsanitary environments (Aronsson et al., 2015) and the destruction of ecosystems (Kopnina, 2016). These injustices involve the domination and oppression of both human and non-human beings, influenced by geo-cultural and political contexts, as well as issues related to gender, age, race and species (Kopnina, 2016; Bell & Russell, 2000) and have extraordinary implications on the lives of future generations.

Not surprisingly, young people, now and in the past, are at the forefront of the fight for environmental causes. From opposition to nuclear power – in the 1980s, a Portuguese rock song by Lena d'Água & Atlântida urged that it was "better to be active today than radioactive tomorrow" (1982, author's translation) – to Fridays for Future (2025), children and young people have made a considerable effort to draw attention to the potentially disastrous consequences of environmental deterioration and climate change. However, not only is the level of transformation needed for actual change to occur paramount, but adults seem unaware and unable to change: far from recognising the political significance of young people's activism, their position, political leaders included, has been patronising and ignorant at best.

Therefore, the impacts of conversations and political mobilisation about the environment and climate change frequently disempower young people. Jones and Davison (2021) stress some unintended consequences, such as feeling overwhelmed and helpless, daunted by the future, between anxiety, loss and hope, while also experiencing an imbalance of power that results in feeling betrayed by previous generations. It is important to understand that emotions are not a by-product of human engagement with social and political phenomena, but are at the core of knowing the world (Damásio, 2022), intertwined with cognition (Todd et al., 2020); politics is not an exception (e.g., Anson, 2018; Marcus, 2000, 2002).

However inevitable, this emotionality is used to devalue and belittle the political significance of youth activists' calls for action. This is not a new strategy; Ryan (1972) has named this phenomenon "blaming the victim," a way of making people affected by injustice appear as guilty of their misfortune;

DOI: 10.4324/9781003480464-10

it is also a sign of the tendency to medicalise social life (Pais et al., 2016). In other words, the vulnerabilities of those already in a social, economic or even health fragility situation are accentuated. An illustrative example comes from the relatively extensive literature on eco-depression, eco-anger and, especially, eco-anxiety that underlies connections with mental health and psychological distress (Cosh et al., 2024), an issue that seems to affect young people across the globe (Hickman et al., 2021).

Nevertheless, as in other areas of political participation (Vasilopoulos, 2018; Wlodarczyk et al., 2017), emotions such as fear, anger and hope play differential roles in individual and collective action, with "anger as a key adaptive emotional driver of engagement with the climate crisis" (Stanley et al., 2021, p1). As such, it is essential to recognise that emotions are at the core of civic and political engagement and participation – now as in the past (Jasper, 2014) – but also that, as stated by Michael Walzer (2002, p. 617), "passionate intensity has a legitimate place in the social world." At the same time, it is vital to create public spaces where controversies, opposing and emotionally charged ideas, can be openly shared, discussed and scrutinised because diversity and pluralism are inevitable in communities and underpin democratic life (Arendt, 1950/1995; Giddens, 1997; Habermas, 1999; Jost, 2006; Marcus, 2002; Nussbaum, 2013).

The relevance of involving young people in these public spaces is evident, as future generations will be most affected by climate change and should have a say in imagining our shared future. The inevitability of climate change calls for communities to identify and confront the local implications of these changes and start considering possible actionable solutions for the problems ahead. Youth movements for climate change have been challenging intergenerational injustice by criticising adult structures and taking politically interventionist positions (Biswas & Mattheis, 2021). They contest the normative thinking that only adults have the power to act politically, and they demonstrate indignation and a willingness to act for the transformation and sustainability of the Earth. This environmental agency is the most positive and hopeful sign for the future of all Earth's beings.

In this chapter, we will illustrate how young people can genuinely and productively be involved in co-creating and co-designing actionable solutions for transformative adaptation to climate change using a combination of participatory action research and "community profiling" in a project with middle and secondary schools in Portugal's Norte Region.

"Community profiling" through community-based participatory action research

"Community profiling" is a research and intervention strategy that was initially implemented in community development to engage local inhabitants in identifying existing resources and needs and creating an action plan to improve the quality of life of their community (Francescato et al., 2002; Hawtin et al., 1998). Since the early 2000s, Italian community psychologists have used community profiling with a stronger emphasis on community engagement in data collection, analysis and discussion while broadening the profile to include different dimensions: territorial, demographic, economic, service, institutional, anthropological, psychological and future (Francescato, 2000; Gelli et al., 2004). While there are obvious links with typical participatory action research, community profiling is distinctive in its focus on the local community; it is a participatory action research project based on the community to create a "profile" of its present characteristics, including both existing "problems" and "resources," but emphasising temporality with a view on the history of the community, but also on imagining how it can become in the future. In fact, the emphasis on the future profile is a distinctive feature of community profiling that opens opportunities for fostering political imagination. Making possible, for better or worse, for people to re-explore possibilities and engage in ways that are both personal and political, individual and social, with the world as it could be (Duncombe & Harrebye, 2020), challenging ideas that things are what they are or that there is no alternative.

Several other authors, including ourselves, started to use a more intentional combination of community profiling and participatory action research with young people (Cicognani, 2014; Menezes & Ferreira, 2012, 2014; Teater & Baldwin, 2009). In Portugal, we used community profiling as a strategy for citizenship education in schools, assuming its potential to address the dictatorial past and the democratic transition through profiles contemplating the past, the present and the future of democracy (Menezes & Ferreira, 2012). Students, supervised by their teachers and researchers, selected a topic of interest (e.g., women's rights, healthcare system, poverty, political participation) and investigated through document analysis, interviews and questionnaires (with experts, but also family members, members of local communities or fellow *schoolmates*) the situation regarding the topic before the 1974 revolution that restored democracy and in the present time; then, they were asked to imagine what could happen in the future. The research findings were presented by the students and discussed in their school, but also in a seminar organised at the University, where all the students from the participating schools presented a poster and jointly discussed their visions of the process with teachers and the research team (Menezes & Ferreira, 2012, 2014). Interviews with students and their teachers suggest that the project fostered students' epistemological empowerment and critical reading of citizenship rights and democracy and, in this sense, their political agency (Menezes & Ferreira, 2014; Pais et al., 2014).

It is important to emphasise that the school is undoubtedly a context with much potential for raising awareness and learning about key societal issues. The community profile, involving participatory research within the community, promotes the development of curricular projects focused on local issues. As such, it fosters the school's role in instigating students' active citizenship through "dialogues with political, social, and economic stakeholders, (...) creating the opportunity for young people to promote change with the support of teachers and stakeholders" (Pinheiro et al., 2024, p. 502). Moreover, it is also an opportunity for young people to act as inquisitive, reflective and critical citizens, exploring issues that impact the daily lives of their community, while also linking those experiences with school knowledge. As such, community profiling has a particular appeal for schools and teachers looking for citizenship education strategies that go beyond a merely normative and discursive approach and that follow Biesta and Lawy's (2006) call for learning democracy.

We have been using variants of this method in the fields of citizenship and environmental education (e.g., Costa et al., submitted; Marques et al., 2020; Prada da Silva et al., 2025; Rios et al., 2022). In brief, the outline of the method is as follows:

- *Phase 1: Setting the participants as researchers of their community.* The goal is to present the project to the group of participants, explaining that they will be involved as researchers of their community, i.e., someone who observes, listens and talks with other people, as real life in their day-to-day contexts will become their "laboratory" and the place where research evolves. This also implies paying attention to media and the Internet, as well as to everyday life events and conversations with family, friends and other people with whom they interact. Suppose the project involves a general topic (democracy, water preservation or climate change, to name some possible examples). In that case, this is the time to present it and suggest that participants open their minds to ideas they might like to explore and share them in the coming session. It is also the time to guarantee that informed consent is possible, explaining that participation is voluntary and that people can opt out whenever – something of particular importance for children and adolescents, as consent from legal guardians is not enough in ethical terms. Given the importance of artefacts as cognitive mediators and archetypal tools of the trade (Latour, 2005; Lave & Wenger, 1991), it makes sense to distribute field notebooks and pencils so that participants can, from the beginning, take notes and start to embody their role as a researcher.

- *Phase 2: Defining the research question.* As anyone working with participatory action research knows – anyone working with research knows – the research questions will be defined and redefined throughout the project. Nevertheless, it is important to focus participants' attention on a specific topic that interests them, and these different interests can become the basis for constituting groups of 3–5 researchers who will work together, as knowledge production is a collective endeavour. These groups will define their research questions based on daily experiences, issues that pop up in the media and curricular content from school subjects (Pinheiro et al., 2024). Teachers can play a vital role in this process by supporting relevant connections with school subjects. This can become a significant way of involving teachers in the project, showing that community profiling is not "something else" but rather an alternative way of relating to school knowledge and operating on it. At the same time, this also allows participating students to address school knowledge as a mediating device to understand the world and generate a broader and situated understanding of "real life." As mentioned above, introducing a historical dimension is particularly significant, and the research questions should explicitly consider exploring the past and the present.
- *Phase 3: Research in the making – observing, listening, talking.* This intensive phase involves preparing the research and collecting and analysing data from various sources. It can begin by sharing some straightforward research papers that students can read and analyse to understand what research is and how it can impact the community (see Marques et al., 2020, for an example on water preservation). It needs to involve some basic training in research methods for the social sciences, adapted to the literacy and age of the participants, that stimulates them to be attentive to the surrounding reality: take field notes or make drawings, plan intentional conversations, and actively listen to what other people are saying or survey community members regarding their views or behaviours. All of this involves planning and designing research instruments in the form of questions to be asked orally or in written form. In our experience, the complexity of these instruments varies widely, but even straightforward devices can generate exciting data, which is the essential thing here. Then, data collection is initiated, and data analysis proceeds. This is a time of intensively discussing the data within the research groups, with other people (teachers, family, community members) and, if possible, with experts from various fields. It might also require looking for documents and knowledge produced by others in various formats (e.g., webpages, books, media news, documentaries and videos). These intensive "conversations" are the basis for a second-order, more in-depth look at the data, making it possible to identify the main findings of the research, tracing a diachronic perspective from the past to the present.
- *Phase 4: Making sense of the research: disseminating and politicising.* Once the main findings are established, it is time to amplify the discussion and engage the community in making sense of the research. This encompasses openly presenting and disseminating the research findings and publicly discussing their significance for the community. It is important to do this in local contexts (such as schools, as in many of our projects with children and adolescents), involving different community actors besides families. It is also important to take a reflexive approach that considers how power

differentials and inequalities in the community contribute to the findings – in other words, politicising the discussion and identifying areas for improvement. We advocate here for a childist perspective (Biswas & Mattheis, 2021) that recognises children and young people as full political actors and stresses that their community research experience involves a learning process for themselves and other people around them, including adults. These discussions should also open the ground for considering the future and possible ways to change its course.

- *Phase 5: Imagining the future and acting for change.* The final phase implies developing a vision for the future that incorporates the different readings of the research and identifies areas where change is necessary. It is also a phase of intensive reflexivity but aligned with praxis in that participants are expected to put (at least) some of their ideas into action. They are also invited to the University to share their community profiles with other participants and academics in a joint event that celebrates and acknowledges their research and investment in imagining and improving their communities.

Our findings reveal positive outcomes on students' civic engagement and political self-efficacy regarding environmental issues (Costa et al., submitted; Marques et al., 2020; Pinheiro et al., 2024; Silva et al., in press). Similar results were obtained with younger children in a project where they got involved in exploring and caring for a local forest – the participatory community profiling not only resulted in critical consciousness regarding the dominant anthropocentric visions of nature but also in fostering their environmental activism (Rios et al., 2022).

In 2021, we started the project *ClimActiC: Connecting Citizenship and Science for Climate Adaptation*, which engaged eight schools and approximately 500 young people throughout the Norte Region in Portugal. The project aimed to bring together scientists, professionals, activists, young people, economic agents and political decision-makers in a collaborative effort to co-create and co-design actionable solutions for a more resilient and climate-prepared Norte. In the next section, we will discuss the implementation of climate community profiling in a secondary school in the Porto Metropolitan Area from 2021 to 2023.

Climate community profiling in action

The ClimActiC project focused on climate change education and involved students and their teachers. The idea was not only to stimulate young people's dispositions and capacities for civic and political action in the context of climate adaptation but also to promote teachers' competencies in climate change education. The project team comprised researchers from Education Sciences, Chemical Engineering, Physics and Psychology who collaborated in teacher training. An important part of the training was how to develop and implement Climate Community Profiling so that teachers could supervise young people in their engagement in participatory action research in the community, focusing on the local implications of climate change. In practice, it allowed teachers to use instruments to co-construct the research project with students, thus facilitating the investigative process and its continuous monitoring. Throughout the process, young people's contact with local experts and actors was favoured by the dynamisation of collaborative laboratories (Malafaia et al., 2024). The laboratories joined students, teachers, representatives of the inter-municipal community, representatives of the local council, local environmental associations and activists and researchers in a joint discussion and reflection to deepen scientific, technical, economic and activist knowledge about the implications of climate change in the local community – and the ways forward. This is in line with the epistemological tradition of Community Psychology that values not only the diversity of perspectives brought about by different people, but also the dialogical pluralism it generates (Kagan et al., 2011; Martin-Baró, 1996).

In the OD School, a group of young students from a humanities course was involved with their history and geography teachers. Teachers supervised the students' research efforts, articulating their advances with the curriculum, but also participating in meetings with stakeholders and supporting the organisation of community field trips. The following description is based on the observation and field notes of the second author, who monitored the process, and the written records kept by teachers. Collaborative work in close partnership between students, teachers and local communities was a major asset of the project.

Research questions: Local climate issues observed and experienced by young people

Over the course of the two years, the young people identified climate issues that they had observed and experienced in their community. In the very first year (2021–22), the environmental problem defined by the young people arose during a field trip to a local Biological Park. During this visit in October, they noticed the rare presence of stork nests, alerting them to climate change's impacts on local biodiversity. Since that visit, they have attempted to understand the impact of climate change on the migratory flow of birds and the extinction of local species (Figure 8.1).

In the second school year, the floods of November 2022, a meteorological event that affected the entire country made young people aware of this issue. They witnessed the local river overflowing, roads flooding and lands collapsing in their locality. This experience led them to adjust the problem of the project to the current situation in which they were living. They, therefore, felt it was pertinent to look more closely at the impact of climate change on the local ecosystem and its consequences on the proliferation of extreme weather events. As a result of this experience, they problematised local deforestation and urban pressure as factors that aggravated the impact of flooding in the town (Figure 8.2).

They also constructed and applied a questionnaire in the local community to collect data on the community's perception of local bird species and their possible fluctuations related to climate change. Family members and acquaintances of the young people took part in this questionnaire.

Another issue widely problematised by young people during the project was the lack of empathy between generations and between people and natural elements. This problem was justified by the excess of human individualism that devalues all other beings, and this was one of the causes attributed to humanity's negligent behaviour towards nature. For example, they said that local urban planning only provides for people's immediate and present wellbeing and neglects the wellbeing of animals and future generations.

Research in the making: Sources used for data collection

During the two years of the project, the young people used various sources to gather information. In field lessons, they observed and researched with and in nature and gathered information from the experts who guided them. For example, in a biological park and a nature reserve in a local estuary, they observed, experienced and researched local nature with the guidance of an expert. They gathered information

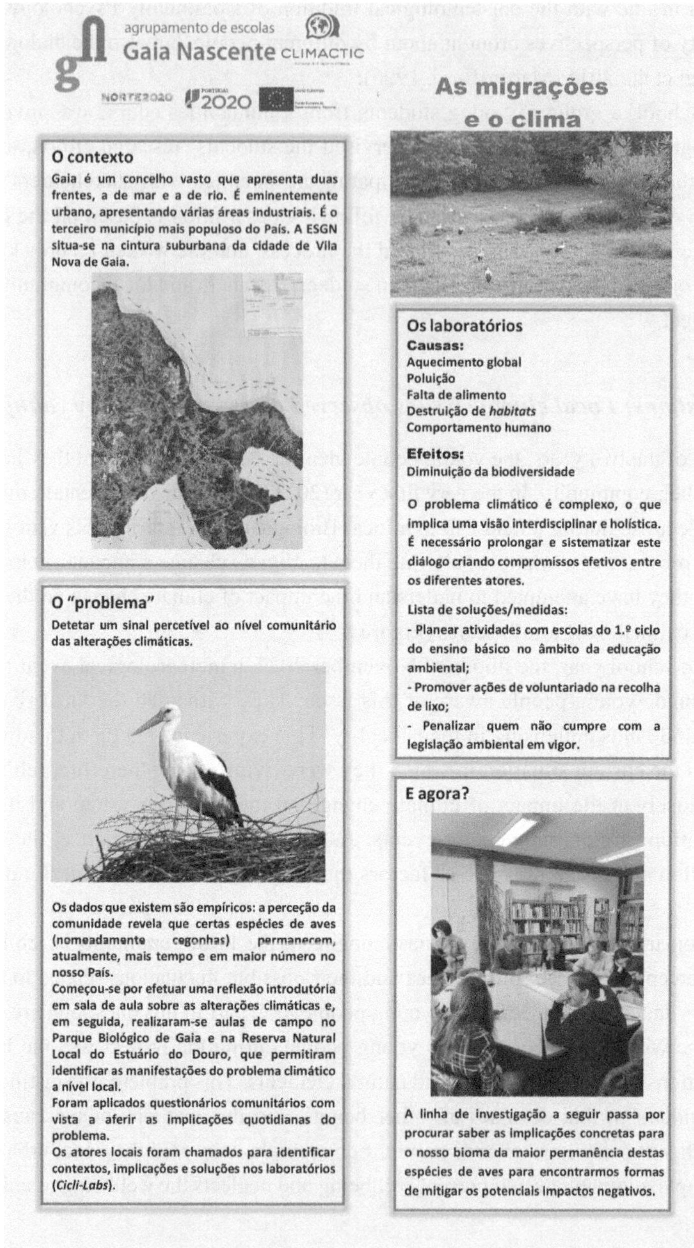

Figure 8.1 Poster presented in 2022 at the ClimActiC annual seminar at the university.

Notes: Translated text: Context: brief description of the municipality in the Porto Metropolitan Area; The "problem": one obvious sign of climate change is that some birds stay in the ecosystem longer, rather than migrating (e.g., storks). This is based on field trips to the local biological park and the River Douro Estuary Reserve, community surveys and talking to community stakeholders in the cicli-labs. The Laboratories allowed the identification of causes and consequences of the "problem," as well as the identification of potential solutions. What now? Proposes the need to research the implications for the biome further.

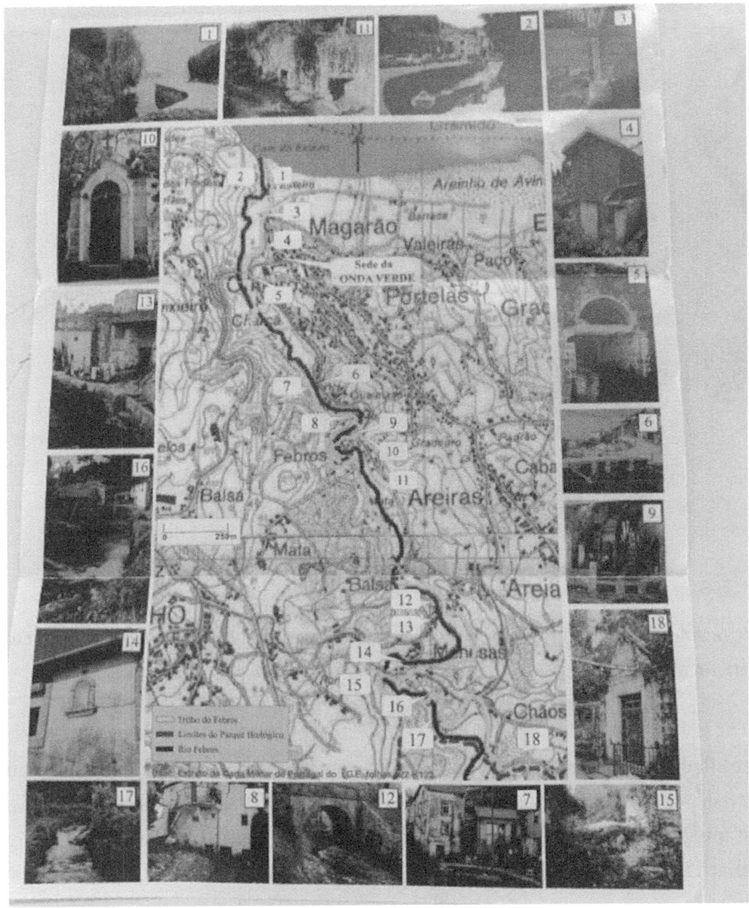

Figure 8.2 Map of the local community river.

about the birds of the region and realised the impact of the extinction of some local species and the change in the migratory flow of some birds.

In geography and history lessons, they deepened their theoretical knowledge and researched climate change. Together with their teachers, they collected information about the issue from local maps from different periods (Figure 8.2), compared current and old photographic records, analysed the local Municipal Master Plan to learn about local land planning, researched news items in local newspapers and looked for legislation on the preservation of common natural spaces.

Research in the making: Data analysis

After collecting the data, participants identified some structural issues regarding the increase in global temperature and the impact these issues have on their locality (Figures 8.3), such as:

- they realised that the agricultural system is almost non-existent at the local river mouth due to the urban pressure that exists.

Figure 8.3 A problem tree developed to consider the causes and consequences of climate change at the local level.

- they identified the urban area as the one that has suffered the most from climate change due to the scarce existence of green spaces and biodiversity, while the seafront and the river were marked as the most important to protect in order to mitigate the extinction of local species.
- they realised that local deforestation has harmed local biodiversity and the population's quality of life.
- they understood that the floods in their town were caused by the fact that there were almost no drainage areas for the river and that this was due to local urban and road pressure.

In developing the climate community profile, they also learned about the history of the population's relationship with the local river: at first, people fished and farmed on the banks of the river; then, industrialisation took people away from the river, and it became a rubbish dump; later, with the support of the local biological park, the river's banks were cleaned up. Today, there is a footpath to bring people closer to the river, and some houses on the riverbank are being redeveloped for local tourism.

Making sense of the research: Suggestions for change

Throughout the project, the young people identified suggestions for change, which stemmed from their reflections on the data they had collected. They suggested changes to lifestyles and environmental behaviour, more conscious urban planning concepts, climate awareness messages adjusted to the generations and promoting activities with the local population.

Regarding suggestions for change, participants focused on the importance of people changing their lifestyles and environmental behaviours. For example, they mentioned the importance of people regularly clearing private land to prevent fires, and they emphasised the importance of better supervision by the authorities, with fines for offenders who do not take care of public or private property.

Other changes suggested highlighted urban planning issues so that construction takes place in cohesion with the river's circulation and in favour of protecting local biodiversity. For the mobility of the population, they mentioned the importance of investing in railway lines to replace motorways, as they are less polluting. They emphasised the importance of identifying more protected areas locally to preserve local biodiversity, as this would make these natural spaces more legally protected and prevent future deforestation.

They emphasised the importance of adjusting climate awareness messages for different generations. For example, they mentioned the importance of having impactful videos to sensitise young people, arguing that they are the most challenging generation to captivate. They gave TikTok videos as an example, as they have impactful messages that can be viewed quickly.

They also said that environmental associations' initiatives are vital for raising awareness among the local population. However, they warned that for them to be successful, they must have an impactful message and good publicity, and the proposed activity must include a way of saying thank you, for example, a get-together at the end.

Imagining the future and acting for change: Actionable solutions and coming together

As actionable proposals, the young people identified actions that could be implemented with local resources. They focused on intergenerational activities, argued that all generations should be sensitised to climate issues and emphasised the importance of the local population being more involved with nature to create bonds and get to know the nature surrounding them.

In this regard, they highlighted awareness-raising activities with the entire school community (students, teachers, parents, etc.). They gave the example of organising talks to publicise this research. With the same population, they also suggested organising volunteer activities in the community, such as cleaning up the riverbanks and other local natural spaces. In fact, they volunteered to participate in an activity with a local environmental association that involved cleaning the trail along a local river. During the cleaning, they collected information about the state of the riverbank and made a photographic report on the local ecosystem. This activity was publicised on the school's social media to publicise their research and encourage similar practices in the community (Figure 8.4).

They also decided to carry out an environmental project on the importance of protecting the local river now and in the future with a group of primary school children. They explained that this project aims to use appropriate and appealing language to captivate the children and include awareness-raising and leisure activities in nature to allow the children to get to know and experience the local natural spaces.

Participation in the ClimActiC project seminars allowed the climate community profiles to be shared with other research peers (students from other schools that participated in the Climactic project) and the academic community. To this end, the young people made a poster to showcase their research and

Figure 8.4 News about the river cleaning activity on the school's website.

Notes: The poster addresses the loss of biodiversity in the banks of the river Febros with the motto "protecting biodiversity is respecting life." While briefly presenting the context, the Gaia municipality, the posters focus on the river closer to the school, a tributary of the main River Douro. The "problem" starts by mentioning the November floods and then presents the various research strategies, including class discussions, document analysis, field visits and the collaborative laboratories. The "what now?" section stresses the importance of involving the local community to generate awareness about climate change and mobilising people to become activists, also recognising the role that leisure activities in nature can play in developing empathy and critical environmental consciousness.

presented it. Afterwards, there was a round table with other young project participants, researchers and local actors where they had the opportunity to take stock of their experience and highlight some aspects that they particularly valued, such as being heard and researching their community in interaction with experts from different areas (politicians, researchers, local experts, local activists).

In fact, across the project, participants from OD emphasised the experience, knowledge and availability of local actors during the investigation and how this was an important part of the development of the climate community profile. However, our observation also showed that, implicitly, some local actors tried to impose their knowledge on young people. This is obviously an important risk when joining groups with such an imbalance of power.

Additionally, participants mentioned other significant experiences. The most mentioned was the opportunity to investigate issues that affect them locally and the fact that they had the time, space and support to investigate them and put them into action. The space and time factors in the research process allowed participants:

- to discover and realise misconceptions about climate change (e.g., the impacts of floods on the community).
- to consider the impact of climate change on the migratory flow of local birds.
- to acknowledge the impact of urban planning on local quality of life.
- to reflect on the political processes related to local climate issues (e.g., protected areas, land-use planning).
- to identify actionable solutions to become environmental, civic and political agents in their contexts (e.g., TikTok climate awareness videos; environmental project with primary school children; volunteer activity).

Conclusion

Participatory research with children and young people is a methodological approach that can problematise and resolve many of the classic issues of power and exclusion in research with children and young people, not least because it assumes that they are seen in the light of a rights-based rather than adult-centred perspective (Gallagher, 2008; Water, 2018). Naturally, this requires a set of theoretical and methodological principles anchored in the ethical commitment involving children (Christensen & James, 2017; Skånfors, 2009). It also requires an active effort to counteract power asymmetries between adults and young people, and how these tend to become dominant and controlling in these contexts (Taft, 2015), especially when not intentionally checked. The role of adults, essential in working modes such as the Climate Community Profiling we propose here, must be carefully considered and reflected upon throughout the intervention, as results show. If adults are important partners in many steps and can be essential in providing conditions and support, they should remember that their partnership should make way for younger participants to find their goals and take the lead (Elsen & Ord, 2021). In this regard, when implementing collaborative laboratories, the guarantee of an intergenerational democratic environment sometimes had to be moderated by ClimActic researchers, as a greater need for control was observed on the part of some local actors, who justified their positions with their professional and life experience, disregarding the position of young people. Despite some constraints, young people valued the existence of these sessions, as they were spaces for debate and exchange of ideas, allowing collaborative research to be carried out with the co-creation of concrete and actionable solutions. Furthermore, these exchanges with local actors allowed young people to put into practice their climate, civic and political agency in their communities, with increased civic and climate awareness on political processes related to local climate issues. In this sense, the community profile approach favoured articulating participatory action research with the local community. It involved obtaining information about your community; the problematisation of their needs; learning about data collection instruments; searching for information from different sources; reflection, analysis and discussion of the collected data; the selection of actionable solutions, foreseeing their implications in the community; and disseminating research for community change.

The active involvement of children and young people in the research process proposed by our version of community profiling sees them as experts in their own lives. This approach recognises the importance of plural and diverse perspectives in research. It assumes that, as co-researchers, children and young people can propose and practise alternative ways of investigating and reading the data. As such, it is important to be open and provide opportunities to explore diverse methods best suited to their expression, such as the visual techniques used in this project. In this regard, the experience can provide the opportunity for children and young people to connect the process of knowing with ways of paying attention to others and engaging with them and their surroundings, of representing what they observe, and of analysing what it may mean in dialogue with others (younger and older, with varying experiences and levels of expertise in different fields). These conversations position (even if not without challenges) children and young people as knowledgeable subjects, with something to say about issues of public concern that powerful adult actors should listen to.

Community profile promotes children and young people's agency by engaging them as researchers in issues that concern them. This idea is combined with the fact that children and young people develop critical thinking from the experience of community profiling, advocating changes that they believe are necessary to build a better world. To stimulate their imagination of alternative futures and their vision of themselves and their communities as agents of that transformation is to foster a sense of collective political hope without which ideas of change, community and future risk becoming pointless.

Acknowledgements

This work was supported by national funds through the Foundation for Science and Technology, IP (FCT), as part of the CIIE's multi-annual funding (project UIDB/00167/2020). The ClimActiC Project (ref. NORTE-01–0145-FEDER-000071) was funded by the European Regional Development Fund (FEDER), through NORTE 2020 – Regional Operational Programme of the North (Norte2020 – Integrated Projects ICDT), North Regional Coordination and Development Commission. The authors thank young people and teachers from the OD School who participated in the ClimActiC Project.

References

Agyeman, J., Schlosberg, D., Craven, L. & Matthews, C. (2016). Trends and directions in environmental justice: From inequity to everyday life, community, and just sustainabilities. *Annual Review of Environment and Resources*, *41*, 321–40. http://dx.doi.org/10.1146/annurev-environ-110615-090052

Anson, I. G. (2018), Partisanship, political knowledge, and the Dunning-Kruger effect. *Political Psychology*, *39*, 1173–1192. https://doi.org/10.1111/pops.12490

Arendt, H. (1995). *Qu'est-ce que la politique?* [*What is politics?*]. Seuil. (Work originally published in 1950)

Aronsson, J., Waite, S., & Clark, M. (2015). Measuring the impact of outdoor learning on the physical activity of school age children. *Education and Health Online*, *33*(3), 57–62. https://sheu.org.uk/sheux/EH/eh333ja.pdf

Bates, D. (2002). Environmental refugees? Classifying human migrations caused by environmental change. *Population and Environment*, *23*(5), 465–477). https://doi.org/10.1023/A:1015186001919

Bell, A., & Russell, C. (2000). Beyond human, beyond words: Anthropocentrism, critical pedagogy, and the poststructuralist turn. *Canadian Journal of Education*, *25*(3), 188–203. https://doi.org/10.2307/1585953

Biesta, G., & Lawy, R. (2006). From teaching citizenship to learning democracy: Overcoming individualism in research, policy and practice. *Cambridge Journal of Education*, *36*(1), 63–79. https://doi.org/10.1080/03057640500490981

Biswas, T., & Mattheis, N. (2021). Strikingly educational: A childist perspective on children's civil disobedience for climate justice. *Educational Philosophy and Theory*, *54*(2), 145–157. https://doi.org/10.1080/00131857.2021.1880390

Cicognani, E. A. (2014). "Lost" youth generation? Reflections from a community assessment study in Italy. *Baskent University Journal of Education*, *1*(1), 112–122.

Cosh, S. M., Ryan, R., Fallander, K., Robinson, K., Tognela, J., Tully, P. J., & Lykins, A. D. (2024). The relationship between climate change and mental health: A systematic review of the association between eco-anxiety, psychological distress, and symptoms of major affective disorders. *BMC Psychiatry*, *24*, 833. https://doi.org/10.1186/s12888-024-06274-1

Costa, H., Menezes, I., & Ribeiro, N. (submitted). Service-learning for sustainability: Transformative learning through the Healthy Waters project.

Cutter-Mackenzie, A., & Rousell, D. (2019). Education for what? Shaping the field of climate change education with children and young people as co-researchers. *Children's Geographies*, *17*(1), 90–104. https://doi.org/10.1080/14733285.2018.1467556

d'Agua, L. (1982). Nuclear Nao, Obrigado. On *Perto de Ti. Valentim de Carvalho.*

Damásio, A. (2022). *Feeling & knowing: Making minds conscious*. Pantheon Books.

Duncombe, S., & Harrebye, S. (2020). Political imagination. In V. P. Glăveanu (Ed.), *The Palgrave encyclopedia of the possible* (pp. 1–10). Springer International Publishing. https://doi.org/10.1007/978-3-319-98390-5_177-1

Elsen, F., & Ord, J. (2021). The role of adults in "youth led" climate groups: Enabling empowerment. *Frontiers in Political Science*, *3*, Article 641154. https://doi.org/10.3389/fpos.2021.641154

Francescato, D. (2000). Community psychology intervention strategies as tools to enhance participation in projects promoting sustainable development and quality of life. In *Proceedings of the Euroconference "quality of life – Sustainability – Environmental changes"* (pp. 35–45). Austrian Research Centres.

Francescato, D., Tomai, M., & Ghirelli, G. (2002). *Fondamenti di psicologia di comunitá: Principi, strumenti, ambiti di applicazione* [*Fundamentals of community psychology: principles, tools, areas of application*]. Carocci.

Fridays For Future. (2025). *Actions on climate emergency*. https://fridaysforfuture.org/

Gallagher, M. (2008). 'Power is not an evil': Rethinking power in participatory methods. *Children's Geographies*, *6*(2), 137–150. https://doi.org/10.1080/14733280801963045

Gelli, B., Mannarini, T., & Bonifazi, A. (2004). The meanings of community: Sense of place and participation. In A. Sánchez-Vidal, A. Zambrano, & M. Palacín (Eds.), *European community psychology: Community, power, ethics and values* (pp. 230–261). Universitat de Barcelona.

Giddens, A. (1997). *Para além da esquerda e da direita: O futuro da política radical* [Beyond left and right: the future of radical politics]. Celta Editora.

Habermas, J. (1999). *Between facts and norms: Contributions to a discourse theory of law and democracy* (3rd ed.). MIT Press.

Hawtin, M., Hughes, G., & Percy-Smith, J. (1998). *Community profiling: Auditing social needs*. Open University Press.

Hickman, C., Marks, E., Pihkala, P., Clayton, S., Lewandowski, E., Mayall, E. E., Wray, B., Mellor, C., & Van Susteren, L. (2021). Climate anxiety in children and young people and their beliefs about government responses to climate change: A global survey. *The Lancet Planetary Health*, *5*(12), e863–e873. https://doi.org/10.1016/S2542-5196(21)00278-3

Jasper, J. M. (2014). *Protest: A cultural introduction to social movements*. Polity Press.

Jones, C. A., & Davison, A. (2020). Disempowering emotions: The role of educational experiences in social responses to climate change. *Geoforum*, *118*, 190–200. https://doi.org/10.1016/j.geoforum.2020.11.006

Jost, J. (2006). The end of the end of ideology. *American Psychologist*, *61*(7), 651–670. https://doi.org/10.1037/0003-066X.61.7.651

Kagan, C., Burton, M., Duckett, P., Lawthom, R., & Siddiquee, A. (2011). *Critical community psychology: Critical action and social change*. John Wiley & Sons.

Kopnina, H. (2016). Of big hegemonies and little tigers: Ecocentrism and environmental justice. *The Journal of Environmental Education*, *47*(2), 139–150. https://doi.org/10.1080/00958964.2015.1048502

Latour, B. (2005). *Reassembling the social: An introduction to actor-network-theory*. Oxford University Press.

Lave, J., & Wenger, E. (1991). *Situated learning: Legitimate peripheral participation*. Cambridge University Press.

Malafaia, C., Diógenes-Lima, J., Pereira, B., Macedo, E., & Menezes, I. (2024). Collaborative climate labs: A youth-led methodology for co-creating community responses to climate change. *Research in Education*, *121*(2), 192–216. https://doi.org/10.1177/00345237241288407

Marcus, G. E. (2000). Emotions in politics. *Annual Review of Political Science*, *3*, 221–250. https://doi.org/10.1146/annurev.polisci.3.1.221

Marcus, G. E. (2002). *The sentimental citizen: Emotion in democratic politics*. The Pennsylvania State University.

Marques, R. R., Malafaia, C., Faria, J. L., & Menezes, I. (2020). Using online tools in participatory research with adolescents to promote civic engagement and environmental mobilization: The WaterCircle (WC) project. *Environmental Education Research*, *26*(7), 1043–1059. https://doi.org/10.1080/13504622.2020.1776845

Martin-Baró, I. (1996). O papel do psicólogo [The psychologist's role]. *Estudos de Psicologia*, *2*(1), 7–27.

Menezes, I., & Ferreira, P. D. (Eds.). (2012). *Educação para a cidadania participatória em sociedades em transição: Uma visão europeia, ibérica e nacional das políticas e práticas da educação para a cidadania em contexto escolar*. CIIE/FPCEUP. https://hdl.handle.net/10216/84682

Menezes, I., & Ferreira, P. D. (2014). Cidadania participatória no cotidiano escolar: A vez e a voz das crianças e dos jovens. *Educar em Revista*, *53*, 131–147. https://doi.org/10.1590/0104-4060.36586

Nussbaum, M. (2013). *Political emotions: Why love matters for justice*. The Belknap Press of Harvard University Press.

Pais, S. C., Menezes, I., & Nunes, J. A. (2016). Saúde e escola: Reflexões em torno da medicalização da educação [Health and school: thoughts on the medicalization of education]. *Cadernos de Saúde Pública*, *32*(9), e00166215. https://doi.org/10.1590/0102-311X00166215

Pais, S. C., Rodrigues, M., & Menezes, I. (2014). Community as locus for health formal and non-formal education: The significance of ecological and collaborative research for promoting health literacy. *Frontiers in Public Health*, *2*, 283. https://doi.org/10.3389/fpubh.2014.0028

Pinheiro, S., Torres, A. C., Pereira, B., Malafaia, C., & Menezes, I. (2024). Citizenship education to promote the participation of young people in climate adaptation: Crossing curricular boundaries through community profiling. *Curriculum Perspectives*. https://doi.org/10.1007/s41297-024-00231-4

Prada da Silva, D. F., Silva, J. B., Barbosa, M. O., Ribeiro, N., & Menezes, I. (2025). Promoting environmental citizenship using participatory school-based community profiling on water (mis)uses. *ECNU Review of Education*, *8*(1), 79–111. https://doi.org/10.1177/20965311241264829

Rios, C., Neilson, A. L., & Menezes, I. (2022). "Let's be heard": Climate activism by children in the local forest. *Educação, Sociedade & Culturas*, *62*, 1–26. https://doi.org/10.24840/esc.vi62.195

Ryan, W. (1972). *Blaming the victim*. Vintage Books.

Skånfors, L. (2009). Ethics in child research: Children's agency and researchers' 'ethical radar'. *Childhoods Today*, *3*(1), 1–22. http://urn.kb.se/resolve?urn=urn:nbn:se:kau:diva-11326

Stanley, S. K., Hogg, T. L., Leviston, Z., & Walker, I. (2021). From anger to action: Differential impacts of eco-anxiety, eco-depression, and eco-anger on climate action and wellbeing. *The Journal of Climate Change and Health*, *1*, 100003. https://doi.org/10.1016/j.joclim.2021.100003

Taft, J. K. (2015). "Adults talk too much": Intergenerational dialogue and power in the Peruvian movement of working children. *Childhood*, *22*(4), 460–473. https://doi.org/10.1177/0907568214555148

Teater, B., & Baldwin, M. (2009). Exploring the learning experiences of students involved in community profiling projects. *Social Work Education*, *28*(7), 778–791. https://doi.org/10.1080/02615470802478220

Todd, R. M., Miskovic, V., Chikazoe, J., & Anderson, A. K. (2020). Emotional objectivity: Neural representations of emotions and their interaction with cognition. *Annual Review of Psychology*, *71*, 25–48. https://doi.org/10.1146/annurev-psych-010419-051044

Vasilopoulos, P. (2018). Terrorist events, emotional reactions, and political participation: The 2015 Paris attacks. *West European Politics*, *41*(1), 102–127. https://doi.org/10.1080/01402382.2017.1346901

Walzer, M. (2002). Passion and politics. *Philosophy & Social Criticism*, *28*(6), 617–633. https://doi.org/10.1177/019145370202800602

Water, T. (2018). Ethical issues in participatory research with children and young people. In I. Coyne & B. Carter (Eds.), *Being participatory: Researching with children and young people. Co-constructing knowledge using creative techniques* (pp. 37–56). Springer. https://doi.org/10.1007/978-3-319-71228-4

Wlodarczyk, A., Basabec, N., Páez, D., & Zumeta, L. (2017). Hope and anger as mediators between collective action frames and participation in collective mobilization: The case of 15-M. *Journal of Social and Political Psychology*, *5*(1), 200–223. https://doi.org/10.5964/jspp.v5i1.471

Yamada-Rice, D. (2017). Using visual and digital research methods with young children. In P. Christensen & A. James (Eds.), *Research with children: Perspectives and practices* (3rd ed., pp. 71–86). Routledge.

PART III

Crafting connection

9 Creative relational wealth building in the context of caregiving

Suzanne Wilson, Rebecca Graber, Katherine Jewell and Hannah Kessler

Introduction

Most of us will encounter unpaid caregiving in some form or another during our lives as caregivers, recipients of care or through mutual exchange. Briefly, caregiving is "the process of helping another person who is unable to do for themselves in a 'holistic' (physically, mentally, emotionally, and socially) manner. Caregiving is facilitated by 'certain character traits, emotions, skills, knowledge, time, and an emotional connection with the care recipient'" (Hermans & Mastel-Smith, 2012, p. 15). This chapter draws on research conducted with caregivers, primarily mothers, to first highlight the relational challenges they may face, such as perinatal loneliness (Naughton-Doe et al., 2025), and then to consider how creative practice can enhance relationships and overall wellbeing. These experiences will be discussed in reference to a Relational Wealth Building Framework (Wilson, 2024), which aims to provide a tool to support the development of relationship practices in institutions and community organisations.

All the authors are women and mothers, and our own personal journeys through motherhood have influenced both our research and our practice. This, along with being our main source of evidence, is why we chose to focus on mothers in this chapter. We hope to offer readers comfort in shared experiences and the courage to have honest reflections on their own. We also hope to inspire others to develop a relational approach within their research and practice with caregivers through sharing examples of our own interpretations and applications of relational practice.

In reflecting as a group on the research and practice presented here, we recognise our own feelings of isolation at times, the relentlessness of caregiving, the experience of a transformative shift in the self and how the fragility of our support network contributed to our own wellbeing. We also recognise points of divergence with our own experiences of motherhood, in terms of material circumstances, personal histories and social identities. We wonder whether caregiving in general, and the transition to becoming a mother in particular, are flattened in academic research, perhaps because they are so intangible and involve "unseen work."

It is worth noting that our own experiences, as well as those of the community members in the case studies, are not universal and should not be taken as such; our biases shape how we perceive and interpret the world. In this chapter, we present a combination of autoethnographic accounts and empirical research that, with careful reflection, we hope represents a diverse range of maternal voices rather than the outcome of our biases. There is a growing shift in using autoethnography in motherhood (Autret & van Eeden-Moorefield, 2024; LeBlanc et al., 2022; Sotirin, 2010) and an emerging literature on the concept of the "Mother Scholars," defined as those who creatively weave their maternal identities into their

DOI: 10.4324/9781003480464-12

scholarly spaces (Abetz, 2019; Jaimes, 2020; Lac, 2021; Lapayese, 2012). Through an autoethnographic process, scholars have reflected on the overlap of their dual identities, and we hope to contribute to this movement by embracing this duality.

As we come from different backgrounds in terms of ethnic identity, religion, socioeconomic class, neurodiversity and citizenship, we recognise that the journey to connection is shaped by numerous processes beyond our individual control, yet is experienced by each individual in the day-to-day through their own way. In practical terms, this can be understood, for example, in how welcome we may feel in a given social or institutional context, such as a toddler playgroup and a GP appointment. This is further compounded by who their child is and what their child's needs turn out to be.

We also recognise our own privilege within our personal circumstances within the context of many of the mothers we engage with in our research practice (see Wilson, 2025). This presents power differentials that must be acknowledged, but we argue, with a relational approach based on the principles of trust, honesty and respect, that these differences need not necessarily impede our research and practice.

Understanding relationships in the context of Community Psychology

People may find meaningful social relationships with family, romantic relationships, friendships, families of choice or fictive kin (where people regard themselves as family despite being unrelated by blood or marriage, e.g., Taylor et al., 2022), as well as ties with colleagues, classmates, community leaders, community members, practitioners and service providers. Most psychological disciplines think about social relationships primarily in terms of their implications for an individual's physical and mental wellbeing so that improvements to wellbeing are identified as an essential reason to improve the quality of social relationships, reduce loneliness and social exclusion, or address the harmful effects of relational dysfunction, abuse or victimisation. This is worthwhile, as broadly speaking, positive relationships are associated with outcomes such as improved immune and endocrine functioning, cardiovascular health, life satisfaction, quality of life, resilience in the face of adversity and growth following trauma (e.g., Adams et al.,2004; Bukowski & Adams, 2005; Cacioppo & Patrick, 2008; Coyle & Dugan, 2012; Graber et al., 2016). The desirability of having "close, meaningful ties to others" is as near a cultural universal as psychology can claim (Ryff & Singer, 2000, p. 31).

From infancy, humans have an innate drive to form meaningful, bonded attachment relationships with caregivers. These relationships significantly shape how a child grows to experience and understand the self, other people and the world, contributing to patterns of thought, behaviour and emotion over time. These patterns are persistent but not fixed, as people remain adaptable throughout their lifespan and are themselves contextualised within other social and structural ties (Burman, 2016). Cumulative bodies of evidence show that perceived access to social support – believing that your needs will be met through your significant interpersonal relationships – is tied to better health and well-being across varying cultures and contexts (Graber, 2019, 2025; Graber et al., 2016). Social support may involve sharing information, offering help, providing validation, fostering emotional intimacy, engaging in fun activities and other valued feelings or resources (Graber et al., 2016). Relationships are also seen to be powerful drivers of change from the individual level to the group level, even in contexts of high polarisation, violence and rivalry. For example, evidence derived from intergroup contact theory (Allport, 1954), a key theory in social psychology, has effectively shown across cultural contexts that when individuals from rival groups make contact under certain conditions, even in contexts of sustained conflict or high perceived discrimination, change in attitudes and behaviour is possible, with significant implications for prevention of discrimination, conflict resolution and prejudice reduction (Turner, 2020; Van Assche et al., 2023).

Theory Summary

Gordon Allport's intergroup contact theory, also known as the contact hypothesis, proposes that positive contact between members of different social groups can reduce prejudice and improve intergroup relations. Allport outlined four key conditions that are believed to be crucial for this positive contact: equal status between groups, intergroup cooperation towards a shared goal, common goals that both groups are working towards, and support from authorities or social norms.

Community psychology complements and deepens this approach in several ways. People are more likely to be healthier in socially cohesive societies, and a lack of empowerment is associated with disease (e.g., Campbell, 2015; Wallerstein, 1992). This suggests that isolation, loneliness and poor access to supportive relationships are social justice issues, with access to quality social relationships across, within and between communities being a way through which marginalisation operates and is exemplified (Graber, 2025). Community Psychology offers a framework and strategies for linking goals of political empowerment, challenging marginalisation and supporting wellbeing. Community Psychology approaches prompt a focus on the relationship between feelings of loneliness and the factors that can contribute to it for communities and community members, which include stigma, functional disability, physical isolation, less social contact and smaller or more fragile social networks (Campbell, 2015). Of particular interest to this context of motherhood and unpaid caregiving, social isolation among mothers of young children has been shown to be associated with feelings of loneliness (Arimoto & Tadaka, 2021). Overall, a Community Psychology perspective on social relationships asks us to consider the broader context of social relationships and groups, including access to different forms of resources and power structures affecting relationship formation, maintenance and quality; aims to facilitate empowerment and social change; and is particularly interested in the relationships of people who are marginalised, excluded or vulnerable.

Psychology often looks at relationships on the individual level, which can neglect relationships within family, community or institutional levels. One way community psychologists apply social relationships in their research and practice is through the lens of ecological systems theory (Bronfenbrenner, 1979), which posits that an individual's development is influenced by a series of interconnected environmental systems, ranging from the immediate surroundings (e.g., family) to broad societal structures (e.g., culture). In this framework, relationships become a key means by which individuals connect to their surroundings, which in turn link to society, and vice versa, so that relationships themselves serve as a mechanism of change. Critiques of ecological systems theory have been that the mechanisms of change are difficult to theorise and harder still to empirically assess, and that issues of power are underdeveloped (Riemer et al., 2020). We suggest that, despite its merits, the ecological systems approach continues to see social relationships mostly as aiming to achieve a particular purpose or as a forum for resource exchange, not unlike more mainstream psychological explanations that suggest that, for example, friends engage in an ongoing assessment of the exchange of love and support (see Crisp &

Turner, 2020, for an overview of mainstream social psychological theories of relationship formation and maintenance).

As we, the authors, have reflected over time on what it means to do Community Psychology, it seems imperative to additionally explore what it means to be in relationship – a softer exploration of what it means to be in relationship with others. This means centring the emotional, intimate and experiential dimensions of relationality – both as the topic of discussion and the practice of "doing" Community Psychology in our corner of the world. Discussions about what it means ideologically to work truly alongside or within marginalised communities are fundamental to Community Psychology, alongside principles of interdependence between persons and of linkages between structural focuses and the individual, between or across communities (see, for example, Kagan et al., 2019; Riemer et al., 2020).

Community Psychology sees critical knowledge creation and liberation practices as happening in dialogue with others, values relational knowledge and uplifts indigenous and Global South perspectives that tend to prioritise interdependence and relationality (e.g., Freire et al., 2018). We "act" and "research" in relationship, and the participatory methodologies emphasised in Community Psychology seem to depend on developing some form of rapport, mutual understanding and respect. Yet, this feels like an increasingly challenging undertaking, as we have observed polarisation and social fragmentation in our communities, as well as noting broader social trends towards loneliness, exclusion and isolation across a range of dimensions. We have each seen personal and professional relationships falter, fail or disappear for various reasons, so that the gap between principles and "on the ground" practice feels wide. Transformative social change depends, in our minds, on an ability to connect with others – whether a colleague, a co-researcher, a community paper or an anonymous reader – often across substantial divides. In this chapter, we are particularly interested in the spaces spanning the self, the subjective experience of social relationships and broader social mechanisms. How do we bring relationships *as relationships* into the working context of Community Psychology?

Now we have offered an introduction to relationships through the lens of Community Psychology, we would like to invite readers to engage in an action for learning activity to reflect on your own social relationships.

Action for learning: Mapping social relationships

This activity provides an opportunity to reflect on how our interpersonal relationships are shaped by broader social inequalities. To do this, we will map our social relationships. Put yourself in the centre of the map diagram below (see Figure 9.1). This is divided into 12 sections, which represent areas of life where you might access social relationships. Concentric circles further divide these areas into three degrees of closeness. The innermost circle contains people you might see most frequently, love the most or feel closest to. The middle circle contains people you know less well, but have a connection to. The outermost circle contains people whom you may know by name but not well. (Everyone defines closeness differently, so consider what feels right to you.) Map your social relationships within this diagram, depicting what domain of life they are concentrated in, and how close or intimate they feel to you. You might do this by listing names in different sections, using colour or pattern to show the number of relationships in different sections, or some other way. You are mapping the people, not the activities in the domains – for example, the people you know at school, not the name of your school or where it is located.

Figure 9.1 Social relationships map.
Source: Author's own.

You can complete this activity in one or more ways depending on your aims.

Option 1: Complete the relationship map for yourself, to reflect your life as it is now (not how it used to be, how you wish it to be or how it may be in the future!). Some people may find it distressing to reflect on their own social relationships; however, allowing for alternative perspectives is important.

Option 2: Complete the relationship map as if you are a person in your community who feels isolated because of their caregiving responsibilities, or some other aspect of life context that you are exploring. Be as specific as possible. This can provide insight into points of isolation and exclusion, especially considering the concept of "closeness" and changes in where people can access social relationships.

Option 3: Complete the relationship map as if you are a member of a particular group or community that you are exploring, being as specific as possible. This can highlight cultural or other group differences in social relationship patterns and resources, as well as systemic exclusion from certain areas of life.

When you have finished, personally reflect or discuss in small groups:

- What patterns of social relationships did you observe? What are the differences between your own map and those from community members or group members?

- How do these patterns reinforce or challenge assumptions about social relationships? Does anything surprise you? Trouble you? Reassure you?
- If you completed Option 2 or Option 3, why do you think these relationship patterns are this way? Try to discuss this with reference to real-life contexts, as well as abstract concepts – for example, the price of bus tickets, scarcity of public toilets and lack of respite care can be meaningful barriers.
- What could be done (and by whom) to help "re-map" a person's relationships to address feelings of isolation and/or wider social exclusion?

This activity was inspired by materials reported in Amado (2013) in the United States of America, where a similar activity was used with individuals with learning disabilities and their supporters to demonstrate the importance of community connections.

Relational and creative practice

Our experiences and work align with the broader context of growing trends towards creative methods and relational approaches in research and practice in the UK (Neuhoff et al., 2022; Wyatt, 2018). The benefit of using creative methods in clinical settings is well-established; visual art, music and other creative activities have therapeutic value in themselves as well as providing an alternative means of communication and expression within counselling sessions or as part of psychiatric treatment programmes (e.g., Malchiodi, 2012). Creative methods are becoming increasingly recognised in social research for similar reasons. Many social scientists are finding that artistic expression is particularly enabling when working with vulnerable groups such as children or ethnic minority participants because of the communicative value alongside the practical potential for levelling the playing field in terms of power dynamics within the researcher–participant relationship (e.g., Kara, 2015).

In terms of relational practice, current developments are more concentrated within therapeutic contexts and relate to extensions on the idea of "enabling environments," which highlights a perceived lack of focus on the cultivation of positive relationships within psychiatric healthcare provision (Benefield & Haigh, 2020; Royal College of Psychiatrists, 2025). Building on this, Haigh and Benefield (2023) are at the vanguard of the "relational practice movement," arguing that traditions within public and health services are based on "a narrow, managerial performance framework" and that practitioners can work to change this culture through relational practice which "gives priority to relationships over procedure" (p259).

Creative-relational inquiry combines these concepts by promoting the use of creative methods as a key enabler for the development of therapeutic relationships within clinical settings, as well as within the fields of health education and research (Centre for Creative-Relational Inquiry, 2025). Some examples include trialling the use of stand-up comedy as part of counselling sessions (Wyatt, 2018) and storytelling within dementia care (Neuhoff et al., 2022). Our work takes the union of creative methods and relational practice out of personal therapeutic settings into the community. Relational practice represents a values-based approach that closely resembles the key pillars of relational wealth building that will be discussed in the next section (Wilson, 2024), which were developed in cooperation with communities, whilst creative-relational inquiry arguably serves as a more clinical reflection of the relational approach that is employed in our praxis case study (presented below). The following section introduces relational wealth building as an emerging approach to creating the conditions for relationships to develop and thrive in various community settings. This will be followed by an analysis of an application of the approach within a family-based creative play setting.

Relational wealth building

Just as financial wealth can be enhanced by working with others to build stronger relationships, our overall wellbeing and quality of life can be enhanced by working with others to build stronger relationships, which we refer to as relational wealth. Relational wealth is defined as:

> *the quality of relationships people experience with each other and with services and institutions. It can be built by creating spaces for people to connect in an equal and accessible way, and is based on the principles of trust, honesty and respect.*
>
> (Wilson, 2024, p. 63)

Relational wealth building is a framework for a process that builds social connections as a resource for community engagement. Informed by the different approaches to relationships we have outlined above, the concept draws on ten years of community research, listening to what families feel are the most important things in creating positive relationships (see for example, Wilson, 2022, 2024; Wilson & McGuire, 2022), and is broken down into five key pillars:

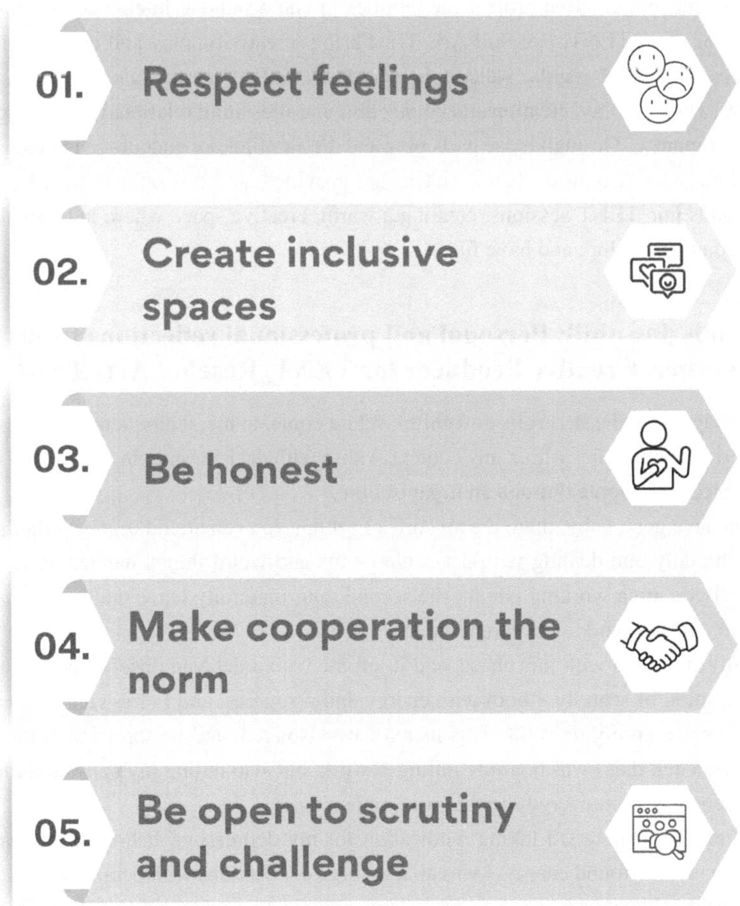

Figure 9.2 The five pillars within the Relational Wealth Building Framework (Wilson, 2024).
Source: Image by author.

Relational wealth building provides an interesting parallel to community wealth building, serving as a metaphor that helps us consider how this wealth is stored or maintained. The concept is evolving, and research is currently underway to explore sustainability, considering how such a resource-intensive set-up can sustain itself in the long term or be replicated (see praxis case study below).

A praxis case study will now be explored through the lens of relational wealth building to show how relational spaces for caregivers can be built in practice. Following an auto-ethnographic account from a Creative Producer who applied relational practice in her work, the relational wealth-building framework will be applied to demonstrate how it can be meaningfully implemented.

Praxis case study: TENT: Intergenerational connections through play

Rosehill Art Trust offers creative projects, workshops, events and social gatherings, creating safe and supportive spaces for people to come together, particularly those who face challenges or have limited access to local opportunities. They work with artists to develop shared experiences, often centred around food, which allow participants to express themselves creatively. They aim to strengthen communities, support personal and collective wellbeing and contribute to the common good.

TENT is a free and creative project for families in and around Whitehaven, a small coastal town in Cumbria, UK. With TENT, Rosehill Arts Trust brings creativity, play and connection to local community centres. They offer regular welcoming spaces around the town where families can explore and grow together. Through play, creation and connection, families build relational wealth together and with their wider community. Through loose parts play and art, families are encouraged to express themselves in new and bold ways. Light meals and snacks are provided, and this offer is free. People of all ages and backgrounds join TENT sessions, creating a warm, creative space where individuals from diverse generations connect, explore and have fun.

The sh1t rolls downhill: Personal and professional reflections from Hannah Kessler, Creative Producer for TENT, Rosehill Arts Trust

My favourite saying is "the sh1t rolls downhill." While crude, to me, it eloquently expresses a sentiment that explains dysfunctionality within any context. Those with decision-making power are responsible for any consequences that ripple through an organisation.

When you have got a baby, there are all sorts of groups you can attend to meet other parents, realise you are not the only one dealing with 3 am blow-outs and weird things happening to your c-section stitches. But if you are a working parent, the second your maternity leave ends, you enter a purgatory where you are either at work or in parent mode.

I personally struggled with this phase, and it left me with a delayed onset of postnatal depression. I felt stuck in a spiral of scarcity – both with energy and resources, and I struggled to do anything other than simply survive on my days off. This meant I was isolated, and on top of that, the guilt was horrendous, as I now felt that I was not only failing at work, but also failing my baby, and the result was an emotional disconnect from everything that was happening.

Around June 2023, I started taking medication for my depression. It helped immeasurably, and I found that with my newfound energy, I was able to forge connections with people, which gave me a support scaffolding that I had not had before. Social mum, happy mum, happy baby. The sh1t rolls downhill.

Figure 9.3 One TENT practitioner's favourite photo from a session.
Source: Photograph by author.

Family activities tend to be targeted at children, and less so at adults. You take your child to see a film, and it's a horrendous experience. But the kids enjoyed it so… You take your child to the softplay, and it's a horrible experience, but they were out of your hair for 90 minutes, and you were able to drink your almost palatable coffee while it was still hot. You take your child to an Easter craft activity, "make your own chick for £15," and it is a horrendous experience. Your child becomes frustrated, and you end up doing most of the work (cutting along pre-drawn lines and gluing the numbered flaps together) to create a soggy, lopsided paper bird that will gather dust on your kitchen dresser for four months before you surreptitiously put it in the recycling.

With my newly medicated clarity, I was able to understand that these kinds of activities were putting me into a state of constant activation. It felt like the conventionally available activities encouraged over-stimulation and dissociation. I was not enjoying my time with my child; I was killing time and wishing it all away, in the name of self-sacrifice. But what if family activities could be genuinely enjoyable for caregivers as well as children?

I went into designing the TENT project using a lot of my own lived experiences, as well as the experiences of others gleaned from many heart-baring conversations. I decided to use it as a space to test the hypothesis that "caregivers need to have space where they can be safely challenged both creatively and intellectually." So I decided to shape the concept TENT around the idea of giving families access to high-quality cultural experiences that are as joyful for adults as they are for children. The sh1T rolls downhill.

We hold weekly creative play sessions at a community hall. The activities we offer vary, but our key ingredients for each session are:

- Artists and staff who are experts in human connection: Building trusting and meaningful relationships with the communities we work with is central to our practice.
- Open-ended creative play: Our artists possess expertise in participatory and exploratory creative practices and play, and all activities are designed to inspire curiosity and imagination.
- Invitational, rather than instructional, activity stations: We offer a range of creative experiences in each session, where all members of the TENT community are free to engage with whatever activity they choose, or none at all if they wish.
- Healthy self-serve food: We find that communion around food creates a shared feeling of connection.
- Openness to suggestions: We are driven by a desire to work in collaboration with communities, providing empowering and enriching environments that allow for shared learning and ownership.

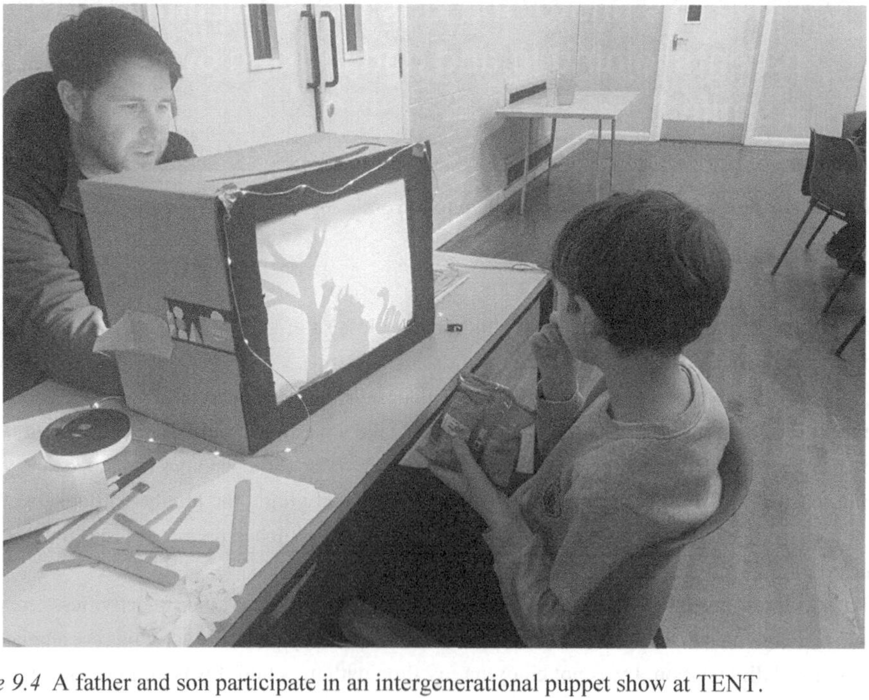

Figure 9.4 A father and son participate in an intergenerational puppet show at TENT.
Source: Photograph by author.

The most important factor behind TENT being a relational space is the facilitation by the staff. From day one, we have made it clear to all families who walk in that they have control over what happens in the hall. The session is intentionally overstaffed to ensure there are enough eyes and hands to keep everyone safe and comfortable. The activities on offer are devised to be easily replicable at home and to trigger play memories in adults. We have found a large contingent of fathers who have taken ownership of the sessions, building carts for the children, designing cardboard swords and even offering to put up extra shelves for our resource storage.

If people feel useful, and like their input is important, they are more likely to engage. This sets a beautiful example to the children, who are always watching, trying to understand how they should be in the world. The more agency, freedom and opportunities to be creative you give a person, the more they will feel like they can contribute to society. In today's political climate, we are seeing more and more of a desire to disconnect and to shut off. To take part in a space where it feels easy to be present, mindful and important makes it easier to build resilience against and therefore resist the Big Scary Things happening in the world.

My ultimate ambition for TENT is that it becomes a movement for mutual support. That it raises the voices of and advocates for caregivers in public conversations and ultimately makes space for families within the mainstream. Through our work, we are collectively redefining what accessibility truly means for families. I believe that creating a space of relational egalitarianism, that is, relational equality, is the first step towards that goal. As with any other effective grassroots work, it is a process that is never complete but always ongoing, involving tweaking, refining, listening, engaging, providing feedback, evolving and responding.

Understanding relational wealth building

The TENT community, comprising family members and practitioners, has been working to develop the concept of relational wealth further, reflecting on how TENT has created conditions for relationships to flourish. These relationships are multifaceted and multi-level, encompassing relationships between adults and children, between different family units, and between practitioners and family members (see Table 9.1).

The concept of relational wealth building continues to be co-produced by the TENT community, and further refinement and testing are needed to identify unifying elements that facilitate relational wealth within different contexts, including social services, education and healthcare. We have different levels on which relationships operate (i.e., individual as a function of a setting) and the power dynamics influencing those behaviours also need further exploration (Avram et al., 2024).

We hope that the context TENT showed how *humanisation* is central to creative relational wealth-building, providing a space for groups of people (children, parents, families) to connect. One area of relational wealth that requires further study is the welcoming of new members into relational spaces, especially in marginalised communities where groups feel a strong sense of ownership over the resources and opportunities and are resistant to others joining. What we have seen so far is a welcome for newly settled refugee families. This has been cultivated by Hannah, who has invested time in building relational wealth through spending one-to-one time with families and creating inclusive spaces. The newly settled families attend weekly and share food from their cultural heritage, as well as participate in new cultural activities. This provides a living example of relational wealth in terms of "the quality of relationships people experience with each other... It can be built by creating spaces for people to connect

Table 9.1 Relational wealth building at TENT

Create an Inclusive Space	• Shared space and communal food. • Focus on using play as a vehicle for establishing a foundation of trust upon which to build. • Knowing your voice stands for something. • Supporting each other shows courage in their creative choices and a willingness to try new things.
Be Honest	• Recognising each person's positionality and differences in lived experiences. • People are being encouraged to express their opinions. • Cultivating a culture of listening to understand versus listening to respond. • Sharing personal experiences as a way to break down barriers.
Make Cooperation the Norm	• Modelling cooperative behaviour. • Building in tidy time at the end of every session. • Cultivating a culture of reciprocity. • Development of TENT chat discussion space. • Looking after the local community, for example, through tree planting.
Be Open to Scrutiny and Challenge	• Approaching relations with the assumption that everyone has a general goodwill towards each other. • Managing expectations and building resilience, whilst being aware of the potential consequences on others when exercising voice. • Agreeing on ways to check in to ensure everyone is encouraged to express challenges or suggest change. • Cultivating a culture of reflective practice that underpins sustainable and communal growth and change.

in an equal and accessible way, and is based on the principles of trust, honesty and respect" (Wilson, 2024, p. 63).

Relational community research

Whilst we appreciate that not all readers will be engaging in research, we wanted to share our experiences of conducting research where we placed relationships at the centre of our practice. Although we explicitly draw on our collective experience in academic research, we hope that the insights we share can be applied both in research and in practice. This stance emphasises the importance of building relationships in conducting authentic community research, moving away from transactional approaches where researchers extract data from communities, taking ownership of something that is essentially not theirs. We argue that relational research can facilitate the honest sharing of experiences (and thus more authentic data), where the ownership of the data (i.e., people's stories and experiences) is shared. Figure 9.5 illustrates a process in which the focus on building relationships is central to all aspects of research.

Our experience has made us well aware of the challenges of building relationships with communities when conducting research in fractious times, particularly when trust in informal institutions, including higher education organisations, is low. Communication barriers and a lack of resources to invest significant time in building relationships can also hinder the process, particularly when the work is conducted within the constraints of an institution, such as higher education or the health service.

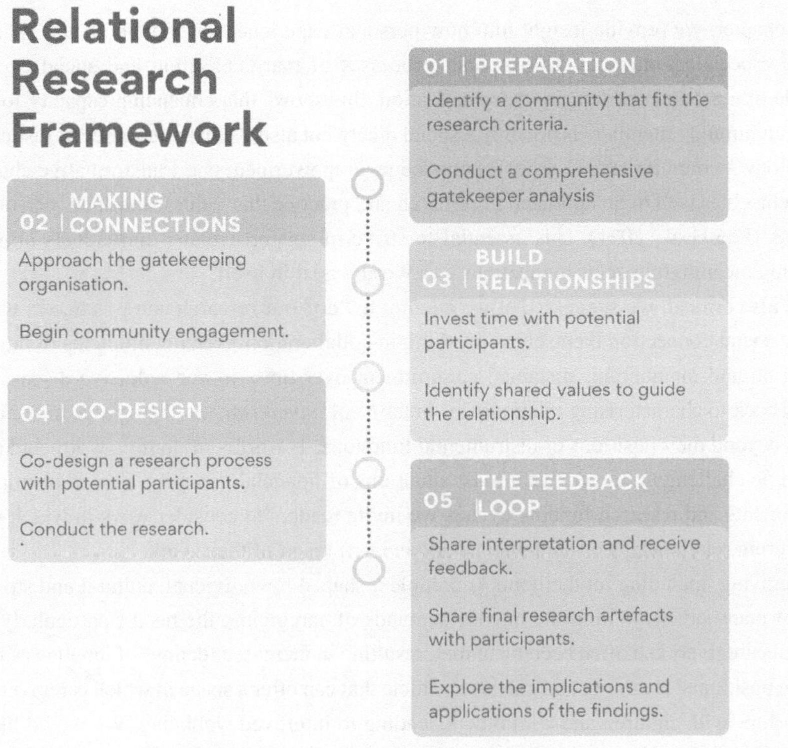

Figure 9.5 Relational community research process (Wilson, 2024).
Source: Image by author.

Institutional funding constraints can significantly impede stages that precede the preparation stage and provide little scope for continued relationships beyond the end of the feedback process. Our long-term, community-embedded approach strongly advocates a shift to focus on collaborative, long-term relationships between communities and community-based organisations rather than one-off, transactional projects.

Action for learning: Relational recruitment

Think about how you could apply the relational community research process in any project you are doing or would like to do, with a particular focus on the ***making connections*** stage.

- How would you go about building relationships with the people you work with?
- What are the barriers you would anticipate?
- How would you try to overcome these?

Use these observations and the relational community research process outlined above to write a recruitment strategy that focuses on building relationships.

Social justice, wellbeing and a relational space for community psychologists

In this chapter, we provide insight into how personal experiences of loneliness and isolation in motherhood, especially, intersect with broader processes of marginalisation and social exclusion. As an example of a group experiencing marginalisation, this shows that enhancing capacity for relationships among community members is not only a social nicety but also a step towards social justice. Community Psychology's commitments to critical knowledge, empowerment and transformative change over time lend themselves well to an approach to research and practice that values sustained, person-centred relationships (Lee et al., 2021). It is essential to strive to support isolated individuals in generating and sustaining meaningful social connections as a worthy goal in itself.

It is also critical, we suggest, that we attempt to "do" our research and practice in ways that foster genuine social connection themselves, working in collaboration, creating moments of human-to-human connection and maintaining sustained commitment over time. In our reflective discussions, we keep circling back to characterising relationships in terms of *humanisation* – being able to see people as individuals beyond their positions or instrumental functions, as worthy of dignity, worth and respect. While this can be challenging to achieve amidst situations of financial precarity, time constraints, caregiving commitments and research funding cycles, we invite readers to consider ways in which they can build empowering relationships through their work and as a result of their work.

Caregiving, including motherhood, is complex, shaped by individual, cultural and structural factors, amongst many others. Within the intense demands of caregiving, the needs, particularly the relational needs, of caregivers can often become unmet, resulting in increased feelings of loneliness. In this chapter, we have positioned creativity and play as a vehicle that can offer a space in which caregivers can cultivate relationships with children and with others, leading to improved wellbeing. We would like to conclude by reflecting on a well-known phrase, "it takes a village to raise a child." In a society whose culture is dominated by individualism, Community Psychology offers a mechanism for building this village.

Reflective questions

- How can Community Psychology be used to promote relational practice?
- How can relational wealth building develop the conditions for social justice and liberation, etc.?
- How do the pillars within the Relational Wealth Building framework resonate with your experience of relational spaces? What is missing? What would you like to add?

Key principles

1. Participation
2. Intervention
3. Empowerment
4. Sense of community
5. Relational knowledge

References

Abetz, J. S. (2019). "I want to be both, but is that possible?": Communicating mother-scholar uncertainty during doctoral candidacy. *Journal of Women and Gender in Higher Education, 12*(1), 70–87. https://doi.org/10.1080/19407882.2018.1501582

Adams, K. B., Sanders, S., & Auth, E. A. (2004). Loneliness and depression in independent living retirement communities: Risk and resilience factors. *Aging & Mental Health, 8*(6), 475–485. https://doi.org/10.1080/13607860410001725054

Allport, G. W. (1954). *The nature of prejudice*. Addison-Wesley.

Amado, A. N. (2013). *Friends: Connecting people with disabilities and community members*. University of Minnesota, Institute on Community Integration.

Autret, M., & van Eeden-Moorefield, B. (2024). An autoethnographic dialogue with motherhood literature. *The Qualitative Report, 29*(1), 1–25. https://doi.org/10.46743/2160-3715/2024.6290

Avram, C. M., Jones, A. E., Lucas, M. L., & Barrett, L. (2024). Reclaiming behaviour settings: Reviewing empirical applications of Barker's behaviour settings theory. *Philosophical Transactions of the Royal Society of London Series B Biological Sciences, 23*(329). https://doi.org/10.1098/rstb.2023.0283

Arimoto, A., & Tadaka, E. (2021). Individual, family, and community factors related to loneliness in mothers raising children less than 3 years of age: A cross-sectional study. *BMC Women's Health, 21*. https://doi.org/10.1186/s12905-021-01365-7

Benefield, N., & Haigh, R. (2020) Personality disorder: Breakdown in the relational field. In J. Ramsden, S. Prince, & J. Blazdell (Eds.), *Working effectively with 'personality disorder': Contemporary and critical approaches to clinical and organizational practice*. Pavilion Publishing and Media Ltd.

Bronfenbrenner, U. (1979). *The ecology of human development: Experiments by nature and design*. Harvard University Press.

Bukowski, W. M., & Adams, R. (2005). Peer relationships and psychopathology: Markers, moderators, mediators, mechanisms, and meanings. *Journal of Clinical Child & Adolescent Psychology, 34*(1), 3–10. https://psycnet.apa.org/doi/10.1207/s15374424jccp3401_1

Burman, E. (2016). *Deconstructing developmental psychology* (3rd ed.). Routledge. https://doi.org/10.4324/9781315727127

Cacioppo, J. T., & Patrick, W. (2008). *Loneliness: Human nature and the need for social connection*. W.W. Norton & Company.

Campbell, C. (2015). Health psychology and community action. In M. Murray (Ed.), *Critical health psychology* (2nd ed., pp. 254–274). Palgrave MacMillan.

Centre for Creative-Relational Inquiry. (2025). *Centre for Creative-Relational Inquiry*. University of Edinburgh. https://health.ed.ac.uk/research/current-research/ccri.

Coyle, C. E., & Dugan, E. (2012). Social isolation, loneliness and health among older adults. *Journal of Aging and Health, 24*, 1346–1363. https://doi.org/10.1177/0898264312460275

Crisp, R. J., & Turner, R. N. (2020). *Essential social psychology* (4th ed.). Sage Publications Ltd.

Freire, P., Ramos, M. B., Macedo, D. P., & Shor, I. (2018). *Pedagogy of the oppressed* (50th anniversary ed.). Bloomsbury Academic.

Graber, R. (2025). Understanding peer support in varying contexts of marginalisation: Implications for and linkages between formal and informal provision. In U. Kumar (Ed.), *Routledge international handbook of psychosocial resilience* (2nd ed.). Routledge.

Graber, R. (2019). Peer support interventions. In C. Llewellyn, S. Ayres, C. McManus, S. Newman, K. J. Petrie, T. Revenson, & J. Weinman (Eds.), *Cambridge handbook of psychology, health and medicine* (3rd ed., pp. 292–296). Cambridge University Press.

Graber, R., Turner, R., & Madill, A. (2016). Best friends and better coping: Facilitating psychological resilience through boys' and girls' closest friendships. *British Journal of Psychology, 107*(2), 338–358. https://doi.org/10.1111/bjop.12135

Haigh, R., & Benefield, N. (2023). The development of a relational practice movement. In S. Boden-Stuart & M. Larkin (Eds.), *Relationships and mental health: Relational experience in distress and recovery*. Palgrave Macmillan.

Hermans, M., & Mastel-Smith, B. (2012). Caregiving: A qualitative concept analysis. *The Qualitative Report*, *17*(75), 1–18. http://www.nova.edu/ssss/QR/QR17/hermanns.pdf

Jaimes, P. (2020). Navigating graduate school and surviving life as a mother–scholar. *Women, Gender, and Families of Color*, *8*(2), 227–234.

Kagan, C., Burton, M., Duckett, P., Lawthom, R., & Siddiquee, A. (2019). *Critical community psychology: Critical action and social change* (2nd ed.). Routledge. https://doi.org/10.4324/9780429431500

Kara, H. (2015) *Creative research methods in the social sciences: A practical guide*. Policy Press.

Lac, V. (2021). A mother-scholar during COVID-19. *Qualitative Inquiry*, *27*(8–9), 1130–1130. https://doi.org/10.1177/1077800420978752

Lapayese, Y. V. (2012). *Mother-scholar: (Re) imagining K-12 education* (Vol. 85). Springer Science & Business Media.

LeBlanc, S. S., Spradley, E., Beal, H. O., Burrow, L., & Cross, C. (2022). Being Dr. Mom and/or Mom, Ph. D.: Autoethnographies of MotherScholaring during COVID–19. *New Horizons in Adult Education and Human Resource Development*, *34*(3), 28–39. https://doi.org/10.1002/nha3.20360

Lee, S., Vibhuti, M., & Sudmann, T. T. (2021). Sustainable person-centred communities design and practice. In *International practice development in health and social care* (pp. 39–51). Wiley. https://doi.org/10.1002/9781119698463.ch4

Malchiodi, C. A. (Ed.). (2012). *Handbook of art therapy*. The Guildford Press.

Naughton-Doe, R., Nowland, R., Kent-Marvick, J., McKenna-Plumley, P., Lovett, E., Nguyen, T., Hunter, L., Wallis, N., Gaughan, F., Hall, K., Colella, C., Wilson, S., Adlington, K., Taylor Buck, E., Shemery, S., Finch, N., & Noone, C. (2025). Exploring perinatal loneliness as a key social determinant of perinatal mental ill health in the UK: Findings from a multidisciplinary consensus statement exercise that mapped knowledge about measurement, prevalence, antecedents, impacts and interventions, and agreed future priorities for research, policy and practice. *BMJ Open*, *15*(5). https://doi.org/10.1136/bmjopen-2024-085669

Neuhoff, R., Dam Johansen, N., & Simeone, L. (2022) Story-centred co-creative methods: A means for relational service design and healthcare innovation. In M. A. Pfannstiel, N. Brehmer, & C. Rasche (Eds.), *Service design practices for healthcare innovation*. Springer.

Riemer, M., Reich, S. M., Evans, S. D., Nelson, G. B., & Prilleltensky, I. (2020). *Community psychology: In pursuit of liberation and well-being* (3rd ed.). Macmillan International Higher Education, Red Globe Press.

Royal College of Psychiatrists. (2025). *Enabling Environments (EE)*. Royal College of Psychiatrists. https://www.rcpsych.ac.uk/improving-care/ccqi/quality-networks-accreditation/enabling-environments-network-ee.

Ryff, C. D., & Singer, B. H. (Eds.). (2001). *Emotion, social relationships, and health*. Oxford University Press.

Sotirin, P. (2010). Autoethnographic mother-writing: Advocating radical specificity. *Journal of Research Practice*, *6*(1), M9. http://jrp.icaap.org/index.php/jrp/article/view/220/189

Taylor, R. J., Chatters, L. M., Cross, C. J., & Mouzon, D. M. (2022). Fictive Kin networks among African Americans, Black Caribbeans, and Non-Latino Whites. *Journal of Family Issues*, *43*(1), 20–46. https://doi.org/10.1177/0192513x21993188

Turner, R. N. (2020). Crossing the divide: Promoting confidence in contact in a diverse society. *Journal of the British Academy*, *8*, 51–59. https://doi.org/10.5871/jba/008.051

Van Assche, J., Swart, H., Schmid, K., Dhont, K., Al Ramiah, A., Christ, O., Kauff, M., Rothmann, S., Savelkoul, M., Tausch, N., Wölfer, R., Zahreddine, S., Saleem, M., & Hewstone, M. (2023). Intergroup contact is reliably associated with reduced prejudice, even in the face of group threat and discrimination. *The American Psychologist*, *78*(6), 761–774. https://doi.org/10.1037/amp0001144

Wallerstein, N. (1992). Powerlessness, empowerment, and health: Implications for health promotion programs. *American Journal of Health Promotion*, *6*(3), 197–205. https://doi.org/10.4278/0890-1171-6.3.197

Wilson, S. (2025). Multiple and fluid positionalities in community research with socially excluded families: A case for reflexive sociology. *Forum Qualitative Sozialforschung / Forum: Qualitative Social Research, 26*(3). https://doi.org/10.17169/fqs-26.3.4346

Wilson, S. (2024). *Levelled up or left behind? A relational approach to social inclusion in low-income coastal communities* (Doctoral thesis). University of Central Lancashire.

Wilson, S. (2022). Can person-centred, strength based programmes impact on parents' engagement in education? *International Journal of Applied Positive Psychology, 7*, 51–71.

Wilson, S., & McGuire K. (2022). "You feel a bit lost": A case study interpreting White, working-class mothers' engagement through Habitus. *British Journal of Sociology of Education, 43*(2), 314–331. https://doi.org/10.1007/s41042-021-00054-y

Wyatt, J. (2018). *Therapy, stand up and the gesture of writing: Towards creative-relational inquiry.* Routledge.

Further reading

Benchekroun, R. (2025). *Precarious motherhood: Navigating relationships and support post-migration in the UK.* UCL Press.

Berry, L. (2018). *The republic of motherhood.* Random House.

Cassels, T. (n.d.). Evolutionary parenting. https://evolutionaryparenting.com/evolutionary-parenting-podcast-2/

Centre for Creative-Relational Inquiry. https://health.ed.ac.uk/research/current-research/ccri

Gordon-Walker, M., & Noughton, C. (Eds.). (2018). *The secret life of mothers: Chronicles of love, sweat and tears.* Silverdart Ltd.

Hollway, W. (2015). *Knowing mothers: Researching maternal identity change*. Springer.

Jones, L. (2023). *Matrescence: On the metamorphosis of pregnancy, childbirth and motherhood.* Random House.

Lamph, G., Nowland, R., Boland, P., Pearson, J., Connell, C., Jones, V., & McKeown, M. (2023). Relational practice in health, education, criminal justice, and social care: A scoping review. *Systematic Reviews, 12*(1), 194.

McNish, H. (2016). *Nobody told me: Poetry and parenthood.* Blackfriars.

Solutions to Perinatal Loneliness. https://perinatal-loneliness.com/

10 Using creative, embodied approaches to prevention of and recovery from substance misuse

A dialogue between research and practice

Rebecca Graber, Raginie Duara, Sangeeta Goswami, Diptarup Chowdhury and Anna Madill

Introduction

This chapter explores three interlinked creative participatory research and practice projects aimed at supporting prevention and recovery to substance addiction in Assam, a North East state of India where substance addiction among young people is a public health concern (Pathak et al., 2017). We aim to show how creative participatory methods support an understanding of addiction that puts possibilities for recovery, social connection and social justice at its heart; provides empathetic insight into the embodied struggle of addiction; and supports forms of research and practice conducive to hope and social change. We refer to "creative participatory methods" as using techniques from the arts (such as photography or drama) to support a participant's active creative production and expression, where the goal of that process primarily is knowledge-making but, if used in a practice context, also therapeutic insight. The resulting creative output may itself be "data," while participant reflections may also be invoked through more traditional methods such as interviews.

We aim to show the value of participatory creative approaches for empowering people to engage with lived experience expertise of recovery and to generate hopeful visions for a healthy and socially connected future. The authors are a group of research psychologists based in the UK and specialising in qualitative, creative methods and mental health (Anna, Rebecca and Raginie, who is from Assam) and research-active clinical psychologists based in Assam (Sangeeta, who directs MIND India, an NGO providing holistic health and wellbeing care and committed to social change, and Diptarup, who provides clinical psychology care for deaddiction and recovery). We share a collective interest and experience in using creative methods for research and healing; the importance of working with people facing stigma and significant challenges in a potentially empowering way; and prevention and treatment of addiction with attention to the wider social context. In case study 1, based on a project we all worked on (The Big Picture), we use photo-led interview techniques to understand lived experience of resilience for recovery to substance addiction. Case study 2 shows how we used our research findings to develop a resource to aid prevention of addiction and insight into recovery journeys using embodied techniques. Case study 3 explores arts-based therapeutic tools for prevention and recovery support based at MIND India. We show how using participatory creative methods can help researchers and practitioners to grapple with the seemingly intractable issues of stigma and marginalisation facing people in substance addiction that contribute to and perpetuate addiction (Graber et al., 2025; Dekkers et al., 2020; Pisarska et al.,

DOI: 10.4324/9781003480464-13

2016). Further, we encourage readers to play with creative processes to provide entry for Community Psychology principles, practices and values.

Substance misuse and addiction: The context for Assam, India

Substance misuse and substance use disorder (SUD) are a major public health concern in India, with adolescents and young people being especially vulnerable to the onset of addiction and its profound implications for physical health, mental health and social inclusion (Ambekar et al., 2019; Gururaj et al., 2016). To give a sense of the scope of the problem, alcohol is the most commonly abused substance by those with substance dependency (19%), followed by cannabis (2.8%), opioids (2.1%), sedatives and inhalants (Gururaj et al., 2016). Addiction can be gendered: in India; men are far more likely to experience misuse and SUD, but women are disproportionately stigmatised for addiction and are underserved by rehabilitation facilities (Kermode et al., 2012).

The Northeastern state of Assam has undergone significant industrialisation and consequent changes to rural and urban areas in recent decades, across castes and religious groupings. It is against this context of tension between structural inequalities on the one hand, and ambitions for achievement and economic advancement on the other, that psychological distress and substance use among adolescents and young people have grown. In our clinical experience, the importance and pressure placed on young people by parents and caregivers on scholastic achievement, the economic and societal disparity between the haves and have-nots and the lack of career opportunities, all contribute to the increase of SUD among young people. Substances are an important part of social life for a minority of young people: young people often experiment with drugs for fun and amusement in the company of friends, particularly in urban areas (Goswami, 2015). A lack of family support, abusive parents, use of substance by parents, parental disharmony and poor attachment between parent and child pose a further hindrance to recovery (Graber et al., 2025; Madill et al., 2022).

Community and non-governmental organisations, such as MIND India and our research partner organisation Nirman Rehabilitation Facility, play a particularly important role in prevention and rehabilitation in Assam. Approaches for addressing substance misuse through de-addiction and rehabilitation range from acute medical detoxification and pharmacological therapies such as opiate substitution therapy primarily in hospital-based settings, to family therapy, individual therapy and 12-step peer recovery programmes (such as Narcotics Anonymous) adapted from the West, across community-based settings (Madill et al., 2022; Perumbilly & Anderson, 2017). Some programmes also integrate Indian cultural practices such as yoga, spirituality and an emphasis on social interdependence including support groups for families (Greene, 2021). There is an ongoing need to better understand prevention, recovery and rehabilitation programmes in the Indian context, especially taking into account gender, caste, spirituality, the centrality of the family and socioeconomic factors (Graber et al., 2025; Kermode et al., 2012; Madill et al., 2022). We suggest using participatory creative methods to support participants in bringing their lived experience of these varying factors to the research, contributing a more contextually specific and culturally sensitive approach.

In the northeastern states of India more broadly, community-based responses to SUD range from coercive measures against drug users by local pressure groups like forced treatment or house arrest by families, to various drug reduction approaches, including grassroots initiatives placing pressure on the state, and central and state government initiatives focusing on psychoeducation of young people and practitioners. For example, in Manipur, women belonging to the All Manipur Women's Social Reformation and Development Samaj (Nupi Samaj) reaffirmed their stand against legalisation of liquor (UT News Service, 2022). Another example is how the community policing wing of Punjab Police is mandated to nudge youth away from drugs (Bajwa, 2025). Psychoeducation to learn about addiction and its presentation is a particular priority. For example, schools and higher education departments are creating more awareness among principals to address the growing issue of drug and substance abuse among students (National Education Policy NEP 2020 No: CBSE/M&PR/Counseling/2025). MIND India, in association with ECHO India, has conducted training for counsellors under the Social Welfare department, Government of Punjab and for counsellors from Bodoland working with community members and families (Bodoland is an autonomous division in Assam which has a large number of young people with SUD). The aim was to understand the red flags of alcohol and SUD and identify positive support for people recovering from alcohol and SUD and their families. Families can benefit from mutual support organisations such as Al-Anon or Nar-Anon which provide opportunities to learn from others affected by SUD. These services started in Guwahati in the 2010s and extend their services to affected families too.

However, these services and approaches are few and far between in Assam and need to be expanded. Further, they continue to draw heavily on models of psychology, public health and education developed in the Global North (Madill et al., 2022). Participatory methods, developed in collaboration with local researchers and practitioners, have strong potential to develop culturally appropriate theory-led knowledge and care practices through centring the experiences and expertise of those who live in recovery in these communities.

A Community Psychology-informed approach to generating knowledge and understanding about substance addiction and recovery

The World Health Organisation recommends community-based care for substance addiction as part of mental health service provision, acknowledging the importance of non-medical, personalised support for outreach and recovery, and involving coordinated service delivery in consultation with community health representatives (WHO, 2021). However, placing care within community settings does not automatically mean that it will empower vulnerable individuals or groups to effect change. Significant structural and individual barriers to de-addiction and recovery include limited or altered life opportunities for those facing addiction, unequal access to recovery facilities and frequency of relapse (Graber, 2025).

Recovery requires some kind of physiological intervention (whether this is abstinence or medical treatment such as opiate substitution), but also psychological change, processes which are partially shaped by factors outside an individual's control. We have therefore found it useful to draw on theories of "psychosocial resilience" to help think about what wellbeing means in the context of substance misuse. Psychosocial resilience is a process through which a person adapts positively to a significantly challenging experience. Most theories of psychosocial resilience suggest a person's positive adaptation through a challenging experience will happen at different times, along different trajectories and include "failed attempts" or delayed change (e.g., Masten, 2014). Social ecological approaches to psychosocial resilience, such as what we use here, further apply a multi-level approach to psychosocial adaptation, understanding change as being shaped by an ongoing process of interactions between mechanisms operating at different levels including individual (such as coping strategies or self-efficacy), relational/social (such as access to supportive social relationships, or opportunities to re-enter education) and structural levels (such as availability of rehabilitation programmes) (Graber, 2025; Liebenberg, 2020). Psychosocial resilience approaches are underdeveloped in addictions *recovery*, although they have been successfully applied to prevention (Graber, 2025; Graber et al., 2025; Rudzinski et al., 2017; Valsala & Devanathan, 2023). A resilience approach encourages researchers and practitioners to identify and use protective assets and strengths available to individuals from themselves and their environments, and to learn from experts-by-experience about what "wellbeing" means in the context of substance addiction, and how it may be achieved (Graber et al., 2025; Madill et al., 2022; Rudzinski et al., 2017).

Community Psychology adds to this by helping us to think about *community-level* processes sitting between individual characteristics (such as family histories of substance misuse) and inequalities in place-based characteristics (such as access to housing or gender-specific recovery programmes) (Fettig et al., 2024; Graber, 2025). A multi-level framework attends to connections between levels and the characteristics of the communities to which people in addiction belong: how communities are shaped by the prevalence of substances themselves, as well as stigma and social exclusion of people living in recovery (Graber et al., 2025; Hugh-Jones et al., 2024; Madill et al., 2022). This has informed our framing of substance addiction as a social justice issue, wherein individual vulnerabilities and suffering interact with criminalisation policies, unequal access to recovery resources and broader social and economic inequalities to drive pernicious substance use which presents in different ways across different geographic and social communities. A multi-level perspective has informed related work outside the scope of this chapter, for example through development of policy briefings (Madill et al., 2022) and examining how research evidence is used to set mental health policy agendas in low- and middle-income countries (Brooks et al., 2023).

Creative participatory methods

Creative participatory methods encompass a broad range of approaches utilising arts-based techniques with people to generate empirical knowledge and understanding through acts of making and engagement with the material world. These can include visual methods such as photo-elicitation and photo-production, videography, sculpture, textile work, interactive mapping; and more (Reavey, 2021) as well as other art forms such as drama or poetry (Cross et al., 2006). In adding the modifier "participatory" we emphasise that the creative act should be driven by the participant, in terms of collecting, producing, organising and/or interpreting creative outputs, as appropriate for the question and context.

Creative participatory methods are especially useful for working with members of marginalised or stigmatised groups because they are often underrepresented in research and excluded from positions of power on the basis of their difficulties and identities (Kramer-Roy, 2015). These methods draw strength from the emergent relationship between researcher and participant underpinned by creative making (or sharing one's creation) and similarly can underpin relationships between groups of people. Because the researcher, or the practitioner, does not exclusively shape the research encounter, the participant has space to claim power and create knowledge in a way that is often less possible in other approaches. Participants can set agendas, create materials, drive topics and conversations, use silence or hesitation and communicate about experiences that are inherently embodied and therefore difficult to put into words. This can contribute to new self-insight by participants and challenges to empirical knowledge.

The researcher cedes some control, and therefore power, over knowledge-gathering: to chance, to serendipity, to place and crucially to the participants or co-researchers who make the process their own. Parameters and boundaries create objectives and promote psychological and physical safety, but creative practice is fundamentally a process of exploration. When used in a therapeutic setting, creativity can accomplish these tasks with the overarching goal being personal healing and connection with the self and others.

We have often been struck by the empathy with which others meet work generated through the creative process. The creative modality therefore offers an opportunity to connect human to human, even in contexts of policy-making, with transformative potential. Engagement in participatory creative methods can be a liberatory tool in the project of raising critical awareness of a social issue, transforming understanding and identifying action to move forward towards a more just future (Martin-Baro, 1994).

Praxis case study 1: Connecting research to lived experience of resilience through the use of photo-led interviews

As part of the Big Picture project exploring prevention and recovery from substance addiction in Assam, directed by Anna, Raginie conducted a series of participatory photo-led interviews with young adults in recovery to explore their lived experience of abstinence and rehabilitation (Graber et al., 2025; Hugh-Jones et al., 2024; Madill et al., 2022). Participants were invited to bring any photos or images to the interview that represented their experience or helped them to tell their story. Some brought personal photographs, some brought internet memes, some brought art or a combination thereof.

We found several strengths to using photo-led interviews. We felt that sharing photos helped establish a rapport between Raginie and participants, as they could show something of their own selves through their selection of images. Further, the photos facilitated insight and reflection. These young adults had not typically been given opportunities to share their stories outside of a medical or rehab setting, where accounts focused on symptoms and struggle. In the interviews, participants could share their stories on their own terms, using imagery to capture hard-to-verbalise feelings and experiences, and bring as much of their selves to the encounter as they wished to, freeing Raginie to focus on following up meaningful aspects of their accounts and being an empathetic presence. We felt breaking from the format of typical interviewing enabled the discussions to also explore how participants navigated into recovery. This enabled interrogation of what it means to be *well* in the context of recovery, and for participants' own meaning-making to take precedence over any theorising we started with, facilitating critical knowledge-making. Finally, because accounts were frequently chaotic and fragmented, the photos also served sometimes as memory aides.

The interview texts and images were qualitatively analysed by Anna, Rebecca and other team members, with frequent checking of developing themes with Sangeeta, Diptarup and other practitioners to see how the analysis related to their own observations, reflected cultural and community concerns and seemed helpful in understanding or improving practice.

We briefly report two key analytical outcomes. One is a multi-level framework of mechanisms for resilience for recovery (Graber et al., 2025), as shown in Figure 10.1. Importantly, "precursors to recovery" are mechanisms of change that may be best addressed through social and community-level approaches, through provision and awareness of appropriate services; enhancing community understanding of addiction; and providing accessible means to interrupt physiological processes of addiction through biomedical means. The "repairing relationships" group of recovery mechanisms underscores

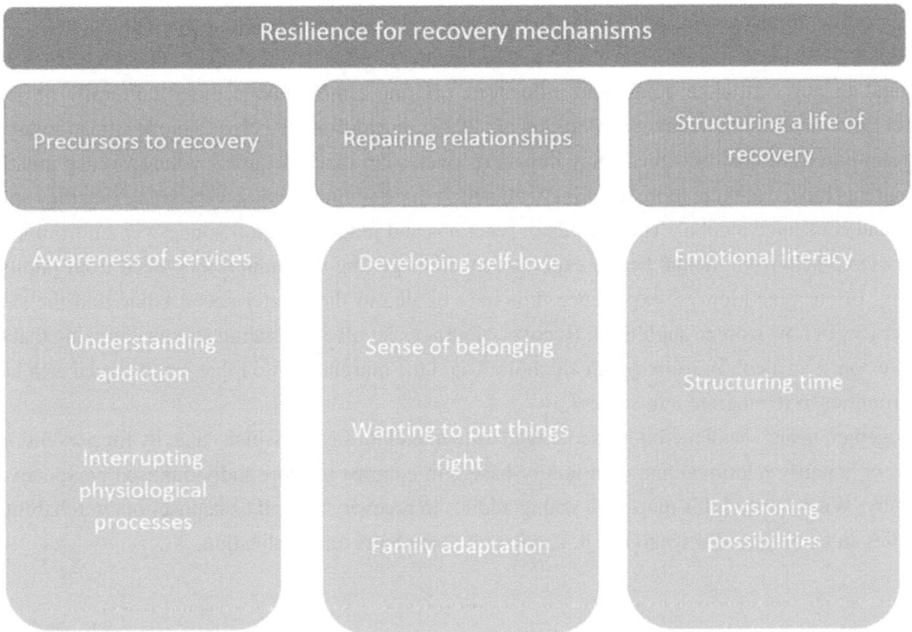

Figure 10.1 Resilience for recovery mechanisms

how substance misuse impacts social relationships within a community over time, creating significant ruptures and divisions between people in addiction and their loved ones or wider communities (Graber, 2025; Rudzinski et al., 2017). Relational repair – with the family unit, with extended kinship circles, with new or sober friends – is crucial. The "structuring a life of recovery" group of mechanisms speaks to building a hopeful future both through individual, intra-psychological change, but also integration into a social milieu that permits new possibilities. Taking the three together highlights the importance of encouraging social connection, relationship formation and self-compassion alongside more structural-level supports such as treatment provision, public health campaigns and opportunities for employment and re-entry into formal education.

This sits alongside our development of the novel Pathways to Recovery model (Madill et al., 2022; Madill et al., 2023) which explains and visualises a nonlinear recovery journey and qualitative differences between abstinence and other forms of non-use. Just as creativity underpinned our encounters with participants, we felt we needed a creative way of detailing their recovery journeys. The model conveys how recovery typically includes multiple routes, setbacks and recalibrations; qualitative differences between misuse, abstinence and real recovery; and the sense that even failed attempts at sobriety can hold wisdom (Madill et al., 2022). This approach diverges from traditional group work exercises commonly used in mainstream Western addiction services, which often rely on structured, linear models such as the 12-step programme or the Transtheoretical Model of Change, a model integral to health psychology and behaviour change fields (Raihan & Cogburn, 2023). However, research increasingly challenges these linear conceptions. For instance, Laudet (2007) highlights that recovery is a multifaceted process that goes beyond just abstinence, involving improvements in health, social functioning and quality of life, influenced by factors like social support, housing and community engagement.

Building on these insights, the *Pathways to Recovery* model makes visible the interplay between personal agency and wider contextual influences, offering a more nuanced and culturally responsive model for understanding recovery (Madill et al., 2023). It additionally helps to pinpoint particular areas of group-based risk and how these may impact recovery. For example, a few young women mentioned that parents looked at them more negatively than their male siblings if they were aware that they smoked weed and consumed alcohol. These kinds of reactions and judgement stop young women from seeking professional help from mental health experts, as well as getting the support they need from family and society. In our practitioners' experience, this may be due to the greater social taboo and the skewed gender lens of how women should act. Recovery journeys involve navigating stigma, knowing that some believe "once an alcoholic, always an alcoholic"; and the marginalisation that results, such as a lack of opportunities to reintegrate into society.

Together, using visual methods encouraged us to attend to ways in which capacity for prevention and recovery is partly relational and community-based, in contrast to more individualised perspectives on recovery. We discussed this map with young addicts in recovery as well as counsellors in rehabilitation facilities and considered ways to use it. Case study 2 explores one application.

Figure 10.2 Pathways to recovery model.

Source: Madill et al., (2023)

Action for learning activity: Imaging "recovery"

This activity develops skill in using photo elicitation techniques to help people think creatively about the process of "recovery." What does it mean to recover from a difficult situation? This could be substance addiction or another difficult situation facing people in your community.

Note: Although creative participatory methods can be meaningful, accessible and rewarding, it is also worth recognising that they can be experienced by some as patronising or childish! We believe creative activities work best when used with the support of peer leaders or coproduced with them, in a context of meaningful relationships with participants and community settings, and when they contribute to a genuine action or outcome so that participants feel they can drive change. It also helps to be flexible in adapting the proposed activity to people's needs and preferences.

This activity should be used within a group that already forms a community – such as members of a school class, youth group or community organisation. This can be used in a workshop or classroom setting. Take care to ensure everyone feels safe to participate. Consider practicalities such as accessibility and physical and psychological safety. Offer appropriate support and adapt the activity for the needs of your community members. There is no "one right way" with creative methods.

Step 1: Decide *how* you will gather your images. Will you take photos? Only take identifiable pictures of people with their permission. Will you use publicly available images from the internet, magazines or other media? Gather the tools you will need (phones, donated magazines, flyers, etc.). Decide on a time frame for generating your images – a week? A day? A few hours?

Step 2: Generate your images. Gather images that represent the experience of "recovery" in some way. Some might take a very literal approach – a picture of a hospital, for example. Some might be more figurative – a sunset, a choppy sea, certain colours. Some might use photographs of times of healing or fracture. Some may even use images of words. Don't be overly restrictive; instead, invite people to include anything they think speaks to the experience of "recovery." You might do this individually or in small groups.

Step 3: Come together as a group and share your images. Discuss how they inform an understanding of "recovery." How do your understandings differ, reinforce or complement each other? Is "recovery" the same in all contexts?

Step 4: Create a poster collage using a small selection of images that the group feels represents the experience of recovery. Use consensus to assemble your poster, ensuring many perspectives are included and that there is a clear message to the viewer. Consider how you might display the poster and to whom.

Step 5: Take action. Using this poster collage as a prompt, consider what changes you could make in your community to support people recovering from a difficult situation, whether this is substance addiction or something else that you identify as a priority for those in your community. Where will you begin?

Praxis case study 2: Embodied learning in addiction prevention education

As a team, we considered how to best convey elements of chance and nonlinearity presented by the Pathways to Recovery model, where recovery can be risky but also open opportunities. Researchers are often asked by funders to "engage stakeholders," an objective that should, to be meaningful, address real needs and allow for learning to happen. We developed several sorts of outputs based on our academic research and returned to the idea that the Pathways model might be turned into a game to promote more active engagement and highlight the nonlinear nature of recovery. Anna and Raginie, working closely with Sangeeta, sought to translate young people's shared experiences into a format that other young people could engage with directly, first through an animation created by Raginie and leading to the creation of a game that provides a space for embodied enquiry into the lives of young people who have personally experienced the arduous journey of addiction and recovery.

One particularly striking aspect from photo-elicitation interviews with Assamese young people who have *avoided* substance addiction was how direct, intimate exposure to the consequences of addiction often influenced their decisions, especially at meaningful turning points (Hugh-Jones et al., 2024). One young person wrote the following lines in a poster she created based on her interview, referring to her brother:

He became hollow
He didn't talk to anybody
He started shivering randomly
Do I ever want to be in a state like that?
Witnessing the consequences of
using substances was
more than enough for me
to know my answer

Her immersion in her brother's reality allowed her to internalise the severe consequences of addiction more effectively than any verbal warnings could have done. Personal stories like these highlight the need for preventive measures that go beyond mere cognitive understanding, to tools that engage the body and emotions to foster a deeper, more visceral comprehension of addiction's grip. However, such intimate exposure to the effects of addiction on one's life is not available to all. The lived experience of addiction is so powerful and disruptive that true insight can be hard to achieve, nested within layers of beliefs about what addiction is, who is vulnerable to it, and how you emerge from it.

This is where the concept of embodied knowledge becomes useful. Todres writes, "the body is intimate to understanding, and such bodily-informed sense-making adds a crucial dimension to the ways we have access to truth and present such truth" (2007, p. 6). The concept of embodied experience suggests that our cognition is deeply rooted in our physical and sensory experiences, rather than being solely a function of the mind (Varela et al., 2017). Addiction and recovery are embodied processes, happening in the body and of the body, but also involving qualitative changes to thinking and relationships. Embodied learning refers to the process by which learning is integrated through bodily engagement, such as through movement, sensation or physical presence, in ways that affect knowledge, identity and behaviour (Clughen, 2024; Sani et al., 2021). This challenges traditional views that separate mind and

Stage: Strategic Self -Management
You feel better and want to stay off substances. Move to Abstinence .
The substances you need are available again. Move back to Addiction .
Your family think you're clean because you did a short detoxification treatment and are no-longer watching you closely. Move back to Addiction .
You can see how much your family love you and how much you are hurting them, so you want to stay off substances for them. Move to Abstinence .
Your family think you're clean because you did a short detoxification treatment and are no-longer watching you closely. Move back to Addiction .
Stage: Supported Treatment
Congratulations. You have stayed clean and found a peer support network to help you create a life without substances. Move to Recovery .
Congratulations. You are staying clean. Move to Recovery . But wait - oh no! You met-up with people who are still using substances and the temptation was too much. Move back to Addiction .
You didn't finish the 90-day programme. Move back to Addiction .
You finished the 90-day programme but have not made a commitment to a life without substances. Move back to Addiction .
You are no-longer using but have made no lifestyle changes and are attending peer-support meetings only now-and-then. Move to Abstinence .
Congratulations. You have stayed clean and found a peer support network to help you create a life without substances. Move to Recovery .

Figure 10.3 Extract of dice move instructions.

body, proposing instead that our bodily experiences are integral to our cognitive processes (Finlay, 2014).

This game employs tactile interactions – rolling dice, moving pieces – to bring the obstacles and progress in addiction, relapse and recovery to life. Physical engagement may facilitate embodied learning by allowing players to experience something of the complex dynamics of risk, choice and consequence in recovery. Figure 10.3 is an extract from our free online educational materials and provides more detail as to how the Pathways to Recovery board game can be played. Rolling dice and relying on chance mirrors the unpredictable nature of addiction, where despite one's intentions, external factors can trigger relapse, echoing the real-life unpredictability and a lack of control faced by addicts (Sayette & Griffin, 2004). It also gives the players a chance to explore different reasons for relapse and positive changes that can move a person nearer to recovery. Moving pieces around the board can simulate the frustrating, repetitive cycles often experienced in addiction, where efforts to move forward can result in setbacks and regression, highlighting the reality that recovery is a non-linear, often gruelling process (Graber et al., 2025; Madill et al., 2022). Engaging multiple senses and physical actions can potentially create a more immersive and impactful understanding of addiction. Embodied enquiry "requires the lived body as the 'place' where intimate understanding of both experience and language happen" (Todres, 2007, p. 5).

Engaging with the game, moving pieces and experiencing the highs and lows through a controlled, yet immersive environment, can help young people empathise with the embodied reality of living with and recovering from addiction. It shifts educational focus from a purely cognitive understanding to an experiential one, where learning is internalised through bodily engagement and emotional connection (Maiese, 2017). Responses were promising from a group of young people (15–17 years old) in Assam who trialled this game with a practitioner as a prevention tool in school. One said: "*The fight with drugs is like a marathon rather than a sprint. It requires a lot of resilience, courage and patience.*" Although clearly a simplification and abstraction, these game dynamics help participants embody the experience of addiction: the setbacks become more than theoretical obstacles – they are felt frustrations. Achieving significant milestones, while not equivalent to real-life recovery, can give players a taste of the relief and achievement that accompanies overcoming addiction challenges. This empathetic, embodied connection can foster a deeper understanding of the complexities and challenges involved in the journey towards recovery.

We used this game based on the Pathways map with community workers, secondary schools, volunteers working at rehabilitation centres under the Government of Assam as well as college students who were interning with MIND India. While this game is not itself a community intervention, the board game may provide a basis for broader work through communal use in schools, community centres, and rehabilitation facilities where groups of young people can, through social interaction with their peers, engage in embodied learning to relate the abstraction of addiction to their own lives, and we are curious as to how the embodied approach may bring something new to information-based or skills-based approaches. Raginie is currently working with young women in recovery in the North of England to understand applicability in a different community context. More broadly, this work poses interesting questions about how embodied learning could be part of a Community Psychology-informed approach within mainstream settings, and whether similar games could be co-produced with people in recovery as part of further efforts to destigmatise, build relationships and create opportunities.

Praxis case study 3: Using creative participatory recovery approaches within a community mental health organisation

In this section, Sangeeta explains how MIND India, which she directs, has been practising different creative methods with students undergoing training in counselling and with other grassroots level community groups since 2018. This has often been in association with Agora, The Space, an art facilitation and wellbeing space headed by Radhika Goswami which teaches counsellors to use theatre and other creative techniques for emotional healing. Similar work has been done with community workers from grassroots level organisations like North East Network (NEN) who work with women and children in vulnerable situations.

Training practitioners to use these methods can be an important way of supporting transformative change in communities, by addressing stigma around substance addiction and recovery and promoting psychological approaches to counter community members' views of addiction as primarily a biomedical issue or an expression of criminality (Graber et al., 2025). As with the creative research methods discussed, arts-based therapeutic practices encourage embodied knowledge, reflection and novel understanding. In our practice, we have found that art therapy can help ease pain by allowing people to explore their feelings and experiences creatively. It can be a good alternative to talking therapy as it doesn't require too much verbal communication and allows the person to use different mediums like craft, pencil art, sketches, water and oil paints, dance and drama. Art therapy can help people work through past traumas in a safe setting, as seen in Figure 10.4. Art and expression therapy has been used as a way of healing and to regulate emotions.

Figure 10.4 Members of Nirmaan Rehabilitation Centers, Guwahati, Assam, participating in art-based recovery approach at Wellness Carnival organised by MIND India (2022).

Using arts-based recovery approaches has been used mostly as a preventive method at different platforms and with different target groups, and to provide opportunities for people in recovery from substance addiction to share their experience, connect with others and engage in public service. For example, school children have put up a mime show at Carnivals organised by MIND India for public awareness, as seen in Figure 10.5. These carnivals also included people in recovery who expressed their recovery path through chart work. These activities reflect the elements of social justice and wellbeing and provide a sense of inclusivity for Assamese young people in recovery from substance addiction in a society which typically stigmatises them, and where they may face challenges to reintegrating as peers disengage from friendships, prospects for romantic relationships are compromised and the chances of rejoining education or employment seem daunting (Graber et al., 2025).

Creative participatory approaches therefore can lend an empowering, embodied and thought-provoking cast to psychoeducation about substances. For example, adolescents from tea garden communities of Assam were exposed to "Forum Theatre" to talk about issues like child abuse, child labour, school drop-out, gender discrimination to name a few, as seen in Figure 10.6. Creative methods have been used with college and university students to enhance self-awareness and positive mental health and wellbeing among young people. Topics varying from knowing oneself, enhancing self-esteem, effects of SUD, understanding rights and protection have been incorporated into these creative methods. These activities helped to create a space to talk about social justice, inequalities, rights and on goals and aspirations of self. Experimentation has been done with creative art with different groups at different platforms. Testimonials of feel-good factor and release of stress and immediate emotional outlet have been shared by participants after the sessions on creative methods. However, more studies need to be conducted to inform evidence-based research.

Figure 10.5 Youth representing Byatikyam Masdo presenting a mime on Anti Tobacco & Liquor Awareness Campaign during the Wellness Carnival organised by MIND India (2022).

Figure 10.6 Radhika Goswami, Director Agora, The Space, Guwahati, facilitating a workshop on the use of arts-based recovery approaches (Forum Theatre) for emotional healing for facilitators working with adolescent groups in Tea Gardens of Assam.

Reflections on social justice, wellbeing and priorities for researchers and practitioners

In writing this chapter, we note how, within our professional roles, we have implicitly or explicitly applied a social justice lens to substance misuse and addiction, viewing "wellbeing" in the context of addiction as a community-level issue with community-level opportunities for support, and aiming to support the empowerment of people in addiction and their wider communities to build healthy, purposeful and interconnected lives. In this section, Rebecca, Diptarup and Sangeeta lead reflections on how creative participatory methods offer a powerful way to understand one's own journey of addiction and recovery, and for someone who has not experienced this directly to peer into visceral lived experience. As well as helping to advance knowledge-making, these methods therefore bridge connection. People struggling with substance addiction, even having entered recovery, experience significant social exclusion in Assam, as elsewhere. Advancing social justice therefore entails acknowledging that social inclusion and the development of meaningful, adaptive relationships with others are critical to addiction recovery, with family and extended community influences playing particularly central roles in Assam (Graber et al., 2025; Madill et al., 2022). Appealing to social obligations and utilising community and relational supports is crucial. This also means developing and using a sense of culturally specific wellbeing. For example, this may mean allowing for practices that are discouraged in other regions because they fulfil important social and cultural functions. Some religious rituals and festivals still require contact with alcohol or other substances, such that complete abstinence may not be feasible or even desired (Graber et al., 2025; Valsala & Devanathan, 2023). The use of alternative addictive substances may also be experienced as positive for supporting cessation from more harmful options (Valsala & Devanathan, 2023). "Wellbeing" may therefore still include contact with alcohol or other substances, even for those in addiction recovery. This is unusual for many Western step-based recovery programmes, so developing and adapting local therapeutic options is important.

Advancing social justice and wellbeing in this context would further entail achieving greater understanding of who takes up different types of treatment and why. Based on our experience working with rehabilitation facilities and in clinical practice, we suggest group-based economic inequalities not only feed into pressures to use substances, but may inform individuals' selection of medical detoxification and opiate substitution therapies that do not necessarily stop cycles of addiction but do address immediate crises and withdrawal symptoms. We wonder about differentiation based on religious group, economic drivers and family pressures that may inform choice of substance, choice of treatment and possibilities of relapse. Our previous research provides partial support, noting that many participants in recovery felt they were viewed by community members as forever tainted or criminal; often pursued detox ineffectually or to strategically self-manage their addictions; and continued to participate in festivals and rituals centring substance use (Graber et al., 2025). Religious, ethnic and caste groups have different norms around substance use, with some suggestion that this is shifting with economic industrialisation as, for example, alcohol use becomes more frequent and less attached to culturally significant meanings (Rose et al., 2015; Valsala & Devanathan, 2023). It will be interesting to see whether efforts to support financial inclusion, community institutions and economic wellbeing in the region, particularly in rural areas (e.g., Kumar, Sengupta & Gogoi, 2023) will impact patterns of substance use. A strength of creative participatory methods is that those engaging with them necessarily bring their own interpretations and lived experience to the material, creating potentially empowering opportunities to explore these tensions in psychoeducation, research and clinical practice.

Our research and practice adapt and challenge treatment paradigms from the Global North with particular emphasis on using creative participatory approaches to reducing and preventing suffering arising from SUD (Madill et al., 2022; MIND India, n.d.). In our collaboration, some of us came to "community psychology" more formally through our experience and training, while others have found this to be a way of naming our values and ways of working in mainstream clinical, medical and academic psychological contexts. We use participatory creative approaches that are accessible and meaningful to service users, providers and others, aiming to empower them to direct and co-construct activities. In practice, this is, of course, not always straightforward, but creativity is seen as personally healing, a way to support people.

Together, these case studies offer insight into applications of participatory creative approaches towards prevention and recovery from substance addiction. We also hoped to show how we, as a group of researchers and practitioners, creatively responded to the problems and opportunities encountered in our work. Participatory creative approaches can prompt novel understandings and embodied moments of insight, challenging biomedical models, stigmatising views and disconnection from the self and others. As addiction recovery is typically a non-linear journey, "wellbeing" should allow for possibilities of learning and deviation; take a holistic approach to understanding and developing a person's needs, vulnerabilities and strengths; be situated within meaningful social relationships and communities; and grapple with the social inequalities contributing to addiction and posing obstacles to recovery. While this is a big task, we suggest that creative participatory methods offer an accessible, human-centric, playful and generative way to get started.

Reflective questions

- In what ways is your understanding of substance misuse shaped by your culture – ceremonies and celebrations, media, shared histories and relationships?
- Do you feel like recovery from substance addiction must be "all or nothing"? Is abstinence the only way, or can some use be permitted? Why?

Discussion questions

- How welcoming is your community to people in recovery from substance addiction? Discuss barriers and facilitators.
- What are three actionable changes that could support people in recovery from substance addiction in your community?

Acknowledgments

The research presented here was funded by the Economic and Social Research Council and Arts and Humanities Research Council Global Research Challenge Fund grant ES/S00047X/1 and an ESRC IAA and Wellcome Trust Institutional Partnership Award. The data that support the findings of Case Study 1 are openly available in ReShare at https://reshare .ukdataservice .ac .uk /855418/. Educational materials can be downloaded from https://licensing .leeds .ac .uk /product /pathways -to -recovery -model-of -substance -use -disorder -youthassam -comics -type -images -and -animations. For the purpose of open access, the author has applied a Creative Commons Attribution (CC BY) licence to any Author Accepted Manuscript version arising from this submission.

References

Ambekar, A., Agrawal, A., Rao, R., Mishra, A., Khandelwal, S. K., Chadda, R. K., & The group of investigators from the National Survey on Extent and Pattern of Substance Use in India. (2019). *National survey on extent and pattern of substance use in India: Magnitude of substance use in India.* Ministry of Social Justice and Empowerment, Government of India.

Bajwa, H. (2025, January 6). Punjab plans to launch drug policy focusing on de-addiction alongside centralised patient registry. *New Indian Express.* https://www.newindianexpress.com/nation/2025/Jan/06/punjab-plans-to-launch-drug-policy-focusing-on-de-addiction-alongside-centralised-patient-registry#:~:text=The%20community%20policing%20wing%20of,chapters%20on%20drug%20abuse%20awareness

Brooks, C., Mirzoev, T., Chowdhury, D., Deuri, S. P., & Madill, A. (2023). Using evidence in mental health policy agenda-setting in low- and middle-income countries: a conceptual meta-framework from a scoping umbrella review. *Health policy and planning*, *38*(7), 876–893. https://doi.org/10.1093/heapol/czad038

Clughen, L. (2024). 'Embodiment is the future': What is embodiment and is it the future paradigm for learning and teaching in higher education?. *Innovations in Education and Teaching International, 61*(4), 735–747.

Cross, K., Kabel, A., & Lysack, C. (2006). Images of self and spinal cord injury: exploring drawing as a visual method in disability research. *Visual Studies, 21*(2), 183–193. https://doi.org/10.1080/14725860600945044

Dekkers, A., De Ruysscher, C. & Vanderplasschen, W. (2020). Perspectives of cocaine users on addiction recovery: A qualitative study following a CRA+ vouchers programme. *Drugs: Education, Prevention and Policy*, *27*(4), 282–296. https://doi.org/10.1080/09687637.2019.1687647

Fettig, N., Mitchell, H., Gassoumis, Z. D., Nizam, Z., Whittier Eliason, S., & Cory, S. (2024). Adult maltreatment risk factors: Adding community-level factors to an individual-level field. *Trauma, Violence, & Abuse, 25*(1), 5–21. https://doi.org/10.1177/15248380221137659

Finlay, L. (2014). Embodying research. *Person-Centered & Experiential Psychotherapies*, *13*(1), 4–18. https://doi.org/10.1080/14779757.2013.855133

Goswami, H. (2015). Substance abuse among youths at Guwahati City, Assam (India): Major instigator and socio-demographic factors. *International Education & Research Journal*, *1*(4). https://ierj.in/journal/index.php/ierj/article/view/35

Graber, R. (2025). Understanding peer support in varying contexts of marginalisation: Implications for and linkages between formal and informal provision. In U. Kumar (Ed.), *The Routledge international handbook of psychosocial resilience* (2nd ed.). Routledge.

Graber, R., Duara, R., Goswami, S., Hugh-Jones, S., Chowdhury, D., & Madill, A. (2025). Young adult resilience for recovery from substance addiction in Assam, India: Lived experience insights from a photo-led interview study. *Journal of Community & Applied Social Psychology*, *35*(1), e70022. https://doi.org/10.1002/casp.70022

Greene D. (2021). Revisiting 12-step approaches: An evidence-based perspective. In W. M. Meil & J. A. Mills (Eds.), *Addictions: Diagnosis and treatment*. IntechOpen.

Gururaj, G., Varghese, M., Benegal, V., Rao, G. N., Pathak, K., Singh, L. K., Mehta, R. Y., Ram, D., Shibukumar, T. M., Kokane, A., Lenin Singh, R. K., Chavan, B. S., Sharma, P., Ramasubramanian, C., Dalal, P. K., Saha, P. K., Deuri, S. P., Giri, A. K., Kavishvar, A. B., & NMHS Collaborators Group. (2016). *National Mental Health Survey of India, 2015–16: Prevalence, patterns and outcomes* (NIMHANS Publication No. 129). National Institute of Mental Health and Neuro Sciences.

Hugh-Jones, S., Duara, R., Graber, R., Goswami, S., & Madill, A. (2024). What protects at-risk young people in India from using and abusing substances? A photo-led study of lived experience. *Journal of Adolescent Research.* https://doi.org/10.1177/07435584241231376

Kermode, M., Songput, C. H., Sono, C. Z., Jamir, T. N., & Devine, A. (2012). Meeting the needs of women who use drugs and alcohol in North-east India: A challenge for HIV prevention services. *BMC Public Health, 12,* 825. https://doi.org/10.1186/1471-2458-12-825

Kramer-Roy, D. (2015). Using participatory and creative methods to facilitate emancipatory research with people facing multiple disadvantage: A role for health and care professionals, *Disability & Society*, *30*(8), 1207–1224. https://doi.org/10.1080/09687599.2015.1090955

Kumar, S., Sengupta, K., & Gogoi, B. J. (2023). Does multifaceted livelihood intervention improve well-being: Reflections on a case study from North-eastern India. *Journal of International Development*, *35*(8), 2446–2464. https://doi.org/10.1002/jid.3777

Laudet, A. B. (2007). What does recovery mean to you? Lessons from the recovery experience for research and practice. *Journal of Substance Abuse Treatment, 33*(3), 243–256.

Liebenberg, L. (2020). Reconsidering interactive resilience processes in mental health: Implications for child and youth services. *Journal of Community Psychology, 48*(5), 1365–1380.

Madill, A., Duara, R., Goswami, S. Graber, R., & Hugh-Jones, S. (2022). Policy Brief 1. Pathways to recovery: Informing solutions to tackle youth substance abuse in Assam. https://projectresilience.co.uk/wp-content/uploads/sites/142/2021/12/BP-Policy-Brief-1.pdf

Madill, A., Duara, R., Goswami, S., Graber, R., & Hugh-Jones, S. (2023). Pathways to recovery model of youth substance misuse in Assam, India. *Health Expectations, 26*(1), 318–328.

Maiese, M. (2017). Transformative learning, enactivism, and affectivity. *Studies in Philosophy and Education, 36*(2), 197–216.

Martin-Baró, I. (1994). *Writings for a liberation psychology*. Harvard University Press.

Masten, A. S. (2014). Global perspectives on resilience in children and youth. *Child Development, 85*(1), 6–20.

MIND India. (n.d.). *MIND India*. Retrieved November 18, 2025, from https://mindindia.org/home

Pathak, K., Deuri, S. P., Gogoi, V., Sobhana, H., Gautham, M. S., et al., & NMHS Collaborators Group. (2017). *Assam state report: National Mental Health Survey, 2015–16*. National Institute of Mental Health and Neuro Sciences. http://indianmhs.nimhans.ac.in/Docs/statereports/Assam-NMHS-Report.pdf

Perumbilly, S., & Anderson, S. (2017). Indian perspectives on treating substance use disorders. *Alcoholism Treatment Quarterly, 35*(3), 298–314. https://doi.org/10.1080/07347324.2017.1322433

Pisarska, A., Eisman, A., Ostaszewski, K., & Zimmerman, M. (2016). Alcohol and cigarette use among Warsaw adolescents: Factors associated with risk and resilience. *Substance Use & Misuse, 51*(10), 1283–1296. https://doi.org/10.3109/10826084.2016.1168442

Raihan, N., & Cogburn, M. (2023, March 6). Stages of change theory. In *StatPearls*. StatPearls Publishing. https://www.ncbi.nlm.nih.gov/books/NBK556005/

Reavey, P. (Ed.). (2021). *A handbook of visual methods in psychology: Using and interpreting images in qualitative research* (2nd ed.). Routledge/Taylor & Francis Group.

Rose, A., Minz, S., Manohari, G. P., Thavamani, T., George, K., Arun, R., & Vinodh, A. (2015). Community perspectives on alcohol use among a tribal population in rural southern India. *The National Medical Journal of India, 28*(3), 117–121.

Rudzinski, K., McDonough, P., Gartner, R., & Strike, C. (2017). Is there room for resilience? A scoping review and critique of substance use literature and its utilization of the concept of resilience. *Substance Abuse Treatment, Prevention and Policy, 12*(1), 1–35. https://doi.org/10.1186/s13011-017-0125-2

Sani, Y., Wardany, O. F., Herlina, H., & Vernanda, G. (2021). The implementation of embodied learning: A literature review. *Edukasi, 15*(1), 8–18.

Sayette, M. A., & Griffin, K. M. (2004). Self-regulatory failure and addiction. *Handbook of Self-Regulation: Research, Theory, and Applications, 3*, 571–590.

Todres, L (2007). *Embodied enquiry: Phenomenological touchstones for research, psychotherapy and spirituality*. Palgrave Macmillan.

World Health Organisation. (2021). *Guidance on community mental health services: Promoting person-centred and rights-based approaches*. WHO. https://www.who.int/publications/i/item/guidance-and-technical-packages-on-community-mental-health-services

UT News Service. (2022, December 29). Women organizations reaffirm stand against alcohol legalization in Manipur. *Ukrul Times*. https://ukhrultimes.com/women-organizations-reaffirm-their-stand-against-alcohol-legalization-in-manipur/https://ukhrultimes.com/women-organizations-reaffirm-their-stand-against-alcohol-legalization-in-manipur/

Valsala, P., & Devanathan, S. (2023). Mental resilience in the context of alcohol use—a qualitative study in a tribal community in South India. *Journal of Ethnicity in Substance Abuse, 22*(1), 213–237. https://doi.org/10.1080/15332640.2021.1925195

Varela, F. J., Thompson, E., & Rosch, E. (2017). *The embodied mind, revised edition: Cognitive science and human experience*. MIT Press.

11 Surviving violence, surviving the system

Secondary victimisation in the context of intimate partner violence

Annalisa Cecconi, Carlo Tomasetto and Cinzia Albanesi

Introduction

In the context of gender-based violence against women, the phenomenon of secondary victimisation has gained renewed attention in recent years. Though the term has been used since the late 1990s, particularly regarding rape victims (e.g., Campbell & Raja, 1999 – see Further readings), research on the topic has increased in the past decade. However, the concept of secondary victimisation in the literature presents a certain degree of vagueness and potential sources of confusion (Pemberton & Mulder, 2023); with this in mind, we will seek to introduce the topic as clearly as possible.

Secondary victimisation occurs when crime victims receive inappropriate responses from institutions or support systems (Pemberton & Mulder, 2023), such as victim-blaming or minimisation of their experiences. Rather than receiving validation and protection, victims may see their experience of violence undermined, questioned, trivialised, or implicitly attributed to their own actions. This results in harm, feelings of betrayal, powerlessness, additional trauma, discouraging help-seeking and further compromising their safety and mental health (Epstein & Goodman, 2018).

The prevention of secondary victimisation is addressed in the EU Victims' Rights Directive (2012) and, in the context of gender-based violence, the Istanbul Convention (2011). Article 15 of the Istanbul Convention, in particular, stresses the need to train professionals interacting with victims to prevent secondary victimisation. This is a crucial point, as it highlights that even professionals working with victims of gender-based violence, such as police officers, healthcare and legal professionals, social workers, and custody evaluators, may (unwittingly) perpetrate secondary victimisation, despite their role in supporting victims. In this chapter, we will discuss specifically this topic, namely when secondary victimisation of victims/survivors is perpetrated by service providers. Moreover, we will focus on intimate partner violence (IPV) victims/survivors who have children, as they must navigate not only interactions with service providers addressing their experiences of violence (e.g., police) but also with those involved in child welfare and/or custody matters. Besides, due to their parenting relationship with the perpetrator, these victims/survivors are reported to face more complex safety concerns and to be exposed to post-separation violence, being often required by service providers to maintain contact with the abusive ex-partner for co-parenting purposes, in addition to dealing with heightened fears for the safety and wellbeing of their child beyond their own one (Calton et al., 2017).

After outlining the phenomenon, which is still underexplored in psychological research, we discuss the role of Community Psychology in addressing this issue, particularly through the contributions on the empowerment of victims/survivors. This exploration is deepened by a case study evaluating a

DOI: 10.4324/9781003480464-14

programme that aims to empower victims, highlighting how secondary victimisation can hinder this process. Finally, the relevance of adopting an ecological perspective that encompasses various levels and actors in addressing secondary victimisation is emphasised, aiming for wider social change.

Given that this research is deeply rooted in gendered power dynamics, it is crucial to reflect on the positionalities of the research team. The team consists of two cisgender women and one cisgender man, all with professional, academic, and advocacy experience in social justice, gender-based violence and engagement with marginalised populations, especially youth. While committed to feminist and intersectional approaches, we acknowledge our own privileges and the potential impact these may have on our research interpretation. As psychologists investigating a phenomenon that can also be perpetrated by professionals in our own field, we are aware of the risk of being unintentionally lenient or protective and engage in reflexive dialogue to remain mindful of these dynamics.

Secondary victimisation of intimate partner violence victims/survivors with children

Manifestations of secondary victimisation. As previously mentioned, the case of victims/survivors with children is of particular interest, as parenting-related matters require women to engage with multiple institutions, such as the police, legal and social services. This not only increases the potential for experiencing secondary victimisation, but also involves specific characteristics that we will explore. In this context, secondary victimisation can manifest in different forms:

- **Victim blaming.** In the context of IPV and children's exposure to IPV, women may be held responsible not only for the violence they suffer, but also for their children's protection. This can lead to the belief that they should have left the abuser sooner to protect their children, thereby attributing fault to the victim/survivor (Wild, 2023).
- **Minimisation**. Perpetrators' behaviour may be reframed as "situational couple violence" or "conflict between partners." Namely, the conflict is perceived as *mutual*, disregarding the dynamics of power and control that define abusive relationships and failing to acknowledge the serious impact and risks of violence (Hay et al., 2023), especially in cases of psychological abuse (Epstein & Goodman, 2018).
- **Questioning or dismissal** of the victim's testimony or account. Professionals may challenge the credibility or plausibility of what victims say (Cattagni Kleiner & Romain-Glassey, 2024). Questioning or dismissing the victim's account overlooks the fact that confusion, fragmentation and inconsistencies in memories and narratives are common results of trauma and abuse (Epstein & Goodman, 2018). Moreover, focus can be placed on the survivor's demeanour or mental health, rather than on the perpetrator's behaviour (Khaw et al., 2021).
- **Prevalence of a pro-contact culture** over safety issues. Service providers involved in child protection often assume that continuous contact with both parents is always in the child's best interests, thus underestimating the impact of IPV on children or even considering IPV and parenting as separate issues. This may result in IPV being insufficiently considered in family-related decisions (Cattagni Kleiner & Romain-Glassey, 2024; Hay et al., 2023) and allows perpetrators to continue exercising control and power over the victim (Heward-Belle et al., 2018). In turn, women who resist or refuse to comply with contact arrangements are often labelled as alienating and vindictive (i.e., "bad mothers"; Hay et al., 2023).

- **Disproportionate responsibility is** placed on women for the safety and welfare of their children, while perpetrators are not adequately scrutinised. Expectations placed on mothers regarding parenting issues and duties are often higher than those for fathers. As a consequence, women may be encouraged to participate in parenting support programmes (e.g., because their parenting skills may be compromised by trauma reactions), whereas the same is not required of the IPV perpetrator. Thus, the focus is placed on changing the mother's behaviour rather than addressing the abuser's actions, overshadowing the need for the perpetrator's accountability (Wild, 2023).

These situations, in which IPV victims/survivors with children find themselves caught due to rigid institutional expectations and stereotypes, have been described by Saunders and Oglesby (2016) as "traps" – no-win scenarios where women face negative consequences regardless of the choices they make. For example, staying in an abusive relationship may lead to accusations of failing to protect their children, while leaving the abuser can result in charges of abandonment and potential harassment by the perpetrator. If victims/survivors are reluctant to co-parent or raise concerns about their children's safety, they may be labelled as vindictive or alienating parents, and ultimately risk losing their children's custody. Seeking therapy may improve survivors' mental health, but could be used against them in court, while avoiding it may hinder recovery and affect their ability to care for their children.

While secondary victimisation can be partly attributed to the fragmentation and inconsistency of procedures and missions within agencies handling gender-based violence cases, Heward-Belle et al. (2018) offer a more profound perspective that digs deeper into the root cause of the phenomenon. The authors argue that, in fact, secondary victimisation is fundamentally rooted in *institutionalised sexism* – namely, sexist practices embedded within the system. The institutional system may adopt tactics, policies and practices that exert power and control over women in a way that precisely mirrors those used by violent men, such as intimidation, coercion, threats and manipulation, especially when children and child protection services are involved. For example, abusers' controlling and coercive behaviours are echoed by service providers' unannounced home visits, threats of removing children and control and scrutiny over women's and children's lives. Similarly, the violent men's dismissive attitude is replicated when IPV is minimised, denied or interpreted as mere conflict by service providers. When women's reactions are viewed as signs of dysfunction or mental disorder, rather than as understandable responses to trauma, service providers may inadvertently reinforce patterns of emotional invalidation.

Experiencing secondary victimisation and its consequences

As a consequence of secondary victimisation, victims/survivors often experience a range of negative emotions, including frustration, confusion, desperation, anger and a sense of being constantly scrutinised (Khaw et al., 2021). Moreover, research highlights the overwhelming powerlessness and loss of control they may feel. For example, within the family court system, many women report feelings of fear, shame, betrayal and mistrust toward societal institutions meant to protect them; they often also experience humiliation and dehumanisation from professionals, leading to mental and physical health consequences like insomnia, fatigue and re-traumatization (Gutowski & Goodman, 2020). Additionally, secondary victimisation can create an "enduring ordeal," where victims/survivors must navigate complex procedures, such as multiple appointments with legal, social and healthcare professionals, while managing practical responsibilities like home visits, housing, employment and childcare duties (Cattagni Kleiner & Romain-Glassey, 2024). Recognising the system's failure to act in their best interests, victims/survivors often feel compelled to comply with such demands, suppressing emotions or compromising their health and safety. For example, they may withhold emotional reactions, fearing that any signs of distress could be used against them (Khaw et al., 2021).

Beyond gender: secondary victimisation, race and socio-economic background

When addressing IPV, research emphasises the importance of considering factors beyond gender that shape the experience of violence and help-seeking. For example, women with a migration background face numerous barriers to accessing services, such as insecure immigration status, fear of deportation, language difficulties, financial dependence and social isolation, making them more reliant on abusive partners; when interacting with service providers, they may also experience racial discrimination, cultural stereotypes and a lack of culturally sensitive training, which leads to mistrust of formal services (Hulley et al., 2023). Ghafournia (2014) points out that IPV case management can be influenced by a culturally relativistic view, which wrongly assumes IPV is inherent to certain minority cultures, or a universalist approach that prioritises "universal rights" while ignoring cultural differences, often reflecting Western values.

Other dimensions of discrimination are also important to consider, particularly for IPV victims with disabilities, homelessness or financial precarity. Goodman and Fauci (2020), for example, highlight the blurred line between poverty and child neglect, which affects how child protection services perceive what a "fit" parent or a "fit" environment are, influencing their decisions in terms of child protection measures – for example, when a mother is monitored or sanctioned, rather than supported financially, because she cannot afford to provide regular meals or adequate clothing for her child(ren).

For service providers, focusing only on gender without considering such intersecting factors may result in a failure to understand the unique needs of each IPV case. To improve IPV policies and services, multiple dimensions of inequality and oppression must be addressed, as gender may not always be the primary lens through which victims/survivors view their experiences (Etherington & Baker, 2018). For example, a woman may attribute her partner's violent behaviour to their situation of financial precariousness and poverty. An intersectional approach, addressing multiple dimensions of inequality and oppression, would also benefit children exposed to IPV, since their stories are often generalised and drawn from their parents' accounts, leaving them with little or no say in their own experiences as the children of an abused mother and without considering their race, gender or socioeconomic status (Etherington & Baker, 2018).

Reclaiming power: A Community Psychology approach to intimate partner violence and secondary victimisation

To date, research on secondary victimisation that specifically focuses on service providers is mostly qualitative and exploratory and lacks a psychological perspective – let alone a Community Psychology lens. Nevertheless, addressing secondary victimisation concerns gender-based discrimination, social justice for women and children, power dynamics and encompasses several ecological levels and community actors, thus strongly aligning with Community Psychology aims and principles. In fact, Community Psychology insights, especially on empowerment processes and their dynamics, can provide a crucial contribution to shed light on secondary victimisation while also offering tools and strategies to contrast it.

In classical Community Psychology theory, empowerment is conceived as a dynamic process through which people (as well as organisations and communities) gain control over issues that matter to them (Rappaport, 1987) and develop a critical understanding of their environment, reflecting both how individuals perceive their ability to influence their context and the actions they take to promote change. Empowerment includes three different components: intrapersonal (perceived control, competence and efficacy), interactional (developing critical awareness, skills and knowledge of resources and systems), behavioural (social actions and active participation to influence change; Zimmerman, 1995) and relational (sustaining the exercise of transformative power in the sociopolitical domain through interpersonal processes; Christens, 2012). In the context of gender-based violence research and intervention, victims/survivors often experience powerlessness and privation or limitation of autonomy as a result of coercive dynamics exerted by their abuser, making empowerment a central goal of the work with victims/survivors (Cattaneo & Goodman, 2015). As highlighted, secondary victimisation by service providers can reproduce dynamics of control and power loss that further undermine victims/survivors' agency and autonomy. Therefore, contributions from Community Psychology, drawing from feminist principles of personal choice, finding voice and transcending oppression (Cattaneo & Goodman, 2015), are essential to promote empowerment in working with IPV victims and survivors, to help them restore the power taken not only by the perpetrator, but also by service providers through secondary victimisation.

A crucial contribution to the discussion is provided by Cattaneo and Goodman's Empowerment Process Model (2015), which is focused on work with IPV victims/survivors (Figure 11.1). The model views empowerment as an ongoing process where victims/survivors set flexible, evolving goals based on their needs (e.g., safety, housing, childcare). To achieve them, women must take action by drawing on their self-efficacy, their knowledge about legal, social and community systems and their ability to

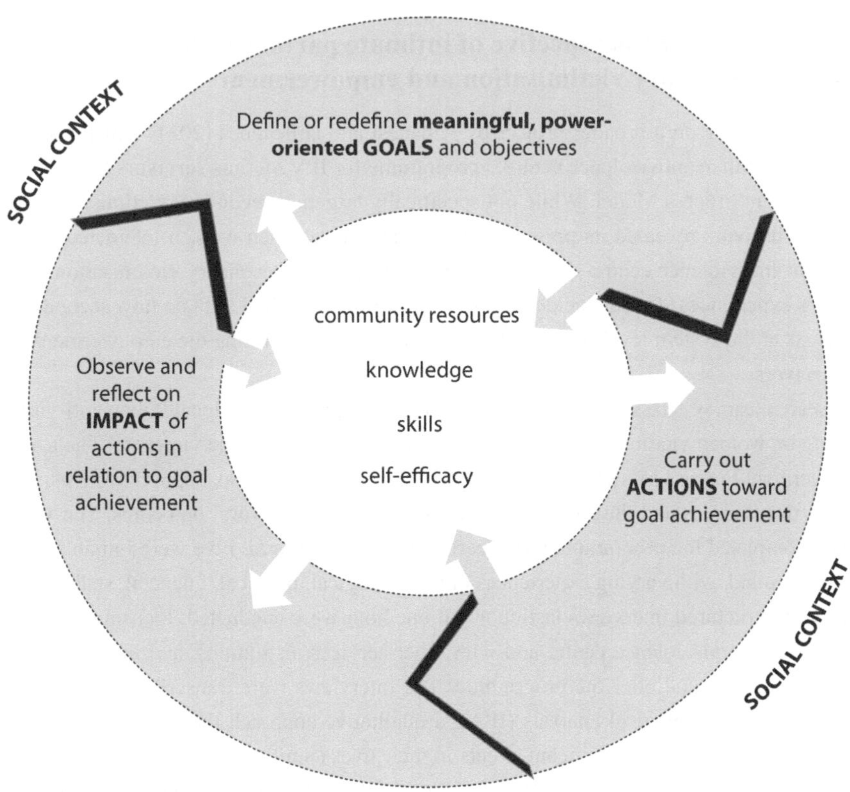

Figure 11.1 Empowerment Process Model.

Source: Copyright: Cattaneo and Goodman, 2015.

identify and use available resources. Regular reflection on progress (namely, on the impact) of such actions helps victims/survivors assess internal and external changes, identify strengths and adjust their strategies. Increased sense of control leads to better interactions with services, improved mental health and long-term positive outcomes like safety. The model also highlights the professional's role in working with IPV survivors: their approach should be individualised, understanding each survivor's unique experience and offering tailored support, as empowerment components such as self-efficacy and resource knowledge vary depending on individual histories and challenges.

In the model, empowerment is presented not only as a process that implies reflecting on and developing understanding of what is needed and achievable, and is influenced by the impact of one's actions, but also as an outcome, referring to the state or level of empowerment that the person has developed. Moreover, empowerment can vary across different areas. This is particularly important, for example, for understanding how victims/survivors may feel empowered in relation to their IPV-related experiences (e.g., trauma, parenting), but powerless when interacting with service providers who perpetrate secondary victimisation.

Thus, empowerment plays a critical role in achieving positive outcomes for survivors, whereas secondary victimisation poses a significant barrier to the empowerment process that manifests when women begin (or attempt to begin) their journey out of violence, or when they believe they have nearly succeeded, and are confronted with a professional who questions them – which will be exemplified in our case study.

Praxis case study: The perspective of intimate partner violence victims/survivors on secondary victimisation and empowerment

This case study draws on a broader project by Albanesi and colleagues (2021) which focused on the evaluation of an Italian anti-violence centre's programme for IPV victims/survivors through the lens of the Empowerment Process Model. While not specifically targeting secondary victimisation, interviews with victims/survivors revealed its presence and pervasiveness when women interacted with services other than the anti-violence centre, thus generating knowledge on secondary victimisation informed by the women's experiences. These "incidental findings" allow us to shed light on how secondary victimisation persists at the system level in the pathway out of violence, limiting the empowerment process of victims/survivors.

The research team was tasked with evaluating an IPV programme at a local Italian anti-violence centre, focusing on women victims/survivors with children who witnessed the violence.[1] The team adopted the Empowerment Process Model to examine aspects like goal formation, support systems, trauma history, access to resources and the role of services in achieving survivors' outcomes. Ten women aged 26–46 who completed the programme were recruited and interviewed. Five were Italian and five had a migrant background, with varying experiences of psychological, physical, financial, stalking and sexual violence. Semi-structured interviews lasting about one hour were conducted, focusing on the women's experiences at the anti-violence centre and with other services/institutions, and the changes they perceived before, during, and after the programme. The interviews were transcribed and analysed using interpretative phenomenological analysis (IPA), a qualitative approach that explores how individuals experience and make sense of significant events in their lives (Smith & Shinebourne, 2012). Grounded in phenomenology and hermeneutics, IPA focuses on the subjective meaning participants attribute to their personal experiences, identifying key themes and turning points in the participants' stories.

The analysis involved multiple readings, detailed coding and comparison of themes across interviews. Findings were then discussed with professionals and participants.

Building empowerment while facing secondary victimisation. The analysis of participants' stories revealed that the programme effectively fostered an empowerment process. Initially, most of them sought protection and support to stop the violence, but over time, their goals evolved to include self-actualisation, economic independence and psychological wellbeing. The programme reinforced survivors' skills and self-efficacy, facilitating access to community resources, though the support network's effectiveness varied across participants; women reported gaining awareness of the violence's impact on themselves and their children, and realised the importance of leaving an abusive partner. Moreover, they were supported in rebuilding personal relationships, developing self-reflection and understanding their experiences of trauma. Despite challenges, many victims/survivors felt empowered and described their progress as a "second life," with anti-violence workers helping them regain control, protect their children and achieve greater autonomy.

The results, however, also highlighted dynamics that can be framed as secondary victimisation, experienced in particular when confronting professionals outside the centre. As previously noted, secondary victimisation was not the primary focus of the research; however, its emergence in the interviews further highlights the pervasiveness of the phenomenon. Some interviewees, for example, reported negative experiences with law enforcement, who were perceived as minimising and underestimating the severity of the violence the victims/survivors suffered and the persistence of danger for them. This led to a lack of trust, low expectations towards institutions, and, above all, a sense of unsafety and fear.

> He threatened me in front of the police, he told me he wanted to see me dead, and threw a bucket at me while leaving... and the police did nothing but tell him 'calm down'. I was scared, and I did not feel protected. (Laura, 46 years old, Italian).

Some women stated that they felt service providers were not considering their testimony sufficient for them to be believed, unless it was supported by material evidence.

> Outside, there is this big billboard saying that victims should file a report. Well, they should take it down, because a woman is not believed until her face is beaten up, and I have seen this with judges, with everyone. I left home with nothing, which means I was desperate. But they just thought I was crazy [...] I do not know why in Italy women are so poorly believed. It is like they think all women go to court and lie to get some financial benefits. (Eva, 42 years old, Italian).
>
> No matter how right you are, unless there is an explicit threat recorded, like 'I will kill you...', you won't be taken seriously. Let alone, I do not have recordings or reports of violence… of course, I am seen as the one in the wrong! (Lina, 32 years old, woman with a migrant background).

An interviewee expressed feeling betrayed when her difficulty in managing the household was seen as neglect towards her children, which led to the involvement of social services. In this case, her suffering as a victim of violence was overlooked, and instead, the focus shifted to her being an inadequate parent, unable to protect or provide a suitable environment for her children.

> We were living in these conditions, I couldn't keep the house clean... bags of cement, paint cans, disassembled wardrobes... the normal cleaning that a woman does in the house, I couldn't do it.

> The police came in and were like 'look how they live...' They even thought about sending me inspections because I did not keep the house clean. I felt stabbed in the back by the people who are supposed to protect you from violence, and whom you trust. (Laura, 46 years old, Italian).

In another case, negative experiences with social services have been reported as social workers and custody evaluators prioritised co-parenting without considering that IPV had occurred.

> I felt targeted, both by the social workers and the psychologists that do custody evaluations. [...] Rather than being incompetent with adults, their incompetence is with children. This is something I have noticed — children tend to be tossed around. For the social workers, the important thing is that the children restore their relationship with both their dad and mom, and I totally agree. But you need to consider what happened before. It is too easy to say that a child without both a dad and a mom is a troubled child. (Sofia, 44 years old, Italian).

This approach was supported even by law enforcement. "Lina" (32 years old, woman with a migrant background) recalled "wherever you went, the police would say, 'he is still the father of the children, he needs to see the children'". Moreover, this separation between IPV and the parenting dimension entails the risk of dismissing the need to care for the victim as a person, and not only as a mother who is under scrutiny for her parenting:

> The judge assigned me to a psychologist to improve my relationship with my children. But the judge did not take into account that I am not just a mother, there is also a woman behind this, and it was not considered. [...] I mean, children are the ones who must be protected first, but what about me? Who can I speak to about what is going on with me? (Eva, 42 years old, Italian).

One participant also felt that her account and story were "twisted" by service providers, who even referred to her as an alienating mother who turned her children against their father.

> My older son, as soon as we stepped out of the house, refused to see his father. When the social worker's report was brought to the custody evaluator, what I had said was completely distorted. I was labelled, these are the exact words, as an alienating mother who turned the children against their father. And unfortunately, this person is still our social worker. The father was portrayed as a martyr, and I was portrayed as a witch. (Eva, 42 years old, Italian).

Besides, in a few of the interviews, participants also reported being placed in a mediation process, which is prohibited by the Istanbul Convention in IPV cases due to its underlying assumptions of shared responsibility and collaboration.

> I expect that a psychologist should be able to understand that at a certain point, some things are pointless. We did six months of mediation, him and I, and it was more shouting and insults than actual mediation. In front of a psychologist, I had to accept everything. A psychologist who just sits there and says nothing [...] It was like being at home with a spectator watching our arguments. (Eva, 42 years old, Italian).

These experiences can be so impactful that they lead women to regret starting the process, to the point where they declare they would not advise other women to leave home and report the abuse, due to the burden and loneliness they felt they had to face.

> The report... you file it, but it is another weight you have to take on [...] After the trial you are on your own, they will tell you to file the report, do this and that, but after you do it, you really find yourself alone, you have no support. You end up managing everything alone. (Clara, 31 years old, woman with a migrant background).

Victims'/survivors' accounts highlight how the work of anti-violence workers effectively initiated a process of support, empowerment, and psychological wellbeing. Drawing on the Empowerment Process Model, the evaluation showed that women were supported in identifying both basic goals (e.g., safety, housing) and progressively more complex ones related to self-actualisation (*goals*), taking steps to achieve them (*action*), and reflecting on their progress to adjust strategies accordingly (*impact*). This iterative process was reinforced through ongoing support in developing personal and social resources such as skills (e.g., professional competences), self-efficacy, knowledge (e.g., self-awareness, information relevant to achieving goals), and access to community resources (e.g., social support, legal aid). Furthermore, the women gained awareness of their own empowerment process - recognising it not only as a journey but also as a tangible outcome.

However, this work of care and the promotion of empowerment and wellbeing cannot be confined to the anti-violence centre or limited to the relationship between victims/survivors and anti-violence workers. Proper support to victims by all professionals and effective collaboration among different agencies and services is essential to create a supportive environment that can sustain victims/survivors in their journey out of IPV and towards empowerment. In our findings, the women's narratives reveal instead gaps, contradictions and even pitfalls within the system, often stemming from a lack of training on gender-based violence and gendered prejudices. This can result in judgemental or victimising attitudes, minimisation of the violence experienced or even overtly sexist responses. Such dynamics risk undermining victims/survivors' progress and limiting their ability to reach their goals and reclaim power, creating a kind of countermovement that weakens the efforts of anti-violence workers.

This work suggests that when empowerment is addressed solely at the individual level and focuses on only one aspect of the system (in this case, the victims/survivors), it becomes a process that cannot be fully realised. At best, it remains confined to the personal level, increasing individual wellbeing but without contributing to real systemic change, and therefore without truly addressing the phenomenon. These reflections lead us to consider the role that Community Psychology and community psychologists can play in addressing these issues, which we explore in the next section.

Action for learning

Behaviours that reproduce secondary victimisation are often supported by internalised implicit beliefs and norms unconsciously held by professionals and citizens. Raising awareness of personal bias is thus a key step in promoting a more supportive and non-judgemental attitude, both personally and professionally.

Interactive group activities may represent an effective tool to help professionals, community members and youth (e.g., school students) recognise and manage different forms of secondary victimisation. For example, consider bringing together different professionals and community members to discuss this topic. Participants may be asked to analyse media coverage of IPV episodes, focusing on how victims/survivors and their children are portrayed. Using search terms like "femicide," "domestic violence" and "children," they may collect samples of news reports or social media content and examine the language, tone and framing. The forms of secondary victimisation described earlier can serve as an analytical grid. This serves as a basis for reflection and discussion: What narrative is conveyed about the victim, the perpetrator and the children? What emotions or judgments emerge in readers? Participants should also be encouraged to consider how aspects like ethnicity, age, migration status or class are presented (or omitted) and how these may fuel bias or stereotypes. For adult groups (e.g., professionals or experienced community members), it is also helpful to identify which professionals are cited (e.g., law enforcement, psychologists, legal experts), and what narratives they reinforce. Are some forms of secondary victimisation linked to specific roles?

This activity can help uncover how secondary victimisation is normalised in public discourse and private opinion, while also promoting media literacy, especially among youth. To ensure safe participation, adaptations should be made based on group context. In adult groups, moderators should ensure that everyone feels comfortable discussing these topics and create space for optional sharing. The activity is not discouraged for victims/survivors, but may be emotionally activating, so facilitators should be prepared to offer support and make sure to offer a safe space. In school settings, we recommend conducting the activity with high school students, under teacher supervision. Teachers should guide article selection to avoid overly distressing content, ensuring a thoughtful and respectful discussion.

Towards transformative practice: Strategies and challenges for intervention in Community Psychology

The case study shows that, when addressing IPV and secondary victimisation, focusing solely on empowering victims is not, and cannot be, sufficient. If secondary victimisation by service providers reflects systemic violence rooted in patriarchal and heteronormative structures, meaningful change must go deeper, tackling the root causes. This requires a radical, transformative approach, one that spans from education (as outlined in our "Actions for learning") to public policy.

As Community Psychology scholars argue, efforts to address any issue should go beyond ameliorative change – i.e., interventions that seek to reform existing systems and often result in merely technical solutions to social problems. Instead, actions should aim to provoke a fundamental shift in the assumptions, values and power dynamics that sustain inequality, thereby achieving transformative change (Nelson, 2013; Nelson & Prilleltensky, 2010). Cattaneo et al. (2014) describe this aim as "status quake" – a disruption of power dynamics that may require those in privileged positions to sacrifice some power. Only such systemic transformation could effectively address the roots of secondary victimisation and lead to lasting change.

However, this process is not always achievable. Rigid institutional structures (Prilleltensky, 2014), along with historical, political and policy-related contingencies that undermine principles of social justice, may hinder deep, structural impact (Nelson, 2013). In the case of secondary victimisation, this challenge is substantial, as the phenomenon is intrinsically linked to institutional systems and roles. Therefore, how can we foster meaningful, but realistic change without merely "settling for amelioration" (Prilleltensky, 2014)?

This question leads us to a key point in our discussion: the need for a multi-level approach. Responding to IPV effectively requires an ecological framework that operates across various levels: individual, organisational and societal. Secondary victimisation itself unfolds across these layers: the individual level (e.g., service providers' internalised gendered norms), the microsystem (e.g., the woman's concerns for children or fear of the perpetrator), the mesosystem (e.g., women are often forced to navigate disconnected and even conflicting systems), the exosystem (inappropriate or harmful responses from professionals) and the macrosystem (patriarchal culture, policies; Pokharel et al., 2020). Community Psychology offers precisely this: a systemic, ecological framework capable of integrating different levels, actors and contexts, while promoting social change.

This perspective allows us to propose concrete actions that, while aware of being situated *within the system* and taking place inside formal settings, still push towards a radical transformation of institutional structures and the disruption of embedded power dynamics. We believe that community psychologists can play a crucial role by engaging at multiple levels, both in research and practice, and addressing the following key points (see Figure 11.2):

- Providing supervision to professionals involved in programmes promoting the empowerment of IPV victims/survivors and their children, while also fostering the production of knowledge on IPV and secondary victimisation through participatory action research (an approach that enhances survivors' awareness and agency by involving them as co-creators of knowledge and change). This is especially important in light of Cattaneo et al.'s (2014) critique that empowerment interventions often fall short when goals are predefined for clients rather than developed with them, ultimately reinforcing systemic norms. In this sense, adopting the Empowerment Process Model is crucial, as it is grounded in the principle that goals should be defined based on their subjective significance to the survivor. However, as previously discussed, focusing only on victims and individual empowerment is not enough for a transformative approach: it must also extend to broader structural and systemic levels, which leads to the next points.
- Ensuring empowerment in IPV goes beyond individual wellbeing, framing it as a contribution to social justice and systemic change. Empowering victims/survivors must not be reduced to "helping" them improve their personal situation, but must involve scaffolding them in reclaiming power and promoting liberation as women, placing individual struggle within a collective movement for social change. This includes raising awareness of gender-based oppression, defending the rights of victims/survivors and women more broadly and improving institutional responses (Sullivan & Goodman, 2019). In practice, victims/survivors' programmes should aim at sociopolitical development, critical consciousness and social action (Prilleltensky, 2008), for example, by building awareness of feminist history and theory and connecting victims/survivors with women's rights groups. Without this collective dimension and a social justice lens, change risks remaining at the individual level, becoming merely ameliorative rather than truly transformative.

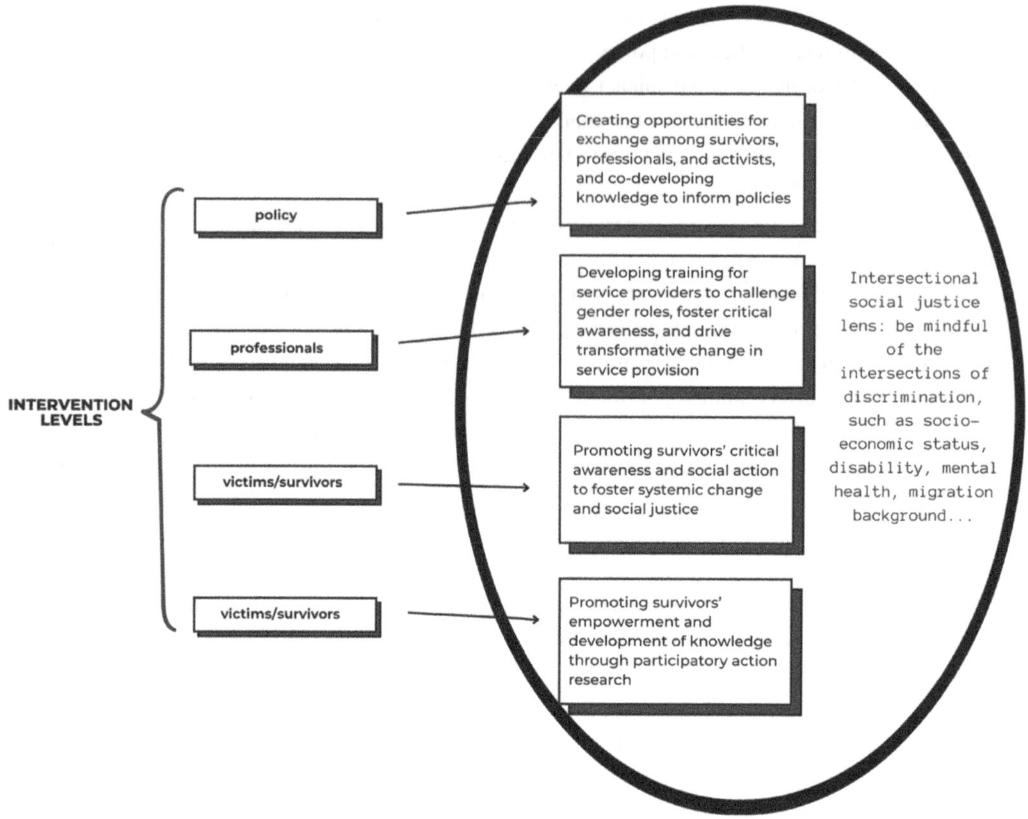

Figure 11.2 Visual representation of intervention strategies

- Identifying and developing training models for service providers is crucial to deconstructing gender roles and stereotypes related to gender-based violence. These models should promote critical awareness of gender inequality and encourage personal reflection on one's role in perpetuating power imbalances. While such training may seem like a technical solution, it has transformative potential, fostering a power shift (or status quake) from those in institutional power positions. However, a key challenge is that service providers could perceive such interventions as judgmental towards their work, potentially discouraging engagement. This is particularly relevant for care workers, who already face high stress, low pay, heavy workloads and emotional fatigue, as research shows (e.g., Lundy & Crawford, 2024, in Further readings, for a review). These factors contribute to burnout, diminished emotional ability to attend to the clients' needs (compassion fatigue) and symptoms of work-induced post-traumatic stress disorder (secondary traumatic stress). To address these challenges, a collaborative and participatory approach is essential. Instead of focusing on blame, this approach should emphasise the positive role service providers can play in driving change, channelling their knowledge and experience to improve victims/survivors' support and to shape policies that impact both their professional practice and society at large. To sustain these actions, it is essential to back potential preventive and educational measures and interventions with dedicated resources and adequate funding. This requires recognising the issue as a political priority and aligning public policies accordingly, which brings us to the next point.

- Fostering interaction between victims/survivors, service providers and women's rights activists to influence policies and policymakers, for example, through structuring participative spaces or co-developing informative documents. Policies should be informed by the experiences of women and the practical knowledge of professionals and activists, shaping interventions at various levels, such as service providers' training, school education programmes and inter-agency collaboration protocols. These policies must always be developed with a social justice-oriented perspective to promote transformative change, rather than merely addressing surface-level issues, never losing sight of the power imbalance and oppression inherent in IPV, beyond the specific missions and objectives of different professions, institutions and agencies.
- Lastly, being aware of the dimensions of discrimination, including socio-economic status, disability, mental health and migration background, is crucial in addressing the unique challenges faced by victims/survivors and their children, as these factors can significantly impact their access to support services and empowerment. Incorporating an intersectional social justice lens (Sullivan & Goodman, 2019) would entail, for example, ensuring that linguistic and cultural mediation is provided when a victim/survivor with a migration background interacts with various services to make sure that her experience is fully understood, or introducing new training models to support service providers in dealing with victims/survivors through a trans-cultural perspective. This holistic, sensitive approach is necessary for addressing the full complexity of IPV and supporting victims in their path towards recovery and justice.

In this chapter, through the analysis of literature and a case study, we explored the phenomenon of secondary victimisation of IPV victims/survivors with children. While we have highlighted the lack of psychological research, we have also emphasised the significant potential contribution of Community Psychology, through its social justice perspective and focus on empowerment, to foster both the well-being of victims and broader societal interventions at the organisational and community levels. This can help address the power loss and deprivation experienced by victims/survivors due to the violence they have endured but also as a result of secondary victimisation in interactions with service providers and institutions. In this perspective, it is essential to adopt a multilevel approach that involves various ecological layers and actors, from victims/survivors to professionals, while also maintaining an intersectional perspective that is sensitive to different dimensions of discrimination.

Key values and principles

- Social justice, empowerment, power

Reflective questions

When you hear or read about a gender-based violence episode, do you ever find yourself focusing on the victim's actions or decisions, rather than on the perpetrator's responsibility? If the episode also involves minors exposed to IPV, do you notice any differences in how you perceive the situation and the women's responsibility or actions? What changes?

Note

1 In the Italian context, the support system for survivors of gender-based violence is commonly referred to as the anti-violence system. It comprises anti-violence centres, which provide support and guidance to victims/survivors, emergency shelters, and specialised workers trained to respond to gender-based violence. Accordingly, the term anti-violence will be used throughout this chapter, and these specialised workers will be referred to as anti-violence workers.

References

Albanesi, C., Tomasetto, C., & Guardabassi, V. (2021). Evaluating interventions with victims of intimate partner violence: A community psychology approach. *BMC Women's Health*, *21*, 1–15. https://doi.org/10.1186/s12905-021-01268-7

Calton, J. M., Grossmann, J. L., & Cattaneo, L. B. (2017). The subjective court experiences of intimate partner violence victims: Does motherhood matter?. *Journal of Interpersonal Violence*, *32*(23), 3577–3600. https://doi.org/10.1177/0886260515600166

Cattagni Kleiner, A., & Romain-Glassey, N. (2024). How the current management of intimate partner violence can endanger victimized mothers and their children. *Journal of Family Violence*, *39*(8), 1593–1607. https://doi.org/10.1007/s10896-023-00596-6

Cattaneo, L. B., Calton, J. M., & Brodsky, A. E. (2014). Status quo versus status quake: Putting the power back in empowerment. *Journal of Community Psychology*, *42*(4), 433–446. https://doi.org/10.1002/jcop.21619

Cattaneo, L. B., & Goodman, L. A. (2015). What is empowerment anyway? A model for domestic violence practice, research, and evaluation. *Psychology of Violence*, *5*(1), 84. https://doi.org/10.1037/a0035137

Christens, B. D. (2012). Toward relational empowerment. *American Journal of Community Psychology*, *50*(1–2), 114–128. https://doi.org/10.1007/s10464-011-9483-5

Epstein, D., & Goodman, L. A. (2018). Discounting women: Doubting domestic violence survivors' credibility and dismissing their experiences. *University of Pennsylvania Law Review*, *167*(2), 399–461. https://doi.org/10.2139/ssrn.3575843

Etherington, C., & Baker, L. (2018). From "buzzword" to best practice: Applying intersectionality to children exposed to intimate partner violence. *Trauma, Violence, & Abuse*, *19*(1), 58–75. https://doi.org/10.1177/1524838016631128

Ghafournia, N. (2014). Culture, domestic violence and intersectionality: Beyond the dilemma of cultural relativism and universalism. *The International Journal of Critical Cultural Studies*, *11*(2), 23. https://doi.org/10.18848/2327-0055/CGP/v11i02/43668

Goodman, L. A., & Fauci, J. E. (2020). The long shadow of family separation: A structural and historical introduction to mandated reporting in the domestic violence context. *Journal of Family Violence*, *35*, 217–223. https://doi.org/10.1007/s10896-020-00132-w

Gutowski, E., & Goodman, L. A. (2020). "Like I'm invisible": IPV survivor-mothers' perceptions of seeking child custody through the family court system. *Journal of Family Violence*, *35*(5), 441–457. https://doi.org/10.1007/s10896-019-00063-1

Hay, C., Grobbelaar, M., & Guggisberg, M. (2023). Mothers' post-separation experiences of male partner abuse: An exploratory study. *Journal of Family Issues*, *44*(5), 1276–1300. https://doi.org/10.1177/0192513X211057541

Heward-Belle, S., Laing, L., Humphreys, C., & Toivonen, C. (2018). Intervening with children living with domestic violence: Is the system safe? *Australian Social Work*, *71*(2), 135–147. https://doi.org/10.1080/0312407X.2017.1422772

Hulley, J., Bailey, L., Kirkman, G., Gibbs, G. R., Gomersall, T., Latif, A., & Jones, A. (2023). Intimate partner violence and barriers to help-seeking among Black, Asian, minority ethnic and immigrant women: A qualitative metasynthesis of global research. *Trauma, Violence, & Abuse*, *24*(2), 1001–1015. https://doi.org/10.1177/15248380211050590

Khaw, L., Bermea, A. M., Hardesty, J. L., Saunders, D., & Whittaker, A. M. (2021). "The system had choked me too": Abused mothers' perceptions of the custody determination process that resulted in negative custody outcomes. *Journal of Interpersonal Violence*, *36*(9–10), 4310–4334. https://doi.org/10.1177/0886260518791226

Nelson, G. (2013). Community psychology and transformative policy change in the neo-liberal era. *American Journal of Community Psychology*, *52*, 211–223. https://doi.org/10.1007/s10464-013-9591-5

Nelson, G., & Prilleltensky, I. (2010). *Community psychology: In pursuit of liberation and well-being*. Palgrave.

Pemberton, A., & Mulder, E. (2023). Bringing injustice back in: Secondary victimization as epistemic injustice. *Criminology & Criminal Justice*, *25*(4), 1181–1200. https://doi.org/10.1177/17488958231181345

Pokharel, B., Hegadoren, K., & Papathanassoglou, E. (2020). Factors influencing silencing of women who experience intimate partner violence: An integrative review. *Aggression and Violent Behavior*, *52*, 101422. https://doi.org/10.1016/j.avb.2020.101422

Prilleltensky, I. (2008). The role of power in wellness, oppression, and liberation: The promise of psychopolitical validity. *Journal of Community Psychology*, *36*(2), 116–136. https://doi.org/10.1002/jcop.20225

Prilleltensky, I. (2014). Meaning-making, mattering, and thriving in community psychology: From co-optation to amelioration and transformation. *Psychosocial Intervention*, *23*(2), 151–154. https://doi.org/10.1016/j.psi.2014.07.008

Rappaport, J. (1987). Terms of empowerment/exemplars of prevention: Toward a theory for community psychology. *American Journal of Community Psychology*, *15*, 121–148. https://doi.org/10.1007/BF00919275

Saunders, D. G., & Oglesby, K. H. (2016). No way to turn: Traps encountered by many battered women with negative child custody experiences. *Journal of Child Custody*, *13*(2–3), 154–177. https://doi.org/10.1080/15379418.2016.1213114

Smith, J. A., & Shinebourne, P. (2012). Interpretative phenomenological analysis. In H. Cooper, P. M. Camic, D. L. Long, A. T. Panter, D. Rindskopf, & K. J. Sher (Eds.), *APA handbook of research methods in psychology, Vol. 2. Research designs: Quantitative, qualitative, neuropsychological, and biological* (pp. 73–82). American Psychological Association. https://doi.org/10.1037/13620-005

Sullivan, C. M., & Goodman, L. A. (2019). Advocacy with survivors of intimate partner violence: What it is, what it isn't, and why it's critically important. *Violence Against Women*, *25*(16), 2007–2023. https://doi.org/10.1177/1077801219875826

Wild, J. (2023). Gendered discourses of responsibility and domestic abuse victim-blame in the English children's social care system. *Journal of Family Violence*, *38*(7), 1391–1403. https://doi.org/10.1007/s10896-022-00431-4

Zimmerman, M. A. (1995). Psychological empowerment: Issues and illustrations. *American Journal of Community Psychology*, *23*(5), 581–599. https://doi.org/10.1007/BF02506983

Further Reading

Campbell, R., & Raja, S. (1999). Secondary victimization of rape victims: Insights from mental health professionals who treat survivors of violence. *Violence and Victims*, *14*(3), 261. https://doi.org/10.1891/0886–6708.14.3.261

Laing, L. (2017). Secondary victimization: Domestic violence survivors navigating the family law system. *Violence Against Women*, *23*(11), 1314–1335. https://doi.org/10.1177/1077801216659942

Lundy, T., & Crawford, J. (2024). Health and wellness outcomes of intimate partner violence support workers: A narrative review. *Trauma, Violence, & Abuse*, *25*(4), 2942–2956. https://doi.org/10.1177/15248380241231604

12 Challenges and opportunities faced by young people in European rural communities

The roles of community psychologists

Francisco Simões and Elena Marta

Introduction

According to demographic and economic criteria, rural areas correspond to depopulated regions (<300 inhabitants per km² and a minimum population of 5,000) (Eurostat, 2018). Such assumptions do not convey, however, the diversity of rural communities' livelihoods regarding their geography, values, economic resources and collective priorities. Seemingly, these criteria perpetuate a limited and often inaccurate representation of rural communities as spaces of decline and decay (Ahlmeyer & Volgmann, 2023). Unfortunately, these dominant, negative narratives are pervasive among young people, meaning those aged 13–30 (Council of Europe, 2024). Take the example below of Ruralia (see Box 12.1) summarising how a rural community is typically represented.

Box 12.1 Ruralia – A standard rural community?

Ruralia is a community of about 15,000 people; 45% are elderly. Most of the residents are dedicated to farming or farming-related activities (e.g., ecotourism). Only a few commute daily to work in a nearby town. More would like to do so, but public transportation is limited. Young people living in Ruralia are not very hopeful about their life in the countryside. The most academic-minded ones leave after completing secondary school, especially young women. Many of those remaining have not completed secondary school and feel they do not have opportunities to find a stable job. The mayor is always talking about "young people" and "the young people's problems" as if they only had problems or were themselves *a* problem or *the* problem. However, most of the youths feel that nobody is listening. Some would like to make their voices heard. They just do not find the right way to do it.

This illustration summarises the purpose of our chapter: to show how community psychologists can contribute to improving rural young people's life circumstances, based on some key principles. Community psychologists can help raise critical awareness and empower European rural young people across domains such as education, employment, mobilities and participation. They can also adopt an ecological lens to read the implications of such challenges and opportunities. Finally, community psychologists can help rural communities address the most pressing issues faced by their younger generations through

DOI: 10.4324/9781003480464-15

participatory methods (e.g., Community-Based Participatory Action Research, CBPAR). In this chapter, we explore each of these points before concluding with a brief reflection about the roles professionals need to play to realise their full potential when serving rural communities.

Are rural young people underperforming in school? Generally speaking, yes, but…

Academic results differ between rural areas and suburban/urban areas across European countries, with the former usually performing worse (Bæck, 2016). The Early Leaving from Education and Training (ESLET), referring to the share of young people aged 18 to 24 years who have not completed secondary education, illustrates this trend as we show in Figure 12.1 (see below in the next section). In 2016, the ESLET proportion was higher in rural areas (11.9%), compared to towns and suburbs (11.2%) and cities (9.3%) across the European Union (EU). ESLET rates declined across all types of territories in 2022, but remained higher in rural areas (10%), compared to towns and suburbs (10.6%) and cities (8.6%). This trend was observed for most European countries in both years, with only a few exceptions (e.g., Belgium, Germany, the Netherlands) (Eurostat, 2024a).

Another useful indicator to assess educational performance across different types of territories is Tertiary Education Attainment (TEA), meaning the share of the population aged 30–34 who has completed a university degree. In 2016, TEA was lower in rural areas (27.4%) compared to towns and suburbs (32.6%) and cities (48.2%) across the EU. The same gaps remained in 2022, although with TEA increases across rural areas (31%), towns and suburbs (36.3%), and cities (53.5%) (Figure 12.1). This trend was observed for most EU countries, except for Finland, Greece, Hungary and Latvia. Importantly, at both time points across all countries except for Malta in 2022, TEA shares were higher in cities (Eurostat, 2024b).

Poorer academic performance in rural areas is explained through structural inequalities. Such differences are driven by social factors such as the mismatch between communities' traditional values and schools' liberal worldviews, parents' lower educational level or students' more vulnerable socio-economic profiles (Bæck, 2016). These inequalities are also justified by educational factors, including lower investments in infrastructure (e.g., school buildings), digital resources and equipment, particularly

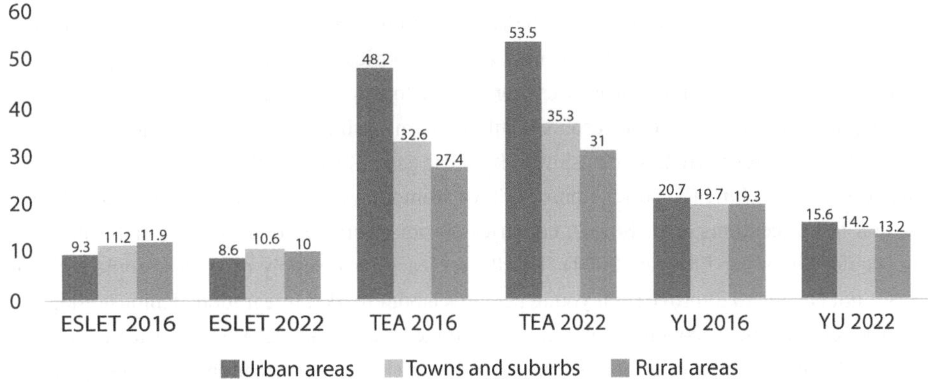

Figure 12.1 Main education and employment indicators by degree of urbanisation from 2016 to 2022 (%).
Source: Eurostat.

in more deprived rural territories with larger shares of vulnerable students (Bæck, 2016), or reduced capacity to retain teachers (Reagan et al., 2019).

There are exceptions to this trend of rural academic underperformance. A recent report shows that Portuguese rural municipalities depicted higher levels of secondary school attainment between 2009 and 2018 and that these differences were significantly greater by 2013 compared to high-density municipalities (Garcia et al., 2023). Between 2012 and 2021, Portugal was among the EU countries showing a more pronounced ESLET decrease (-14.6 pp) above France (-11.4 pp) and Finland (-8.1 pp), which came second and third, respectively. It is, therefore, important to understand how educational improvements are spreading across different types of territories to target best practices in rural areas. Meanwhile, the gap between rural and urban areas may continue to shrink, but not for the best reasons. High-density areas in the suburban belts of major cities are becoming more diverse from a cultural point of view, but also socially more vulnerable. For instance, these areas host a greater number of first-generation migrant families as well as their children. A disproportionate number of them are among students with lower educational attainment (Organisation for Economic Co-operation and Development - OECD, 2023). These communities often depend on low-resourced public programmes to access education. Subsequently, suburban schools struggle to respond to students' growing diverse backgrounds, leading to worse school outcomes (Garcia et al., 2023).

What about employment: Is farming the only way out for young people settled in rural areas?

It is a bit more complicated than that. Youth Unemployment (YU) rates in the EU in 2016 were lower in rural areas (19.3%), compared to towns and suburbs (19.7%) and cities (20.7%). Overall, these figures (see Figure 12.1) improved for rural areas (13.2%), towns and suburbs (14.2%) and cities (15.6%) by 2022 (Eurostat, 2024c). However, in Southern (e.g., Spain, Greece) and Eastern countries (Bulgaria, Hungary, Romania) as well as in the Baltic States, YU shares are consistently higher in rural areas, opposite to many Central (e.g., Germany) or Northern (e.g., Sweden) European countries. Further reports demonstrate that regions displaying lower Gross Domestic Product (GDP) and lower demand for more qualified jobs are disproportionately rural regions of Southern and Eastern Europe (Cefalo & Scandurra, 2021).

The structural West/East and North/South divides in European youth labour markets are multidetermined. Firstly, rural territories in Southern and Eastern countries still rely on a dominant primary sector, especially family-owned farming businesses more averse to innovation and showing low levels of entrepreneurship able to transform local resources into modern business models (Mujčinović et al., 2024). Secondly, the policy response has been slow to fill these gaps. Recent analyses of the Reinforced Youth Guarantee, the overarching EU policy framework for promoting youth employment and education, show that with a few exceptions (e.g., Spain), countries do not prioritise policies for (disadvantaged) rural young people (Simões & Erdogan, 2024). Thirdly, increasing the supply of young people with college degrees is not enough to improve rural young people's labour market integration, demonstrating that job supply also relies on local economic conditions (Cefalo & Scandurra, 2021). These structural constraints often translate into youth leaving for cities and suburban areas, the perpetuation of the inter-generational cycle of poverty and inequalities due to longer or more recurrent unemployment spells, and delays in the accumulation of work experience/specialisation across rural communities (Simões & Rio, 2020).

There are still some opportunities for rural young people's labour market integration. Sustainable agriculture and ecotourism are creating new businesses and feeding socially responsible entrepreneurship that may help retain younger generations in their territories. Within agriculture, some niches (e.g., wine production) or the preference for local and responsible consumerism add an impulse to sustainable farming that resonates with rural younger generations' worldviews (Simões & Rio, 2020). Moreover, the possibilities offered by remote work and, in turn, the housing crisis affecting urban centres can bring more high-skilled young people into rural areas, but these trends still need to be better understood. Finally, some rural areas closer to urban centres are developing transportation means for young people to commute, whether to study or to work (Mujčinović et al., 2024).

Is moving away the only pathway for rural young people to improve their life prospects?

Not entirely. Rural areas face a shrinking demography and ageing. The population aged 15 to 24 in rural areas has decreased by more than 2 million from 2016 to 2022. This trend is evident in most countries apart from Cyprus, France, Greece, Ireland and the Netherlands. This outcome is largely credited to youth leaving rural areas or changes in the administrative classification of the territory (in the case of France) (Eurostat, 2024c).

The migratory movements of rural young people to more affluent, urban areas within the country or abroad have frequently been depicted as a standard. These movements are caused by young people's intentions to improve their education and skills, access better jobs and reach a better socioeconomic condition (Silva et al., 2021). Rural youth migration has been interpreted as the result of unequal territorial distribution of resources or a triumph of a narrative limiting young people's future and opportunities to urban places. Consequently, those staying are often less academic-minded youths, especially men, lacking the financial resources to move out, further stretching social gaps between younger generations living in rural areas and (sub)urban territories (Farrugia, 2016).

We think there are important nuances to rural young people's outmigration trends that must be highlighted. Firstly, for the past decade, the increasing shares of young people living in rural areas in some European countries (e.g., Ireland) require further understanding. Likewise, rural young people's mobilities are becoming more diverse, including short-term or returning movements. Studies following this approach have shown that the emotional bond to local communities and places is an important predictor of rural young people's returning intentions. Thus, leaving and staying can coexist, and returning can also be an option under certain circumstances, even if moving out to (sub)urban areas continues to be the dominant mobility trend among rural younger generations (Simões et al., 2021; Silva et al., 2021).

Are rural communities providing enough room for young people's participation?

There is limited evidence of that. By youth participation, we mean young people's engagement in an activity to achieve a collectively determined goal through social action, volunteerism, collective action, voting or protesting. Youth participation can, however, range from mere attempts by adults to control the process (e.g., tokenism) to youth-led initiatives (Pozzi et al., 2017). Youth participation should rely on youth-directed initiatives, based on decision-making processes shared with adults. Several reasons prevent that from becoming a standard. Rural communities' decision-making platforms are frequently dominated by older generations that set local agendas and reproduce local values/traditions. The space for participation is further constrained by strong informal relationships and loyalty to local values. This limits young people from expressing their worldviews (Simões et al., 2023). Moreover, initiatives aiming at youth participation in rural areas struggle to combine resources at multiple levels, including

Table 12.1 Challenges and opportunities faced by rural young people

Domain	*Challenges*	*Opportunities*
Education	Mismatch between communities' traditional values and the school's liberal worldviews. Parents lower educational level. Students' more vulnerable socioeconomic profiles. Lower investments in infrastructure. Limited access to high-quality preschool experiences. Reduced capacity to retain teachers and prevent teacher turnover.	In some countries (e.g., Portugal) rural areas are performing well in terms of educational results. More case studies of best practices in rural education will be informative.
Employment	Dominant family-owned farming businesses are innovation-aversive. Continued dismantling of industrial capacity. Loss of experienced workers who can mentor younger generations in developing skills. Slow reaction from decision-makers to address the gaps of rural youth labour markets in Southern and Eastern countries.	Sustainable agriculture and ecotourism are feeding new ways of socially responsible entrepreneurship. Production niches and local consumerism are adding an impulse to sustainable farming aligned with younger generations' values. Remote work or the housing crisis may lead to retain more high-skilled in rural areas. Rural areas closer to urban centres are establishing the transportation means for young people to commute.
Mobilities	Youth outmigration associated to access to better jobs and increase the odds of upwards social mobility. Youth outmigration reflects unequal distribution of opportunities and resources across territories.	Rural young people's mobilities are becoming more diverse including short-term or returning movements. Place attachment to rural communities is an important predictor of rural young people circular and returning mobilities.
Participation	Rural communities' decision-making is frequently dominated by older generations setting local agendas and reproducing local values/traditions. Initiatives aiming at rural youth participation in rural areas struggle to combine policies and programs, institutional support systems and informal social networks.	Rural younger generations are interested in solving concrete local problems. Municipalities are starting to target local young people for participating in decision-making platforms. The twin transition can facilitate greater youth participation in multiple ways. The settlement of more young people and newcomers in rural areas will intensify the dialogue between local traditions and urban/foreign cultures.

policies and programmes, institutional support systems and informal social networks (Ferreira et al., 2024).

There is evidence that younger generations in rural areas have been found to be interested in being socially active to help solve concrete local problems (Simões et al., 2023). Meanwhile, some rural municipalities are starting to engage local young people in committees or informal interest groups to support decision-making (Silva et al., 2021). Moreover, the digital and green transitions will certainly pressure greater youth participation, further strengthening intergenerational relationships in rural areas in terms of developing and using new skills and knowledge or managing local resources. The settlement of newcomers in rural areas may intensify the collaboration between local traditions and urban/foreign cultures. Although such intercultural contact can create tensions between different social groups, it might also lead to a creative dialogue between different generations in the long term. Specifically, local heritage and goods may be resituated in the global culture, with rural young people helping to shape that process (Simões et al., 2023).

Box 12.2 pinpoints how the main topics raised in this section as the most relevant for rural young people's livelihoods can be transformed into topical discussions or guided discovery exercises. Furthermore, Table 12.1 provides a comprehensive list of the different topics by domain (e.g., education), whether they represent challenges and opportunities, that might be used for inspiring these practical activities.

Box 12.2 Using key topics as a training and learning tool

The key topics presented in this section can be used in classes to spark discussions about rural young people from a Community Psychology perspective. You can:

- transform them into ice-breaking questions to initiate debates.
- distribute them into small groups to promote time-limited discussions.
- implement a world café series, with each topic presented as a talking point for asking students for opinions/comments.

Our topics can also be used as drivers for a **pros and cons discussion**. Transform each of them into a one-sided statement (e.g., Rural young people are school underperformers). Then, ask the students to position themselves for, against, or somewhat in between regarding that statement. Afterwards, open a plenary discussion for 5/10 minutes. Finish up the discussion by highlighting arguments in favour and against the statement using the challenges and opportunities listed in Table 12.1.

Why is Community Psychology well-suited to understand of rural young people's challenges and opportunities?

Community Psychology offers a promising avenue to address and manage challenges and emerging opportunities faced by rural younger generations. We consider that some of Community Psychology's main features can contribute to that in a historical period of transition complicated by prejudice, negative stereotypes and stigmatisation phenomena. These features include:

- openness to interdisciplinary and transdisciplinary approaches.
- emphasis on individuals through the lens of emotions and cognitions that shape subjectivity, accounting for the role of cultural, economic and social factors.

- relevance of individual agency, by embracing a circular concept of knowledge and action, where the individual not only influences but is also influenced by the context in which he/she is embedded.
- focus on promoting the "melior," that is, the resources and potential of both individuals and contexts, from a salutogenic (health-promoting) perspective.
- priority given to the development of participatory methodologies.
- commitment to social change and social justice – i.e., each person should receive what is due to him or her, fairly and equitably (Prilleltensky, 2012).

Within Community Psychology, Trickett and Rowe's (2012) ecological-systemic approach is a theoretical framework that we find particularly relevant for fulfilling the field's potential for addressing rural young people's current circumstances. This framework considers the different levels of reality and the dynamic processes occurring between them. Overall, the model involves moving from a contextual analysis – focusing on specific settings such as schools, neighbourhoods or organisations – to a systemic analysis examining the interrelationships among the various parts of a system and their mutual influences. This perspective is grounded in values such as inclusion and maintaining a moral commitment to individuals and their contexts.

Each ecological-systemic approach level provides guidelines to gather information about a certain phenomenon and to establish, design and implement adequate interventions (see Figure 12.2). We depict these levels by applying them to research or intervention efforts targeting young people Not in Education, Employment, or Training (NEET) from Ruralia who are deciding whether to stay or seek opportunities in an urban setting (for a more detailed discussion, see Simões & Erdogan, 2024).

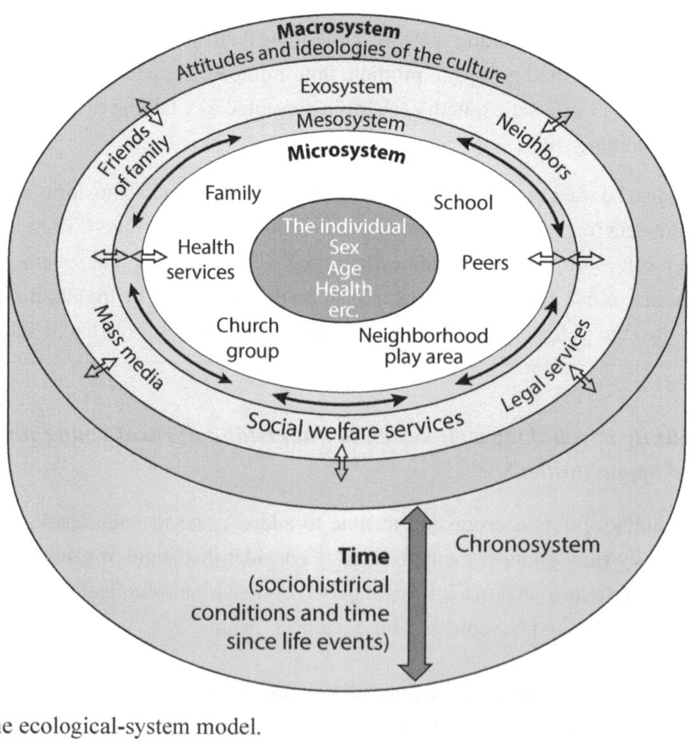

Figure 12.2 The ecological-system model.
Source: Santrock, 2011.

The *individual level* of the ecological-system model covers organic-heritage characteristics (e.g., gender, age, ethnicity), cognitive features (e.g., self-efficacy) and lifestyle behaviours. At this level, for NEETs living in Ruralia it is essential to consider gender and migration background. In many countries, a significant share of youths in the NEET condition are female and migrants who are in a more vulnerable situation. Additionally, it may be important to assess skills, whether specific subsets (e.g., soft skills) or those that need to be further developed. Regarding lifestyle, it may be relevant to compare, for instance, the time these youths spend outdoors or in sports versus the time spent in digital interactions.

The *micro-level* refers to the person's social network, including family, peer groups and neighbours. The relevant features at this level include the network's size and density, the quality of the relationships (communication patterns, rules, habits) and their roles (e.g., instrumental, emotional, informational and/or affiliative support). In the case of NEETs from Ruralia, research and programme development may be required to explore the nature and quality of their relationship with their parents and friends and if they receive appropriate support – emotional or otherwise – from them.

The *meso-level* corresponds to the structured network of micro-systems such as schools, workplaces and service systems in which individuals are directly involved. At this ecological level, examining how NEETs living in Ruralia are shaped by educational opportunities and resources (e.g., provision of career guidance) or social organisations (e.g., trade association benefits for the children of its members) may be key for delivering proper research efforts or programme design.

The *exo-level* corresponds to the interconnection between people and the territory and how that generates opportunities for participation. This is also known as the community level. Making sense of NEETs' livelihoods in Ruralia might require understanding if they are involved in organised groups or activities, how public institutions, third-sector organisations or political entities encourage youth participation and networking, and if these opportunities generate social goods such as care and promotion of young people or a sense of community and social justice.

Finally, the *macro-level* of the ecological-systemic approach pertains to the cultural and value systems of the community, including policies at the regional and national levels, as well as the media's role. The cultural messages media convey about Ruralia, the social representations about the community or how these representations influence local organisations and institutions' actions are key elements at this level that may add to a full comprehension of local NEETs' life circumstances. Box 12.3 summarises key principles and illustrative guiding questions using an ecological-systemic approach to rural youth challenges. The proposed guiding questions are organised by the layers of the ecological-systemic model and focus on the specific challenges associated with the school-to-work transition.

Box 12.3 Using ecological-systemic principles and guiding questions to promote rural youth participation

Consider Ruralia – whether you live, work or volunteer there. Imagine you have to develop a project to support the local young people's school-to-work transition. Using the various levels of the ecological-systemic model, what key research questions would you need to ask?

In carrying out the project, consider the fact that:

- it is important to involve young people and give them a voice.
- in addition to needs, map endogenous resources at different levels.
- community involvement must promote its development.

In Table 12.2 you can find some examples of questions by levels of the ecological-systemic model.

Table 12.2 Examples of questions by levels of ecological-systemic model

Level	*Issues*
Individual	How do Ruralia youths look to at and understand school-to-work transition? What are their expectations, attitude, beliefs, values and skills? What do they want to change in Ruralia to provide them better job prospects?
Micro-level **Family**	How are typical family interactions and relationships? How can families promote/ prevent smooth transitions to the labour market?
School	Do Ruralia schools include employment as a topic in their agenda? Do they encourage young people participation on discussions related to labour markets? Do they provide counselling services?
Meso-level	How do the interactions between different settings and people affect the transition to the labour market in Ruralia? How and to what extent do these interactions encompass the voice of young people?
Exo-level	How do organisations/institutions at this level provide opportunities/resources for easing the transition to the labour market? Have they considered designing solutions with them based on promising economic activities?
Macro-level	How do the cultural and economic Ruralia characteristics influence the transition? How does the media address this issue? How much does the business world contribute to develop decent work conditions?

What methodological approach addresses rural young people's needs from an ecological-systemic perspective?

The ecological-systemic model is upheld by participatory methods. We understand participation as an intentional, voluntary, collective and organised process in which social actors are involved in the action-research process in diverse ways. It involves a relational dynamic leading to further relationships, aimed at achieving shared values, goals and the common good among the different actors involved (Ferreira et al., 2024). Participatory methods facilitate research, intervention and change processes. These methods involve varying degrees of participation, from being a research participant to acting as a co-researcher.

Fostering participation strongly relies on building a relational environment based on trust. To help rural young people face their specific challenges, we believe it is essential that community psychologists use a Community-Based Participatory Action Research (CBPAR) lens, which merges elements of Community-Based Participatory Research (CBPR) with Participatory Action Research (PAR).

> CBPR involves the equitable involvement of community members, organizational representatives, and researchers throughout the research process, identifying the community as a unit of identity, building on the community's strengths and resources, promoting co-learning and capacity building for everyone involved, and achieving a balance between research and action.
>
> (Israel et al., 2008) (Kral & Allen, 2016)

CBPR links science with social activism, recognising community members as active, decision-making participants (Wallerstein & Duran, 2008). Thus, PAR emphasises community empowerment, democratic social change, a participatory worldview and practical solutions to pressing community needs.

A specific form of CBPAR is Youth-led Participatory Action Research (YPAR), which involves training young people to identify key issues in their communities, conduct research to understand these problems and take a leadership role in shaping policies and decisions to improve their living conditions

(London et al., 2003). YPAR shares CBPR's emphasis on empowering marginalised groups through an iterative process of inquiry and action, and democratising research by including the expertise and voices of those most affected by it (Ozer, 2016).

The CBPAR and YPAR are methodological approaches that can help to address rural young people's challenges for at least three reasons (Simões et al., 2023):

- **Involving rural young people in CBPAR or YPAR activities as co-researchers or co-leaders can lead them to recognise their skills while also developing new ones.** This engagement, through, for instance, group-based initiatives promoted by community psychologists, also allows rural young people to contribute meaningfully to community development, fostering a stronger sense of belonging, responsibility, and commitment to social justice.
- **Participatory methodologies offer a structured and "safe" environment for intergenerational collaboration.** They allow different generations to compare perspectives, understand each other's viewpoints and negotiate actions that respect and value contributions from all age groups. This collaboration in interventions can sustain collective efforts over time. Community psychologists can facilitate forums for debate, where young people's voices are incorporated into discussions about solutions for pressing challenges. Adopting a common working method and embracing a dialogue-participation approach can shift the community's value structure, with each generation's contribution increasingly recognised in intergenerational relations.
- **CBPAR and YPAR provide outstanding opportunities to develop trust, reciprocity and cooperation within and between different groups, while promoting participation within institutions (in other words, developing social capital).** This approach can reduce widespread distrust and generate innovative solutions. Through co-construction of solutions, community psychologists can help bridge the gap between institutions and citizens, fostering trust – particularly among young people.

In Box 12.4, we provide an example of the use of CBPAR in a rural community setting involving rural young people as well as other generations. This is an intervention co-led by a community psychologist, Francesca Mercuri, and a sociologist, Lidia Piattini (Mercuri, 2024). The method involved three stages: preparation, profiling and action.

Box 12.4 Example of CBPAR implementation

Preparation: The local administration of a rural municipality approached a community development firm – comprised of community psychologists, educators, social workers and sociologists, expressing concern over the lack of citizen participation, particularly among young people, in local, social and political life. The administration also highlighted concerns about rising school dropout and NEET rates, and prevailing negative stereotypes about young people due to acts of vandalism perpetrated by some young people against a public facility. The team initially encouraged the administration to reflect on their understanding of youth, the broader community and the local participatory processes based on some driving questions (e.g., who are the young people in the community? What do they want?). Following a period of listening and discussion with the administration, the team initiated a CBPAR process, involving the administration, a group of young people referred by multiple stakeholders (schools, third-sector organisations and personal networks) who formed a Youth Council, and several stakeholders and third-sector bodies were interested in the project. All these actors co-designed the project together.

Profiling: The team used a community profiling strategy to map and engage the community to develop four community profiles presented below:

Territorial profile – The Youth Council identified, explored and analysed the municipality's strengths (what is there) and weaknesses (what is missing) through group discussions and with the help of a town councillor who had the task of aggregating and summarising the information. A Future Lab, composed of school-age children, through focus groups, reread the data and made proposals for territorial development.

Productive activities profile – Developed using statistical data from the Chamber of Commerce of the provincial capital and data from semi-structured interviews held with companies and craft activities. The Youth Council, in cooperation with the Councillor for the Budget and a municipal councillor, selected the interviewees and the interviews.

Future profile – Children participating in the parish's Summer Centre (95% of all children in the municipality) who were also involved in the Future Lab were engaged in various age-related activities. Children aged 6–7 designed a game following the life stages of an imaginary child they named IVAN and whom they also imagined living in the country in the future. Children aged 8–10 were video interviewed: they were asked what they liked or disliked about the country and were taken through its past, present and future. Youths aged 11–14 identified two significant places in the municipality and critically explored them to suggest improvements. This work was included in the territorial profile.

Psychological profile – The project's team prepared a survey to be distributed among the residents including, for instance, a scale of sense of community. The Youth Council and the middle school children identified suitable places and times for survey dissemination (the market, the church square, the school exit), after analysing and sharing the instrument. The children and youth divided into small groups with a Youth Council "tutor," administered the questionnaire to the citizens. The team processed the data from the questionnaires and the young people summarised their experiences and impressions in a short video.

Action: Young people took the lead in designing and implementing these profiles with the team's support. The eight-month project yielded relevant short-term results such as (1) providing the administration with a detailed diagnosis of the area, i.e., a participatory analysis of the village's problems, resources and potential, helping to guide future actions; (2) stimulating constructive dialogue between generations and different segments of the community; and (3) facilitating the creation of shared, sustainable proposals based on an analysis of the community's strengths and weaknesses. In the long term, the project led to (1) consolidating the Youth Council, which expanded its territorial reach; (2) establishing a permanent working group of local associations; and (3) developing a project titled "When Culture Brings People Together," focusing on intergenerational cultural initiatives and secured funding from a private foundation.

In conclusion, how can community psychologists address the challenges faced by rural young people?

As we explored throughout this chapter, community psychologists can address rural young people's needs based on three key Community Psychology principles. Firstly, community psychologists can contribute to raising critical awareness and empower rural younger generations in facing the pressing challenges and emerging opportunities in areas such as education or employment. Secondly, community psychologists can provide an ecological reading of their challenges and opportunities, guaranteeing that the multiple factors shaping complex social issues affecting rural young people are duly considered. Finally, community psychologists can offer extensive expertise in promoting participation to address this group's needs, using the most appropriate methods (e.g., CBPAR, YPAR).

The combination of the outlined Community Psychology principles is key for providing rural young people a platform to express their views, experience supportive relationships, access resources and contradict stereotyped and negative representations spread about them. Overall, we consider that the strategic use of these principles promotes rural young people's mattering as an experience of feeling valued and adding value (Elliot et al., 2004). This, in turn, prioritises social justice in rural communities and upholds younger people's wellbeing.

To fully adopt these principles and fulfil social justice and wellbeing outcomes, community psychologists must consider their multiple roles. As intermediary figures, community psychologists can ensure continued negotiation between the needs of rural young people and the community services, between youth initiatives and decision-maker choices, between practice and research, and between theoretical research, applied research and action-research (Simões et al., 2023). As "travel companions," community psychologists can help to reconnect fragmented or divided parts and different generations in rural communities. They are, thus, catalysts for change who are skilled in managing social dynamics and conflicts. As a "repository of trust" (Kelman, 2005), community psychologists can nurture relationships during times of crisis or when trust has been eroded – a common feature in rural areas.

For all these reasons, we believe that the work of community psychologists not only supports young people in rural areas in coping with their daily challenges but also empowers the entire community, helping it to become more resilient.

Acknowledgements

This work was developed in the context of the European Rural Youth Observatory (EURYO). EURYO is an international research-led association committed to moving rural young people forward through knowledge and collaboration between multiple stakeholders. www.euryo.org

References

Ahlmeyer, F., & Volgmann, K. (2023). What can we expect for the development of rural areas in Europe? Trends of the last decade and their opportunities for rural regeneration. *Sustainability*, *15*(6), 5485. https://doi.org/10.3390/su15065485

Bæck, U.-D. K. (2016). Rural location and academic success: Remarks on research, contextualisation and methodology. *Scandinavian Journal of Educational Research*, *60*(4), 435–448. https://doi.org/10.1080/00313831.2015.1024163

Cefalo, R., & Scandurra, R. (2021). Territorial disparities in youth labour market chances in Europe. *Regional Studies, Regional Science*, *8*(1), 228–238. https://doi.org/10.1080/21681376.2021.1925580

Council of Europe. (2024). *Youth*. https://pjp-eu.coe.int/en/web/youth-partnership/glossary

Elliot, G. C., Kao, S., & Grant, A. (2004). Mattering: Empirical validation of a social- psychological concept. *Self and Identity*, *3*(4), 339–354. https://doi.org/10.1080/13576500444000119

Eurostat. (2018). *Methodological manual on territorial typologies*. https://ec.europa.eu/eurostat/documents/3859598/9507230/KS-GQ-18-008-EN-N.pdf

Eurostat. (2024a). *Early school leavers from education and training by sex and labour status*. https://ec.europa.eu/eurostat/databrowser/view/edat_lfse_14/default/table?lang=en

Eurostat. (2024b). *Population by educational attainment level, sex and age (%) - main indicators*. https://ec.europa.eu/eurostat/databrowser/view/edat_lfse_03/default/table?lang=en

Eurostat. (2024c). *Population by sex, age, country of birth, labour status and degree of urbanization*. https://ec.europa.eu/eurostat/databrowser/product/page/LFST_R_PGAUWSChttps://ec.europa.eu/eurostat/databrowser/view/une_rt_a/default/table?lang=en&category=labour.employ.lfsi.une

Farrugia, D. (2016). The mobility imperative for rural youth: The structural, symbolic and non-representational dimensions rural youth mobilities. *Journal of Youth Studies*, *19*(6), 836–851. https://doi.org/10.1080/13676261.2015.1112886

Ferreira, T., Ellena, A. M., Jonsson, F., Barbosa, B., Uyan-Semerci, P., Tuna, E., Kvieskienė, G., Marta, E., Unay-Gailhard, I., & Fernandes-Jesus, M. (2024). Building bridges: Community-based projects for participation and social inclusion of rural NEETs. In F. Simões & E. Erdogan (Eds.), *NEETs in European rural areas* (pp. 17–33). Springer. https://doi.org/10.1007/978-3-031-45679-4_2

Garcia, D., Simões, F., Bettencourt, L., Aguiar, C., Ferreira, I. A., Mendonça, J., Moleiro, C., Rocca, A., & Lendzhova, V. (2023). Predictors of secondary education completion across Portuguese municipalities: Evidence from the 2009–2018 period. *Societies*, *13*(9), 200. https://doi.org/10.3390/soc13090200

Israel, B. A., Schulz, A. J., Parker, E. A., & Becker, A. B. (2008). Critical issues in developing and following community-based participatory research principles. In M. Minkler & N. Wallerstein (Eds.), *Community-based participatory research for health* (pp. 47–62). Jossey-Bass.

Kelman, H.C. (2005). Building trust among enemies. *International Journal of Intercultural Relations*, *29*(6), 639–650. https://doi.org/10.1016/j.ijintrel.2005.07.011

Kral, M. J., & Allen, J. (2016). Community-based participatory action research. In L. A. Jason & D. S. Glenwick (Eds.), *Handbook of methodological approaches to community-based research: Qualitative, quantitative, and mixed methods* (pp. 253–263). Oxford Academic.

London, J. K., Zimmerman, K., & Erbstein, N. (2003). Youth-led research and evaluation: Tools for youth, organizational, and community development. *New Directions for Evaluation*, *98*, 33–45. https://doi.org/10.1002/ev.83

Mercuri, F. (2024). Lezione Profili di comunità Lurano 2020 dott.ssa Mercuri [Lecture Community Profiles Lurano 2020 Dr. Mercuri] [Power Point slides]. https://blackboard.unicatt.it/ultra/courses/_135610_1/outline

Mujčinović, A., Bojnec, S., Nikolić, A., Tonković, A. B., Gašparović, S., Lazereg, M. Stojanović, A., & Bojadjieva, D. (2024). Pathways for young farmers' entrepreneurship in sustainable rural development. In F. Simões & E. Erdogan (Eds.), *NEETs in European rural areas: An interdisciplinary, transnational reader* (pp. 69–87). Springer. https://doi.org/10.1007/978-3-031-45679-4_5

OECD. (2023). *Indicators of immigrant integration*. https://www.oecd.org/en/publications/indicators-of-immigrant-integration-2023_1d5020a6-en/full-report.html

Ozer, E. J. (2016). Youth-led participatory action research: Developmental and equity perspectives. In S. S. Horn, M. D. Ruck, & L. S. Liben (Eds.), *Equity and justice in developmental science: Theoretical and methodological issues* (pp. 189–207). Elsevier Academic Press. https://doi.org/10.1016/bs.acdb.2015.11.006

Pozzi, M., Pistoni, C., & Alfieri, S. (2017). Verso una psicologia della partecipazione [Towards a psychology of participation]. *Psicologia Sociale*, *12*(3), 253–276. https://doi.org/10.1482/87884

Prilleltensky, I. (2012). Wellness as fairness. *American Journal of Community Psychology*, *49*(1–2), 1–21. https://doi.org/10.1007/s10464-011-9448-8

Reagan, E. M., Hambacher, E., Schram, T., McCurdy, K., Lord, D., Higginbotham, T., & Fornauf, B. (2019). Place matters: Review of the literature on rural teacher education. *Teaching and Teacher Education*, *80*(1), 83–93. https://doi.org/10.1016/j.tate.2018.12.005

Santrock, J. W. (2011). *A topical approach to life-span development*. McGraw-Hill Education.

Silva, S. M., Silva, A., González, G., & Braziene, R. (2021). Learning to leave and to return: Mobility, place, and sense of belonging amongst young people growing up in border and rural regions of mainland Portugal. *Sustainability*, *13*(16), 9432. https://doi.org/10.3390/su13169432.

Simões, F., & Erdogan, E. (2024). *NEETs in European rural areas: Individual features, support system and policy measures*. Springer.

Simões, F., Fernandes-Jesus, M., Marta, E., Albanesi, C., & Carr, N. (2023). The increasing relevance of European rural young people in policy agendas: Contributions from community psychology. *Journal of Community and Applied Social Psychology*, *33*(1), 3–13. https://doi.org/10.1002/casp.2640

Simões, F., & Rio, N. (2020). How to increase rural NEETs professional involvement in agriculture? The roles of youth representations and vocational training packages improvement. *Journal of Rural Studies*, *75*, 9–19. https://doi.org/10.1016/j.jrurstud.2020.02.007

Simões, F., Rocca, A., Rocha, R., Mateus, C., Marta, E., & Tosun, J. (2021). Time to get emotional: Determinants of university students' intentions to return to rural areas. *Sustainability*, *13*(9), 5135. https://doi.org/10.3390/su13095135

Trickett, E. J., & Rowe H. L. (2012). Emerging ecological approaches to prevention, health promotion, and public health in the school context: Next steps from a community psychology perspective. *Journal of Educational and Psychological Consultation*, *22*(1–2), 125–140. https://doi.org/10.1080/10474412.2011.649651

Wallerstein, N., & Duran, B. (2008). The theoretical, historical, and practice roots of CBPR. In M. Minkler & N. Wallerstein (Eds.), *Community-based participatory research for health: From process to outcomes* (pp. 25–46). John Wiley.

PART IV

Troubling medicalisation

Perspectives from the UK

13 Family wellbeing, Community Psychology and social prescribing

Amy Edwards-Smith, Sam Pywell, Fiona Routh, Koser Khan and Natalie Hicks

Overview

This chapter integrates practice and academic perspectives on family wellbeing through Social Prescribing (SP) and Community Psychology. Family wellbeing is a complex, multidimensional concept shaped by health, community and social cohesion. Given their shared focus on holistic well-being and the social determinants of health, SP and community psychology intersect as complementary approaches. This chapter explores how integrating these disciplines can enhance family wellbeing by addressing both individual and systemic needs. SP connects individuals and families to non-clinical community resources, promoting wellbeing. Community Psychology, meanwhile, focuses on social justice, empowerment and collective approaches to health. Together, these disciplines have the potential to support families experiencing financial hardship, marginalisation and structural barriers. This chapter defines family wellbeing, discusses the importance of community connection and presents two case studies to illustrate how SP can meet the diverse needs of families. It also examines structural barriers such as poverty, housing and legal status and explores the role of community psychologists in creating lasting change.

Introduction

From a community psychologist perspective, SP bridges between traditional services and community-led solutions, offering responses to the social determinants of health conventional services may overlook. Family wellbeing is a flexible and contested term with various definitions across health and social care. While often idealised, family wellbeing is shaped by real-world challenges, poverty, displacement and inequality. This multidimensional concept encompasses physical, emotional, social and environmental health within family systems (Centre for Mental Health, Children and Young People's Mental Health Coalition, & Save the Children, 2024; Garthwaite et al., 2022; Rainer et al., 2024).

The UK National Health Service (NHS) describes family wellbeing as a state where family members experience positive physical and mental health and maintain strong relationships in a supportive environment (NHS, 2024). This aligns with contemporary guidance defining wellbeing more holistically, emphasising social connection, stable housing, education and economic stability (National Institute for Health and Care Excellence, 2022; World Health Organization (WHO), 2025). SP connects individuals and families to non-medical activities promoting wellbeing, such as peer groups, arts and nature-based

DOI: 10.4324/9781003480464-17

activities (Hayes, et al., 2023). The NHS England (n.d.) model of SP helps people (including families) address the social determinants of health by linking them with local support.

While SP is typically seen as an individual intervention, its potential to support whole families is increasingly recognised (Muir et al., 2024). This overlaps with community psychology, particularly around relational health and collective wellbeing. The Family Quality of Life (FQoL) framework stresses wellbeing is not simply the sum of individual wellbeing; it arises from shared relationships and collective experiences (Borilli et al., 2022). Clear, inclusive definitions of family wellbeing are critical to ensuring interventions are responsive to diverse family structures and needs. Terms like "citizen" often shape policy eligibility but can exclude vulnerable families, especially those without settled status, from basic services. This has direct implications for children's access to education and healthcare (UK Visas and Immigration, 2024). SP offers a practical route by meeting people where they are and supporting whole family needs. SP challenges rigid eligibility frameworks and supports those who are at risk of being marginalised within existing support systems.

Poverty as a systemic barrier to family wellbeing

Family wellbeing is fundamental to the health and development of children and young people (CYP). While community psychology offers a framework for enhancing wellbeing, implementation is hindered by structural inequalities. Organisational systems and social norms often fail to recognise or address interconnected issues of poverty, social exclusion or access to services (Marmot et al., 2020; Russell, 2022). Barriers are particularly evident among marginalised families, as illustrated in case study 1.

Praxis Case study 1: Supporting immigrant families through Social Prescribing

A newly arrived immigrant family in the UK is placed in poor housing conditions (damp walls, no access to green space) and struggles with social isolation. Due to their unsettled immigrant status, the children cannot attend school. The parents lack support networks and face challenges navigating public services.

A Manchester-based charity (Afrocats, n.d.), led by schoolteachers, provides educational support to CYP without settled status, effectively acting as a form of SP through the Community Enhanced SP Model (Morris et al., 2022). Referred by local services, families engage in structured learning, social activities and community connection. The charity's open-door policy allows for ongoing engagement, and many families later return as volunteers, fostering long-term cohesion and resilience.

Impact and relevance to Social Prescribing

This case study illustrates how SP can address policy-driven gaps in education and social care, offering relational and rights-based support formal systems often exclude (Bos et al., 2023). Families without "citizen" status face barriers shaped by legal definitions not aligning with human need (Zambelli et al., 2023). Through community-led models, SP creates more inclusive pathways to wellbeing. Yet as powerful as community responses are, they exist within, and are often constrained by, larger systemic forces. Poverty remains a persistent barrier to family wellbeing, influencing everything from housing to healthcare access (Bidmead et al., 2024). Charity-led support can partially address the effects of poverty, but it cannot eliminate them. A persistent North/South divide in UK child poverty exists with 1.05 million children in the North living in deprivation (N8 Research Partnership, 2024). Poverty impacts access to housing, health care, education and social participation, factors directly linked to family wellbeing (Oxford Poverty and Human Development Initiative (OPHI), 2013).

The Multi-dimensional Poverty Index (MPI) identifies three types of child poverty:

- Material poverty: Inability to afford or access essential items and activities deemed necessary for an acceptable standard of living, which is largely beyond the influence of services (Hodgkins & Prowle, 2023).
- Opportunity poverty: A child's limited access to fulfilling life choices, often due to systemic exclusion (Domínguez & Navarro, 2021).
- Relational poverty: Recognises the lack of social capital and support networks weakening a child's sense of belonging (Crane et al., 2020).

Community psychologists and SP practitioners must recognise relational poverty and the significance family and local community relationships have upon a child's sense of self-worth and belonging. Chronic poverty (especially when combined with housing instability or immigration stress) can reduce parenting capacity. Daily "toxic stress" reduces the emotional resources caregivers need to support their children, disrupting attachment and developmental outcomes (Banihani et al., 2025). SP interventions are strength-based, thus helping families build secure attachments and reconnect with supportive environments (Hodgkins & Prowle, 2023). When properly resourced, SP contributes to resilience, not by "fixing" families, but by enabling them to navigate systemic challenges with greater support.

The case for integrated SP models for CYP

Emerging evidence supports SP for CYP (Barnados, 2023) by reducing pressure on services, e.g., CAMHS, yet most SP models are adult oriented. Scaling SP nationally requires resourcing acknowledging the distinct needs of CYP and their families (Jarvis & Mitchell, n.d.). Without such integration, poverty risks becoming a syndemic; driven by interconnected structural inequalities perpetuating disadvantages across generations. Family wellbeing depends not just on individual interventions, but on systemic, collaborative approaches including education, housing and community-based care (Ellis et al., 2022).

Solutions: SP for CYP and families

Case study 2 illustrates how a Social Prescribing Link Worker (SPLW) in a GP practice can provide holistic support – addressing families' practical, emotional and developmental needs (National Children's Bureau, 2023).

Praxis Case study 2: Family wellbeing and Social Prescribing

Lena has three children and visited her GP, struggling with symptoms of loneliness, low mood and anxiety. She declined a mental health referral and was instead referred to a SPLW who guided her through a "what matters to you" conversation. Lena identified her priorities as reducing family conflict and engaging in activities outside the home.

Social Prescribing interventions and solutions

The SPLW introduced a range of support options, guided by the NHS's "Five Ways to Wellbeing" framework (Gilliver, 2021):

- Immediate support: Benefits check, food bank vouchers, pre-loved uniform access, transport and budgeting assistance.
- Health and wellbeing: Connection to a free online perimenopause support group, bereavement counselling service and a family inclusive Nature-Based SP (NBSP) initiative, with the SPLW.
- Support for her children: CAMHS "Wait Well" programme for her neurodiverse son and forest school for her youngest child to enhance confidence and social skills, along with enrolling at Afrocats, a Manchester charity supporting CYP without settled status.
- Technology access and education: A donated computer and digital literacy enabled Lena to access job resources. She also joined online language classes.
- Social inclusion: Access to community yoga and a local resources guide tailored to her family's needs.

Outcomes after six months

Lena's case demonstrates SP as a whole family intervention, addressing practical and emotional challenges. When built around "what matters" to individuals and families, SP can serve as a vital connector across services, reducing isolation and fostering resilience (National Academy for Social Prescribing, n.d.). However, success depends on access to flexible, well-funded services. Without these, the most marginalised families risk remaining excluded from support networks potentially enhancing wellbeing (Marmot et al., 2020).

How SP can address inequalities

Barriers including poverty, isolation and systemic inequities hinder family wellbeing and require targeted, long-term solutions. Integrating SP with PU and community psychology can bridge these gaps by improving access to support, education and wellbeing services (Marmot et al., 2020). The following solutions build on earlier challenges, showing SP's potential to drive meaningful change.

Emerging evidence on SP for children and young people

Current research suggests SP activities can improve mental health outcomes for CYP (Hayes et al., 2023; National Academy for Social Prescribing, n.d.; Polley et al., 2023) for example:

- The Linking Leeds programme demonstrated how SP fosters social connectedness and behavioural activation, promoting positive mental wellbeing (Brettell et al., 2022).
- (Rosehill, n.d.) An SP model within a Child and Adolescent Mental Health Service (CAMHS) was found to reduce loneliness and improve service outcomes (Fancourt et al., 2023).

These findings align with broader literature which suggests SP can enhance community engagement and mitigate social isolation (Howarth et al., 2018).

Nature-based Social Prescribing: A tailored approach for CYP and families

The neurodiversity movement views neurodivergence as natural variations in human experiences rather than disorders requiring a cure (Kushwaha, 2023). SP aligns with this philosophy by creating individualised support pathways rather than imposing medicalised solutions (National Academy for Social Prescribing, n.d.). SP can provide opportunities for developing social interactions in a structured manner (Zahir et al., 2023). Animal-assisted therapeutic activities and forest schools have demonstrated positive impacts on neurodivergent CYP helping develop empathy, self-regulation, social belonging, positive mental health and purpose (Haywood et al., 2024; Rich et al., 2024).

Creating the conditions for Social Prescribing to work

While SP is central to this chapter, SP depends on broader conditions like housing, food security, transport and accessible services – the wider determinants of health (Marmot et al., 2022). Without investment in these areas, SP risks offering only short-term relief. Two key factors shaping its success are Proportionate Universalism (PU) and education.

Equity in action: Proportionate universalism as a foundation for SP

Two critical levers shaping the success of SP are PU and education. PU provides a framework for distributing resources according to level of need (Marmot et al., 2010). Marmot et al. (2020) highlights PU is inconsistently applied in the UK, meaning the most disadvantaged are frequently underserved. A parent referred to a local parenting group via SP who cannot afford transport will fail to benefit. Likewise, education systems can provide early, low-stigma access to SP and act as anchors for family wellbeing. Without equity in these broader systems, SP risks becoming a surface-level solution to deep-rooted inequality. Family wellbeing is shaped not just by services but by how resources are distributed across society. Without equitable resourcing, including access to food, transport or childcare, SP interventions may remain inaccessible to families who need them most (Pickett et al., 2021).

Schools as SP hubs: The role of education in supporting family wellbeing

Schools function as community hubs, sites of community cohesion, health promotion and social support (Riley, 2013; Wilson, 2013). They can provide early, low-stigma access to SP and act as anchors for family wellbeing. Without equity, SP risks becoming a surface-level solution to deep-rooted inequalities. Schools can identify unmet needs early and facilitate SP referrals. Embedding SP within schools can enhance early, low-stigma intervention. Staff might refer a parent to a peer group, building protective networks and promoting resilience. Successful examples include school-based health centres and local partnerships offering integrated care for families (Fehrer & Leos-Urbel, 2016; Love et al., 2019). However, schools cannot fulfil this role without adequate funding and collaboration with external partners (Kellezi et al., 2021). By embedding SP within schools and scaling support based on need, services can work together to create a more equitable foundation for family wellbeing.

Community Psychology in practice

Reducing parental isolation through Community Psychology and SP

Community connectedness plays a vital role in reducing loneliness and social isolation (Morris et al., 2022), both of which impact parental wellbeing and, by extension, family functioning. SP has demonstrated positive outcomes in improving mental health and reducing isolation (Cooper et al., 2023; Stock et al., 2022; Thompson et al., 2023; Wilkinson et al., 2020) particularly when it involves accessible localised activities (Jarvis & Mitchell, n.d.). Despite this, there is limited evidence on how SP supports parents, especially for those with limited income or caregiving capacity. Addressing parental loneliness requires a multi-sector collaboration. Nowland, Charles and Thomson (2024) highlight its intergenerational impacts, stressing the need for coordinated services across health, education and community services. Community psychologists play a crucial role in fostering belonging, especially for marginalised families, by advocating for inclusive and responsive services.

Referral to Social Prescribing for family wellbeing

While SP is typically designed as an all-age service, research shows CYP need tailored models to benefit (Bertotti et al., 2020; Jarvis & Mitchell, n.d.; Social Prescribing Youth Network, 2020). Youth-friendly SP differs from traditional approaches in several ways:

- Flexible service delivery – Home visits, support with using public transport, or after-school appointments (Jarvis & Mitchell, n.d.; Social Prescribing Youth Network, 2020).
- Youth-centred communication – Using text messaging or app-based contact instead of formal phone calls or paperwork (Jarvis & Mitchell, n.d.; Social Prescribing Youth Network, 2020).

CYP are more likely to engage when SP reflects their lives, goals and communication styles (Social Prescribing Youth Network, 2020).

Barriers to effective SP referrals

Despite growing interest in CYP SP, systemic barriers persist:

- Limited awareness among health and education professionals (Hazeldine et al., 2025; Simpson et al., 2021).
- Inconsistent provision across regions due to funding disparities (Pilkington et al., 2025).
- Fragmented services, limiting collaboration between education, health and community organisations (Sandhu et al., 2022).
- Engagement challenges for families facing poverty, language barriers or service distrust (Fixsen et al., 2021).

The case for whole family Social Prescribing

Research suggests a family-centred approach to SP offers several advantages:

- addresses intergenerational challenges by supporting children and caregivers together (Cooper et al., 2023).

- improves service engagement, especially when parents feel supported (Rothe & Heiss, 2022).
- breaks cycles of disadvantage by addressing structural inequality across households (Hassan et al., 2020).

Despite its potential, whole family SP remains undeveloped. Community psychologists can help design and evaluate family-based models reflecting real-world complexity. This includes training professionals to identify when family needs extend beyond individual support and advocating for policies making SP more accessible and equitable.

Action for learning: Putting theory into practice

Challenging cognitive biases in system level thinking

Supporting family wellbeing requires an understanding of how poverty, health inequalities and systemic barriers shape outcomes. Training plays a critical role in helping professionals reflect on their own cognitive biases and assumptions (Susanto & Novitasari, 2024), Reflective practice can support more compassionate, equity-focused service delivery (Gabarda, 2019). For example, smoking is often viewed as an individual behaviour issue. Yet, Marmot (2015) highlights smoking as an indicator of poverty, shaped by social and economic stressors such as childcare demands, financial insecurity and isolation. Instead of applying shame-based approaches, services can provide holistic support, such as benefit advice, mental health resources and access to community resources, to address root causes (Eyal, 2014). In case study 2, Lena's smoking was a coping mechanism. SP interventions addressed stress and isolation to improve her wellbeing.

Rethinking waiting lists – "Wait well" as an upstream SP solution

Long wait times for services like CAMHS are common. SP can offer "upstream" alternatives, allowing CYP to "wait well" by engaging in meaningful, structured support while awaiting specialist interventions (Gordon et al., 2023). In case study 2, Lena's eldest child was referred to a bereavement service with a two-year wait. Instead of receiving no support, her child was referred to a "wait well" initiative providing structured activities and peer mentoring, maintaining wellbeing and reducing emotional distress.

Social justice and wellbeing

Achieving social justice in family wellbeing

Social justice in family wellbeing means ensuring equitable access to health, education and support, regardless of income, immigration status or social background (Hailemariam et al., 2020).

For social justice to be meaningful in practice, families must have:

- equitable access to services and support – including health care, education and financial assistance (Kellezi et al., 2021).
- personalised care tailored to diverse needs – ensuring resources address both individual and community challenges (Kellezi et al., 2021).
- freedom from structural barriers – financial burden of transport services, inaccessible childcare and exclusion from community programmes (Beardon et al., 2021).

When social justice is embedded in service design, families can move beyond survival and begin to thrive, becoming active participants in their communities (Kellezi et al., 2021).

Rawls (2012), defines social justice through human rights, liberty and equal opportunity. Cohen (1986) expands this into five dimensions:

- Distributive justice: Ensuring a fair and just distribution of a society's resources, opportunities and burdens including education, health care and financial assistance.
- Procedural justice: fair and just means of decision-making in institutions, organisations and policies, creating transparent and inclusive decision-making processes.
- Retributive justice: Addressing harm and providing reparations for families affected by systemic injustice.
- Restorative justice: Repairing damage done through compensation or rehabilitation, potentially through community-led solutions.
- Intergenerational justice: Benefits or burdens left from one generation to another, ensuring families do not pass down cycles of disadvantage to future generations.

Family services reflect these principles of justice in their models, working to remove barriers and foster empowerment. Justice should not stop at compensation. True equity requires investment in inclusion (Hellman et al., 2019) e.g., designing services that reflect the lived realities of diverse families. Community participation, cultural responsiveness and long-term structural change must be embedded in how family wellbeing services are planned and delivered (Devaney et al., 2024).

Action for learning: Applying Social Prescribing and Community Psychology

This section invites readers to critically explore how SP and Community Psychology intersect with real-life challenges.

Using proportionate universalism in Social Prescribing

The Marmot et al. (2010) principle of PU advocates scaling support to levels of need.

Scenario

Sarah has two children living in an area of high deprivation from another country. She has been referred to a SP Link Worker (SPLW) by her GP. She is hesitant to engage due to negative past experiences with statutory services.

Discussion Questions

1. What practical barriers might Sarah face, and how can they be addressed?
2. How can SP enhance Sarah's engagement with the community for improved family wellbeing, leaning into social justice?

Policy advocacy through practice

Community psychologists can play a key role in challenging policy barriers.

Activity

Write a 250-word policy brief or a 2-minute pitch to a local authority outlining:

- key barriers families face in accessing SP.
- solutions.

The role of community psychologists: Challenges and opportunities

System barriers to family wellbeing

Community psychologists are key to enhancing family wellbeing, yet their work is often constrained by systemic barriers overlooking the social determinants of health and the criticality of applying resources to need (Marmot et al., 2020). Limited resources for community services contribute to inequitable health outcomes. When services families rely on, such as early childhood programmes, mental health support and SP initiatives, are underfunded, vulnerable groups face the greatest disadvantage (National Academy for Social Prescribing, n.d.). Removal of the SureStart programme is one example, disproportionately impacting low-income families and deepening health and education disparities (Laxton et al., 2024).

Expanding SP for CYP

Deployment of SP in England initially focused on older adults, reducing GP workloads and responding to the COVID-19 pandemic (Fancourt & Steptoe, 2024). With rising demand for CYP health services and long CAMHS waiting lists, interest in SP as an alternative grows (Hickey et al., 2023). However, limited funding remains a major barrier for governments, local organisations and charities. Integrating SP into Family Hubs and schools could improve access, but gaps between signposting and actual service access must be addressed (Graaf et al., 2022). Without adequate support for adults and caregivers, SP risks falling short of its potential to support families holistically (Radež et al., 2020).

Addressing intergenerational transmission of trauma and vulnerability

Community psychologists understand the impact early childhood trauma has on development and overall life experiences (Ravishankar & Sathiyaseelan, 2022). "Complex" trauma is used to describe a chronic, ongoing exposure to adversity, such as poverty, abuse and neglect. This shapes neurological, emotional and behavioural outcomes. Early trauma is linked to long-term health disparities, with many adult conditions rooted in adverse childhood experiences (Bowers & Yehuda, 2019; Shonkoff & Garner, 2012). Embedding trauma-informed, systemic approaches into Social Prescribing (SP), guided by frameworks, e.g., Self-Determination Theory (SDT) can enhance SP effectiveness by promoting autonomy, competence and relatedness – key to fostering genuine engagement (Hanlon et al., 2021).

However, interventions must align with families' readiness and cultural context (Freeman & Dolan, 2001). SP must be inclusive, as those most in need often face the greatest barriers to access (Gibson et al., 2021; Kiely et al., 2022). Underfunded services and inconsistent provision further limit impact, highlighting the need for community psychologists to advocate for equitable, evidence-based policy and practice.

Building community capacity in research – families as researchers

Participation and the rights of children and families

Community psychologists play an important role in promoting the rights of children and families, particularly when those voices are excluded from decisions impacting their wellbeing. The United Nations Convention on the Rights of the Child calls for meaningful participation, particularly in Articles 3, 12 and 13, which supports children's rights to express their views and influence decisions affecting them (United Nations Convention on the Rights of the Child, 1989). The Lundy Model of Participation (Lundy, 2007) offers a framework to operationalise Article 12 by focusing on four core elements (Figure 13.1).

Although widely endorsed, implementation is often inconsistent. Cuevas-Parra (2023) and Clark (2010) notes adult perceptions frequently limit children's opportunities to participate fully. Participation must go beyond tokenism and be embedded in practice as a vehicle for empowerment.

Community-based participatory research

Community-Based Participatory Research (CBPR) (Hacker, 2013) offers a way to embed participation at research and policy level. It treats families and communities not as subjects, but as co-creators of knowledge (Wilson et al., 2024). This collaborative approach is especially useful when working with families affected by systemic inequality.

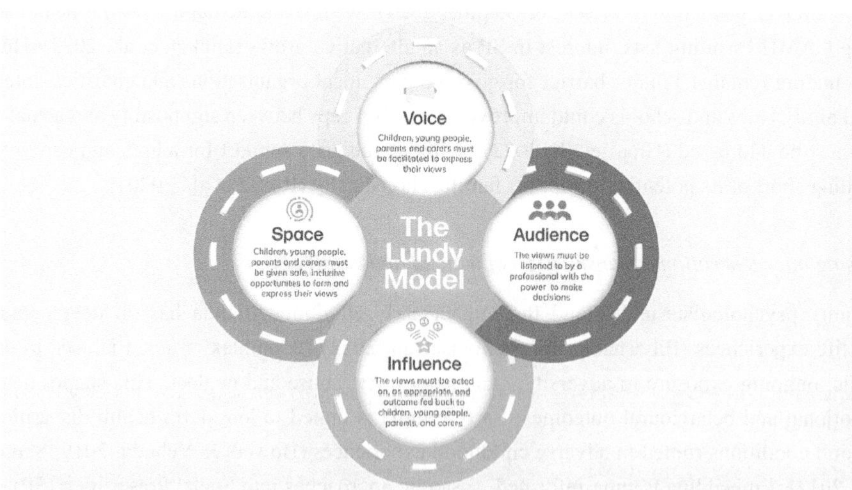

Figure 13.1 The Lundy Model.

Source: Lundy, 2007.

CBPR emphasises four components (Chanchien Parajón et al., 2021):

1. Self-Assessment: Communities define their own needs.
2. Compliance review: Ensure research aligns with ethical and community-based principles.
3. Recognition and acceptance: Acknowledging lived experience of families as valuable sources of knowledge.
4. Dispute resolution and enforcement: Establishing mechanisms for addressing conflicts and ensuring integrity.

By applying CBPR, community psychologists can support more inclusive service design and shape policies reflecting the lived realities of diverse families. This also enables families to challenge how local funding decisions are made and advocate for resources aligned with their actual needs.

Conclusion

This chapter presents insights from practitioners and academics on how Social Prescribing (SP) and Community Psychology can enhance family wellbeing. It addresses systemic barriers like underfunding and social inequalities limiting access to support. By applying *Proportionate Universalism*, it argues for resource allocation based on need. When grounded in health equity and community involvement, SP can drive inclusive, sustainable change – reducing disparities and strengthening families through integrated, cross-sector collaboration. By embedding SP into integrated care systems and expanding its role within Community Psychology, we can create long-term, equitable solutions empowering families, reducing health disparities and strengthening the social fabric of communities.

Discussion questions

- How can SP contribute to equitable health creation for family's wellbeing?
- In what situations might SP negatively impact family wellbeing?
- How can SP be delivered in line with PU?

Reflective questions

- How might SP empower family wellbeing if aligned with Marmot's concept of "PU"(Sandford, 2019)?
- How can families be meaningfully involved in co-producing their own support?

Key principles

- social prescribing,
- family wellbeing,
- health inequalities,
- proportionate universalism,
- poverty.

Author positionality statements

Amy Edwards-Smith is a neurodivergent mother of three, educator, and lifelong advocate for social justice with 17+ years in higher education. Her background spans mainstream, specialist and autism-focused services. She currently teaches widening participation students from underrepresented communities.

Fiona Routh is an educator, mother of two, and doctoral researcher focused on Social Prescribing for children and young people. With over 16 years' experience across early years, primary, further, and higher education, she brings deep insight into participation, equity and social mobility. A first-generation university student, Fiona's work is rooted in community, advocacy and listening to children's voices to shape services.

Natalie Hicks is an occupational therapist, educator and mother of three autistic sons. Living with a genetic disability and chronic pain, she has extensive lived and professional experience in disability, caregiving and community-led support. Formerly a charity coordinator, she now teaches SP to adult learners, combining her OT training, personal experience and passion for inclusion.

Koser Khan is a researcher with the NIHR-funded ARC Northwest Coast, with a background in welfare rights, local government and public health. A first-generation graduate, she brings lived and professional insight into systemic challenges communities face. Her work champions co-production, collaboration and meaningful engagement to tackle health inequalities from the ground up.

Sam Pywell is a neurodivergent mother of two, senior lecturer and occupational therapist with a decade of NHS experience supporting families in high-deprivation areas. Deeply rooted in community, her work centres on health creation.

References

Afrocats. (n.d.). *Youth of the World supports young people to broaden their horizons, develop skills and importantly have lots of fun*. https://www.afrocats.org.uk/youth-of-the-world

Banihani, S., Zimmer, S., Tagvoryan, A., Setaghiyan, H., Novák, D., & Osei, A. (2025). The impact of a caregiver's chronic illness on childhood psychosocial functioning. *Families Systems & Health*. https://doi.org/10.1037/fsh0000951

Barnados. (2023). *The missing link: Social prescribing for children and young people*. https://www.barnardos.org.uk/research/missing-link-social-prescribing-children-young-people

Beardon, S., Woodhead, C., Cooper, S., Ingram, E., Genn, H., & Raine, R. (2021). International evidence on the impact of health-justice partnerships: A systematic scoping review. *Public Health Reviews, 42*. https://doi.org/10.3389/phrs.2021.1603976

Bertotti, M., Frostick, C., Sharpe, D., & Temirov, O. (2020). *A two-year evaluation of the Young People Social Prescribing (YPSP) pilot: Project report*. Institute for Connected Communities, University of East London. https://repository.uel.ac.uk/item/88x15.

Bidmead, E., Hayes, L., Leggott, E., Wildman, J. M., Rankin, J., Bramhall, L., Todd, L., & Smith, L. M. (2024). Poverty proofing health care: A qualitative study of barriers to accessing health care for low income families with children in northern England. *PLoS One, 19*(4), e0292983. https://doi.org/10.1371/journal.pone.0292983.

Borilli, M. C., Germano, C. M. R., Avó, L. R. d. S. d., Pilotto, R. F., & Melo, D. G. (2022). Family quality of life among families who have children with mild intellectual disability associated with mild autism spectrum disorder. *Arquivos De Neuro-Psiquiatria, 80*(4), 360–367. https://doi.org/10.1590/0004-282x-anp-2020-0537

Bos, C., Weger, E. d., Wildeman, I., & Kemper, P. (2023). Implementing and embedding social prescribing successfully: What works, for whom and in which context? *International Journal of Integrated Care*, *23*(S1), 61. https://doi.org/10.5334/ijic.icic23027

Bowers, M. E., & Yehuda, R. (2019). Intergenerational transmission of stress vulnerability and resilience. In A. Chen (ed.) *Stress resilience: Molecular and behavioral aspects* (pp. 257–267). Elsevier. https://doi.org/https://doi.org/10.1016/B978-0-12-813983–7.00017-3

Brettell, M., Fenton, C., & Foster, E. C. (2022). Linking Leeds: A social prescribing service for children and young people. *International Journal of Environmental Research and Public Health*, *19*(3), 1426. https://doi.org/10.3390/ijerph19031426

Centre for Mental Health, Children and Young People's Mental Health Coalition, & Save the Children. (2024). *A dual crisis: The hidden link between poverty and children's mental health.* https://cypmhc.org.uk/wp-content/uploads/2024/07/A-Dual-Crisis.-Parliamentary-briefing-.pdf

Chanchien Parajón, L., Hinshaw, J., Sanchez, V., Minkler, M., & Wallerstein, N. (2021). Practicing hope: Enhancing empowerment in primary health care through community-based participatory research. *American Journal of Community Psychology, 67*(3–4), 297–311. https://doi.org/https://doi.org/10.1002/ajcp.12526

Clark, R. (2010). *Childhood in society for early childhood studies*. Sage Publications.

Cohen, R. L. (1986). *Justice: Views from the social sciences*. Springer Science & Business Media.

Cooper, M., Flynn, D., Avery, L., Ashley, K., Jordan, C., Errington, L., & Scott, J. (2023). Service user perspectives on social prescribing services for mental health in the UK: A systematic review. *Perspectives in Public Health*, *143*(3), 135–144. https://doi.org/10.1177/17579139231170786

Crane, A., Elwood, S., & Lawson, V. (2020). Re-politicising poverty: Relational re-conceptualisations of impoverishment. *Antipode*, *52*(2), 339–351. https://doi.org/10.1111/anti.12603

Cuevas-Parra, P. (2023). Multi-dimensional lens to article 12 of the UNCRC: A model to enhance children's participation. *Children's Geographies*, *21*(3), 363–377. https://doi.org/10.1080/14733285.2022.2071598

Devaney, C., Mac Donald, M., & Holzer, J. (2024). A social justice perspective on the delivery of family support. *Children and Youth Services Review*, *159*, 107494. https://doi.org/https://doi.org/10.1016/j.childyouth.2024.107494

Domínguez, M. Á. S., & Navarro, M. (2021). Public policies of welfare state and child poverty in the European Union. *Sustainability*, *13*(5), 2725. https://doi.org/10.3390/su13052725

Ellis, W., Dietz, W. H., & Chen, K.-L. D. (2022). Community resilience: A dynamic model for public health 3.0. *Journal of Public Health Management and Practice, 28*(Supplement 1), S18-S26. https://doi.org/10.1097/phh.0000000000001413

Eyal, N. (2014). Nudging by shaming, shaming by nudging. *International Journal of Health Policy and Management*, *3*(2), 53–56. https://doi.org/10.15171/ijhpm.2014.68

Fancourt, D., Burton, A., Bu, F., Deighton, J., Turner, R. E., Wright, J., Bradbury, A., Tibber, M. S., Talwar, S., & Hayes, D. (2023). Wellbeing while waiting evaluating social prescribing in CAMHS: Study protocol for a hybrid type II implementation-effectiveness study. *BMC Psychiatry*, *23*(1). https://doi.org/10.1186/s12888-023-04758-0

Fancourt, D., & Steptoe, A. (2024). Can social prescribing reach patients most in need? Patterns of (in)equalities in referrals in a representative cohort of older adults in England. https://doi.org/10.1101/2024.03.26.24304891

Fehrer, K., & Leos-Urbel, J. (2016). "We're one team": Examining community school iImplementation strategies in Oakland. *Education Sciences*, *6*(3), 26. https://doi.org/10.3390/educsci6030026

Fixsen, A., Barrett, S., & Shimonovich, M. (2021). Supporting vulnerable populations during the pandemic: Stakeholders' experiences and perceptions of social prescribing in Scotland during covid-19. *Qualitative Health Research*, *32*(4), 670–682. https://doi.org/10.1177/10497323211064229

Freeman, A., & Dolan, M. (2001). Revisiting Prochaska and DiClemente's stages of change theory: An expansion and specification to aid in treatment planning and outcome evaluation. *Cognitive and Behavioral Practice*, *8*(3), 224–234. https://doi.org/https://doi.org/10.1016/S1077-7229(01)80057-2

Gabarda, A. (2019). *Level of understanding and attitudes towards poverty, confidence working with individuals experiencing poverty, and active learning of health coaches participating in a poverty simulation* [Doctoral dissertation, University of Pittsburgh]. https://core.ac.uk/download/pdf/224781636.pdf

Garthwaite, K., Patrick, R., Power, M., Tarrant, A., & Warnock, R. (2022). *Covid-19 collaborations: Researching poverty and low-income family life during the pandemic*. Policy Press. https://doi.org/10.51952/9781447364504

Gibson, K., Pollard, T. M., & Moffatt, S. (2021). Social prescribing and classed inequality: A journey of upward health mobility? *Social Science & Medicine, 280*, 114037. https://doi.org/10.1016/j.socscimed.2021.114037

Gilliver, C. (2021). The five ways to wellbeing model: A framework for nurses and patients. *Nursing Times, 117*(5), 48–52. https://www.nursingtimes.net/nurse-wellbeing/the-five-ways-to-wellbeing-model-a-framework-for-nurses-and-patients-06-04-2021/

Gordon, K., Gordon, L., & Basu, A. P. (2023). Social prescribing for children and young people with neurodisability and their families initiated in a hospital setting: A systematic review. *BMJ Open, 13*(12), e078097. https://doi.org/10.1136/bmjopen-2023-078097

Graaf, G., Baiden, P., Keyes, L., & Boyd, G. A. (2022). Barriers to mental health services for parents and siblings of children with special health care needs. *Journal of Child and Family Studies, 31*(3), 881–895. https://doi.org/10.1007/s10826-022-02228-x

Hacker, K. (2013). *Community-based participatory research*. Sage.

Hailemariam, M., Felton, J. W., Key, K., Greer, D., Jefferson, B. L., Muhammad, J., Miller, R., Richie, F., Robinson, D., Saddler, S., Spencer, B. R., Summers, M., White, J. M. C., & Johnson, J. E. (2020). Intersectionality, special populations, needs and suggestions: The flint women's study. *International Journal for Equity in Health, 19*(1). https://doi.org/10.1186/s12939-020-1133-9

Hanlon, P., Gray, C. M., Chng, N. R., & Mercer, S. W. (2021). Does self-determination theory help explain the impact of social prescribing? A qualitative analysis of patients' experiences of the Glasgow 'deep-end' community links worker intervention. *Chronic Illn, 17*(3), 173–188. https://doi.org/10.1177/1742395319845427

Hassan, S., Giebel, C., Morasae, E. K., Rotheram, C., Mathieson, V., Ward, D. L., Reynolds, V., Price, A. D., Bristow, K., & Kullu, C. (2020). Social prescribing for people with mental health needs living in disadvantaged communities: The life rooms model. *BMC Health Services Research, 20*(1). https://doi.org/10.1186/s12913-019-4882-7

Hayes, D., Jarvis-Beesley, P., Mitchell, D., Polley, M., & Husk, K. (2023). *The impact of social prescribing on children and young people's mental health and wellbeing*. National Academy for Social Prescribing. https://socialprescribingacademy.org.uk/media/lrif2emh/evidence-review-the-impact-of-social-prescribing-on-children-and-young-peoples-health-and-wellbeing.pdf

Haywood, A., Dayson, C., Garside, R., Foster, A., Lovell, R., Husk, K., Holding, E., Thomson, J., Shearn, K., Hunt, H. A., Dobson, J., Harris, C., Jacques, R., Witherley, D., Northall, P., Baumann, M., & Wilson, I. (2024). *National evaluation of the preventing and tackling mental ill health through green social prescribing project: Final report*. Department for Environment, Food & Rural Affairs. https://beyondgreenspace.net/wp-content/uploads/2024/09/21194_gspevaluationfinalreport-mainreportjan2024-4–1.pdf

Hazeldine, E., Westwood, S., Hassannezhad, M., Tierney, S., Gavens, L., & Husk, K. (2025). Routes to social prescribing outside National Health Service (NHS) structures: A systematic map. *BMJ Public Health*, 3(1), e000941. https://doi.org/10.1136/bmjph-2024-000941

Hellman, T., Schmidt, P., & Heller, S. M. (2019). *Social justice in the EU and* OECD. Bertelsmann Stiftung. https://www.sgi-network.org/docs/studies/Social_Justice_in_the_EU_2019.pdf

Hickey, L., Harms, L., Evans, J., Noakes, T., Lee, H., McSwan, A., Bean, H. R., Hope, J., Allison, L., Price, S., & Harris, N. E. (2023). Review: Improving access to mental health interventions for children from birth to five years: A scoping review. *Child and Adolescent Mental Health, 29*(1), 84–95. https://doi.org/10.1111/camh.12652

Hodgkins, A., & Prowle, A. (2023). *Strength-based practice with children and families*. Critical Publishing.

Howarth, M., Rogers, M., Withnell, N., & McQuarrie, C. (2018). Growing spaces: An evaluation of the mental health recovery programme using mixed methods. *Journal of Research in Nursing*, *23*(6), 476–489. https://doi.org/10.1177/1744987118766207

Jarvis, L., & Mitchell, D. (n.d.). *Children & young people's social prescribing toolkit*. Streetgames. https://www.streetgames.org/wp-content/uploads/2023/12/NHS-Children-Young-Peoples-Social-Prescribing-Toolkit.pdf

Kellezi, B., Wakefield, J., Bowe, M., Bridger, K., & Teague, K. (2021). Adapting social prescribing to meet the needs of migrant populations: Challenges and solutions to service access and effectiveness. *Community Psychology in Global Perspective*, *7*(2), 1–21. https://doi.org/10.1285/i24212113v7i2p1

Kiely, B., Croke, A., O'Shea, M., Boland, F., O'Shea, E., Connolly, D., & Smith, S. M. (2022). Effect of social prescribing link workers on health outcomes and costs for adults in primary care and community settings: A systematic review. *BMJ Open*, *12*(10), e062951. https://doi.org/10.1136/bmjopen-2022-062951

Kushwaha, R. K. (2023). Neurodiversity approaches and autism (ASD): A scoping review. *Qistina Jurnal Multidisiplin Indonesia*, *2*(2), 780–787. https://doi.org/10.57235/qistina.v2i2.612

Laxton, S., Moriarty, C., Sapiets, S. J., Hastings, R. P., & Totsika, V. (2024). Neighbourhood deprivation and access to early intervention and support for families of children with intellectual and developmental disabilities. *Journal of Policy and Practice in Intellectual Disabilities*, *21*(2). https://doi.org/10.1111/jppi.12486

Love, H., Schlitt, J., Soleimanpour, S., Panchal, N., & Behr, C. (2019). Twenty years of school-based health care growth and expansion. *Health Affairs*, *38*(5), 755–764. https://doi.org/10.1377/hlthaff.2018.05472

Lundy, L. (2007). 'Voice' is not enough: Conceptualising Article 12 of the United Nations convention on the rights of the child. *British Educational Research Journal*, *33*(6), 927–942. https://doi.org/10.1080/01411920701657033

Marmot, M., Allen, J., Goldblatt, P., Boyce, T., McNeish, D., Grady, M., & Geddes, I. (2010). *Fair society, healthy lives: The Marmot review*. Institute of Health Equity. https://www.instituteofhealthequity.org/resources-reports/fair-society-healthy-lives-the-marmot-review

Marmot, M. (2015). The health gap: The challenge of an unequal world. *Lancet*, *386*(10011), 2442–2444. https://doi.org/10.1016/s0140-6736(15)00150-6

Marmot, M., Allen, J., Boyce, T., Goldblatt, P., & Callaghan, O. (2022). *A hopeful future: Equity and the social determinants of health in Lancashire and Cumbria*. https://www.instituteofhealthequity.org/resources-reports/a-hopeful-future-equity-and-the-social-determinants-of-health-in-lancashire-and-cumbria

Marmot, M., Allen, J., Coldblatt, P., Herd, E., & Morrison, J. (2020). *Build back fairer: The COVID-19 Marmot review. The pandemic, socioeconomic and health inequalities in England*. Institute of Health Equity. https://www.instituteofhealthequity.org/resources-reports/build-back-fairer-the-covid-19-marmot-review

Morris, D., Thomas, P., Ridley, J., & Webber, M. (2022). Community-enhanced social prescribing: Integrating community in policy and practice. *International Journal of Community Well-Being*, *5*(1), 179–195. https://doi.org/10.1007/s42413-020-00080-9

Muir, C., Kedzior, S. G. E., Barrett, S., McGovern, R., Kaner, E., Wolfe, I., & Forman, J. (2024). Co-design workshops with families experiencing multiple and interacting adversities including parental mental health, substance use, domestic violence, and poverty: Intervention principles and insights from mothers, fathers, and young people. *Research Involvement and Engagement*, *10*(1). https://doi.org/10.1186/s40900-024-00584-0

N8 Research Partnership. (2024). *Developing a platform for collaboration, high-quality research and policy engagement that will improve the lives of children living in the North of England*. https://www.n8research.org.uk/research-focus/child-of-the-north/

National Academy for Social Prescribing. (n.d.). *The future of social prescribing*. https://socialprescribingacademy.org.uk/media/ti2e1inx/the-future-of-social-prescribing-in-england-3-pager.pdf

National Children's Bureau. (2023). *Children and young people's social prescribing good practice guide*. https://www.ncb.org.uk/sites/default/files/uploads/attachments/NHSE%20social%20prescribing%20good%20practice%20guide.pdf

National Institute for Health and Care Excellence. (2022). *Mental wellbeing at work (NG212)*. https://www.nice.org.uk/guidance/ng212

NHS England. (n.d.). Social prescribing. https://www.england.nhs.uk/personalisedcare/social-prescribing/

NHS England. (2024). *Improving personal health and wellbeing*. https://www.england.nhs.uk

Nowland, R., Charles, J., & Thomson, G. (2024). Loneliness in pregnancy and parenthood: Impacts, outcomes, and costs. *The Yale Journal of Biology and Medicine*, *97*, 93–98. https://doi.org/10.59249/NKTK3337

Oxford Poverty and Human Development Initiative (OPHI). (2013). *Constructing a multidimensional poverty measure*. OPHI Briefing 18, Oxford Poverty and Human Development Initiative (OPHI), University of Oxford. https://ophi.org.uk/publications/B-18

Pickett, K., Taylor-Robinson, D., & Erlam, J. (2021). *Child of the North: Building a fairer future after* COVID-19. https://www.thenhsa.co.uk/app/uploads/2022/01/Child-of-the-North-Report-FINAL-1.pdf

Pilkington, G., Johnson, M. I., & Thompson, K. (2025). Social prescribing for adults with chronic pain in the UK: A rapid review. *British Journal of Pain*, *19*(3), 176–186. https://doi.org/10.1177/20494637241312064

Polley, M., Hayes, D., Husk, K., Jarvis-Beesley, P., Mitchell, D., & Keohane, J. (2023). *Social prescribing for children and young people: A summary of findings from our recent snapshot survey*. National Academy for Social Prescribing. https://socialprescribingacademy.org.uk/media/ovvek3j2/summary-of-children-and-young-people-survey-findings.pdf

Radež, J., Reardon, T., Creswell, C., Lawrence, P. J., Evdoka-Burton, G., & Waite, P. (2020). Why do children and adolescents (not) seek and access professional help for their mental health problems? A systematic review of quantitative and qualitative studies. *European Child & Adolescent Psychiatry*, *30*(2), 183–211. https://doi.org/10.1007/s00787-019-01469-4

Rainer, C., Treloar, N., Abdinasir, K., & Edwards, P. (2024). *A dual crisis: The hidden link between poverty and chilldren's mental health*. Centre for Mental Health. https://cypmhc.org.uk/wp-content/uploads/2024/07/CentreforMH_ADualCrisis.final_.pdf

Ravishankar, A., & Sathiyaseelan, A. (2022). Perceived reality of self and others with two childhood trauma survivors – An idiographic case study. *ECS Transactions*, *107*(1), 3143–3153. https://doi.org/10.1149/10701.3143ecst

Rawls, J. (2012). Classical utilitarianism. In G. Sher (Ed.). *Ethics: Essential readings in moral theory* (pp. 262–265). Routledge.

Rich, S., Hickey, B., & Kaprielian, E. (2024). Trauma informed farm animal assisted neurotherapy and green care farming for neurodiverse conditions. In H. Friedman (Ed.), *Neuropediatrics - Recent advances and novel therapeutic approaches*. https://doi.org/10.5772/intechopen.1002513

Riley, K. (2013). Walking the leadership tightrope: Building community cohesiveness and social capital in schools in highly disadvantaged urban communities. *British Educational Research Journal*, *39*(2), 266–286. https://doi.org/10.1080/01411926.2012.658021

Rosehill. (n.d.). *TENT*. https://www.rosehilltheatre.co.uk/get-involved/children-families/together-tent-artist-and-playworker-lab

Rothe, D., & Heiss, R. (2022). Link workers, activities and target groups in social prescribing: A literature review. *Journal of Integrated Care*, *30*(5), 1–11. https://doi.org/10.1108/jica-09-2021-0047

Russell, C. (2022). *Asset-Based Community Development (ABCD): Looking back to look forward: In conversation with John McKnight about the heritage of ABCD and its place in the world today* (3rd ed.). Published independently.

Sandford, M. (2019). *Local government: alternative models of service delivery*. House of Commons Library. https://commonslibrary.parliament.uk/research-briefings/sn05950/

Sandhu, S., Lian, T., Drake, C., Moffatt, S., Wildman, J., & Wildman, J. M. (2022). Intervention components of link worker social prescribing programmes: A scoping review. *Health & Social Care in the Community*, *30*(6). https://doi.org/10.1111/hsc.14056

Shonkoff, J. P., & Garner, A. S. (2012). The lifelong effects of early childhood adversity and toxic stress. *Pediatrics*, *129*(1), e232–246. https://doi.org/10.1542/peds.2011-2663

Simpson, S., Furlong, M., & Giebel, C. (2021). Exploring the enablers and barriers to social prescribing for people living with long-term neurological conditions: A focus group investigation. https://doi.org/10.21203/rs.3.rs-403346/v1

Social Prescribing Youth Network. (2020). *Social prescribing for children and young people*. https://www.streetgames.org/wp-content/uploads/2022/12/Principles-for-All-Age-Social-Prescribing.pdf

Stock, S., Bu, F., Fancourt, D., & Mak, H. (2022). Longitudinal associations between going outdoors and mental health and wellbeing during a COVID-19 lockdown in the UK. *Scientific Reports*, *12*(1). https://doi.org/https://10.1038/s41598-022-15004-0

Susanto, E., & Novitasari, Y. (2024). Implications of the Dunning-Kruger effect for counselors in counseling practice: A systematic review. *Guidena Jurnal Ilmu Pendidikan Psikologi Bimbingan Dan Konseling*, *14*(4). https://doi.org/10.24127/gdn.v14i4.12054

Thompson, J., Holding, E., Haywood, A., & Foster, A. (2023). Service users' perspectives of a national social prescribing programme to address loneliness and social isolation: A qualitative study. *Health & Social Care in the Community*, 1–8. https://doi.org/https://10.1155/2023/5319480

UK Visa and Immigration. (2024). *Guidance: Registration as British citizen: children.* https://www.gov.uk/government/publications/children-nationality-policy-guidance/registration-as-british-citizen-children-accessible

United Nations Convention on the Rights of the Child. (1989). Treaty no. 27531. *United Nations Treaty Series*, *1577*, 3–178. https://treaties.un.org/doc/Treaties/1990/09/19900902%2003-14%20AM/Ch_IV_11p.pdf

Wilkinson, E., Lees, A., Duncan, G., Weekes, S., Meads, G., & Tapson, K. (2020). A collaborative, multi-sectoral approach to implementing a social prescribing initiative to alleviate social isolation and enhance wellbeing amongst older people. *Journal of Integrated Care*. https://10.1108/JICA-02-2020-0004

Wilson, H. F. (2013). Multicultural learning: Parent encounters with difference in a Birmingham primary school. *Transactions of the Institute of British Geographers*, *39*(1), 102–114. https://doi.org/10.1111/tran.12015

Wilson, S., Ridley, J., & Morris, D. (2024). Understanding the impact on children's citizenship of participating in community-based action research. *Citizenship Studies*, *28*(2), 222–242. https://doi.org/10.1080/13621025.2024.2360404

World Health Organisation (WHO). (2025). *Promoting well-being.* https://www.who.int/activities/promoting-well-being

Zahir, R., Alcorn, A. M., McGeown, S., Mandy, W., Aitken, D., Murray, F., & Fletcher-Watson, S. (2023). Short report: Evaluation of wider community support for a neurodiversity teaching programme designed using participatory methods. *Autism*, *28*(6), 1582–1590. https://doi.org/10.1177/13623613231211046

Zambelli, E., Benson, M., & Sigona, N. (2023). Brexit rebordering, sticky relationships and the production of mixed-status families. *Sociology*, *58*(3), 605–622. https://doi.org/10.1177/00380385231194966

Suggestions for further reading/viewing/listening

The following resources provide deeper insights into SP, family wellbeing and related social issues:

"What Matters? for family wellbeing" • A podcast on Spotify for Podcasters

Ideas about Family (ted.com): A collection of TED Talks exploring the evolving definition of family in contemporary society

What Is SP ? | The King's Fund (kingsfund.org.uk): An explanation of social prescribing and its impact on health and wellbeing

14 Using photo-elicitation to gain an in-depth understanding of service user and staff experience

An ethical framework for mental health research

Penn Smith and Anna Madill

The study on which this chapter is based sought service user and staff perspectives on a novel style of deep third sector community in-reach within a National Health Service setting in the UK designed to smooth the transition to community living. We examine how service users and staff can be included in research underpinned by Community Psychology principles of *empowerment* and *social justice* (Taquette & Borges da Matta Souza, 2022). Specifically, we reflect on ethical and methodological considerations of using photo-elicitation in the context of the challenges of conducting research within complex mental health settings and offer a relational, ethical praxis.

Community Psychology, service user voice and research in mental health settings

Since the 1980s, involving service users in research has been limited despite ongoing requests by this group and its advocates to acknowledge social context and user experience in service development (Repper & Perkins, 2004). In the past, staff perspectives have been given greater credibility than that of service users, with the latter embedded in a deficit-based framework (Branfield et al., 2006). More recently, however, emphasis has been placed on the importance of *empowering* those suffering psychological disorders to improve their own wellbeing and the services that support them by encouraging them to take part in research (National Institute for Health Research, 2021). However, mental health staff are struggling to apply this approach due to challenges such as limited funding (British Medical Association, 2023).

An important goal of mental health services is to facilitate service users to thrive as integrated members of a supportive community, whether this is temporarily within in-patient care or in a sustained manner in their own neighbourhood. This commences with Community Psychology principles of *empowerment* and *social justice*, discussed here in relation to informing services through inclusive research.

Empowerment to speak is a key consideration and not straightforward in mental health settings in which gaining and maintaining informed consent requires sensitivity to the ways in which both service users and staff may feel unsafe (Nyttingnes et al., 2016). Service user voice can be lost under the weight of the different teams and organisations involved in their care, and they regularly feel omitted from decision-making processes. Similarly, staff who work in complex mental health settings exist within a powerful hierarchical system dominated by the medical model. This can create tensions around

DOI: 10.4324/9781003480464-18

priorities, approach to care and attitude to risk and leave staff feeling unsure about speaking out (Wright et al., 2016).

Empowerment to speak is foundational for *social justice*. Service users need to inform the system designed to support them and staff need to inform the work in which they have invested. Hence, taking time to build positive trusting relationships in mental health care cannot be overestimated (Bacha et al., 2020). Good relationships enable vulnerable people to reconnect to a world from which they often feel excluded and encourage active involvement in their care (Erdner et al., 2009). Similarly, feeling valued can enhance trust and encourage active engagement from staff (Rössler, 2012). However, gaining the trust and engagement of service users and staff in research can be challenging. Because they can feel unheard, service users often have little trust in the healthcare system, which can make it difficult to talk about their experiences (Sandhu et al., 2013). Moreover, mental health staff experience high workloads and a lack of resources, which impacts their ability or desire to engage in additional tasks (Rössler, 2012).

Praxis case study: Using photo-elicitation with service users and staff in a complex mental health setting

The Service featured in this case study consists of a novel partnership between the National Health Service (NHS) inpatient and community voluntary organisations. The approach to mental health care offers multidisciplinary and multi-agency assessment, formulation and intervention within a stepped intensive pathway through inpatient care to better support transition and reintegration into the community. Through the application of recovery-focused principles and the biopsychosocial model, support is offered to promote independence and facilitate living fulfilling and meaningful lives. At the time of data collection, approximately 78 NHS and 12 community voluntary organisation staff within psychiatry, psychology, nursing, occupational therapy and mental health recovery worked for the Service in various service locations. These included an inpatient "ward-environment" with 36 inpatient beds, an inpatient staffed "house-environment" located on the same site away from NHS acute care and supportive living in the community with support from Service staff for up to six months post discharge. Those accessing the Service were termed "service users" to describe individuals with complex mental health needs, predominantly psychotic disorders, who have found it difficult to live safely outside a hospital environment and/or have been detained under the Mental Health Act 1983.

We addressed the research question: *What are the experiences of service users and staff who work in a novel in-reach rehabilitation and recovery service for people with profound and enduring mental health needs?* Inclusion criteria comprised adults (i.e., ≥18 years) who were current inpatients or within six months of leaving the inpatient Service and staff who had worked within the Service for at least six months. Fifteen purposefully sampled service users (ten men, five women) and fifteen purposefully sampled staff (four men, eleven women) were recruited from across the Service to broadly mirror the service user and staff demographic and structure. Photo-elicitation interviews were conducted (see below), transcribed and analysed using interpretative phenomenological analysis (IPA). IPA is a method of thematic qualitative analysis very focused on the ways in which people make sense of their lived experiences (Smith et al., 2009). For a more detailed account of the analytical process see Smith et al. (2021, 2023).

We believe a key element of our research which promotes the Community Psychology principles of *empowerment* and *social justice* is our use of photo-elicitation interviews. Collier (1957) first highlighted the value of using photographs as a starting point for discussion in research interviews. Since then, the use of photography in research has been well documented using several different methods including photo-elicitation. Photo-elicitation is a powerful tool in which photographs are used as a reference point in the interview to facilitate a curious enquiry of how the participant makes sense of brought images and how they link to past experiences. Photographs can present literal meanings, such as people and places, but the method invites participants to consider also metaphorical representations of their experiences of the social world (Richard & Lahman, 2015).

The therapeutic value of using photography in research is well documented as is its potential for *empowering* disadvantaged groups (e.g., Duara et al., 2022). Disadvantaged groups are likely familiar with power inequities with respect to the request to tell their story because this usually occurs in the context of being assessed. In redress, the act of taking photographs to discuss during interview can provide a positive experience of *empowerment* (Smith et al., 2021). Photographs can also enhance collaboration with community partners, as in Erdner et al.'s (2009) study of a community day centre, encouraging staff to develop their understanding of self and others and to express their views about service delivery. Despite the extensive literature on visual methods, there is a dearth of studies exploring how to navigate ethical and methodological concerns in applied community settings serving vulnerable people (Kyololo et al., 2023).

Nine-step ethical framework

We now present our nine-step ethical framework for good practice when using photo-elicitation with vulnerable participants within complex mental health settings. We set out what we have learned in detail in order to facilitate other researchers wishing to employ this method which, we believe, will translate to many applied community settings (Figure 14.1).

Step 1: Build relationships and become familiar with the setting

The researcher (first author) embedded herself in the Service by working on-site a few days each week until the end of the data collection phase and for a more limited period afterwards. This meant securing an honorary NHS contract and a desk within the Service. She shadowed staff and engaged with service users in social activities and, with permission, some treatment meetings to learn more about the Service. This also allowed service users and staff to become familiar with her and to influence the study through informal conversations.

Step 2: Form a steering group and invite gatekeepers to take part

The steering group included the lead researcher, her supervisor (second author), the Service operational manager, the local NHS head of Research and Development, third sector staff representatives and a service user group representative. The steering group was consulted on key matters such as project design, participant welfare, study material development, NHS ethics and Service policies and procedures throughout the length of the project. Recovery workers were invited to act as gatekeepers to assess the suitability of approaching specific service users to take part in the study. They were also asked to put forward any interested service users who fitted the inclusion criteria and might benefit from being involved, as well as asked to offer support with technical equipment and to check in with service users post interview.

Step 1: Build relationships and become familiar with the setting
Spend time within the service/organisation and with participant groups to build relationships and knowledge of complexities involved.

Step 2: Form a steering group and invite gatekeepers to take part
Steering group to include key members of the service/organisation, research team, and participant group representatives to consult on project design, participant welfare, technical equipment, service/organisation polices, study material, and ethics. Consider inviting gatekeepers to assist with recruitment and offer support to vulnerable participants.

Step 3: Develop study materials
For example: consent form, information sheet, instruction guide for taking photographs, guide to safe and appropriate internet use, device contract, and staff checklist.

Step 4: Apply for ethical approval
Apply to an appropriate research ethics committee (REC) and consider if other approvals or permission needs to be in place before commencing the research.

Step 5: Recruitment
Consider organising a dedicated project launch meeting or attending pre-existing forums to provide information, share study materials, and create opportunities to practice using the technical equipment.

Step 6: Initial one-to-one meeting
Opportunity to provide or revisit guidance on the process and for participants to reread the study materials, ask questions, practice using the technical equipment, and provide informed consent.

Step 7: Taking photographs
Additional support may be needed at this stage regarding the use of technical equipment such as electronic tablets, digital cameras, mobile phones etc. Suggested number of photographs 5-7.

Step 8: Photo-elicitation interview
To take place approximately 10-14 days following the initial meeting. Consider how to collect and view the photographs during the interview. Include a lightly structured protocol of open-ended questions.

Step 9: Post photo-elicitation interview check in and time to reflect
Participants to take time to reflect post interview if needed. Gatekeepers to check in with vulnerable participants.

Figure 14.1 Nine-step ethical framework for good practice when using photo-elicitation with vulnerable participants within complex mental health settings.

The use of mobile phones to take photographs was ruled out due to concerns over service users potentially accumulating unexpected mobile phone charges and because staff were not allowed to have personal mobile phones on the wards. Therefore, the Trust bought electronic tablets for use in the research. Complications over how to delete personal images and data from returned devices led to the decision to gift all participants the electronic tablet as a thank you for taking part. However, it was agreed that service users who might become more vulnerable to theft by owning an electronic device would, unfortunately, not be considered for the study.

Step 3: Develop study materials

The steering group consulted on the development of the study material, which consisted of (i) consent form; (ii) information sheet; (iii) instruction guide for taking photographs; (iv) guide to safe and appropriate internet use; (v) device contract; and (vi) staff checklist (Table 14.1). To aid inclusivity, the same study materials containing straightforward language were used in both staff and service user recruitment, and key contact details were included in case participants needed further information or support.

Table 14.1 Study materials and suggested content within the nine-step ethical framework

Study material	Included content
(i) Consent form	What it means to take part and give consent. *Including permission for photographs to be disseminated in public and professional settings.*
(ii) Information sheet	Information about the study, research team, signposting details and ethical considerations. *Including limits to confidentiality and anonymity such as disclosures of harm to self or others.*
(iii) Guide to taking photographs	Instructions and guidelines for taking photographs. *Including instructions to seek verbal consent before taking anyone's photograph and advice against taking inappropriate imagery such as anything offensive or photographs of children.*
(iv) Safe and appropriate internet use guidelines	Organisations expectations, guidelines and policies. *Including safe and appropriate internet use and how to protect others' confidentiality.*
(v) Device contract	Clarity over use, responsibility and ownership of device. *Including a statement that clearly states responsibility in the case of damage or loss.*
(vi) Staff checklist	Guidelines for staff supporting participants. *Including a tick list to monitor the participants understanding, willingness to be involved, engagement with taking the photographs and impact post interview.*

Step 4: Apply for ethical approval

NHS ethical and NHS research and development approval was granted by Yorkshire and The Humber, Leeds East Research Ethics Committee and Leeds and York Partnership NHS Foundation Trust. Considerations around information sharing, informed consent and confidentiality were key in achieving participant autonomy and avoidance of harm. This formed an important part of achieving ethical approval, in addition to examining specific considerations applicable to both participant groups, the research setting, and the creative methodology used. Due to the complexity of service users' challenges and the unpredictable nature of their diagnosis, a recovery worker signature was added to the consent form in addition to that of the service user to ensure any additional needs were fully supported.

Participants were informed that their involvement was voluntary, and that they were free to leave the study without prejudice or impact on care, role within the organisation, or right to services.

It was made clear in the study materials and via discussions with the researcher that the project could not ensure full anonymity for participants, as photographs had the potential to identify participants, others who use or work in the Service, and people with whom participants interact. For these reasons, staff were expected to adhere to Trust regulations and not include service users in their photographs. This safeguarded the service users' right to confidentiality and protected those who might lack the confidence to withhold their consent. However, service users were only restricted from taking photographs of children. Additional steps were taken to protect individuals, such as asking service users to get verbal permission from anyone appearing in photographs. Moreover, the researcher pixelated or removed all identifying features from photographs used in reports (e.g., faces, place names). Permission to use anonymised photographs in reports was given on the condition that the steering group also approved the release of each photograph as part of information governance.

Step 5: Recruitment

Initially, a pilot study was conducted with one service user and two members of staff to test the photo-elicitation interview, preparation and procedure. Challenges noted in the service user's photo-elicitation interview included slurred speech as a side effect of taking regular medication, reduced concentration and slow thought and speech processing time. Taking the time to check understanding to gain maximum clarity became essential when communicating with anyone experiencing similar challenges. The main recruitment strategy was guided by the steering group and informed by the researcher's growing understanding of the two participant groups.

The main recruitment drive began with staff in the anticipation that by experiencing the research process themselves they would be in a good position to support service users interested in taking part. The study was communicated widely throughout the Service, and staff were introduced to the study through an initial project launch meeting and through word of mouth. Service users were recruited via Service User Views Meetings, which provide a regular forum to discuss issues with staff and to hear about upcoming events. During the meetings, the researcher introduced the study, shared the study materials, and provided an opportunity for questions, as well as a space for participants to practise using the electronic tablets.

Staff questions focused on the viability of taking photographs within the Service, whilst service users' questions focused on how to use the technical equipment. This was managed sensitively to avoid triggering shame in those who were unfamiliar with using the equipment. Service users were encouraged to discuss their interest in the project with their recovery workers to ensure they were aware of their involvement in the project and to offer additional support in re-reading the study materials to facilitate understanding and discuss any potential concerns.

Step 6: Initial one-to-one meeting

Due to the large volume of responses, not all staff who showed an interest in the project were invited to the initial meetings with the researcher, whereas all interested service users were invited to talk about the project further. All service users' suitability for the study was regularly monitored by recovery workers throughout their involvement with the research. Having space before the photo-elicitation interview in this initial meeting enabled participants to voice their concerns and feel more confident about the process. For example, some staff initially felt uncomfortable accepting electronic tablets that could have been used for the benefit of service users and only agreed to keep them due to the complications around deleting data. Moreover, some service users required extra reassurance with regard to the motivations and reasoning behind being gifted a tablet.

During the initial meeting, participants were assessed for capacity to consent, and a signature was obtained. Informed consent was sought only after participants had been given the opportunity to reread the study material, ask questions and practise using the electronic tablets. Recovery workers were welcome to attend the initial meetings if requested to do so by service users. This happened once with an individual who had complex needs and who later experienced a serious decline in their mental health, which inhibited their ability to maintain informed consent. Some service users were wary about signing the consent form, and one service user chose not to be involved as a result, despite being offered extra time and further information, as well as the opportunity to provide verbal consent and speak to their recovery worker. Another service user withdrew after the initial meeting due to struggling to understand the conditions of consent because of language difficulties and expressed concerns at having an interpreter speak for them in this context.

Step 7: Taking photographs

During the initial meeting, an open research question was provided to all participants as a focus for their photographs in the hope that their narratives would relate appropriately to the research aims without being overly primed: "*What are your experiences of the Rehabilitation and Recovery Service?*" Participants were invited to take an optimum number of 5–7 photographs. The pilot study proved this to be the most appropriate number for the time allocated to the photo-elicitation interview (approximately one hour). All photo-elicitation interviews aimed to take place within 10–14 days following the initial meeting. However, as time went on, a flexible approach was taken that allowed for the daily challenges faced by participants.

Most people who came forward felt confident in their photography skills and in reflecting on their experiences; however, some voiced concerns regarding their ability to be creative. Participants were advised that any photograph they chose to take has its own meaning and is therefore valuable. As such, they were encouraged not to worry too much about what to photograph, but to consider what were the most important parts of their experiences they wanted to convey. On the three occasions where service users struggled with the electronic tablet, adjustments were made or additional support was offered. For example, one service user filmed short videos by accident instead of taking photographs. The researcher supported the participant in taking stills from the videos that best represented what they wanted to capture. Another service user arrived at their interview with the impression they had taken photographs, but their tablet was blank. Additional help was offered by their recovery worker, who ensured they had photographs to bring to a rearranged meeting. A third service user took all their photographs an hour before their interview in the garden and arrived with five very similar images. However, interestingly, they were still able to provide a rich insight into their experiences.

Step 8: Photo-elicitation interview

Photo-elicitation interviews took place in service user accommodation in the community, staff offices or private meeting rooms within the Service and were audio recorded on a Dictaphone with consent. All recordings were removed immediately after the interview and held securely on a university system. Most of the staff selected specific photographs to discuss prior to their photo-elicitation interview, whereas many service users selected theirs during the interview. A lightly structured protocol supported participants in reflecting on the meaning and content of their photographs and included the following open-ended questions:

(i) *Which photograph would you like to share first?*
(ii) *What can you tell me about this photograph?*
(iii) *What does this photograph express about your experience of the Service?*
(iv) *Which photograph would you like to share next?*

A question asking what photographs were *not* taken was also included at the end to provide insight into what participants might have found difficult to express. Flexibility was offered around interview length and was dependent on how much the participants wanted to share. For example, staff interviews lasted between 55–95 minutes, whilst service user interviews lasted between 12–98 minutes.

A few different ways of working with photographs were trialled. For example, prior to their interview, participants were initially encouraged to email their photographs to the researcher so they could be printed, and participants could physically choose a photograph to talk about. However, this only worked for staff because many of the service users did not have an email account or access to a reliable internet connection. Therefore, a portable printer was purchased so that chosen photographs could be printed during the interview. However, this took too long, which was problematic as staff were already stretched for time and some service users had limits to their concentration. In the end, transferring chosen photographs from the participants' electronic tablets to the researcher's laptop at the start of the interview to view on screen proved to be the most practical way of working with the photographs. Finally, at the end of each interview, a further opportunity to censor or withdraw any photograph was offered.

Step 9: Post photo-elicitation interview check in and time to reflect

Working with service users required the careful balance of responding to and supporting their complex needs in the moment and following the photo-elicitation interview. For example, one service user experienced hearing voices during their interview, and another became paranoid about the process and technical equipment being used. In both situations, the researcher paused the questions and recording to respond to the individual's immediate needs. In the case of the first service user, space was given for their voices to be present so as not to cause any unnecessary distress. For the second service user, time was given to revisit the information sheet, answer questions about the research and technical equipment being used and confirm boundaries around confidentiality. Both were then supported by their recovery workers post-interview to reflect on their experience further.

A couple of participants voiced anger over the care they had received from different services and wanted the researcher to support them in making a complaint. This was handled sensitively in the moment, and appropriate signposting information was given, including suggestions of who could best support them within the Service. Following the pilot study, surprise was communicated by participants regarding the speed at which the photo-elicitation process enabled them to access in-depth thoughts and feelings. At their recommendation, staff were offered time and space post-interview to reflect internally on their experiences before returning to work, and recovery workers were asked to support service users post-interview with any further reflections they may have had. This proved to be an invaluable process that enabled participants to feel supported and encouraged service users to continue the conversation with their recovery worker about their experiences of being in mental health services and how this might inform their recovery journey.

Diverse visions of empowerment *and* social justice *revealed through this case study*

We now provide a selective overview of the findings of our case study, demonstrating what it reveals in terms of diverse visions of the Community Psychology principles of *(dis)empowerment* and *social justice* through our participants' use of photographs. For a more detailed account of the full range of themes, see Smith et al. (2021) for service users and Smith et al. (2023) for staff.

Service user visions of (dis)empowerment: Challenge and Power

Service users used their photographs to represent the powerful impact their experience in the Service has had on them. Their photographs enabled them to express a variety of challenging experiences and, in this way, were *empowered* to express their experiences of *disempowerment*. For example, Jackie used a photograph of her feet (Figure 14.2, left) to describe feeling trapped by her illness: *"I took that because I spent months and months either lying or sitting on my bed [...] that was what I saw most of the time."* Similarly, Ethan used a photograph of a light shining through a door window (Figure 14.2, right) to share his experience of being sectioned: *"It's slightly prison-like [...] it's got the style of door where people can look in [...] it's got this sense of lack of privacy."*

Service user visions of social justice: Connection and awareness

Photographs could also be a vehicle through which service users can develop awareness and reflect on the supportive connections they have made. Arguably, these are important aspects of *social justice* from the service user perspective because they indicate a cycle of increasing ability to integrate with, and be accepted within, the community which is central to equal rights and human dignity. For example, Heather used a photograph of leaves pushing up against green metal railings (Figure 14.3, left) to reflect on her sense of personal growth and relationship with others: *"...they're still managing to flourish, the flowers, the leaves. They're growing through all the bars."* In another example, Tim used a photograph of a house in the process of being built (Figure 14.3, right) to reflect on his journey with a sense of pride: *"I think it's made me realise how far I've come."*

Staff visions of empowerment: Hope and limitations

Staff used the opportunity to talk about the ways in which they were limited in their role, but also what gave them hope, *empowering* them to deliver meaningful care. For example, using a photograph of two chairs together in a room (Figure 14.4, top) Aimee considered the importance of peer support: *"It can*

Figure 14.2 Jackie's photograph (left), Ethan's photograph (right)

be quite lonely making these decisions [...] but if you've got the resources there to share [...] learn from each other, why wouldn't you?" In another example, Louise used a photograph of a half empty carpark (Figure 14.4, bottom) to express what she needed to make her job easier: *"...there are still spaces for more people, we need more people."*

Staff visions of social justice: Culture and confidence

Staff evidenced that photographs offered an opportunity to challenge barriers to *social justice* embedded in the work culture. For example, Faye used a photograph of a brick wall (Figure 14.5, top) to explore the challenges she experienced working within a multidisciplinary team which she felt limited her ability to provide the best possible service: *"I just felt really frustrated [...] trying to bring a psychological perspective into the Service, it is really difficult, and a lot of people are very resistant to it."* However, photographs also provided an opportunity for staff to highlight aspects of their work that gave them confidence that they were supporting *social justice* through the seemingly small things they were able to do for vulnerable people. For example, using a photograph of a succulent plant (Figure 14.5, bottom) Holly reflected on the positive impact of her work with service users: *"...when something really positive does happen it can sometimes be really, really, small but it makes a massive difference."*

Figure 14.3 Heather's photograph (left) and Tim's photograph (right)

Challenges and opportunities for community psychologists using photo-elicitation in complex applied settings

The multidisciplinary, multi-agency setting of our case study in which health and third sector professionals serve a vulnerable population likely resonates with many initiatives in which community psychologists are involved. We now reflect critically on the challenges and opportunities of our use of photo-elicitation in this complex applied setting to encourage community psychologists to consider the potential of the approach to enhance their work.

There are challenges using photography with organisations in which client confidentiality is vital and with high-need participants with, sometimes, compromised ability to engage. Our nine-step ethical framework demonstrates how risks can be managed through a relational, ethical praxis. This means communicating well throughout the project and prioritising the agency of participants within required regulations. One restriction which requires careful communication and monitoring is the content of photographs. However, we found this to be an opportunity to encourage creativity through inviting participants to take photographs of objects which conveyed a feeling or association to the people they valued if, for example, they could not, or did not want to attempt, to get verbal consent (e.g., Figures 14.3 and 14.4).

Good communication and support were also required to enable the more vulnerable participants to take the photographs that best expressed their perspective. This included building their confidence to use the technology and avoiding any implication that photographs were expected to be "perfect." It must

Figure 14.4 Aimee's photograph (top) and Louise's photograph (bottom)

be remembered that photo-elicitation is a powerful method with the potential to evoke and explore difficult emotions and traumatic memories (Bates et al., 2017), hence our articulation of a nine-step ethical framework. However, the approach was also an opportunity for our participants, including the most vulnerable, to explore positive experiences, supportive relationships and personal achievements. Indeed, service user feedback included how they appreciated the chance to explore their experiences and mental health challenges in a stigma-free context and staff valued the opportunity to reflect on their practice.

Finally, a perennial challenge of conducting research in organisations and with vulnerable populations is achieving "buy-in" from potential participants. Service users often experience low motivation, dips in mood or health and forgetfulness, whereas staff have continuous demands on their time. Again, our nine-step ethical framework outlines how relationship building is vital. Taking part in research is, however, an opportunity for the community constituting the organisation to feel valued through

Figure 14.5 Faye's photograph (top) and Holly's photograph (bottom)

contributing to service development and building confidence to express themselves. Our experience is that photo-elicitation provides an opportunity to make this valuable outcome particularly attractive and concrete. For example, an exhibition of the photographs generated in our study won a community citizenship award in recognition of the staff and service users who engaged with the project. Moreover, following participation, one service user joined a photography group and won first prize in a competition.

Conclusion

We argue that *empowerment* to speak is foundational for *social justice* and have explored these principles of Community Psychology through a case study employing photo-elicitation to support service users to inform the system designed to support them and staff to inform the work in which they have invested. We provide a nine-step ethical framework for good practice using photo-elicitation with vulnerable participants within complex mental health settings. In particular, we highlight the potential of photo-elicitation to help people locate themselves in wider community contexts (see also Hodgetts et al., 2007), to inform systems central to their wellbeing and livelihoods, and hope to inspire the use of similar methods in other complex applied community settings.

Key principles, values and principles: *Empowerment* and *social justice*

Action for learning

Consider using photo-elicitation to draw attention to a community project you care about. Ask people contributing to the project to take photographs illustrating why it is important to them, explaining the ethical limits on content such as not including children. Print out the images and ask the photographers to add a caption which explains evocatively what the picture means to them. Organise a display of the work in a public space and celebrate the opening.

Discussion questions

To what extent are photographs impactful in the promotion of *social* justice? How might you use photography ethically with people who are physically unable to use a camera and in a way that *empowers* them to express their needs?

Reflective questions

What photograph would you take to capture what you care about in a particular community project and what caption would you provide? Think of a photograph that has made a deep impression on you. Reflect on what it is about the image that has achieved this effect and what meaning it holds for you.

Acknowledgements

This research on which this chapter is based was funded by Leeds and York Partnership NHS Foundation Trust and NHS Leeds North Clinical Commissioning Group. We thank all the service users and staff who supported and who took part in the research.

References

Bacha, K., Hanley, T., & Winter, L. A. (2020). 'Like a human being, I was an equal, I wasn't just a patient': Service users' perspectives on their experiences of relationships with staff in mental health services. *Psychology and Psychotherapy: Theory, Research and Practice*, 1–20. https://doi.org/10.1111/papt.12218

Bates, E. A., McCann, J. J., Kaye, L. K., & Taylor, J. C. (2017). "Beyond words": A researcher's guide to using photo elicitation in psychology. *Qualitative Research in Psychology*, *14*(4), 459–481. https://doi.org/10.1080/14780887.2017.1359352

Branfield, F., Beresford, P., Andrews, E. J., Chambers, P., Staddon, P., Wise, G., & Williams-Findlay, B. (2006). *Making user involvement work*. Joseph Rowntree Foundation. https://www.nsun.org.uk/wp-content/uploads/2021/05/making-user-involvement-work.pdf

British Medical Association. (2023). *Mental health pressures in England*. https://www.bma.org.uk/advice-and-support/nhs-delivery-and-workforce/pressures/mental-health-pressures-data-analysis

Collier, J. (1957). Photography in Anthropology: A report on two experiments. *American Anthropologist*, *59*(5), 843–859. https://doi.org/10.1525/aa.1957.59.5.02a00100

Duara, R., Hugh-Jones, S., & Madill, A. (2022). Photo-elicitation and time-lining to enhance the research interview: Exploring the quarterlife crisis of young adults in India and the United Kingdom. *Qualitative Research in Psychology*, *19*(1), 131–154. https://doi.org/10.1080/14780887.2018.1545068

Erdner, A., Andersson, L., Magnusson, A., & Lützén, K. (2009). Varying views of life among people with long term mental illness. *Journal of Psychiatric and Mental Health Nursing*, *16*(1), 54–60. https://doi.org/10.1111/j.1365–2850.2008.01329.x

Hodgetts, D., Chamberlain, K., & Radley, A. (2007). Considering photographs never taken during photo-production projects. *Qualitative Research in Psychology*, *4*(4), 263–280. https://doi.org/10.1080/14780880701583181

Kyololo, O. B. M., Stevens, B. J., & Songok, J. (2023). Photo-elicitation technique: Utility and challenges in clinical research. *International Journal of Qualitative Methods*, *22*, 1–8. https://doi.org/10.1177/16094069231165714

National Institute for Health Research. (2021). *Best research for best health: The next chapter*. https://www.nihr.ac.uk/documents/best-research-for-best-health-the-next-chapter/27778

Nyttingnes, O., Ruud, T., & Rugkåsa, J. (2016). 'It's unbelievably humiliating'– Patients' expressions of negative effects of coercion in mental health care. *International Journal of Law and Psychiatry*, *49*, 147–153. https://doi.org/10.1016/j.ijlp.2016.08.009

Repper, J., & Perkins, R. (2004). *Social inclusion and recovery. A model for mental health practice*. Elsevier Health Sciences.

Richard, V. M., & Lahman, M. K. (2015). Photo-elicitation: Reflexivity on method, analysis, and graphic portraits. *International Journal of Research & Method in Education*, *38*(1), 3–22. http://dx.doi.org/10.1080/1743727X.2013.843073

Rössler, W. (2012). Stress, burnout, and job dissatisfaction in mental health workers. *European Archives of Psychiatry and Clinical Neuroscience*, *262*(2), 65–69. https://doi.org/10.1007/s00406-012-0353-4

Sandhu, A., Ives, J., Birchwood, M., & Upthegrove, R. (2013). The subjective experience and phenomenology of depression following first episode psychosis: A qualitative study using photo-elicitation. *Journal of Affective Disorders*, *149*(1–3), 166–174. https://doi.org/10.1016/j.jad.2013.01.018

Smith, J. A., Flowers, P., & Larkin, M. (2009). *Interpretative phenomenological analysis: Theory, method and research*. Sage.

Smith, P., Simpson, L., & Madill, A. (2021). Service user experiences of a novel in-reach rehabilitation and recovery service for people with profound and enduring mental health needs. *International Journal of Mental Health Nursing*, *30*(5), 1106–1116. https://doi.org/10.1111/inm.12861

Smith, P., Thompson, A., & Madill, A. (2023). Staff experiences of a novel in-reach rehabilitation and recovery service for people with profound and enduring mental health needs. *International Journal of Mental Health Nursing*, *32*(5), 1289–1300. https://doi.org/10.1111/inm.13160

Taquette, S. R., & Borges da Matta Souza, L. M. (2022). Ethical dilemmas in qualitative research: A critical literature review. *International Journal of Qualitative Methods*, *21*, 1–15. https://doi.org/10.1177/16094069221078731

Wright, N., Rowley, E., Chopra, A., Gregoriou, K., & Waring, J. (2016). From admission to discharge in mental health services: A qualitative analysis of service user involvement. *Health Expectations*, *19*(2), 367–376. https://doi.org/10.1111/hex.12361

Further reading

https://www.bacp.co.uk/ethical-framework; https://assets.publishing.service.gov.uk/media/5a81d57de5274a2e8ab56140/A_framework_for_mental_health_research.pdf; Fullana, J., Pallisera, M., & Vila, M. (2014). Advancing towards inclusive social research: Visual methods as opportunities for people with severe mental illness to participate in research. *International Journal of Social Research Methodology: Theory & Practice*, *17*(6), 723–738.

15 Radical health care

Community action to shape person-centred health care for trans and non-binary people

Gray Hutchins

Overview

Radical approaches to health care start with community leadership, involvement and empowerment. The aim is for radical change. Change informed by the authenticity of those it serves, change that results in reform.

This chapter demonstrates the importance of underpinning projects from a trauma-informed and intersectional feminist perspective, and its critical requirement in order to invite authenticity: relevant to *all* marginalised and under-represented groups. Intersectional feminism goes beyond pushing back on misogyny, and at its core challenges transmisogyny: "the impersonal or state violence meted out to people who are perceived as transfeminine, whether they would understand themselves that way or not" (Peterson, 2021). Transmisogyny holds a strong undercurrent of racism, ableism and antisemitism, in addition to the medical pathologisation and demonisation of those affected. Using a trauma-informed approach involves understanding and compassion that every person's mind and body is also affected by both systemic, community and/or direct traumas they experience. Both elements are utilised as a loose framework for this chapter.

This lens is through the grassroots work of the transgender and non-binary (TNB) community of whom many stand shoulder to shoulder in the intersectional feminists' fight for bodily autonomy, respect and dignity – including and beyond gender-affirming care.

For those who are not familiar, gender-affirming care refers to any practice, exploration and/or intervention that affirms a person's gender identity. This is sometimes called "transitioning." This can include medical care, such as Hormone Replacement Therapies (HRT) or Speech and Language Therapy (SALT), but for most people, it extends to social aspects, such as changing our name and/or gender expression through clothing, hair, etc. Some people also consider psychotherapeutic input part of this, such as counselling or embodiment coaching. Gender-affirming care and "transition" looks different for everyone, and access to this varies immensely, as covered later in this chapter, in the context of England, UK.

Note: I am an activist, as are many of those who share and are invited to our table.

I am not a scholar, healthcare professional, or a community psychologist, but I work using some Community Psychology principles and would like to invite more community psychologists into this space, where they have opportunities to leverage change in healthcare practice. I've spent the last 15 years in community organising, the last 10 in particular in grassroots, community-led trans and non-binary specific organising.

DOI: 10.4324/9781003480464-19

Our TNBI population

The chapter is based on my reflections generated from my years in this community and supported as appropriate with academic research. The evolution of my own lived experience of gender and sexuality has led me to spend the majority of this time in settings which focused on the development and mobilisation of trans, non-binary and/or intersex (TNBI) community organising. My insight and reflections shared throughout this chapter are not built on academic or experimental grounds; however, they have come from years of organically generated lived, learnt and observational experiences. I would like to start by thanking the members of The Clare Project, colleagues, collaborators, chosen family and friends across the community for gifting me with this opportunity and insight.

Gender identity and its recognition is increasingly complex and vastly variable throughout the world. For the purposes of this chapter, we will be referring to the UK context of trans and non-binary people as anyone whose gender identity does not align with the sex assigned at birth. Anecdotally, across the community itself and allied professionals (e.g., academics, sexual health services), this is considered to be anywhere between 1–4% of the UK population (Brighton & Hove City Council, 2015; British Medical Association, 2024; Heath & Bunn, 2023; Holland et al., 2023). It is also important to note the more recent development of intersex communities' experiences, who make up a further 2–3% of the population, being considered alongside the inequalities faced by trans and non-binary people (Peterson, 2021). This has particularly increased since the development of the LGBTQIA+ Global Inclusive Flag, which includes the intersex flag (The Global Inclusive Pride Flag Project, n.d.). Redeveloped in 2021 by Valentino Vecchetti of Intersex Equality Rights UK, it requires acknowledgement that although our communities face similar inequalities with particular regard to health and social inclusion, being trans or non-binary is not the same as being intersex – and you can be both. You can have a variation in sex characteristics (also known as being "intersex"), be transgender, and of a minority sexuality (bisexual, asexual etc.), just as much as you can be of other intersecting marginalised communities (e.g., Person of Colour, care experienced, person of faith or belief, etc.) (Peterson, 2021). As a result of variations in diagnostic criteria for certain health conditions, constraints on reporting and stigma and inequalities, it is difficult to determine an exact prevalence in the population.

Similar to the evolution of the LGBTQIA+ acronym, our communities continue to join forces in tackling the inequalities we face and although there are clear examples of parallel experiences for both trans/non-binary people and intersex communities (e.g., long waiting times for "specialist" healthcare provision), it is an evolving area of knowledge for me. Gratefully, there are an emerging number of resources, speakers and organisers, some of whom are referenced in this chapter and references. There is a desperate need for recognition of struggles shared and often exacerbated by being intersex, a small number shared here.

What do we mean by "Inadequate Healthcare"?

Our health, our body, our choice. Without oversimplifying, it seems appropriate to begin this chapter with the basics which underpin the countless, relentless battles surrounding inadequate health care. In many parts of the world, the healthcare system is unattainable, failing, being destroyed and/or entirely absent, so it is important to start by outlining *what I really mean* when discussing "inadequate health-care." In the UK, there are two routes to accessing health care: the state-funded National Health Service (NHS) and/or Public Health services and secondly, the private sector.

Familiar examples of state-run and taxpayer-funded provision often include urgent care such as A&E or childbirth provision. Parallel to this sits a growing number of private providers of health care which generate income via state-funded contracts to help address escalating NHS waiting times or attainable by individuals who can afford to pay the price. Going private, in most cases, means drastically cutting waiting times to be seen by medical professionals and specialists, alongside the potential to access services or treatments not available on the NHS (TransActual, 2025a).

In this context, I am not only considering the context of a lack of funding to our state-run services. I am also referring to the wider systems and everything that underpins them – since their inception – not being made with us or by us. In our UK context, extending to many parts of Europe and North America, a few headline examples over the last few decades include: access to life-saving drugs after contracting HIV (Rodriguez-Hart et al., 2023), the rising mortality rates in Black women following childbirth (Rahman et al., 2022), on-going unnecessary surgical interventions on intersex children (Richmond, 2021), the demonisation and exclusion of support surrounding the menopause (Glyde, 2022; Westwood, 2024). Underpinned by centuries of racism, misogyny and homo/inter/transphobia, it is deeply structural and systemic.

To simplify, our UK healthcare systems originated from being written, designed, staffed and led by everyone but us. Whether its healthcare guidelines, medical school curriculum, the engineering of medical equipment, placement or design of our hospitals – it is grossly inadequate. As a result, they are often not for us at all, making them unfit for purpose – or at the very least, inadequate. In some cases, this goes beyond inadequacy, and at its peak becomes actively exclusionary: discriminatory.

Key examples having an increasingly adverse effect on TNBI people include:

- Vast mismanagement of/lack of recognition in NHS data systems, resulting in no national "joined up" approach to ensuring TNBI people's health needs are both known and respected with dignity: for example, all people are "coded" within NHS systems as male, female or indeterminate – depending on what you are coded as it will dictate what health screenings you are called for (regardless of anatomy), how bloods/tests are interpreted, etc. Although some improvements have been made in areas such as cancer screenings, this progression in silo feels to be weighed down by an ineffective system.
- Failure to update NICE guidelines and guidance which reflects World Professional Association for Transgender Health (WPATH) stating the need to move away from the medicalisation of being TNB considered only as someone experiencing gender dysphoria/incongruence, coded as a mental health condition (American Psychiatric Association, 2013; Fernandez Rodriguez et al., 2018; WPATH, 2025).
- A lack of consistency among NHS trusts and service providers with regard to TNBI inclusive practices among day-to-day operations (General Medical Council, 2024), including how to treat TNBI patients with dignity and respect, e.g., recording and respecting pronouns, gendered ward allocation, access to introductory training, etc. (Bachman & Gooch, 2018; Holland et al., 2023; White et al., 2023).
- Trans and non-binary people are facing an increasing rate of refusal for shared care relating to hormone replacement therapy, despite being recommended by specialists, while it continues to be prescribed for other conditions among the cis population (Bachman & Gooch, 2018; TransActual, 2021, 2024).

- Intersex people have no single defined treatment and/or support pathway, particularly with regard to care only attainable via Gender-Affirming Care pathways (e.g., genital reconstruction) and/or specialist endocrinology (Peterson, 2021).

Despite amounting challenges facing our TNBI communities, there are a growing number of examples of impactful activism taken up by many grassroots and growing organisations which seek to highlight and challenge health systems providing such inadequate care. Recent examples include ACT UP (Spencer, 2022), Intersex Equality Rights UK (n.d.), the Love Tank CIC (n.d.), Black Beetle Health (2023). Notably, the common thread between many of these ongoing battles is the fight for bodily autonomy, the enabling, empowerment and embrace of our choice.

Over recent years, I've seen the boom in "Co-production" – however throughout my own observations, I have rarely seen community involvement go beyond one-offs or short-term. We need to make space to actively, *really* involve the communities that these services are there to serve. This goes beyond the realm of cookie-cutter "co-production," curated consultations and simply put, inauthentic acts of what we might otherwise call tokenism. We're here for enabling community-led initiatives, resourced and supported by those who know themselves best, the communities they seek to support and serve (White, 2024). Simply put, sowing seeds for authenticity and what will eventually become: Radical Care.

Example of gender-affirming care

Like many marginalised groups, TNBI people are juggling many other intersecting challenges surrounding inadequate health care. Over recent years, it has become increasingly clear due to the escalating waits of up to seven years for a first appointment (Heath & Bunn, 2023; Holland et al., 2023; TransActual, 2025a), for alongside exclusionary/discriminatory rhetoric on the rise, that many in our community see gender-affirming care as the ultimate front door to health and wellbeing. For example, it is uncommon among our community to seek and/or acquire trauma therapy, and/or assessment for neurodivergence, out of fear of any results could have on accessing gender-affirming treatment (White, 2024). When looking at the harrowing statistics of poor mental health, suicidality, increasing deaths by suicide, homelessness, experiences of domestic violence, family estrangement – all of these desperately increase the need for support surrounding health and wellbeing (Holland et al., 2024).– For many, a lack of gender-affirming care is not only a contributing factor in causing these challenges, but can exacerbate them to last longer and be more intense (Heath & Bunn, 2023; White, 2024).

Many trans and non-binary (TNB) people have received, are receiving, (or more likely) awaiting some form of gender-affirming care. At present, the NHS limits this to a small number of surgeries, some elements of hormone therapy treatment, a few sessions of speech therapy and/or means-tested fertility preservation. If your GP agrees to a referral to one of the UK's Gender Identity Clinics, there will be a painful 3–7 year wait to access a first appointment for psychological assessment for "Gender Incongruence," previously known as – but for some continues to be defined as – Gender Dysphoria or Transexuallism (Heath & Bunn, 2023; TransActual, 2025a; Winter et al., 2016). These diagnoses currently fall under the umbrella of mental health conditions, despite being deemed not so by the World Health Organisation (Heath & Bunn, 2023).

Aside from the fact that many TNBI community members desire other support and/or resources to affirm their gender, such as hair transplants/removal, hormone suppressants, clothing/make-up, non-surgical fillers/botox, etc., many community members and professionals consider the current diagnoses model, service provision and guidelines which govern such services: wholly, if not grossly, inadequate. So much so, many community organisations continue to generate their own resources such as the Gender Construction Kit (n.d.), TransActual's (2025a) Gender Identity Clinic information page and The Clare Project's community resource booklets (TCP, 2024a).

In recent years, due to the escalating number of cases of shared-care refusals by GPs, community organisers suspect there may have been a rise in self-medicating activity (e.g., acquiring HRT from sources outside of the NHS and/or private realm) and community organising surrounding this including knowledge sharing and safety information (Bachman & Gooch, 2018; TransActual, 2025b).

In summary, our biggest takeaway from recent years' organising is that for many in our community, gender-affirming care, its continuity and "success," is only the front door into addressing ***all*** health needs.

Imagine a game of snakes and ladders (also Westernised, known as Gyam Chauper in Northern India):

- Snakes: a lack of recourse to funds, you're of another marginalised identity, unsupportive family/friends, undocumented, unhoused, etc.
- Ladders: binary, living in the same area, have money, already obtained relevant diagnoses.

The importance of place, people and space

As mentioned previously and observed consistently throughout my years of community organising, location in England can have a huge impact on your ability to access gender-affirming care. Whether it be due to being securely housed, having a GP who will agree to refer you to a Gender Identity Clinic, or whether you have more progressive initiatives happening in your area. Sussex, and in particular the city of Brighton & Hove, has held a long-standing reputation for being TNB community inclusive. Of course, that does not mean it is well-rounded or intersectional in its inclusion, but similar to London and Manchester, it does have a rather relentless magnet effect. Led by local community activists and groups, it was the first city in the UK to host the first and Europe's largest Trans Pride event (Trans Pride Brighton, n.d.), Trans Needs Assessment (Hill & Condon, 2015), TNB-specific sexual health clinic "Clinic T" (2025), and local ICB hosted the countries' first Trans Health Improvement Board (NHS Sussex, 2022), although short-lived. Unsurprisingly, the city also acted as a hub to The Beaumont Society (2025), and the UK's longest standing TNB-led support service The Clare Project (2024b); it is now home to over 20 TNB-centred groups (TCP, 2024a). Albeit far from perfect, it has become quite the sanctuary for many.

Something which really struck me when I started getting involved in community organising/activism in Brighton and Hove was the inherent lack of TNB representation in our voluntary sector, where most community organising that becomes funded/resourced in any way often ends up. This is particularly stark amongst the LGBTQIA+ sector, where you might expect to see trans and non-binary people more visibly/knowingly represented. Noted, it might be that there is representation of TNB people who are not visibly "open" with this aspect of their identity, and nor should they be expected to be. However, what is noticeable is the parallels of perceivably low numbers in TNB representation, alongside the low levels of ring-fenced funding for TNB-specific services/projects within those organisations, and subsequently, often low footfall of TNB service users.

Because of the way most VCSO and funders' monitoring data is captured and many commissions coming from statutory sector data systems (e.g., dictated by the NHS), it is simply too binary and vastly outdated for many intersectional groups. Alas, community representation and insight are light years away from permitting our community to be seen through tools such as Gender Pay Gap reporting or annual monitoring. Although some organisations are beginning to share data surrounding TNB communities' attendance to services, representation in teams, etc., it is difficult to source for past years, making very little opportunity for comparison. Admirable organisations such as Charity So White (n.d.) continue to shine a light on the inherent lack of Black & PoC representation, shining a much-needed light on both systemic and structural racism in the history and existence of the voluntary sector. In our sector, we continue to capture other groups such as ex-armed forces, age, etc., causing us to question how much we really know about our communities' engagement, needs and/or scale of the absence of such.

Observationally, it could be said this under-representation of community space alongside the struggle for cohesion among the LGBTQIA+ sector itself could be a contributing factor as to why TNB-centred space has been so valuable when it has come about. As myself and others continue to see in our area of work, it is common for under-represented and under-served groups within wider communities to break off and make space for themselves; similarly with TNB communities, we continue to see similar success with the asexual community, QTIBIPoC groups, queer women, and so forth. Many of our communities begin our organising by existing among demand, either our own lived experience or from peers; it is often the point of inception. The demand is what brings people together, often a common thread bonding people, whether it be an aspect of identity, a struggle such as social isolation, a shared trauma or perhaps something to celebrate. Our collective response to such demand, particularly in those rare and valuable moments which are bonded by this shared lived experience, is equally mountainous, relentlessly challenging, and as a result: resoundingly fruitful. The desperate desire for one thing: space.

The Clare Project

Starting off in the autumn of 2000, The Clare Project began as an informal meet-up in the back room of a beauty salon. The salon became popular with a number of local transgender women for inclusive and friendly laser hair removal, and the salon owner suggested using the salon after hours for an informal meet-up. After a few years of growing in popularity, one of the co-founders – a local chaplain, Christina Beardsley – was offered a low-cost weekly meeting space at Dorset Gardens Methodist Church in Kemptown, Brighton & Hove. For over 20 years, The Clare Project's ever-popular Tuesday Drop-in continues to meet there, regularly welcoming 25 or more visitors every single week of the year.

In the earlier years, the majority of those using and mobilising TCP were middle-aged to older trans women, sometimes gender questioning, or cross-dressers – those deeply affected by transmisogyny. Attendees would meet and simply enjoy coffee, biscuits and a chat; others would make use of the basement meeting room to do speech practice or the occasional offer of low-cost 1:1 counselling. A few years later, around 2011, those attending the group were beginning to diversify, including trans men and non-binary people, who also began meeting outside of TCP at "FTM* Brighton," now called "Navigate Brighton" (2020). Following mounting dissatisfaction with Brighton Pride and the overall lack of community space to come together, 2013 saw the beginning of Trans Pride Brighton, which quickly became Europe's largest Trans Pride event, now welcoming 40,000+ attendees every year. The Brighton & Hove City Council did England's first ever Trans Needs Assessment (Hill & Condon, 2015), a collaborative effort of all three organisations known as "The Trans Alliance" (Switchboard, 2025). In the following year, The Clare Project became formally constituted as a charity in 2016 (TCP, 2024b), opening doors to obtaining their own bank account for obtaining funding, a Board of Trustees to oversee the volunteer "committee" and so on.

The seed of frustration at the lack of community-led organisations for trans and non-binary people in the city was sown the day I set foot in The Clare Project as their first employee in late 2018. However, there was a catch – although I was working for TCP, I was employed by Brighton & Hove LGBT Switchboard, a larger charity operating support services for LGBT adults in the city. Having volunteered with Trans Pride Brighton doing Community Outreach and Partnerships two years previously, I was taken aback to hear our community groups were dependent on other organisations and/or cis allies for our existence. TCP had recently seen cis members of the Board and counselling team amicably leave their roles, and here they were – although constituted – under the umbrella of an LGBTQ+ organisation.

Under the Charity Commission's setup and guidance, by being hosted in this way, it arguably subjected TCP to operate under the policies, practice and guidance of an LGBTQ+ organisation. Although a by-and-for charity at the time, 40+ years strong, there was very little – if any – TNB leadership, input or co-creation. A lack of community-led existence in our sector is rife, and often, inaccurately claimed. I was frustrated that despite being in one of the countries' most "radical" areas for TNB inclusion and action, our community groups had so few of our community organising from leadership at Trustee or Director level, through to front-line team members, or even existing substantially enough to make room for such a structure.

It is certainly a very honourable and inspiring story that TCP has spent the last 18 years propped up by a small team of volunteers, vastly made up of courageous trans women. Only more recently were they joined by a couple of low-wage facilitators – their turnover around £2-4k a year – mostly generated by the lovely Julia Trangmar, who enjoyed vigorously shaking a donation box (or maybe ash tray) at the Drop-in. At that time in the city there were a number of growing LGBTQ+ support organisations, with much larger teams of volunteers and paid staff, incomes ranging between £150k and 400k, tens of volunteers and several paid staff. Their LGBTQ+ organisations were rapidly growing, while TNB representation continued to be under-resourced. Sadly this has been pretty consistent year-on-year, and gross inequity of representation in funding is only just beginning to be highlighted. (Consortium, n.d.)

Notably, TCP would perhaps not be where it is today if it wasn't for a number of allied individuals within those organisations, particularly those who encouraged and enabled it to be community-led with a leg-up in times of need. Switchboard hosted me as their first worker and put an end to us being the only voice in the room that went unpaid. Undeniably, it was disheartening. Among the hundreds of community organisations in the area – why do so few hold our community in leadership? Even on a national scale, why were there so few – if any – community-led organisations in a position to deliver services and receive funding for doing so? Grassroots groups, led by our communities, were severely lacking in recognition and resources, resulting in a resounding absence of our presence at the many tables it was so desperately needed.

The road to radical health care

The Clare Project continued its trajectory of being radical when it continued to concretise its foundations by being solely built on community leadership. Our Board of Trustees was steered by a community GP (Dr Sam Hall) and a leading clinician in sexual health (Dr Kate Nambiar), alongside expertise from those with a background in health systems policy and improvements (Dee Humphreys). Supported by further expertise and valuable lived experience of several others across both the Board and Management Committee, TCP had already begun generating understanding of our communities' health and wellbeing needs. Through the Trans Alliance, Trans Needs Assessment, and the founding of Clinic T, it was increasingly evident to all involved that there was a significant, and rather desperate need, for not only community-led psychosocial support, but even more so: a helping hand to the front door of health care (White, 2024).

It was in this setting that the following priorities became part of the practise.

Priority 1: Voice

Generate equitable existence for our community. Underpinning everything was the priority to enable and empower voice, which was initiated by both the need and generosity of these bold women. Building on this, it was clear TCP had many more intersecting communities it needed to more effectively support, particularly those who are racially minoritised, disabled and/or neurodivergent. This naturally also evolved over time to actively include non-binary people, and more recently movement towards including people with a variation in sex characteristic (also known as intersex). This priority never stops.

Priority 2: Resilience

Develop and strengthen our position as an entirely community-led organisation able to be a competitive provider of funded services. In those earlier days, the aim was to obtain funding from our NHS to deliver community awareness training to local GPs (White, 2024). However, this did also mean looking inwards and being in a position to bid for either statutory funding or grants for further resources to meet community needs such as mental health support, advocacy, information or advice, etc.

Alongside professional resilience, it also required personal and emotional resilience. Existing within a structure designed by and for everyone but you is hard, but vital work.

Priority 3: Action

Empower and enable our community's voice to be heard, organise and act. This work began early in the COVID-19 pandemic as activism-inspired community involvement projects such as co-written/designed resources (2021-), the start-up of pop-up health clinic The Trans Health Hub (2021-) and quickly extended to longer-term community development projects such as Sussex Transcendence (2022-). Many of these community-led initiatives continue today, with great strength but not without challenge, thanks to those who have worked and/or volunteered to take them on.

Following a rather relentless crash course involving many challenges, 2023–24 saw our local TNBI communities' rapid increase in health-related involvement projects. It was during this time TCP facilitated over 1500 hours of paid community involvement – alongside a further 2000+ hours of our own team's involvement, input and organising. Projects wildly varied, including over 750 hours throughout the mobilisation of the NHS England funded Sussex Gender Service Pilot, to the running of our Trans Health Improvement Group, co-creation of TNB Health Screening timelines and ongoing development of TCP's training content/resources. Whether it was sitting on the 20 NHS staff recruitment panels, attending the ICB's Trans Health Improvement Board meetings, scrutinising NHS Trust's approach to gender-affirming care pathways, developing innovative ways of improving the inclusivity of Public Health's Towards Zero HIV initiative – it was relentless, it was great.

Beyond everything, it was hard. Hard for our community, even with the recent privilege of being in a paid and supported capacity, to work towards rebuilding trust, understanding and relationships with these systems. Not only was there historical damage, many also experienced personal traumas at the hands of our health system, whether through negligence due to inadequacy of services or everyday discrimination. Harm throughout all of the work was unavoidable, and although there were many moments of pain and difficulty, there was an extremely courageous effort from all involved. Notably, this project's lifetime existed throughout the tail end of a pandemic (impacting all marginalised populations even further), community-specific upheaval of gender-affirming care for young people, rising numbers of deaths by suicide in the community – on the local and global backdrop of amounting discrimination and violence – the pressure was unimaginable.

The risk of re-traumatisation would not only be disengagement, but long-lasting, perhaps even irreparable damage, is huge in these environments. This is particularly fragile when there are glimmers of hope or trust built over time – as ultimately it results in being dropped from even greater heights. Throughout my experience of community organising, including and beyond The Clare Project, common instances of this were often repeated:

- A result of a lack of clear, harmful and/or accessible communication between the community and NHS, e.g., acronym use, jargon, bureaucracy, only operating Monday to Friday 9–5, "othering" TNB participants by not taking time to share context or briefing before/after meetings.
- Mismanaging expectations, false promises and tokenism: often for secondary gain such as a project to appear inclusive, although sometimes out of naivety statutory partners assume success, although our community groups are operating in an inherently exclusionary system. People begin rebuilding trust, only to have it broken again, heightened by unclear communication as to how or why.
- Direct and indirect discrimination, often underpinned by a lack of understanding and/or influence in popular culture. Invasive questions, issues/complaints not being considered seriously, misgendering, erasure from data, inaccessible options for payment or employment, and at its peak – action and/or inaction surrounding transphobia and transmisogyny.
- The health and social care system does not appear to have time, capacity and/or resources to be genuinely, authentically, trauma-informed. There is no time to nurture relationships.

Both observationally throughout my work, and increasingly shared throughout blogs and publications, trans and non-binary workers are finding being within the health system as both staff and patients increasingly challenging. Particularly clinicians or those working in health systems, not only are they existing within the system as employees, they studied or trained in it, in some ways perpetrating its harm further; they are also on the receiving end of it for their own care. If you are not institutionalised by it, or falling victim to your own internalised discrimination, the vicarious trauma and distress of operating against your own moral standards in this field are potentially all-consuming. This is of course immensely exacerbated by a healthcare system with multiple layers of discrimination with its roots in misogyny and subsequent transmisogyny, added to by racism if you are also Black or Brown, and/or layered with the communities' common overlap with neurodivergence. In some instances, the escalating pathologisation of our lived experiences – our identities – can be effectively utilised very quickly to undermine any validity of our professional voice, particularly if it is coming from a place of desperation.

A harrowing observation, but at several points throughout my work I have questioned if TNB existence as internal stakeholders in statutory systems is considered "too radical" to fit into such an archaic, discriminatory system. Counter to this, sometimes isolated from their own or allied communities for being part of a harmful system. Added to this, too radical to be taken seriously in the system, or even be perceived as a threat, but also ostracised from the community for sitting alongside a system believed to cause harm. However, to bridge the gap between radical and realistic, being akin but not within. Our communities continue to try, try and try again.

In action/In practice

The beauty of what our TNB community continued to work so tirelessly to create at The Clare Project doesn't simply amount to co-production: it is creation, it was existence and it was empowerment of voice. Wherever possible, whether through TCP, our peers in other TNBI or allied groups, it resulted in action – whenever it is community-led, it is always community-centred. In the simplest of terms: "it is as good as what you put in." The wealth of our work went beyond the realms of authenticity, and often fed into action – ranging from the doing or delivery of services, creating resources, community organising and supporting the creation of entirely new community-led groups. In some cases, it also resulted in making informed decisions to withdraw our part in projects entirely.

Appreciatively, being in a position of privilege as an organisation where you have the option to withdraw is not one for which to be complacent. Our lived experience involvement (or action, one might say) is non-prescriptive and aims to be non-hierarchical. In particular, our communities require the opportunity to lead, not to be led. Our communities want to be paramount in the doing, not having it done for us. Understandably, I have worked alongside both community members and peers who would advocate that any seat at a table is better than none, which is one of the reasons why Priority 2 became so important for The Clare Project. Ultimately, if your presence as a provider is known, or even previously present, holding organisational autonomy can shift power in a room. It takes a long time to obtain a position of strength in which withdrawal can be used as a tactic to negotiate, and certainly is a risky one. In some cases, this absence of known existence, in many ways, demonstrates resistance.

Enabling authenticity: A vision for social justice and wellbeing for TNB people

Having reflected on The Clare Project's activities of previous years, I have given a light-hearted attempt at summarising our learning as to *what is needed* to enable, empower and ultimately mobilise our radical approach to community action. This is my vision of how social justice can look, in order to enable wellbeing, and although it is centred on the experiences of trans and non-binary people, particularly those affected by transmisogyny, I hope it can sow seeds of inspiration for other intersecting communities. Whether it be creating the existence of space, a creation project, learning or remedial conversations, meetings, or otherwise – the initiating aim is to harvest rich and diverse perspectives. As previously discussed, enabling these perspectives to be authentic is not without significant risks, particularly of re-traumatising those with marginalized identities – for example, disclosing or re-sharing traumatic experiences with healthcare professionals or through participation learning that what they experienced was discrimination. It cannot be underestimated how much these activities require adequate reflection and support for both participants and workers, as highlighted below.

Evolving components

- **Supporting participation, courage and vulnerability**
  For example, this can involve making information and/or education accessible, such as easy-read formats; providing trauma-informed support following sessions, e.g., debriefs or clinical supervision; outsourced or professional support based on specific needs, e.g., PoC supervisors if requested; encouraging and enabling brave and courageous approaches through training or offers of mentorship.
- **Recognising fears: difficult conversations**
  This involves making space for people to share *what they really mean*, guided or supported communication, allowing time, self-awareness and reflection. This is part of preparation; however, it requires constant re-visiting through support provided (above). For example, providing induction/training on anti-oppressive or trauma-informed communication.
- **Agreeing shared values**
- Starting with shared, concrete principles is key to building the equitable foundations you wish to build on. Having a solid values-based approach to everything gives all participants something to return to. It can be both applied and compassionately scrutinised, particularly when it comes to addressing challenges and decision making.
- For example, a shared value for many is "respect" – whether that embeds itself in a team practice or Group Agreement as: respecting another's lived experience may be very different from your own, challenging the topic and not one another, etc. This has been particularly key for TCP when addressing disagreements between participants, and particularly when needing to uphold our trauma-informed approach.
- It is important these values evolve as the group/individuals' dynamic does, while also being mindful they aren't formed or used to undermine one another. For example, if another shared value acquired is "honesty," participants need to work towards how this can be applied respectfully.
- **Owning – and where possible, addressing – limitations**
  Continue to recognise and name limitations, discuss risks, expertise or experience among those currently present, remind yourselves what you are here to achieve and manage expectations to avoid disappointment. This can include agreeing core objectives or aims of the space; it doesn't necessarily mean you have to limit long-term goals. These objectives may also be fixed or evolving, provided it is equitably agreed.
- **Inviting others to come with you**
  Underpinning everything, and a key part of all community development, organising and collaboration – is inviting those who are invested in working towards progress to come with you. Recognisably, many significantly under-resourced communities rely on allyship at times of inception and/or through challenging periods; however, community leadership, and certainly centring, should always take priority over all else where possible. Allies can support, but the community leads.

Once attempts at enabling authenticity of communities, whether a team of volunteers or staff, participants of a new consultation group, a 1:1 mentorship, or members of a meeting – you then need to invite perspective (in some examples, characterised as voice or creation). Throughout our organising, I've begun to recognise that four key components of practice have significantly enabled the existence of perspective in our teams and collaborations and throughout many of our activities and projects:

- Presence

  This centres itself on accessibility in both the practical sense (e.g., paid attendance, accessible language through the aid of induction or working glossary, clear aims of the space, etc.) as much as it does emotionally support those involved through being trauma-informed and providing reflective/debrief space. This can also include the active involvement of others involved, for example, coming to activities prepared or active listening in the space.
- Patience

  Recognition and acknowledgement for all involved that in order to invite and enable diverse perspectives, it requires both compassion and understanding for one another and subject matter. This is embodied by patience for both ourselves and our learning, alongside one another joining us on the journey. Knowledge, education and exposure to perspectives are a privilege, and for many this may be the first environment where it is welcomed. For example, recognition that many LGBTQ+ people have differing associations with terms such as "Queer." Depending on their lived experience and/or access to learning or community, where this word was used as a hateful slur predominantly towards LGBTQ+ people, and now many reclaim or repurpose the word as part of their identity. Application of its use often varies across geographies, class, generations and experiences of violence; although not exclusively. Generating understanding and appreciation for this perspective requires patience.
- Practice

  Community empowerment, organising and action requires practice. This work is going to be difficult, at points potentially re-traumatising or triggering. As seen frequently throughout our activity, there is often a need to share personal, emotional challenges in order to generate or implement solutions. This could be on an individual basis, such as sharing lived experience as a TNB patient who had a traumatic experience of discrimination. Another common experience was often encountered through exposure to harmful policy and/or practice, such as assessment criteria for gender dysphoria as mentioned previously. A significant, escalating factor was the political environment – entirely beyond our control. It may be turbulent at many points, with both successes and challenges; revisiting the approach to enabling authenticity here is key in ensuring remedial action. This can include revisiting your meeting structure, or Group Agreement, practising what works best for participants in times of political uncertainty, etc.
- Progress

  Finally, but importantly, our ongoing reflection and evaluation of all elements – the ripple effect included. All highs and lows play a key part, and progress is underpinned by learning and growth, regardless of outcome. Personal growth, emotional growth, organisational learning, etc. need to be considered. This has previously manifested as physical outputs, such as diversifying recruitment practices or health screening resources, but has also been rather personal, such as individual learning or inspiration.

Because TCP's experience of TNB engagement has been so new, it is key to recognise that the lack of community engagement is just as valuable as fuller participation. Similar to our own absence/abstaining from participation, it is helpful to know what people do not want to do, are fearful of, or misunderstand regarding what is being proposed.

Going forward, community psychologists can actively enable opportunities for community involvement. This starts by being an advocate "on the inside," and in particular, when there is no known representation of our communities. Inviting perspective, involvement and input might not always be possible when you join a particular project; however, approaching this dynamically and

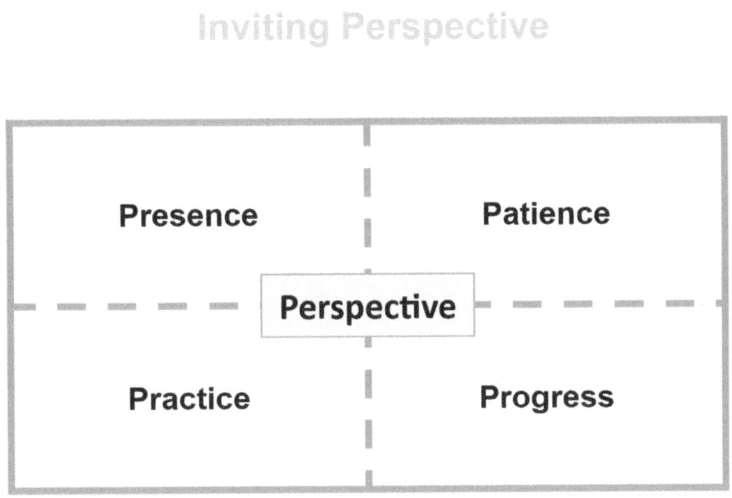

Figure 15.1 Inviting Perspective

embedding perspective in your practice will not only enhance delivery but activate others to do so as well.

A good place to start, when presented with a project, policy or idea, is by asking yourself "what might this look/feel/be like for someone from the TNB community?" "how might we find out? Is there something I can read/look to for more information? Has a TNB person already written about this? Who from the TNB community could we meaningfully invite in to contribute?" The role of allyship plays a consistent role in your everyday life, not limited to the TNB community; you can apply "perspective checks" – and although this will not replace lived experience, you can certainly generate learnt experience. As mentioned previously, I and other community organisers regularly take inspiration from activists whose vision for social justice and wellbeing is rooted in the right to autonomy. I would encourage every community psychologist to activate their inner-activist by continually advocating and enabling perspective (See Figure 15.1).

Action for learning: Perspective framework activity (Individual task or group)

An aspect of our identity that affects everyone is gender. You/your group have been invited to join a steering group on working towards gender equality.

Take a few moments on your own to reflect on what you might individually need to enable authenticity in the steering group.

What do these four components mean to you?

What do they look like when you're wanting to participate authentically?

What concerns do you have? How might they be mitigated?

What would enable your participation?

Using the template in Table 15.1, and based on your wishes, draft up a working/live Group Agreement/Terms of Reference:

Table 15.1 Template for group agreement/terms of reference

Presence	Patience
Practice	**Progress**

References

American Psychiatric Association. (2013). *Diagnostic and statistical manual of mental disorders* (5th ed.). https://doi.org/10.1176/appi.books.9780890425596.

Bachman, C. L., & Gooch, B. (2018). *LGTB in Britain: Trans report.* Stonewall and YouGov. https://files.stonewall.org.uk/production/files/lgbt_in_britain_-_trans_report_final.pdf?dm=1724230505

Black Beetle Health. (2023). *Home*. https://www.blackbeetlehealth.co.uk/

Brighton & Hove City Council. (2015). *Trans people in Brighton & Hove: A snapshot report.* https://www.brighton-hove.gov.uk/files/sites/bhconnected/files/Brighton%20&%20Hove%20Trans%20Data%20Snapshot%202015.pdf

British Medical Association. (2024). *Managing patients with gender dysphoria.* https://www.bma.org.uk/advice-and-support/gp-practices/gp-service-provision/managing-patients-with-gender-dysphoria

Charity So White. (n.d.). *Home*. https://charitysowhite.org/

Clinic, T. (2025). *Clinic T for trans and non binary*. Brighton & Hove Sexual Health & Contraception Service. https://brightonsexualhealth.com/service/clinic-t/

Consortium. (n.d.). *The LGBT+ fund report: The UK LGBT* voluntary *&* community sector finances, funding *and* future. Retrieved October 7, 2025, from https://www.consortium.lgbt/wp-content/uploads/2019/07/LGBT-Fund-Report-11-GG.pdf

Fernandez Rodriguez, M., Mendez Granda, M., & Gonzalez, V. (2018). Gender incongruence is no longer a mental disorder. *Journal of Mental Health and Clinical Psychology*, *2*(5), 6–8.

Gender Construction Kit. (n.d.). *Gender Construction Kit*. https://genderkit.org.uk/

General Medical Council. (2024). Trans healthcare. https://www.gmc-uk.org/professional-standards/ethical-hub/trans-healthcare#mental-health-and-bridging-prescriptions

Glyde, T. (2022). LGTBQIA+ menopause: Room for improvement. *The Lancet*, *400*(10363), 1578–1579. https://doi.org/10.1016/s0140-6736(22)01935-3

Heath, L., & Bunn, S. (2023). *Factors shaping gender incongruence and dysphoria, and impact on health services*. Parliamentary Office of Science and Technology (POST). https://researchbriefings.files.parliament.uk/documents/POST-PB-0053/POST-PB-0053.pdf

Hill, A., & Condon, R. (2015). *Brighton & Hove trans needs assessment, 2015*. Brighton & Hove City Council. https://www.brighton-hove.gov.uk/files/sites/bhconnected/files/Brighton%20&%20Hove%20Trans%20Needs%20Assessment%202015.pdf

Holland, D., White, L. C. J., Pantelic, M., & Llewellyn, C. (2023). The role(s) transgender adults want general practice to have in their healthcare: A qualitative study in Southeast England. *Bulletin of Applied Transgender Studies*, *2*(3–4), 175–194. https://doi.org/10.57814/w0e6-xy86

Holland, D., White, L. C. J., Pantelic, M., & Llewellyn, C. (2024). The experiences of transgender and nonbinary adults in primary care: A systematic review. *European Journal of General Practice*, *30*(1), https://doi.org/10.1080/13814788.2023.2296571

Intersex Equality Rights. (n.d.). *Home*. https://www.intersexequalityrights.com/

Navigate Brighton. (2020). *Home*. https://www.navigatebrighton.co.uk/

NHS Sussex. (2022). *NHS Sussex trans healthcare report*. HOSC. https://democracy.brighton-hove.gov.uk/documents/s180280/Final%20NHS%20Sussex%20Trans%20Healthcare%20Report%20HOSC%20-%20July%202022%20_%20002.pdf

Peterson, J. K. (2021). *A comprehensive guide to intersex*. Jessica Kingsley Publishers.

Rahman, S., Igwe, S., & Nazmeen, B. (2022). *Systemic racism, not broken bodies: An inquiry into racial injustice and human rights in UK maternity care*. Birthrights. https://birthrights.org.uk/wp-content/uploads/2022/05/Birthrights-inquiry-systemic-racism-May-22-web-1.pdf

Richmond, E. (2021). The rights of intersex children: Meet the Manchester academic and the activist hoping to help intersex children get a better start. *The University of Manchester Magazine, Winter 2021 Issue*. https://www.manchester.ac.uk/about/magazine/features/rights-of-intersex-children/

Rodriguez-Hart, C., Zhao, G., Goldstien, Z., Radix, A., & Torian, L. (2023). An exploratory study to describe transgender people with HIV who accessed Medicaid and heir viral suppression over time in New York City, 2013–2017. *Transgender Health*, *8*(5), 429–436. https://doi.org/10.1089/trgh.2021.0195

Spencer, S. (2022). The British AIDS activists you might not know about. *BBC*. https://www.bbc.co.uk/bbcthree/article/7b375363-45e9-4a60-927a-456a8f305948

Switchboard. (2025). *Trans Alliance*. https://www.switchboard.org.uk/trans-alliance/

The Beaumont Society. (2025). *Home*. https://beaumontsociety.org/

The Clare Project. (2024a). *Resources*. https://clareproject.org.uk/resources/

The Clare Project. (2024b). *About us*. https://clareproject.org.uk/about-us/

The Global Inclusive Pride Flag Project. (n.d.). *The home of the global inclusive pride flag*. https://www.globalinclusiveprideflag.com

The Love Tank CIC. (n.d.). *Home*. https://www.thelovetank.info/

TransActual. (2021). *Trans lives survey: Enduring the UK's hostile environment*. https://transactual.org.uk/wp-content/uploads/TransLivesSurvey2021.pdf

TransActual. (2024). *GP refusal to prescribe HRT: Summary report*. https://transactual.org.uk/wp-content/uploads/GP-refusal-to-prescribe-HRT-October-Report-V2.pdf

TransActual. (2025a). *Gender clinics*. https://transactual.org.uk/medical-transition/gender-dysphoria-clinics/

TransActual. (2025b). *Bridging prescriptions*. https://transactual.org.uk/bridging-prescriptions/

Trans Pride Brighton. (n.d.). *About*. https://transpridebrighton.org/about/

Westwood, S. (2024). A bloody mess? UK regulation of menopause discrimination and the need for reform. *Journal of Law and Society*, *51*(1), 104–129. https://doi.org/10.1111/jols.12469

White, L. (2024). *TNBI healthcare report 2024*. The Clare Project. https://clareproject.org.uk/tnbi-healthcare-report-2024/

White, L. (2024). *TNBI healthcare report 2024*. The Clare Project. https://clareproject.org.uk/tnbi-healthcare-report-2024/

White, L. C. J., Holland, D., Pantelic, M., & Llewellyn, C. (2023). "I carry so much anger, and that is not good for my health": The mental health impact of current gender-affirming healthcare pathways on transgender adults in England. *Bulletin of Applied Transgender Studies*, *2*(1–2), 47–65. http://doi.org/10.57814/0dbe-4w50

Winter, S., Diamond, M., Green, J., Karasiz, D., Reed, T., Whittle, S., & Wylie, K. (2016). Transgender people: Health at the margins of society. *The Lancet*, *388*(10042), 390–400. https://doi.org/10.1016/s0140-6736(16)00683-8

World Professional Association for Transgender Health. (2025). *WPATH*. https://wpath.org/

Suggestions for further reading

Beardsley, C., & Dowd, C. (2020). ***Trans Affirming Churches: How to celebrate gender variant people and their loves ones***. Jessica Kingsley Publishers.

16 Promoting the use of Community Psychology in clinical psychology settings

Carl Harris, Jan Bostock, Teresa Hagan, Alex Stirzaker and Juliet Young

A critical discussion of a social problem: UK clinical psychology's response to the impact of social determinants on mental health

There has been an increase globally in mental health difficulties, with a billion people experiencing this issue worldwide (World Health Organisation, 2025). Nationally, in 2019, the UK had the highest number of people experiencing moderate or severe symptoms of depression among the 29 countries in the OECD.

The UK is experiencing significant growth in the prevalence of mental health difficulties, particularly among young people. According to the latest Adult Psychiatric Morbidity Survey, 22.6% of adults aged 16 to 64 were identified with a common health condition, such as depression and anxiety. This represented an increase from 18.9% in 2014 and 17.6% in 2007, with women showing a higher prevalence than men at each point. The numbers for young adults are worse, the latest being 25.8%, compared to 17.5% in 2007 (NHS Digital, 2025). These developments have been described as a mental health crisis (The Economist, 2023).

The mental health gradient would predict (Allen et al., 2014) that the prevalence of mental health difficulties would be higher among those who are less well off. Indeed, the rate for depression was particularly noticeable amongst the bottom 20% income bracket in the UK, where more than 20% of people were experiencing symptoms (OECD, 2019).

UK healthcare providers, responding to the crisis in young people's mental health, express concern that capacity is being outstripped by demand and call for action to reduce waiting times for mental health services. There are calls for the integration of digital technologies and new partnerships among health, education and the voluntary sector. There are also calls for a whole government approach, acknowledging that health care only accounts for 20% of our health outcomes, with the other 80% being affected by other determinants, such as poverty, deprivation, insecure housing and unemployment (National Health Executive, 2025) as well as insecure, poorly paid employment (Royal Society of Arts, 2024).

And yet, despite awareness of the importance of social determinants, the Department of Health and Social Care's (DHSC) response to the growing need for mental health services continues to focus on spending on front-line mental health services (DHSC Media Team, 2023).

NHS figures show that a total of 8.6 million patients in England were prescribed antidepressants in 2022–23, almost double the number prescribed in 2011 (Thomas, 2023). The rate of prescription is highest in areas of deprivation (Ruddock et al., 2023). Prescription rates are high amongst those with

DOI: 10.4324/9781003480464-20

mild and moderate depression, even though the evidence indicates that antidepressants may only benefit people experiencing severe depression (Mahase, 2023).

IAPT: A neoliberal solution to a neoliberal problem?

In 2008, the UK also set up a service, based on a stepped-care model, to address the impact of the more common mental health difficulties (such as anxiety and depression) on the population. This service was called Improving Access to Psychological Therapies and was later renamed NHS Talking Therapies.

This service employs a predominantly Cognitive Behavioural Therapy (CBT) approach to address the challenges that those referred are experiencing. Understanding the service's effectiveness is somewhat complicated. There are claims that the service achieves 50% recovery rates among those referred to it (Wakefield et al., 2020). There are, however, significant concerns about the performance of IAPT and its assessment.

The IAPT service has a very high attrition rate, so that only one-sixth of those referred (289,551 out of 1,245,225 April 2023–March 2024) achieve "reliable recovery." There are almost no follow-up studies for those who have completed treatment.

There are no measures of IAPT practitioners' fidelity to the CBT model, making it impossible to know what intervention those attending the service actually receive. A recipient of the service is considered to have completed treatment if they have attended two planned sessions, which is undoubtedly not an evidence-based parameter for CBT (Scott, 2020).

In terms of outcomes, those people who do complete treatment are judged to show a degree of "recovery" which is not, however, diagnostically meaningful and which is comparable to the impact of placebo (Barkham & Lutz, 2021; Bschor et al., 2024). Furthermore, IAPT data over a ten-year period demonstrated poorer access and outcomes for people from Black and minoritised ethnic groups (National Collaborating Centre for Mental Health, 2023) and poorer levels of access for older people with limited engagement amongst younger adults (Pettit et al., 2017).

The IAPT service represents a recent trend in psychological provision within mental health services. Before the last 25 years, clinical psychologists in the UK were trained and recognised for their ability to formulate unique problems at different levels, in collaboration with those affected, thus enabling complex clinical decision-making. More recently, however, there has been a focus on standardised, protocol-based, evidence-based treatments, marking a change in how psychologists think and behave. They have become much more likely to accept the diagnostic categories of psychiatry and have reduced psychology to a set of techniques (Cooke, 2017).

The IAPT service has been characterised as a neoliberal construct in both its aims and its methods. Conceived by an economist who was critical of the economy's ability to deliver human happiness, its initial aim was to support people experiencing depression in returning to work (Layard et al., 2006). Layard, supported by the clinical psychologist Andrew Clark, decoupled people's emotional experience from the performance of the economy and the nature of society and suggested that the government spend less time attempting to relieve poverty and focus instead on treating depression.

Providing people with access to therapy may be a laudable social goal, but the IAPT approach assumes that all individuals will find CBT helpful and makes this offer of therapy contingent upon the economic benefits to wider society. More broadly, the IAPT service places the burden of unemployment and/or depression on the individual. This fits with the individualising and victim-blaming aspect of neoliberalism. (Burton & Kagan, 2003). It also supports the role that psychology has played in the wider workfare environment of psychocompulsion – whereby the unemployed are expected to modify their "attitudes, beliefs and personality notably through the imposition of positive affect" (Friedli & Stearn, 2015, p. 40).

Layard and Clark's approach of treating individual cases of depression with little consideration of the social context places them at odds with the celebrated public health expert George Albee (1999):

> If our goal is the reduction or elimination of emotional disorders in our country, or in the world, a major social revolution is required. Individual psychotherapy is available to a select few. No mass disorder has ever been eliminated by treating one person at a time.
>
> (Albee, 1999, p. 133).

In terms of its methods, the principal approach of IAPT, CBT, has also been characterised as neoliberal in its nature, being both short-term and standardised. CBT is also normative in its goals: the recipient is expected to conform to the clinician's "supposedly benevolent rationalism" (Ferraro, 2016, p. 19).

CBT focuses on the aspects of clients' experience over which they have some control. There are clearly areas of people's lives where we can use this to, for example, reduce negative self-appraisal. For instance, we can reframe our thinking from, "I got a poor result on my test, therefore I am stupid" to "I got a poor result on my test, I could do better if I did more revision." However, if the negative self-appraisal comes from a more structurally imposed process, such as racism or discrimination on the basis of class, it is inappropriate to frame this as something the individual can control. If the client experiences a therapist as lacking awareness in this regard, it is likely to make the therapeutic space feel unsafe (Ahuvia & Schleider, 2023).

The therapeutic space can also feel unsafe for the IAPT practitioners. The target-driven culture results in them being expected to select "IAPT-friendly" candidates for treatment and even to falsify records to improve results (Davies, 2021).

What about the wider context?

The UK population resides in the most unequal country in Europe (Francis-Devine, 2026). This has significant implications for their health and wellbeing. Inequality is correlated with a range of adverse outcomes which affect health and mental health both directly and indirectly. These outcomes include: reduced life expectancy, increased prevalence of mental health problems and teenage pregnancy, as well as other indicators such as levels of trust and violence in society. As a consequence, countries with higher levels of inequality experience higher levels of mental health difficulties (Wilkinson & Pickett, 2009).

The UK population has been exposed to social policies described as "austerity" since 2010 (subsequent to the 2008 financial crash), with consequent negative impacts on life expectancy and health. The growth in life expectancy has stalled for the first time in 100 years and has even reduced for women living in the most deprived 10% (Marmot et al., 2020).

Austerity and its associated policies have increased the overall burden of mental health in the UK. The wider social responses to the mental health crisis are often manifested in calls for more investment in our mental health services. These mental health services and, importantly, their surrounding ecosystem of non-statutory agencies have, however, been significantly affected by the policies of austerity (Cummins, 2018).

The widespread agreement and established evidence base for the influence of the social determinants of mental health makes clear that, although there is talk of a mental health crisis, there is actually another set of crises which lie beneath. As mentioned earlier, the social determinants of mental health include income, employment, socioeconomic status, education, food security, housing, social support, discrimination, childhood adversity, neighbourhood conditions and access to affordable health care. The likelihood of anyone encountering these determinants in either a protective or harmful way is influenced by the distribution of money, power and resources at global, national and local levels (McGorry et al., 2025).

Suicide rates are two to three times higher in the most deprived areas compared to the most affluent. Men in the lowest social class, living in the most deprived areas, are up to ten times more at risk of suicide than those in the highest social class, living in the most affluent areas (Samaritans, 2017).

In the UK, in 2011, 3.2 million people were in insecure work. By 2024, this had increased to 4 million, representing a net rise in insecure employment of around 800,000 (TUC, 2025). The Living Wage Foundation put the figure for insecure work at 6 million, the health and social care sector having the highest numbers (Richardson, 2023).

The description "mental health crisis" obscures the social determinants which drive mental health difficulties. This serves both those who wish to distract people from these concerns, as well as those who are involved in responding to the crisis through individual therapies. When we take the social determinants into account, the "mental health crisis" can be described more accurately as a crisis of the various social determinants: poverty, poor housing, loneliness and precarity.

Many members of the clinical psychology profession are aware of this contradiction and feel ethical, professional and personal dissonance as a consequence. When they engage in discussions about these concerns and are suggested that a more community-focused approach might be more appropriate, they often agree with the principle but feel that there are no opportunities to operate in this way.

During their training, clinical psychologists are taught a range of approaches; however, the interventions they deliver in the UK tend to be individualised, with little consideration given to the person's broader context beyond their immediate family or care environment (Hagan et al., 2018). There is no requirement from the British Psychological Society for clinical psychology trainees to receive any input on Community Psychology.

Trainees are often exposed to only a small amount of community psychology training, often as little as one day over a three-year programme. Nevertheless, trainees are often interested in the approach and want to know what Community Psychology looks like in practice (Jozefowicz-Simbeni et al., 2005). Clinical psychology trainees in community psychology training sessions have also reflected that this work sits most appropriately in a leadership curriculum for them.

Data also show that the clinical psychology profession remains skewed towards those from more affluent and privileged backgrounds, meaning that they often lack an understanding of how the social distribution of power has worked in their favour, while working against others (Clearing House, 2024).

This problem and psychology's response raise issues of social justice:

- individualising and decontextualising distress, e.g., through diagnosis.
- facilitating the medicalising of distress, notably through the use of antidepressants.
- offering treatments that have questionable evidence base.
- offering treatments that are culturally inappropriate or coercive.
- distracting people from the true sources of distress and supporting the status quo.

- focusing people's attention "downstream" and neglecting prevention.
- using society's resources for ineffective activities. Is psychology working in the interests of the people, as Liberation Psychology says it should be?
- "Gaslighting the precariat?" committing epistemic injustice.

What does Community Psychology look like in this field?

Community Psychology in the UK has not developed to the same extent as it has in other parts of the world (Burton & Kagan, 2003). There are, however, psychologists in the UK who have specialised in Community Psychology and have been leaders in the field (Kagan et al., 2019). Manchester Metropolitan University has been a fertile space for the discipline, as well as for critical psychology. Mark Burton (a clinical psychologist) has hosted a Community Psychology website in the UK for more than 20 years, which connects all interested practitioners to activity globally.

Several clinical psychologists have employed Community Psychology approaches in their work with adult clients in mental health services. Some of them will go beyond this to try to empower/increase agency in a group/community. For instance, Sue Holland worked in a deprived housing estate in London. She supported women through a process that started with individual therapy and progressed to collective social action, aiming to mitigate some of the immediate challenges they faced (Holland, 1992). Also in London, since 2008, MAC UK has used an ecological systems framework to engage with excluded young people in their communities. Members of the team set out to meet young people in "non-problem defined spaces" and work alongside them to build bridges to mainstream services. MAC-UK supports the training of agencies by young people and promotes young people's social action, both in their communities and with the agencies that have influence in their lives (Peddi et al., 2017).

Teresa Hagan and David Smail (Hagan & Smail, 1998) developed a tool for mapping an individual's power and resources across a range of meaningful social domains, all of which have significant impacts on mental health, thereby making those links more straightforward. Joe Miller and Lynn McLelland (Miller & McLelland, 2006) described an approach to individual therapeutic work which acknowledged structural social inequalities. Their model of formulation showed how these inequalities operated at different levels to produce internalised conflict within the individual. This internalised conflict then manifested itself in thoughts and behaviours which could be seen as reflecting "domination" or "subordination."

In the field of child and family work, Gordon Jack and Owen Gill (both social workers) brought an awareness of previously unconsidered evidence surrounding environmental factors to the assessment of children's development (Jack & Gill, 2003). Bostock and Freeman (2003) conducted participatory action research with young people in the North East of England to co-design the mental health services they would engage with.

The Gwent Community Psychology service undertakes community formulation with the communities it serves, creating community profiles and utilising its clinical psychologists' skills to formulate at a community level, rather than an individual or family level (Burns, 2022). Others have practised participatory action research to co-produce accounts of community experiences from different perspectives, reducing the victim-blaming, epistemic injustice of inappropriate, diagnostic labelling (Harris, 2014).

The Power, Threat, Meaning Framework (PTMF) has presented a significant challenge to the dominant diagnostic framework (Johnston & Boyle, 2018). The framework highlights the role of power in human distress and explains how individuals respond to the threats they encounter. This important shift is characterised as a change in the approach of the clinical services from asking "what's wrong with you?" to "what has happened to you?" The group of authors included two survivor campaigners. The project was also supported by a consultancy group of mental health service users. The PTMF has reconceptualised psychologists' understanding of how distress manifests. Although it isn't a Community Psychology approach in itself, the PTMF highlights the benefits of responses which acknowledge and address the abuses of power that produce and perpetuate human distress and shows significant promise (Nikopaschos et al., 2023).

Other psychologists will operate collectively in what Bronfenbrenner calls the exosystem to try and influence policy but do not necessarily operate as community psychologists; in fact, they are usually working in traditional therapy roles, often in the NHS. These psychologists often form networks with other practitioners who operate in community settings but are not psychologists and do not employ a psychological framing.

At this level of the exosystem, several clinical psychologists have written about the shortcomings of the current approach to mental health and have advocated for the use of socially informed constructs and Community Psychology approaches (Bostock, 2017; Bostock et al., 2021; Hagan et al., 2022). It has been argued that psychologists need to look beyond individual therapy and consider public health and Community Psychology approaches (Harper, 2016). The Midlands Psychology Group (2022), comprising practitioner-authors, expands on David Smail's concept of "outsight" and argues for a social-materialist understanding of human experience, critiquing an individualising, neoliberal therapeutic agenda.

There are groups of psychologists who have come together with other practitioners and activists to address the issues of social determinants of wellbeing. Psychologists Against Austerity came together to raise awareness of the psychological impact of the UK government's austerity programme after noticing that the psychology profession appeared to be unique in not having organised a response to the programme of cuts to services and further impoverishment of the poor. They highlighted the psychological mechanisms through which austerity harms those who experience it. They identified five ailments of austerity: humiliation and shame, fear and distrust, instability and insecurity, isolation and loneliness, and being trapped and powerless (McGrath et al., 2016). This group continues under the name Psychologists for Social Change (PSC).

The Housing and Mental Health Network focuses on the impact of housing policy on mental health. This group originated through a partnership between the Newham E17 housing activist organisation and Sheffield University (Hardy & Gillespie, 2016). Not all members of these groups are psychologists, and only a few would describe themselves as community psychologists; however, they are both concerned with and actively involved in issues that impact human environments, with an emphasis on mental health and wellbeing.

Community Psychology needs to address social factors in partnership with marginalised communities, sharing power and helping all parties form a better understanding of the situation. There is a risk that psychologists can believe that they understand what a community needs. Alternatively, a psychologist may extract information from a community for their own purposes. A meaningful partnership means that both the psychologist and the community gain a deeper understanding of the situation and their respective roles within it.

There have been community development workers and activists who have formed alliances with psychologists. For instance, Cathy McCormack, a housing activist in Glasgow (and later a United Nations ambassador), formed a productive 25-year collaboration with critical psychologist David Fryer (Fryer & McCormack, 2019). Alliances with those who are directly experiencing marginalisation are key to the development of a community psychologist. Without building such understanding, practitioners can continue to hold their own views on what change is necessary and unwittingly reproduce existing power imbalances.

There is no protected title of Community Psychologist in the UK, although Master's courses in the subject have been taught at Manchester Metropolitan University and the University of Brighton. Furthermore, there is no overarching structure to community psychology in the UK; it is eclectic in its methodologies, and practitioners from diverse backgrounds contribute to work that is relevant to its values and aims. There are undoubtedly benefits and drawbacks to this situation but:

> With ... a permeating notion of liberatory practice, any debate about who is really doing CP, and about how to organise to do it, perhaps fades away as only of interest to careerist professionals.
>
> (Burton et al., 2007, p. 232)

There is an annual festival of community psychology in the UK. The first of these was called a conference and was held less frequently. At the Great Yarmouth conference in 2006, a vote was held which led to the network becoming a section within the British Psychological Society. There was some concern that the BPS was a socially conservative organisation, which might limit the degree to which members could be critical; however, the potential opportunity to benefit from the organisation's influence was sufficient to overcome this. The section has been established for a considerable time and often supports the organisation of the annual festival.

Contradictions experienced by clinical psychologists

Clinical psychologists undertake training across four main areas: child, adult, older adult and learning disabilities. Their training equips them with an understanding of research processes, interpersonal processes, and organisational and clinical settings. At the core of their skills is formulation: the ability to understand a person's thoughts, feelings and behaviour in the context of their life experience, but this is almost always with little reference to the social context within which these developments took place.

Clinical psychologists' experiences, whether pre-, during, or post-training in clinical practice or service management, often present them with a contradiction between the perceived (or presented) evidence base for the effectiveness of individual therapies and the experience of delivering therapies in the context of disadvantage and the social determinants of mental health difficulties. More than 40% of psychological practitioners in the NHS report feelings of depression and feelings of failure in their work (Rhodes, 2016).

Different way of working using Community Psychology principles

For a newly qualified Psychologist starting work in a locality that is confronted by years of poverty, where social determinants are stacked against the health of local residents, it can be hard to know where to begin. Saira felt overwhelmed and very concerned about the length of the waiting list for psychological therapy when she started her job after qualifying in Clinical Psychology. Her supervisor suggested an enquiring approach that started with a look at local public health data and some community mapping, rather than immediately filling all of her time with individual psychological consultations. They aimed to understand the challenges facing people as well as assets in the community. What resources are available to support Saira and others in their work to help people address poverty, racism, unemployment and poor physical and emotional health?

Saira started by visiting local places and talking with professionals, locals and volunteers at the mosque, church, Health Centre, a Women's Refuge, a food bank and a Refugee service. She found a range of sources of support and identified initiatives committed to social justice and change. She listened to stories of hardship and significant threats to people's financial security, their physical safety and their dignity. She also heard about more resources and how people are leading changes, such as growing their own food and advocating for changes to road safety and traffic pollution.

Saira also began working with a group of women who used the refugee and asylum service, and they shared information on a low income, their experiences of racist attacks and aggression, the frustration of unemployment, and how they could support each other. They developed these ideas into a participatory action research project that the women led, and they shared these insights with neighbouring schools and health staff. This led to co-produced training for staff about influences on wellbeing and public health across the lifespan, which highlighted the strengths in the community and a non-medical analysis of social threats and their repercussions. These insights also informed Saira's direct psychological work with individuals and groups, which she based in primary care and the premises of a partner organisation.

Praxis case study

This case study describes the construction of a document, "Using Community Psychology approaches to reduce the impact of inequality through the Community Mental Health Framework" (BPS, 2022). The document is designed to support clinical psychologists and health service leaders to use Community Psychology ideas to address the growing demand for mental health services while recognising the underlying causes of this demand. These ideas help us to understand that the factors underlying this ever-increasing demand are beyond the control of our services, but that there are things we can do to mitigate their impact and to respond to the "crisis" in a more collaborative way.

The implementation of new ideas, a concept which is perhaps more familiar to us from our NHS work, is a long process and requires a set of factors to be in place. The successful implementation of research into practice is a function of the relation between the nature of the evidence, the context in which the proposed change is to be implemented and the facilitation of the change. (Harvey & Kitson, 2015).

The document compiles the evidence for the application of Community Psychology principles. It does so at a time of change, when the NHS in England made a significant investment in a community transformation in mental health services. This, alongside the NHS long-term plan's vision for modernised, whole-person, whole-population approaches, creates a more supportive context for community-focused ideas. We set out this rationale at the beginning of the document.

We also considered the pressures on our commissioners and service providers and sought to produce a brief, visually impactful, evidence-based document. We hoped that it would be a useful tool for them in responding to the call to produce a service specification that would allow them to access Community Transformation funding, and we aimed to maximise the appropriate influence of Community Psychology principles in this transition.

We need to present these ideas as relevant, understandable and feasible to implement. For the ideas to make a difference, we needed to use them to help psychologists reconceptualise the context of our

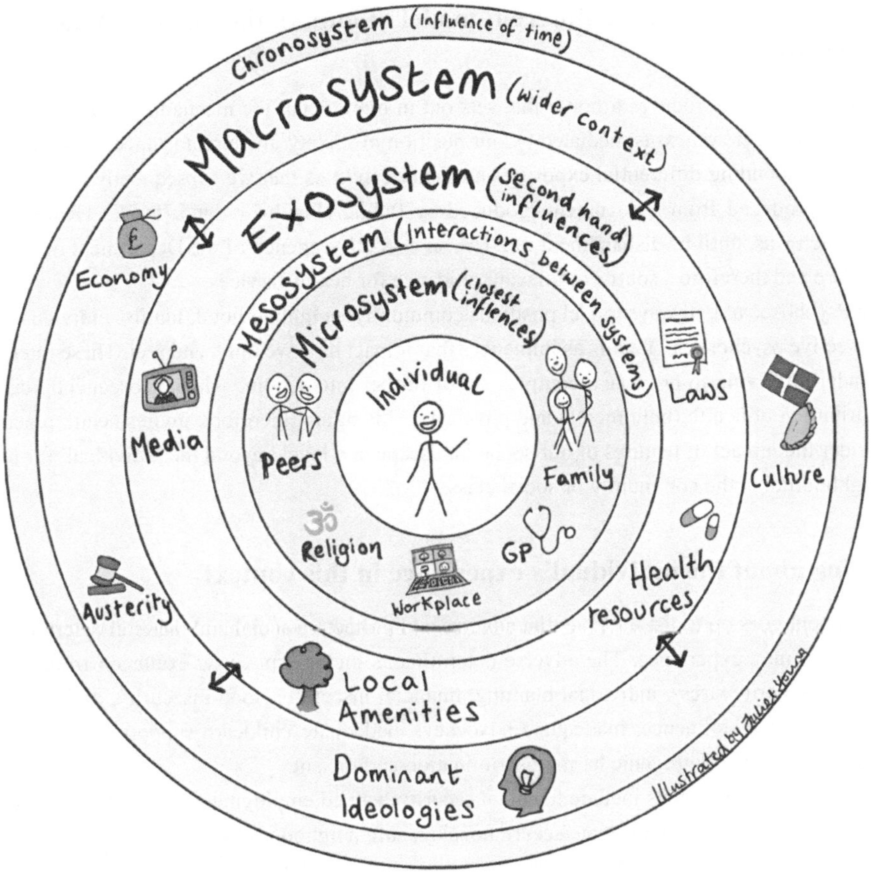

Figure 16.1 Bronfenbrenner's Ecological Systems Theory.
Source: Author's Own.

clients and the wider population. We also needed to help them utilise their power in order to begin shifting the focus and activity of their practice. To this end, we shared a narrative of change. We also shared concrete examples of change in practice, as well as a sample job description for a Neighbourhood Psychologist (BPS, 2021).

Reconceptualisation

In order to offer psychologists (and particularly leaders and commissioners of services) a reconceptualisation of how the social determinants of health impact their local population's mental health, the document used an illustration of Bronfenbrenner's ecological systems theory (1979) (see Fig 16.1). This model shows how people live in systems that impact on their development and life experiences. The model is familiar (certainly in terms of its appearance) to many psychologists and other mental health professionals and continues to be relevant (Cameron, 2025).

Supporting evidence for a different model of human thoughts, feelings and behaviour

The document then introduces a figure that sets out in more detail the mechanisms through which the impact of our wider context is mediated by our position in society, the circumstances in which we live, and the corresponding differential exposures and vulnerabilities that we subsequently experience. The figure is reproduced from a document produced by Public Health England (Public Health England, 2017), which was, until its disbandment in 2020, an executive agency of the Department of Health and Social Care and therefore a source of relevant guidance for health services.

The Psychosocial Pathways model positions community, neighbourhood, family, individual adverse and protective psychosocial factors as influences that impact how we think and feel. These interact with our standard of living to produce a complex set of further interactions, which subsequently determine the distribution of health (both mental and physical). This figure, therefore, invites health practitioners to consider the impact of features of our social landscape at a level beyond the individual, for instance, the neighbourhood, the community or social class.

Thinking about the individual's experience in this context

The document goes on to list the potential adverse and protective social and material determinants that an individual may experience. The adverse determinants include: poverty, exclusion from amenities, stigma and minority stress, individual blaming, financial insecurity, food insecurity, digital exclusion, inadequate level of influence, inadequate advocacy, inadequate childcare support, lack of transport, isolation, exploitation, iatrogenic harm, discrimination and racism.

The positive determinants include financial security, valued employment roles, social support, food security, access to travel, appropriate/secure housing, safe neighbourhoods, quality education (valuing diversity, retention, and success), good transport access and good quality and appropriate mental health services. These were all represented in an illustration by Juliet Young. Juliet is a clinical psychologist and a member of our authorship team, who communicates complex issues through images and has a significant social media following.

The point is made that determinants can be both protective and adverse, but that the more adverse determinants a person experiences, the higher their risk of mental health difficulties, especially if there are fewer protective factors to compensate. This image makes the impact of social determinants on the experience of the individual clearer. The therapy process and mental health services are unlikely to draw them to attention, and this image makes their impact more visible on those who are affected.

These structural factors often operate through processes of microaggressions or repeated, chronic traumas and are less easily brought to a conscious discussion, being simply part of a person's daily experience. Their effect is similar to the concept of "weathering" (Geronimus, 2023), which is also mentioned in the document.

Different ways of working – recognising and responding to the influence of power

Every risk factor for poor mental health reflects power inequalities, but this reality is rarely highlighted or investigated in psychological theory or practice. The document identifies the need for a change of narrative in mental health, which privileges an understanding of power as an alternative to traditional

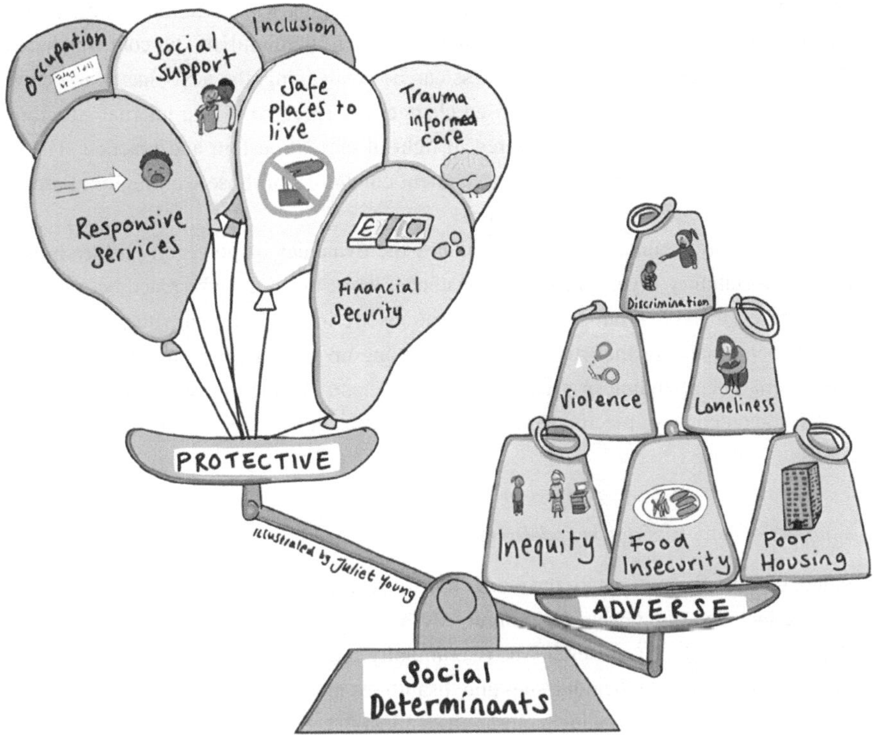

Figure 16.2 Protective and adverse factors in mental health.

Source: Author's Own.

psychiatric models that predominate in psychiatry and psychology. In the document, we refer to The Power, Threat, Meaning Framework (PTMF), which provides a comprehensive account of how different kinds of power are socially mediated and perpetuated, and how this impacts people physically, psychologically, culturally and socially, particularly through ideological power.

The structural factors that shape the processes in the Psychosocial Pathways are also embedded in our health organisations, our professions and our practices. The document considers various examples of different working practices that address these processes. These different ways of working are particularly aimed at the process of planning services: commissioning, community formulation, evidence and service changes. In addition to highlighting relevant aspects of this process, such as power-sharing, this section provides examples of the skills, knowledge and support required – many, but not all, of which are familiar to psychologists.

A narrative of how to make this happen in reality

After introducing the importance of building trusting relationships with the community for any partnership working and providing an illustration of Arnstein's Ladder of Participation (1969), the document proceeds to describe how the changes described in different ways of working can be implemented in practice. This section owes its appearance to a document produced by the Rethink charity (Rethink, 2021), which was subsequently modified in collaboration with the charity to reflect the experiences of the document's contributors.

Rethink's original document described the process of engaging with community partners very helpfully, which can often be a challenging task for all parties, as it is unfamiliar. Our contributors, however, highlighted that while the "reaching out" process can be challenging, the next phase can be even more difficult to manage. This is where the proposed changes are received by the internal structures of the statutory organisation and must be considered in light of current custom and practice. The proposed changes must also be filtered through the employment conditions of those working in related roles, as well as the context of clinical governance and risk.

This element of the document clearly articulates the dynamics of power in partnerships between statutory and non-statutory organisations. For instance, when meetings take place between NHS providers and charities, the staff from the two organisations are in very different situations. The statutory professional is being paid for their time and is not giving up valuable personal time. In contrast, the charity worker may be attending in a voluntary capacity and outside of their regular working hours. Consequently, the outcome of meetings may be disproportionately influenced by the paid staff of large organisations.

Giving examples of models of different delivery

The document then briefly outlines for the reader five diverse examples of these principles being put into practice. These included: the Gwent Community Psychology Team, supporting local organisations to support their young people; Even Better CIC (Community Interest Company) working to reduce social isolation for adults with mental health issues and disabilities in employment and education; Rococo (an organisation connecting people to wider communities); Just Psychology CIC, working with children and families in Manchester with an emphasis on cultural diversity, cultural competence and social justice; The Grenfell Health and Wellbeing Service, promoting the emotional health and wellbeing of all those affected by the tragic fire which claimed the lives of 70 people in North Kensington, London.

The document's final page showed a Neighbourhood Psychologist job description (British Psychological Society, 2021). This document was compiled by all members of the BPS COVID-19 Workstream Community Action and Resilience, with the assistance of external reviewers. This highlighted a set of skills and practices for the psychologist to carry out: participatory action research projects; work in partnership with or for community groups; training on psychologically informed topics; psychologically informed expertise to support policy development; enhancing psychological sense of community; recognising and building on the strengths of the community.

The final page also includes a link to a supporting document, which provides additional evidence for the importance of social determinants and community psychology approaches (British Psychological Society, 2022). The other is a link to contact us to join together in this endeavour.

Discussion

To advance this work, our team members spoke with senior leaders in clinical psychology departments. An account emerged of their perspective, which was that they were aware of these issues, but that change was difficult because of the governance arrangements for departmental spending. They described the limiting impact of "risk" when it comes to dedicating precious resources to unfamiliar or preventative approaches. This barrier pertains, even when the current practice might be based on little or questionable evidence of its effectiveness.

Subsequently, we learned more about the role of leaders in such situations. Such leaders are often encouraged to "be brave." This seems to be a relevant value to hold in such an influential position, but it appears to be one that requires considerable support from those in positions of power, as well as in policy guidance and clinical governance arrangements. This drew our attention to the facilitation aspect of implementation.

As a result, members of the authorship team have now set up a learning group within the BPS leadership faculty to support such thinking and action. We continue to pursue this enterprise, not least because our personal and professional experience tells us that collectivising and working together in solidarity builds confidence, and we want to support our leaders in growing their confidence in using such approaches.

During our ongoing work in this area, we have developed a conceptual tool to help us understand where we operate as individuals and as groups of psychologists: the Ladder of Influence. The Ladder of Influence organises action from individual to collective and from intrapersonal to social-structural-political. The ladder is incorporated into the Action for Learning exercise at the end of this chapter. In Figure 16.3, the ladder is represented as a rainbow.

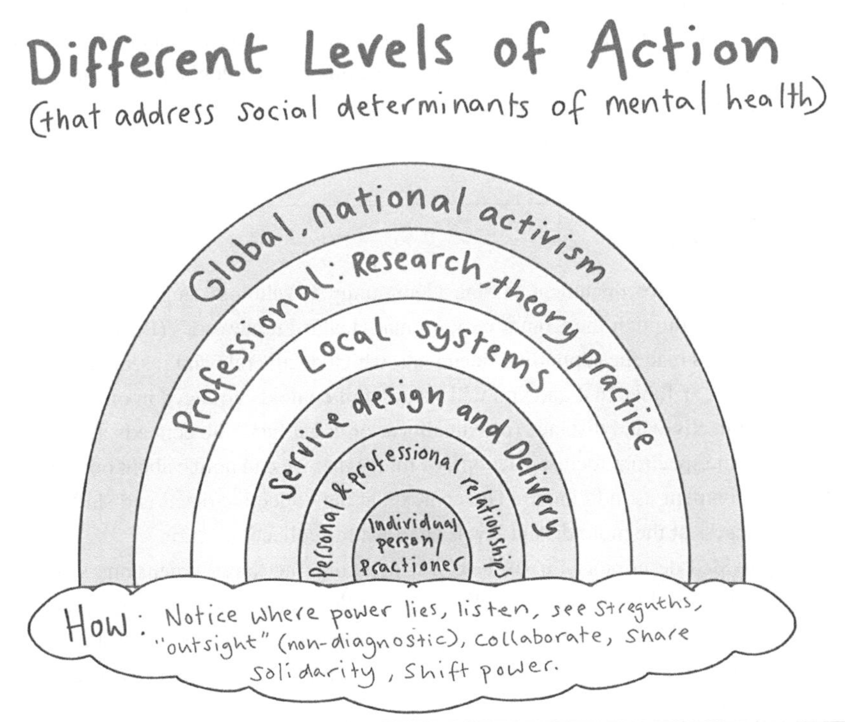

Figure 16.3 The Ladder of Influence Rainbow.

Source: Author's Own.

Conclusion

"Do not make the perfect the enemy of the good."

This document is the product of a series of decisions and compromises. We have been guided by an intention to make it legitimate for clinical psychologists to pursue Community Psychology approaches and to provide tools for their successful implementation.

The guidance document is less critical of clinical psychology than it could be. The document bears the hallmark of the BPS, which is often associated with conservative perspectives and the promotion of individual therapies, but which also has a worldwide membership of 60,000. The document has also been disseminated through the BPS's structures, including the Division of Clinical Psychology and the Public Health and Prevention subcommittee. In terms of implementation, as well as evidence and context, we need to ensure that there is facilitation of the introduction of these ideas, and the BPS structures are a potential source of support for this.

We recognise that mainstream clinical psychologists in the UK are influenced by an individualistic perspective on human experience, which focuses on the interpretations that people make of their circumstances as the primary determinant of their wellbeing, rather than the circumstances themselves. This bias prevents them from adopting a social materialist perspective where problems are addressed at a level above the individual. It also provides a valuable bulwark for those who would prefer to attribute such matters to individual, internal factors, a clear political implication for maintaining the status quo.

We will continue to raise critical awareness (or conscientization) and a social materialist perspective among clinical psychologists. We also want to encourage other psychologist practitioners to join us, as collectivising is the most effective way to promote change.

"If you want to go fast, go alone. If you want to go far, go together."

Action for learning

Firstly, read the guidance document "Using Community Psychology approaches to reduce the impact of inequality through the Community Mental Health Framework" (BPS, 2022). You may also find it helpful to read the supporting document, which details relevant research findings.

Then take a look at Table 16.4 and you will see a set of contexts arranged in order of their focus (individual or collective) and distance (proximal/near or distal/far). The contexts at the individual/proximal end of the spectrum focus on actions, or things that we can notice about ourselves and our immediate environment as individuals. The contexts at the collective/distal end shift our focus to actions or awareness at the more distant levels and towards collective action.

We have provided descriptors for six levels, which combine these dimensions in ways which are hopefully meaningful for those in the clinical psychology profession (although practitioners in other professions should also be able to identify issues relevant to them using this table).

We have provided examples of actions in the second column which fit with a Community Psychology approach.

For the purposes of this exercise, please find at least one other person with whom you can discuss this table and think together about some of the potential actions you could carry out between you. Give yourself time to consider the factors which inhibit or promote each action (we suggest an hour to consider all levels) and then choose one action to carry out. Write the chosen action in the box below, set a date for it to be completed by, meet (at that date) to discuss how it went and make a plan for your next action.

Level at which Action taken	Examples of Action	Proposed Actions
Global, national, political context	Join a national activist group, such as Psychologists for Social Change	
Professional, research, theoretical processes	Examine the evidence for current practice and it's effectiveness	
Local systems	Build relationships with local allies and partner with them to research social determinants	
Service design and delivery	Notice which client group isn't represented in your service	
Work with clients	Notice client strengths: resist using pathologising terminology	
Individual person and practitioner	Notice how you use power: how it flows through you	

Figure 16.4 Table to support the ladder of action exercise.

Key principles

- Social justice
- Intervention
- Praxis
- Power
- Ecological analysis

References

Abdul, S. (2025). *The experience of insecure work.* Trade Union Congress. https://www.tuc.org.uk/research-analysis/reports/experience-insecure-work

Albee, G. (1999). Prevention, not treatment, is the only hope. *Counselling Psychology Quarterly*, *12*(2), 133–146. https://doi.org/10.1080/09515079908254084

Ahuvia, I., & Schleider, J. L. (2023). Potential harms from emphasizing individual factors over structural factors in cognitive behavioral therapy with stigmatized groups. *The Behaviour Therapist*, *46*(7), 248–254. https://doi.org/10.31234/osf.io/n65fj

Allen, J., Balfour, R., Bell, R., & Marmot, M. (2014). Social determinants of mental health. *International Review of Psychiatry*, *26*(4), 392–407. https://doi.org/10.3109/09540261.2014.928270

Arnstein, S. R. (1969). A ladder of citizen participation. *Journal of the American Institute of Planners*, *35*(4), 216–224. https://doi.org/10.1080/01944366908977225

Barkham, M., & Lutz, W. (Eds.). (2021). *Bergin and Garfield's handbook of psychotherapy and behavior change* (7th ed.). John Wiley & Sons, Inc.

Bostock, J. (2017). Understanding power in order to share hope: A tribute to David Smail. *The Journal of Critical Psychology, Counselling and Psychotherapy*, *16*(1), 25–36. https://doi.org/10.53841/bpscpf.2017.1.297.13

Bostock, J., & Freeman, J. (2003) "No limits": Doing participatory action research with young people in Northumberland. *Journal of Community and Applied Social Psychology*, *13*(6), 464 –474. https://doi.org/10.1002/casp.751

Bostock, J., Hartley, N., & Lai, S. (2021). Community psychology, Covid-19 and beyond: What can clinical psychologists learn and contribute? *Clinical Psychology Forum*, *345*, 12–18. https://doi.org/10.53841/bpscpf.2021.1.345.9

British Psychological Society. (2021). *A neighbourhood community psychologist: Potential and possibilities* https://cms.bps.org.uk/sites/default/files/2022-08/Neighbourhood%20Community%20Psychologist.pdf

British Psychological Society. (2022). *Using Community Psychology approaches to reduce the impact of inequality through the Community Mental Health Framework* https://cms.bps.org.uk/sites/default/files/2022-07/Reducing%20the%20impact%20of%20social%20inequalities.pdf

Burns, G. (2022). It's all about relationships: Creating a whole system response to meeting the emotional and mental health needs of children and young people. *Clinical Psychology Forum*, *357*, 24–29. https://doi.org/10.53841/bpscpf.2022.1.357.24

Burton, M., Boyle, S., Harris, C., & Kagan, C. (2007). Community Psychology in Britain. In S. Reich, M. Reimer, I. Prilleltensky, & M. Montero (Eds.), *International community psychology: History and theories* (pp. 219–237). Kluwer/Springer.

Burton, M., & Kagan, C. (2003). Community psychology: Why this gap in Britain? *History and Philosophy of Psychology*, *4*(2), 10–23. https://doi.org/10.53841/bpshpp.2002.4.2.10

Bronfenbrenner, U. (1979). *The ecology of human development: Experiments by nature and design.* Harvard University Press. https://doi.org/10.2307/j.ctv26071r6

Bschor, T., Nagel, L., Unger, J., Schwartzer, G., & Baethge, C. (2024). Differential outcomes of placebo treatment across 9 psychiatric disorders: A systematic review and meta-analysis. *JAMA Psychiatry*, *81*(8), 757–768. https://doi.org/10.1001/jamapsychiatry.2024.0994

Cameron, C. (2025). Introduction. In C. Cameron (Ed.), *Urban childhoods: Growing up in inequality and hope.* https://doi.org/10.14324/111.9781800089341

Clearing House for Postgraduate Courses in Clinical Psychology. (2024). Equal opportunities data. https://www.clearing-house.org.uk/about-us/equal-opportunities/equal-opportunities-data

Cooke, A. (2017). Training that domesticates or education that liberates? Tensions and dilemmas related to teaching critical psychology in the context of UK clinical psychology training. In C. Newnes & L. Golding (Eds.), *Teaching critical psychology: International perspectives* (pp. 259–277). Routledge/Taylor & Francis Group. https://doi.org/10.4324/9781315209319-13

Cummins, I. (2018). The impact of austerity on mental health service provision: A UK perspective. *International Journal of Environmental Research and Public Health*, *15*, 1145. http://dx.doi.org/10.3390/ijerph15061145

Davies, J. (2021) *Sedated: How Modern Capitalism Created Our Mental Health Crisis*. London: Atlantic Books.

Department of Health and Social Care Media Team. (2023). How we are supporting mental health services in England. https://healthmedia.blog.gov.uk/2023/06/09/how-we-are-supporting-mental-health-services-in-england/

Ferraro, D. (2016). Psychology in the age of austerity. *Psychotherapy and politics international*, *14*(1), 17–24. https://doi.org/10.1002/ppi.1369

Friedli, L., & Stearn, R. (2015). Positive affect as coercive strategy: Conditionality, activation and the role of psychology in U.K. government workfare programmes. *Medical Humanities*, *41*, 40–47. https://doi.org/10.1136/medhum-2014-010622

Francis-Devine, R. (2026) Income inequality in the UK, House of Commons Library. https://researchbriefings.files.parliament.uk/documents/CBP-7484/CBP-7484.pdf

Fryer, D., & McCormack, C. (2019). The war without bullets: Socio-structural violence from a critical standpoint, *The Journal of Critical Psychology, Counselling and Psychotherapy*, *19*(1), 7–15. https://doi.org/10.17161/gjcpp.v3i1.20885

Geronimus, A. (2023) Weathering. The Extraordinary Stress of Ordinary Life in an Unjust Society. Little Brown

Hagan, T., Armstrong, N., & Bostock, J. (2018). Putting the social into psychotherapy. In J. Lloyd & R. Pollard (Eds.), *Cognitive analytic therapy and the politics of mental health.* Routledge. https://doi.org/10.4324/9780203728857

Hagan, T., Bostock, J., Harris, C., & Zlotowitz, S. (2022). *How can we address the negative impact of inequalities on our mental health? New BPS guidance to inform prevention.* Inequality and Mental Health. *Clinical Psychology Forum, 356*, 29–32. https://doi.org/10.53841/bpscpf.2022.1.356.29

Hagan, T., & Smail, D. (1998). Power-mapping – 1. Background and basic methodology. *Journal of Community and Applied Social Psychology*, *7*(4), 257–267. https://doi.org/10.1002/(SICI)1099-1298(199709)7:4%3C257::AID-CASP428%3E3.0.CO;2-P

Hardy, K., & Gillespie, T. (2016). Homelessness, health and housing: Participatory action research in East London. *The Sociological Review.* https://thesociologicalreview.org/collections/urban-sociologies/homelessness-health-and-housing/

Harper, D. (2016). *Beyond individual therapy.* The British Psychological Society. https://www.bps.org.uk/psychologist/beyond-individual-therapy

Harris, C. (2014) *The Impact of Austerity on a British Housing Estate. The Psychologist*, April 2014.

Harvey, G., & Kitson, A. (2015). PARIHS revisited: From heuristic to integrated framework for the successful implementation of knowledge into practice. *Implementation Science*, *11*, 33. https://doi.org/10.1186/s13012-016-0398-2

Holland. (1992). From social abuse to social action. In J. Usher & P. Nicholson (Eds.), *Gender issues in clinical psychology*. Routledge.

Jack, G., & Gill, O. (2003). *The missing side of the triangle.* Barnardo's.

Johnstone, L., & Boyle, M. with Cromby, J., Dillon, J., Harper, D., Kinderman, P., Longden, E., Pilgrim, D., & Read, J. (2018). *The power threat meaning framework: Towards the identification of patterns in emotional distress, unusual experiences and troubled or troubling behaviour, as an alternative to functional psychiatric diagnosis*. The British Psychological Society. https://www.researchgate.net/profile/Lucy-Johnstone-3/publication/326864047_The_Power_Threat_Meaning_Framework_An_Alternative_Nondiagnostic_Conceptual_System/links/5ca4770e458515f785203739/The-Power-Threat-Meaning-Framework-An-Alternative-Nondiagnostic-Conceptual-System.pdf

Jozefowicz-Simbeni, D. M. H., Israel, N., Braciszewski, J., & Hobden, K. (2005). The "big tent" of community psychology: Reactions to Paul Toro's 2004 presidential address. *American Journal of Community Psychology*, *35*, 17–22. https://psycnet.apa.org/doi/10.1007/s10464-005-1886-8

Kagan, C., Burton, M., Duckett, P., Lawthom, & Siddiquee, A. (2019). *Critical community psychology: Critical action and social change*. Routledge. https://doi.org/10.4324/9780429431500

Layard, R., & CEP Mental Health Policy Group. (2006). *The depression report: A new deal for depression and anxiety disorders.* Centre for Economic Performance https://cep.lse.ac.uk/_new/publications/abstract.asp?index=2404

Mahase, E. (2023). Curb antidepressant prescribing to improve mental health, say campaigners. *British Medical Journal, 383*, 2873. https://doi.org/10.1136/bmj.p2873

Marmot, M., Allen, J., Boyce, T., Goldblatt, P., & Morrison, J. (2020). *Health equity in England: The Marmot Review 10 years on.* Institute of Health Equity. https://www.instituteofhealthequity.org/resources-reports/marmot-review-10-years-on/the-marmot-review-10-years-on-full-report.pdf

McGorry, P., Gunasiri, H., Mei, C., Rice, S., & Gao, C. (2025). The youth mental health crisis: Analysis and solutions. *Frontiers in Psychiatry*, *15*, 1517533. https://doi.org/10.3389/fpsyt.2024.1517533

McGrath, L., Griffin, V., & Mundy, E. (2016). The psychological impact of austerity: A briefing paper. *Educational Psychology Research and Practice*, *2*(2), 46–57. https://doi.org/10.15123/uel.885xw

Miller, J., & McLelland, L. (2006). Social inequalities formulation: Mad, bad and dangerous to know. In L. Johnstone & R. Dallos (Eds.), *Formulation in psychology and psychotherapy making sense of people's problems.* Routledge. https://doi.org/10.4324/9780203087268

National Collaborating Centre for Mental Health. (2023). *Ethnic inequalities in Improving Access to Psychological Therapies (IAPT): Full report.* National Collaborating Centre for Mental Health.

https://www.nhsrho.org/wp-content/uploads/2023/10/Ethnic-Inequalities-in-Improving-Access-to-Psychological-Therapies-IAPT.Full-report.pdf

National Health Executive. (2025). *Report highlights deepening mental health crisis.* https://www.nationalhealthexecutive.com/articles/report-highlights-deepening-mental-health-crisis

Pettit, S., Qureshi, A., Lee, W., Stirzaker, A., Gibson, A., Henley, W., & Byng, R. (2017). Variation in referral and access to new psychological therapy services by age: An empirical quantitative study. *British Journal of General Practice*, 67(660). https://doi .org /10 .3399 /bjgp17X691361

NHS Digital. (2025). *Adult psychiatric morbidity survey: Survey of mental health and Wellbeing, England.* https://digital.nhs.uk/data-and-information/publications/statistical/adult-psychiatric-morbidity-survey

Nikopaschos, F., Burrell, G., Clark, J., & Salgueiro, A. (2023). Trauma-informed care on mental health wards: The impact of power threat meaning framework team formulation and psychological stabilisation on self-harm and restrictive interventions. *Frontiers in Psychology*, *14*, 1145100. https://doi.org/10.3389/fpsyg.2023.1145100

Peddi, J., Jones-Hewitt, K., Steadman, S., McGillivary, R., Foss, M., Hatton, P., Casale, L., & Zlotowitz, S. (2017). Putting smail's ideas into practice: Introducing MAC-UK and the INTEGRATE approach. *Clinical Psychology Forum*. https://doi.org/10.53841/bpscpf.2017.1.297.43

Platt, S., Stace, S., & Morrissey, J. (Eds.). (2017). *Dying from inequality: Socioeconomic disadvantage and suicidal behaviour, Summary report 2017.* Samaritans. https://media.samaritans.org/documents/Samaritans_Dying_from_inequality_report_-_summary.pdf

Public Health England. (2017). *Psychosocial pathways and health outcomes.* https://www.gov.uk/government/publications/psychosocial-pathways-and-health-outcomes

Rethink. (2021). *Keep thinking differently: Continuing your journey of community mental health transformation.* https://www.rethink.org/media/4391/certified-rmi-keep-thinking-differently_final-220221.pdf

Rhodes, E. (2016) *Wellbeing Issues Facing Psychological Professionals. The Psychologist*, April 2016.

Richardson, J. (2023). *Precarious pay and uncertain hours: Insecure work in the UK labour market.* https://www.livingwage.org.uk/precarious-pay-and-uncertain-hours-insecure-work-uk-labour-market

Royal Society of Arts. (2024). *State of paralysis: Young people's health and economic security in the UK.* https://www.thersa.org/wp-content/uploads/2024/02/state-of-paralysis-report.pdf

Ruddock, M., Watt, J., Kurth, M., Lamont, J., Mooney, L., & Fitzgerald, P. (2023). A review of the prescribing culture of anti-depressants across government districts in Northern Ireland. *Frontiers in Drug Safety and Regulation, 3.* https://doi.org/10.3389/fdsfr.2023.1303572

Scott, M. (2020). Ensuring that the Improving Access to Psychological Therapies (IAPT) programme does what it says on the tin. *British Journal of Clinical Psychology*, *60*, 38–41. https://doi.org/10.1111/bjc.12264

The Economist. (2023). *Britain's mental-health crisis is a tale of unintended consequences.* https://www.economist.com/britain/2023/12/07/britains-mental-health-crisis-is-a-tale-of-unintended-consequences?utm_campaign=shared_article

The Midlands Psychology Group. (2022). *Outsight: Psychology, politics and social justice*. PCCS Books.

Thomas, T. (2023). Experts call for fewer antidepressants to be prescribed in UK. *The Guardian.* https://www.theguardian.com/society/2023/dec/05/experts-call-for-fewer-antidepressants-to-be-prescribed-in-uk

Wakefield, S., Kellett, S., Simmonds-Buckley, M., Stockton, D., Bradbury, A., & Delgadillo, J. (2020) Improving Access to Psychological Therapies (IAPT) in the United Kingdom: A systematic review and meta-analysis of 10 years of practice-based evidence. *British Journal of Clinical Psychology*, *60*(1), 1–37. https://doi.org/10.1111/bjc.12259

Wilkinson, R. D., & Pickett, K. (2009). *The spirit level: Why more equal societies almost always do better.* Bloomsbury Publishing; Allen Lane/Penguin Group UK.

World Health Organisation. (2025). *World mental health today: Latest data.* https://www.who.int/publications/i/item/9789240113817

17 Liberation without oppression

Reimagining hope, power and solidarity

Maria Fernandes-Jesus, Suzanne Wilson, Rebecca Graber and Carl Harris

Throughout this book, we have devoted considerable attention to critically discussing how community psychologists, activists, practitioners, and students can apply Community Psychology principles to advance social justice and wellbeing in their communities. We offer practical tools and strategies that can be used in classrooms as well as with communities on the ground. Based on research, teaching experience, activism and practice, the authors of the chapters presented in this book bring together a range of diverse perspectives, approaches and methodologies. They have offered a contemporary and timely collection of how Community Psychology looks like across several countries (e.g., Italy, Portugal, Brazil, India), around concrete and everyday challenges (e.g., housing, gender violence, climate justice) and with multiple and diverse groups and communities (e.g., Quilombolas, migrants, children, low-income coastal communities). Each chapter illustrates the role of Community Psychology in mobilising collective action, resistance and social change in the face of marginalisation and oppression. While the four editors initiated the process of envisioning this book a couple of years ago, we could not have done it without the perspectives and contributions of the many authors involved in the chapters. Grounded in critical theories, methodological creativity, rigour and commitment to social justice, their work offers hope in challenging times, and they have shaped and built this edited collection in many ways.

As discussed in many chapters, communities all over the world are facing multiple and interconnected crises, each with severe social implications. Addressing these challenges requires approaches that go beyond the individual level and tackle the structural causes responsible for them in the first place. This requires attention to the struggles of communities through their own eyes and experiences. For example, right-wing politicians and the media are increasingly articulating populist narratives, and radical right parties have secured representation at various levels, from local governments to national parliaments and the European Parliament (e.g., Aktas, 2024; Campo, 2024). Evidence suggests that communities considered "left-behind" are increasingly turning to right-wing parties as an alternative to mainstream politics, which they feel is a system that has failed to meet their needs (Schraff & Pontusson, 2024; Snegovaya, 2024). An increasing proportion of children within these communities are also demonstrating right-wing and nationalist attitudes (Ciccolini, 2025; Nilan & Gentles, 2024).

This poses a threat to social and community cohesion (Schonert-Sieber, 2025) and is considered a policy priority in many contexts (e.g., Dotti et al., 2024). It is challenging to see through another's eyes, especially when that community has been marginalised time and time again. This is therefore not an inherently comfortable exercise, and where there is discomfort, it often feels natural to resist forging a connection or experiencing empathy. A danger of oppressive ideologies is in offering platforms that

DOI: 10.4324/9781003480464-21

promise solutions to subjective and objective ills while actually enhancing social divisiveness, entrenching existing power structures and frequently threatening basic welfare to persons and planet. Community Psychology can be used to foster critical dialogue among people, enabling communities to co-create recommendations for inclusive policy development (Hill & Wilson, 2003; Huddy, 2001; Hunter, 2003). Through participatory approaches, community psychologists can mobilise creative methods to facilitate the sharing of stories, promote critical consciousness and develop critical pedagogical materials (Pinedo et al., 2024) with all political actors, including community members, grassroots organisations, local authorities, the central government and beyond.

As we write these concluding remarks in late 2025, we are inundated with news about the growing oppressions, challenges and uncertainties faced by many communities worldwide, from the untold acts of violence and dehumanisation committed in the names of politics and power the world over, to the devastations of abuse, addiction, illness and disenfranchisement – which lack geopolitical boundaries but are also informed by systemic injustices. We recall a quote attributed to Maya Angelou (American poet and well-known civil rights activist) about freedom: "The truth is, none of us can be free until everybody is free." Highlighted – yet in different ways – by the many authors involved in this book, Community Psychology is deeply embedded in struggles for freedom and anti-oppression of all. In a world dominated by power inequalities, political conflicts, climate crisis and numerous other interconnected crises, we acknowledge the work of those who have come before us, such as Ignacio Martín-Baró and Maritza Montero, and who have worked to place liberation at the centre of psychologists' work. We must continually question how to do this in practice, without inadvertently perpetuating existing harms and creating new forms of oppression at this political moment, as our authors have grappled with throughout these chapters in their quests to challenge injustice and envision new pathways of wellbeing and social justice.

Community Psychology, through its commitment to social justice and critical action, can support communities in their pursuit of liberation and freedom. As a discipline and praxis, Community Psychology can create spaces for working within discomfort towards transformative change, disrupting the status quo and fostering more hopeful futures. The chapters in this book discuss some of the ways community psychologists can work towards liberation, which "in its fullest sense requires the securing of full human rights and the remaking of a society without roles of oppressor and oppressed" (Watts & Serrano-García, 2003, p. 187). In a world that is urgently calling for its "remaking," we believe this book offers pathways to build hope, solidarity and power.

Returning to the main title of our concluding chapter, "Liberation without oppression," we further invite our readers to envision the liberation of groups and communities in a manner that does not oppress others. This seems quite obvious, but throughout our history, we have seen many instances where the oppressed have become the oppressor or where the freedom of some implies the oppression of others. Moreover, this should not be limited to people and communities. It is crucial that we acknowledge the intersection of structural issues that are responsible for the current state of the world, as well as how the oppression of Nature is having devastating impacts on communities. Community Psychology can offer a bridge between the individual and the structural, people and nature, helping to transcend the human and non-human dichotomies. This is particularly important within the current neo-liberal and capitalist world in which we live, where individuals, communities and nature are commodified and services consumerised. For example, the way migrant and refugee communities are "moved" to different locations, with little warning and no control over their placement, represents a complete dehumanisation and commoditisation of their lives (Coddington et al., 2020; Morris, 2023; Nassar, 2025). A

Community Psychology approach instead would consider the psychological, social, cultural and political impact on the individuals and the wider community while taking a stance against the oppressive regimes and violence that migrants and refugees often face (e.g., Esposito et al., 2023). As the chapter authors in our book discuss, Community Psychology recognises the structural limitations which may impact those facing adversity and works together with migrants – and other underserved groups and communities – towards their wellbeing and empowerment. Community Psychology's potential also lies in its acknowledgement of the capacity of individuals and communities to take action, reclaim power and strive towards liberation and empowerment. To oppose, to challenge, to resist and to overcome these structural challenges.

We understand that this is easier said than done, particularly given our privileged positions, which afford us a certain level of stability and security in our lives. We do not face the multiple daily challenges and struggles that many of the communities we have covered in this book face. This inherently gives us an unfair, structural advantage over the communities we seek to work with. However, what we have done in this book is to very carefully consider what is within our gift as committed community psychologists and community activists. We have also attempted to bring diverse voices from different contexts to join us in building this book. We encourage all readers, regardless of their personal and professional background, to consider the resources and skills they can mobilise towards social change, as we all have a role to play in cultivating a more equal and socially just world. The chapters in this book offer practical recommendations on how to do this by supporting communities in their own struggles for liberation without oppressing others.

As a final remark, we would like to emphasise that the central message of this book is ultimately a call to action. A call to action to join, foster and support existing community social justice struggles. To all of us, to come together to create spaces for radical imagination to happen (e.g., Fernandes-Jesus et al., 2025) and build futures that are embedded in liberation and social justice. This implies acknowledging that Community Psychology is unavoidably a political field where "liberation is a never-ending task" (Montero, 2007, p. 529). It also requires looking beyond the borders of our own discipline and accompanying the work of activists, communities and social movements on the ground (Fernandes-Jesus et al., 2025). We invite readers to engage with structural and political issues, contest power and oppression in their local communities and join international struggles for solidarity. Only by doing so can we achieve the social change urgently needed.

References

Aktas, M. (2024). The rise of populist radical right parties in Europe. *International Sociology*, *39*(6), 591–605.

Campo, F. (2024). Differentiated tolerant opposition: League and five star movement. In A. K. Bourne (Ed.), *Democratic defence as normal politics: Everyday opposition to populist parties in multilevel Europe* (pp. 219–243). Springer Nature Switzerland.

Campo, F., Giunti, S., & Mendola, M. (2024). Refugee crisis and right-wing populism: Evidence from the Italian Dispersal Policy. *European Economic Review*, *168*, 104826.

Ciccolini, G. (2025). Who is left behind? Economic status loss and populist radical right voting. *Perspectives on Politics*. Advance online publication. https://doi.org/10.1017/S1537592724002858

Coddington, K., Conlon, D., & Martin, L. L. (2020). Destitution economies: Circuits of value in asylum, refugee, and migration control. *Annals of the American Association of Geographers*, *110*(5), 1425–1444. https://doi.org/10.1080/24694452.2020.1715196

Dotti, N. F., Fratesi, U., & Oberst, C. (2024). Regional economic theories as drivers of the EU Cohesion Policy. In N. F. Dotti, I. Musiałkowska, S. De Gregorio Hurtado, & J. Walczyk (Eds.), *EU cohesion policy: A multidisciplinary approach* (pp. 30–46). Edward Elgar Publishing.

Esposito, F., Rebelo, D., Olanrewaju, M., Vine, M., Fernandes-Jesus, M., Bodden, D., Kalokoh, A., & Olson, B. (2023). A community psychology for migrant justice: Critically examining border violence and resistance during the COVID-19 syndemic. *American Journal of Community Psychology*, 1–17. https://doi.org/10.1002/ajcp.12669

Fernandes-Jesus, M., Trott, C., D., Barnes, B., & Barnwell, G. (2025). Towards a critical psychology of climate justice: Encouraging radical political imagination to shape our collective futures. *International Perspectives in Psychology, 14*(3), 162–173. https://doi.org/10.1027/2157-3891/a000130

Hill, J., & Wilson, T. (2003). Identity politics and the politics of identities. *Identities: Global Studies in Culture and Power, 10*(1), 1–8. https://doi.org/10.1080/10702890304336

Huddy, L. (2001). From social to political identity: A critical examination of social identity theory. *Political Psychology, 22*(1), 127–156. https://doi.org/10.1111/0162-895X.00230

Hunter, S. (2003). A critical analysis of approaches to the concept of social identity in social policy. *Critical Social Policy, 23*(3), 322–344. https://doi.org/10.1177/02610183030233002

Montero, M. (2007). The political psychology of liberation: From politics to ethics and back. *Political Psychology, 28*(5), 517–533. https://doi.org/10.1111/j.1467–9221.2007.00588.x

Morris, J. C. (2023). (Im) mobility economies: Extractivism of the refugee as a human commodity. *International Development Policy| Revue internationale de politique de développement*, 15. https://doi.org/10.4000/poldev.5430

Nassar, J. (2025). Commodified by displacement: The effects of forced displacement on Syrian refugee women in Lebanon's agricultural sector. *Migration Studies, 13*(1), mnae052. https://doi.org/10.1093/migration/mnae052

Nilan, P., & Gentles, T. (2024). Thinking sociologically about young people and the far-right. In J. Bessant, P. Collin, & P. O'Keeffe (Eds.), *Research handbook on the sociology of youth* (pp. 39–52). Edward Elgar Publishing. https://doi.org/10.4337/9781803921808.00011

Pinedo, A., Diemer, M. A., & Frisby, M. B. (2024). Critical consciousness and youth political activism. *Annual Review of Developmental Psychology, 6*, 351–372. https://doi.org/10.1146/annurev-devpsych-010923-113449

Schraff, D., & Pontusson, J. (2024). Falling behind whom? Economic geographies of right-wing populism in Europe. *Journal of European Public Policy, 31*(6), 1591–1619. https://doi.org/10.1080/13501763.2023.2278647

Schonert-Sieber, C. (2025). *The growing right-wing populism as a practical theological challenge.* Unum Press.

Snegovaya, M. (2024). *When left moves right: The decline of the left and the rise of the populist right in postcommunist Europe*. Oxford University Press.

Watts, R. J., & Serrano-García, I. (2003). The quest for a liberating community psychology: An overview [Editorial]. *American Journal of Community Psychology, 31*(1–2), 73–78. https://doi.org/10.1023/A:1023022603667

INDEX

For Product Safety Concerns and Information please contact our
EU representative GPSR@taylorandfrancis.com Taylor & Francis
Verlag GmbH, Kaufingerstraße 24, 80331 München, Germany